R. H. (Robert Hogarth) Patterson

The new golden Age and Influence of the precious Metals upon the World

R. H. (Robert Hogarth) Patterson

The new golden Age and Influence of the precious Metals upon the World

ISBN/EAN: 9783743313958

Manufactured in Europe, USA, Canada, Australia, Japa

Cover: Foto ©ninafisch / pixelio.de

Manufactured and distributed by brebook publishing software (www.brebook.com)

R. H. (Robert Hogarth) Patterson

The new golden Age and Influence of the precious Metals upon the World

CONTENTS OF THE SECOND VOLUME.

BOOK THIRD.

PERIOD OF RENEWED SCARCITY.

CHAP.		PAGE
XII.	RENEWED SCARCITY OF THE PRECIOUS METALS—A.D. 1800-1830,	3
XIII.	THE PERIOD OF SCARCITY. PART II.—EFFECTS UPON GREAT BRITAIN,	26
XIV.	THE SCARCITY LESSENS.—BEGINNINGS OF A NEW GOLD-SUPPLY,	112
XV.	GENERAL DISTRESS BEFORE THE GOLD-DISCOVERIES,	163

BOOK FOURTH.

"CHEAP" AND "DEAR" MONEY.

XVI.	ON THE EFFECTS OF CHANGES IN THE QUANTITY AND VALUE OF MONEY,	229

BOOK FIFTH.

THE NEW GOLDEN AGE.

XVII.	FIRST GETTING OF THE NEW GOLD,	289
XVIII.	FIRST DIFFUSION OF THE NEW GOLD,	314

CHAPTER XII.

RENEWED SCARCITY OF THE PRECIOUS METALS.
1800–1830 A.D.

At the beginning of the present century, full thirteen hundred millions sterling of gold and silver had been extracted from the earth for the use of mankind, and poured into Europe, since the year 1500. But one-third of this enormous quantity had been exported from Europe, chiefly to Asia; a still larger quantity had been converted into plate and ornaments; while about one-eighth (or 170 millions) had been lost to the use of mankind, by casualties and abrasion.[1] The total quantity of gold and silver existing as coin in Europe at the beginning of the present century is reckoned to have amounted to about 380 millions sterling. This was more than ten times as large as the stock existing at the date of the discovery of America; and the annual supply was in a still larger proportion to what it had been in A.D. 1492. Some of the American mines had become exhausted, but these were more than replaced by the

[1] See *supra*, note to chap. x.

progressive discovery of new ones; and thus the annual supply of gold and silver which had amounted to about two millions sterling in the middle of the sixteenth century, after the discovery of Potosi in 1544, had increased by steady gradation until the beginning of the present century, when it amounted to fully ten millions sterling,—of which annual sum £2,634,000 was gold, and £7,733,000 was silver.[1]

Despite this large increase in the existing stock of gold and silver, and not less so in the annual supply, the growth of population and of trade, especially foreign trade—nay, even the growth of Wealth, which of itself needs more money as a means of storing and utilising it—had rendered the stock of the precious metals in Europe less adequate for men's wants than it had been in 1640 and for a century and a half thereafter. Gold and silver had been growing somewhat dearer, and the value of money had perceptibly risen, before the present century began. But now a great and serious change was at hand; and in both of its shapes, and also in its causes, the direful change may be regarded as a legacy from the closing events of the eighteenth century. The renewed scarcity was occasioned by

[1] Humboldt states the total produce of the gold and silver mines of the world (exclusive of Asia), in the year 1809, as follows:—

	Gold (francs).	Silver (francs).
Europe,	4,467,444	11,704,444
Africa,	855,111	4,824,122
America,	59,557,889	176,795,778

—*Nouvelle Espagne*, iii. 400.

the operations of a great War, and also by the consequences of the Revolt of the American Colonies of Spain. Certainly from no love of freedom or of political independence, but in order to damage a rival Power, the French Court had aided the rebellion of the British Colonies in North America; and some of the crack regiments of the French army—including the regiments of Touraine and Agénois and the Royal Auvergne, which bore for its proud motto "*sans tache*"—had played the leading part in the capitulation of the British General, Cornwallis, at Yorktown;[1]—the upshot being that these French troops, with Lafayette and other officers, brought

[1] German troops, also, under Baron Steinbein, took part in the siege of Yorktown; and the discomfiture of the British troops in the American War was really due to the jealousy and hatred of all her Continental neighbours. The Americans played only a third-rate, and of itself wholly inadequate, part in the operations which led to the capitulation of Lord Cornwallis at Yorktown in October 1781. The British troops consisted of only 5000 men and about 1500 sailors, holding an open and unhealthy town, where sickness, more than the fire of the enemy's batteries, soon left the British General with less than four thousand effective combatants. The besieging army consisted of 8000 French troops under Lafayette, and 8000 "Continentals" chiefly under General Steinbein, together with 5000 American Militia, under Washington, and possessing also a formidable park of artillery, greatly superior to that of the beleaguered British force; and finally, the mouth of the York river was occupied by the French fleet under Admiral De Grasse, numbering 27 ships of the line, and which had just beaten off Admiral Hood, commanding a British fleet of inferior numbers. Cornwallis, after a gallant defence, capitulated on the 19th October 1781; and on the 27th February following, a motion was carried against the Ministry in the House of Commons to the effect that the subjugation of the revolted Colonies by force was impracticable.

The centenary of the memorable surrender of Cornwallis has been recently celebrated (October 1881) by the Americans by two days of

home with them the revolutionary spirit, which speedily overthrew the ancient monarchy of France, and plunged all Europe into war. Spain had likewise taken part against Great Britain in her troubles, in the hope of recovering impregnable Gibraltar, memorably defended by the iron-hearted Elliott; and ere long the tables were turned against herself by the revolt of her own vast and valuable colonies or dominions in the New World;—the completion of the revolt, too, being mainly a consequence of the Revolutionary War,—the allegiance of the Colonies being loosened by the enthroning at Madrid, in 1809, by French bayonets, of a Buonaparte in place of the old line of the Spanish Bourbons. That was the origin of the Revolt. Finally when, in the year 1819, the revolutionary spirit seized upon the Spanish army of twenty thousand men at Cadiz, ready to embark to suppress the American Revolt, the die was cast, and the proud royalty of Spain in the New World came entirely to an end. The days of the

public festivities at Yorktown, including a military and naval review. And it is a most gratifying fact, as a proof of the friendly regard now established between the two great branches of the British race—a mutual regard which has been notably augmented by the national sympathy excited in Great Britain by the assassination of President Garfield—that at the close of the review a decree from the new President was read ordering a salute to be fired in honour of the British flag. An eyewitness says:—" It was impossible to make any mistake about the heartiness of the salute of the British flag. Every vessel, including the French, hoisted colours at the foremast, and each ship fired twenty-one guns. As the echoes of the naval salute rolled between the York and Gloucester shores, there came from distant camps down river answering echoes, showing that the Army had joined the Navy in the salute. Meanwhile, the crowd sent up cheer after cheer."—*Standard* newspaper, Oct. 22, 1881.

galleons and Flota were over. Indeed almost the last of the treasure-ships from Lima and Acapulco, conveying to Spain the silver and gold from the mines of the Andes, had been attacked and captured, or sunk with two millions sterling of bullion, by a British squadron off Cadiz in October 1804.[1]

Thus, while the War in Europe was growing fiercer and wider,—peremptorily absorbing for its own use a larger and larger portion of the precious metals, the supply from the New World—it may be said, the entire supply—was suddenly interrupted. Mankind

[1] Attacks upon the Spanish galleons or treasure-ships from Lima and Acapulco were a constant feature in our naval operations whenever war broke out between the two countries. And it is a curious fact that it was one of those attacks upon the galleons which chiefly originated the use of snuff-taking in England, which, like tea-drinking, dates from the reign of Queen Anne. At the beginning of last century a fleet under Sir George Rooke paid a visit to Vigo, where the Admiral had advice that a number of galleons from the Havannah, richly laden, had put in. Here our fleet got in and destroyed most or all of the Spanish shipping, and the plunder was exceedingly "rich and valuable,"—including, among other merchandise, "prodigious quantities of gross snuff from the Havannah, which were designed for manufacture in different parts of Spain." Moreover, in an earlier part of the cruise, the Fleet had made a descent at Port St Mary, near Cadiz, where, it is stated, "besides some rich merchandise, plate, jewels, pictures, and a great quantity of cochineal, several thousand barrels and casks of fine snuffs were taken." In consequence of these captures, we are told, "it now came to the turn of the sea-officers and sailors to be snuff proprietors and merchants. And thus, though snuff-taking was very little known or practised in England at that period, the quantities taken in this expedition (which was estimated at fifty tons weight) plainly show that in the other countries of Europe snuff was held in great estimation, and that the taking of it was considered not at all unfashionable." When the Fleet returned to England, " waggon-loads of this Vigo snuff were sold at Portsmouth, Plymouth, and Chatham for not more than three or four pence per pound."

pay dearly for their follies and frailties even when making a change for the better, a step in advance. In particular, almost every Revolution, even when adopted as a cure for intolerable popular hardships, has for its first effect to aggravate the hardships of the masses and increase the burdens of the State: a result which is apt to impel the revolutionary leaders to extreme measures and unpremeditated changes, which, instead of bringing relief, only widen or augment the general distress. No Revolution ever looked more full of promise or more free from drawbacks, whether political or social, than that by which the Spanish States or Colonies in the New World threw off the burdensome yoke of the Court of Madrid, and, with that, the noxious restrictions of the selfish dog-in-the-manger commercial policy of the mother country. It seemed to onlookers that a new epoch alike of mining and of commercial prosperity was about to dawn upon Spanish America. The British nation, who had themselves suffered so keenly from the intervention and the military aid given by previously neutral Powers to the revolt of our own Colonies in the New World, nevertheless eagerly assisted the Spanish Colonies in their revolt, —being prompted not merely by political objects and a love of freedom, but by a covetous desire to acquire free trading powers with these long-secluded and jealously restricted States, and also to obtain a new and valuable region for British enterprise and the investment of British capital.[1]

[1] It is a fact to be remembered that it was the intervention of the

How disappointing was the result! Instead of the reign of political freedom and of wise and orderly constitutional government, which offered so attractive a prospect to free England at a time when Autocracy was resuming its old supremacy in Europe, and which tempted Canning in an exuberant moment to boast that he had "called into existence a New World to redress the balance in the Old,"—anarchy, interspersed with shortlived despotisms, overtook the whole emancipated region. Released from Spanish thrall, the Colonies gave birth to a series of native despots. Desultory but often merciless warfare became the order of the day. Spanish rule had at least maintained peace and order, and Industry, although grievously and foolishly fettered, could at least carry on her pursuits in security. But now Peace became a rare thing, and all but the commonest kinds of industry became impossible. The revolutionary convulsions destroyed alike the powers of production and of consumption; and the large and

British Government, and the fighting power of the British Volunteers —not a few of whom were disbanded veterans of Wellington's army— which won the decisive victories in South America, and defeated Spain in her resolute attempt to restore her dominion in the New World. But for these victories, Spain would have retained her dominion not only in South America, but over Mexico, Texas, and California: and, unless the United States had been willing to engage in a very serious and costly war, the two latter provinces would still have owed allegiance to the Spanish Crown, instead of being enrolled as States of the American Republic. Thus, in truth, it was British policy and British arms which alone made possible the "Monroe doctrine," which the Government of the United States is now evoking in obstruction of that grand triumph of commerce and civilisation, the canalisation of the Isthmus of Darien.

lucrative trade which had excited the cupidity of British merchants rapidly dwindled, leaving merely a shadow to be grasped as the spoils of conquest.[1] The mineral resources of the country fared not less badly. The glowing visions cherished by outsiders and onlookers (as among our own people) of enhanced productiveness of the treasure-bearing rocks of the Andean Cordillera—which seemed to teem with gold or silver all along the chain, from the Desert of Atacama in the south to the northern extremity of Mexico—were doomed to total disappointment. Even the existing Mines became neglected, or had wholly to be abandoned, owing to the prevalent insecurity and ever-recurring hostilities and distress; and forthwith the deep shafts and branching galleries became flooded with water,—requiring more skill and more capital to reopen the mines than the population possessed or could command. Even British capital, largely advanced or invested upon delusive information, failed in such mining operations; and, whether from exhaustion or from other causes, the Mexican and South American mines have never recovered from the catastrophe which overtook them during the revolutions which effected the downfall of Spain's ancient and splendid dominion in the New World.[2]

---

[1] The exports from Spain to her American Colonies before the Revolutions (in 1808) had amounted to £15,250; but in 1827, the entire imports of these Colonies, alike from Great Britain and from Spain, amounted only to £1,630,000! In 1836, they still amounted only to £2,248,644. — Humboldt, *Nouvelle Espagne*, iv. 153-4; and Porter's *Progress of the Nation*, ii. 104.

[2] The annual produce of the gold and silver mines of America

To Europe, its peoples and its Governments, this change came as suddenly as it was felt severely. In the year 1810, friendly communication ceased betwixt Spain and her treasure-bearing colonies beyond the Atlantic Ocean. The supply of the precious metals from America did not gradually dwindle and disappear, like as the streamlets from the foot-hills of the Sierra Nevada gradually dry up in the summer noonday as they advance into the great central Plain of California. The diminution speedily attained its maximum, and at a time when our need was at the sorest. Cut off by the Transatlantic Revolt, the cessation of the annual stream of gold and silver was to Europe like what the drying up of the Euphrates river was to mighty Babylon of old, when the engineering of Cyrus suddenly diverted the flood into a new channel, leaving the great city shorn of defence, as well as of a prime necessary of life for its inhabitants; and never again did the Euphrates river return completely into its old bed, but formed the marshes and began the overflowings which in course of time by

(namely, of Mexico, Bolivia, Chili, and Peru) fell rapidly to only $2\frac{1}{4}$ millions sterling (£2,252,088) in 1816,—the first year of the Peace in Europe, and also the date of the demonetisation of silver by the British Parliament. During the next four years the annual produce of these American mines averaged $3\frac{1}{2}$ millions. From 1820 to 1830, it averaged less than $2\frac{3}{4}$ millions. During 1831 and 1832 it averaged considerably less than one million (only £888,000!), its lowest point: rising in the next three years to an average of $3\frac{1}{2}$ millions sterling. (See Table given in Porter's *Progress of the Nation*, v. 170.) This is little more than one-third of the annual produce of the American mines in 1809, as given by Humboldt, viz. 236,353,667 francs, or £9,454,000.

devastations and insalubrity produced the decay and destruction of the grandest of the ancient cities of the world.[1] Only, as already stated, in the case of the precious metals in 1810, the cutting off of the supply was accompanied by a drying up of the sources, which never since then have been fully reopened. The annual supply of full ten millions sterling of gold and silver suddenly dropped to one-half, and in five years sank to only one-quarter of their previous yield,—the produce of the mines in 1816 being only two and a quarter millions sterling. The mining regions of the New World temporarily cut their connection with the Old; and Europe, in a great crisis of her fortunes, was suddenly left without her usual supply of the canonised metals which constituted her Money, her circulating medium—the means of making every kind of purchases and of payments—the sole medium for effecting exchanges of property, whether goods or labour,—the wheels of Trade and the sinews of War.

At this time the Great War was at its height. Every quarter of Europe, if not every country, was involved in it. France, led by the peerless genius of Napoleon Buonaparte, was carrying everything before her. The Tricolor, the flag of the French Revolution, had been carried in military triumphs to Rome

---

[1] What Cyrus designed was but a passing manœuvre, to render him master of the richest and most powerful city of the world; but the enduring effects of that manœuvre were to destroy the splendid spoil which he coveted, and condemned Babylon the Great to gradual decay and final ruin,—until the White Race of Europe come (at a time now near at hand) to rebuild anew on its marshy site the great commercial Emporium of the Old World.

and Naples in the south, to Berlin and Copenhagen in the north; and from Madrid and Lisbon to Vienna and Warsaw. Russia, engaging in the contest, had seen her armies beaten on each successive venture,— first driven from Switzerland by the generals of the Revolution, then routed by the new Emperor at Austerlitz and Friedland. Even Egypt and south-western Asia had become the theatre of war; and Constantinople had to be rescued from French supremacy, and the passage of the Dardanelles had been forced, by a British fleet. All Europe was involved in the war, while its echoes were heard from beyond the seas, and literally in every part of the world. Each country of the Continent was a camp where nations were being drilled; fortresses were erected or enlarged, and foundries and arsenals were ceaselessly busy in supplying the weapons and material of war. All over the Continent, armies— larger and in greater number than the Modern World had beheld—were on the march, manœuvring or fighting; and along with each of them went the Treasure-chest, as indispensable as the Commissariat itself. Common trade and industry languished on the Continent, but the stern Trade of War, the one universal trade of that time, created even a greater demand for the precious metals than would have been caused by a simple continuance of commerce and the arts of peace. Great Britain alone (France for a while excepted) maintained her domestic industry unimpaired, and indeed steadily progressing. Behind her "wooden walls," England was secure from invasion or even from attack; and Napoleon from his camp on the heights of Boulogne had watched and wearied in vain for a single day's mastery of the Channel. By the time of which we write, England had fairly won for herself the dominion of the seas. Nelson had actually destroyed—had sunk, burnt, or captured—the entire hostile fleets of France and Spain, while that of neutral Denmark had been snatched out of the grasp of Napoleon, and was kept in English harbours for its owners at the return of peace. The commercial as well as the military navies of the hostile Continent were as good as extinct; and the sea-trade of the world was virtually in the hands of Great Britain. Foiled in every attempt to reach our shores, Napoleon the Great— discerning that, like Carthage and Venice of old, Britain derived her main and peculiar power from Foreign Trade, and that without foreign markets our industries would perish and that the resources with which we fed the war must dry up—employed his political supremacy and military dominion to close all Europe against our ships and merchandise. But the policy of Pitt and the victories of Nelson had thwarted in advance his far-reaching project; and in the world at large, and especially in her now vast colonial dominions, Great Britain found markets for all her manufactures, and a new resource in the warwon carrying-trade of the world. Events, these, not here mentioned because memorable in general history, but as illustrating the position of Great Britain under the sudden cessation of the supply of the precious metals,—a calamity which affected her to a peculiar degree, inasmuch as, when the dearth of bullion and coin was at its worst, our country was carrying on simultaneously the trades of war and of peace—alike fighting and trading on the largest scale.

In France, the heavy expenditure of the Revolutionary Government, accompanied by a temporary paralysis of the national industry, had produced a dearth of the precious metals nearly twenty years before the epoch of which I now write. While public articles of iron and bronze, including the bells of parish church or stately cathedral, were carried to the Government foundries and converted into cannon; the plate and ornaments of churches, every utensil or symbol of religion composed of gold or silver, had been seized and melted down into coin by the Revolutionary Government, which also, and chiefly, had recourse to a vast issue of Assignats, or paper-money issued upon the credit of that portion of the Crown-lands for which it had been found impossible to procure purchasers. This was, in substance, a revival of Law of Lauriston's system. And it failed, as the Mississippi Scheme failed,—namely, from the amount of the paper-money thus issued being immensely in excess of the public requirement for such money,—so that, in any case, its value must have fallen, even although the notes had not exceeded the natural or ordinary value of the property upon which they were issued. The very fact that no further purchasers could be found for the Crown-lands, showed that this kind of property had wholly lost its ordinary value. Land, in France, had temporarily become a drug in the market; there was far more of it offered for sale than there were persons ready to purchase it. In fact, the unsold portion of the Crown-lands had lost all present value, retaining only that part of their value which consists in the permanent existence and usefulness of land—in other words, merely that part of its value which is prospective. Only under very exceptional circumstances can Land possess the ready negotiability which is requisite in a basis or security for paper-money; and this was far from being the case with the Crown-lands of France. Thus the security upon which the *assignats* were issued was a kind of property which retained only one part of its normal or ordinary value, and had lost the prime element of value,—namely, immediate exchangeableness, resting on a demand to purchase it whenever offered for sale.

Except as a revolutionary measure, and one of absolute necessity to the State, the system of the Assignats stood self-condemned. This paper-money was issued upon the credit of lands which the Government had tried to sell, and could not: therefore the security was bad, being an unsaleable kind of property, and not an equivalent for the money issued upon the credit of it. But, further, the issue of assignats soon became, in amount, utterly irrespective of the value, whether present or prospective, of the Crown-lands: and thus the issue failed trebly, and altogether; (1) because the lands, or security for the notes, had lost any present or current value in exchange; (2) because the issues of the paper-money became so large as to exceed not merely the permanent or prospective value of the lands, but even what was the original and what may be called the normal and ordinary value of the Crown-lands; (3) the paper-money was issued immensely in excess of the current monetary requirements of France,—and on this account alone it must quickly have fallen in value, whatever might have been the value of the property upon which the notes were issued. In truth, the Assignats were issued totally irrespective of their fitness to be a currency, or circulating medium. The sole thought of the Revolutionary Government was to find a means of paying its own debts,—which doubtless, in the emergency, it would have done even although there had been no Crown-lands: but, having this large and unsaleable amount of property on its hands, the Revolutionary Government attached it as a security (wholly unsuitable, yet by no means worthless) for the paper-money with which it paid the national creditors. In short, it is a mistake to regard the Assignats as a deliberately devised currency, and one which failed because of mistakes in its conception. It was simply a political necessity, —a rough-and-ready scheme adopted by a revolutionary Government, which, in adopting it, had no higher or wider object in view than to pay its debts by the help of despotic power. It was never their acceptableness which floated the Assignats. They were really a currency issued upon the security of the guillotine.

Under Napoleon Buonaparte, France was brought back to a metallic currency — a currency of gold and silver coin. And in considering what befell Europe when the American supply of the precious metals was interrupted, and while a Great War was in progress, one of the most remarkable features of the case is the exemption of France, the most warring State of all, from the dearth of the precious metals which prevailed more or less severely in every other country of Europe. War — certainly all foreign war, all military operations in foreign countries — may be aptly likened to a "ready-money" branch of Trade, in which, also, only coin passes current by voluntary acceptance. And the great wars carried on by France under Napoleon were wars of aggression, wars for conquest and European ascendancy, — in other words, pre-eminently foreign wars. Yet, except for one single critical moment, that master in the science of war and in the art of conquest was able to keep his country amply supplied with the precious metals, — maintaining a stable currency of coin at home, while every other leading nation in Europe was forced to have recourse to inconvertible paper-money. Indeed, even at the close of his marvellous career, Napoleon possessed a large stock of gold and silver, as a private reserve, in the vaults of the Tuileries.

Changes in the value of a currency, especially in the direction of a monetary dearth, constitute one of the most serious, although most subtly operating, evils which can befall a community. Most of all, is this the case when such changes come suddenly, as they always do when occasioned by war. The steady recognition of this fact by the Emperor Napoleon, and the ceaseless care which he bestowed upon the maintenance of the established metallic currency and entire financial condition of France, was not the least striking proof of the statesmanlike sagacity of that Great Conqueror. Nevertheless a severe crisis of this kind occurred in the year 1805, soon after the commencement of his reign, and before he had systematised his civil and military administration. For some years previous, the public expenditure of France had exceeded the revenue-receipts to the amount of four or five millions sterling annually; and further, the revenue-collectors had to account to the Government each year, while the revenue could not be wholly collected until the middle of the following year. Also, owing to the deficit of revenue, the Government contractors had to wait long for payment of their accounts. It was the boast of Napoleon that he never would issue a Government paper-money: but what he scrupulously refrained from doing, had at this time to be done, in substance at least, by his subordinates. The Bank of France and the great capitalists advanced money to the Government contractors and collectors, whose bonds, representing Government debt, were at first accepted freely. But in the autumn of 1805 matters were brought to a crisis, owing to a sudden dearth of coin in the Bank.

When Napoleon set out from the camp at Boulogne to carry the war into the valley of the Danube, he took two millions sterling in coin from the Bank of France, in order to support his army in foreign territory. Thereupon the Bank became unable to continue its advances; Recamier and several other great capitalists failed; and the bonds of the contractors and others, representing Government debt, became so depreciated that soon they passed current at merely one-tenth of their nominal value; and credit gave way in all quarters. In this emergency, the Bank invoked assistance, among others, from the great Government contractors, Ouvrard & Company, whose influence was so vast that M. Ouvrard actually obtained from the Court of Spain a treaty intrusting to him a year's supply of the precious metals from America; the whole of which, then amounting to about eleven millions sterling, he was authorised to import. This supply would have been ample to relieve the monetary crisis in France, but a considerable interval must elapse before the specie could come to hand; and, despite every effort on the part of the Bank and the great capitalists, a Government bankruptcy, or indeed a general bankruptcy throughout France, became imminent; and it was only averted by means of the rapid and brilliant successes of the Emperor in the war. The campaign of Ulm and Austerlitz was the most rapid and triumphant ever waged by Napoleon. Breaking up his camp at Boulogne in September 1805, Mack's army in the fortified camp at Ulm was captured, Vienna was occupied, the Russians were routed at Austerlitz in the heart of Moravia, peace was signed, and the Emperor was back in Paris before the end of January. Travelling post-haste, and arriving in Paris at night, the Emperor, without a moment's rest, summoned his Minister of Finance, minutely inquiring into everything; and at eleven o'clock next forenoon a Council of Ministers was held. The crisis was at an end; but no one knew better than Napoleon the formidable character of the peril which he had escaped, and which thereafter he so sedulously and successfully guarded against. Indeed it was a desire to get possession of the gold and silver from the American mines which was one of the motives which, soon after this, led to Napoleon's invasion of the Peninsula, and to his placing his brother Joseph upon the throne of Spain. He had already begun his famous system of "making war support war;" and thenceforth he made it imperative upon all his Generals to find supplies for their troops from the foreign territory which they occupied. The vast armies of France were kept abroad, and, as a rule, not a shilling was sent to them from the French Treasury. At the same time, very considerable sums in coin, wrung as indemnities from conquered States, were brought into France, and were expended in developing the means of trade and traffic, and stimulating the general industry of the country.

Napoleon Buonaparte was the first great ruler or military chief in modern times who systematised international warfare on a basis of pecuniary returns and of immediate and direct compensation for its costs. He adopted the principle of making war defray its own expenses, irrespective of the realisation of the ordinary objects for which war is undertaken,—a system which, judging from recent memorable examples, appears to have recommended itself to the utilitarian spirit of the present age. Nations and their rulers go to war chiefly, almost exclusively, for the sake either of defending or of extending their territories and rights. And the old usage was, to accept as natural the costs of war, and to be fully satisfied if the war was successful in attaining the objects, chiefly patriotic and territorial, for which it was undertaken. "To the victor, the spoils!" was a maxim never forgotten; but in every case—we speak of civilised warfare—the costs of the war were regarded as an unavoidable expenditure, as a means to the desired end, while the spoils came at the close of the war like the profits on the outlay, and in the shape of the realisation of the objects for which hostilities had been engaged in. Indeed so little was there of the utilitarian spirit or pecuniary objects in the wars antecedent to the close of last century, that successful generals paid more regard to destroying the property of their enemies than of appropriating it to their own use. Napoleon Buonaparte, enamoured of military contests, and whose soaring ambition desired for himself—or for France as connected with himself—the political supremacy or actual dominion of Europe, discerned that if his victories were to be popular with the French, and if France was to continue capable of the military contests in which he delighted, he must present her with the glories and spoils of war without any deduction for the costs of the contest. Hence, especially from the year 1805 onwards, the moment his army crossed the frontier, his generals were taught and strictly required to supply their troops by levying contributions in the foreign territories,—usually giving *bons* or acknowledgments of the debt so contracted; while the treaties of peace which he dictated frequently imposed heavy charges upon the conquered States, by means of which (besides the sums which he expended on public works in France) he replenished his arsenals and created a war-treasure, ready to meet any unusually great emergency.

Thus, throughout the great European War, which raged without intermission from the accession of Napoleon to the French throne down to his defeat and final overthrow at Waterloo, France never had to abandon a currency of gold and silver, and continued to be amply supplied with the precious metals, although these had wholly forsaken her during her Revolutionary period. Although easily explained, the fact was a striking one. At a time when the supply of bullion from the Mines had wellnigh ceased, and when the requirements of War had created a dearth of coin (in some cases a total absence of gold and silver) throughout the other countries of Europe, in France there was no lack of coin, while the precious metals were lavishly employed in ornamental splendour and the arts of peace. Napoleonic France, in fact, repeated the example of imperial Rome, and made Conquest the means of supplying herself with the precious metals.

Every country in Europe became involved in the Napoleonic wars; but it was the leading Powers of the Continent, and especially the great military States—Austria, Prussia, and Russia—which suffered most severely in the contest, and in which the dearth of the precious metals became most complete. Their own military expenditure, together with the sums of money exacted by the Emperor Napoleon, soon ruined the finances of the various States, while coin became unprocurable within their territories. Before the end of the eighteenth century, there was hardly a State on the Continent which could put an army in the field without the aid of loans from Great Britain; and as the War progressed, all the leading Powers were forced to issue "inconvertible" paper-currencies,—that is to say, paper-money not exchangeable into coin, but in substitution for coin, which was then unprocurable in those States. This dearth of the precious metals became memorably conspicuous in Prussia in 1813—the year of the uprising of Germany against Napoleon, after his disastrous invasion of Russia,—when, in order to procure coin for the "War of Liberation," the Prussian Government appealed to all Germans to send their plate and all ornaments of gold and silver into the Treasury; each contributor receiving in return similarly shaped ornaments of iron (giving rise to the subsequently famous manufacture of "Berlin iron"), each stamped with the motto "*Iron for Gold.*" So excessive were the issues of these State paper-currencies on the Continent, owing to the great emergencies of the Powers which issued them, that the notes became enormously depreciated; so much so that in the concluding and ultimately decisive campaigns of the War, the guarantee of Great Britain, indeed a joint guarantee of the Allied Powers, was needed to uphold their value and usefulness,—a measure which alone rendered possible the vast military operations of the Allies, and the assembly of the armies of all Europe upon the banks of the Rhine, which resulted in the defeat of the French armies and the downfall of Napoleon the Great. Paper-money overthrew him, although metallic money was one of his best props.

NOTE.

The following tabular statements, from Mr Jacob's work, show what had been the general course of the production, and of the distribution and consumption, of the precious metals (including the exports to Asia, and conversion into articles of use and ornament) from 1492 down to end of 1829. The figures represent millions sterling :—

	Produced.	Existing as Coin.		Exported to Asia.	Converted.	Loss.
1492,	...	33	1492-1600,	14	28	5
1600,	177	130	1601-1700,	33	60	77
1700,	514	297	1701-1809,	352	352	93
1810,	1396	380	1810-1829,	40	112	18
1829,	1497	313				
				439	552	193

Total Production, £1497 millions; Lost, Exported, &c., £1184 millions; Existing as Coin in 1830, £313 millions.

CHAPTER XIII.

THE PERIOD OF SCARCITY.   PART II.—EFFECTS UPON GREAT BRITAIN.

Upon Great Britain, the prevalent dearth of the precious metals fell with extreme severity. She was the great fountainhead of opposition to the imperious military aggressions of France,—ceaselessly feeding the war on the Continent, as the best means of keeping it from her own shores. At a very early period of the war, Great Britain became Paymaster of the Forces to Europe, in the struggle against the domination of France. Undoubtedly this was a wise course. It was the best means of utilising her peculiar power—namely, her Wealth,—and of compensating the smallness of her military strength, consequent upon the smallness of her territory and population. But for her subsidies and resolute policy, the Continental Powers, defeated in turn by the military genius of Napoleon, would soon have been compelled to make peace with victorious France; and Napoleon would have been able to carry out his clearly-planned design of finally crushing Great

Britain by combining against her the military and naval forces of the entire Continent, besides closing Europe against her trade, and cutting off the supplies of food which were necessary to the maintenance of her population whenever a succession of bad harvests occurred.

And so, as an unavoidable consequence, there occurred a dearth of coin in England, similar both in cause and character to that which had been experienced a century previous under William III. in connection with the war against France under Louis XIV. France had now an Emperor, instead of a "Grand Monarch," and the range and intensity of the contest were far greater; but in their essential features there was little difference between the dearth of coin in 1694 and in 1797. Partly owing to the military operations of the British Government on the Continent (comparatively insignificant as these at first were), but chiefly owing to the subsidies paid in specie to our Continental Allies, a heavy drain had been made upon the stock of coin in this country, and especially (as was natural) upon the reserve-stock of coin kept by the banks to meet the legitimate demands of the public, whether as note-holders or depositors. The actual crisis, which necessitated a general suspension of specie-payments, was precipitated, or somewhat prematurely occasioned, by panic on the part of the public, arising from the apprehensions of a French invasion,—with which calamity our country was then menaced, and to which it remained liable until the victory at Trafalgar finally swept every hostile fleet from the seas. The invasion-panic became largely prevalent in the autumn of 1796; and the banks in various parts of the country were beset by depositors who claimed repayment of their deposits in coin. It was impossible to meet such a demand. In fact, a "run" is absolutely incompatible with the existence of Banking,—just as a great Plague, were it to sweep away both old and young whose lives were insured, would be destructive to Insurance Companies. If persisted in, a "run" must compel even the wealthiest of banks to close their doors.

And so, in the closing months of 1796 the English banks in large numbers were forced to close their doors; and as the run upon the banks extended to London, in February 1797 the Bank of England itself was on the brink of a similar catastrophe, and had recourse to making payments in sixpences, in order to gain time and allow the Government to come to its help. The Bank (as shown in the subsequent Parliamentary investigation of its accounts) at that time actually possessed a surplus of assets over liabilities to the amount of £3,800,000, or upwards of one-fourth; but the Bank was totally unable to meet the large demands thus suddenly made upon it for payment of its deposits in coin. Had the Bank been compelled to close its doors, the panic throughout the country, as well as the universal stoppage of discounts and other forms of banking accommodation, would have been most disastrous. Accordingly the Government, with the full concurrence of Parliament, authorised a temporary suspension of specie-payments. This is just what every State finds it necessary to do during a great war,—unless it is able, and chooses, to "make war support war" in the manner adopted by Napoleon. As has recently been witnessed, even during a Civil War the United States of America were forced to adopt a similar course. But, as will be shown immediately, the suspension of specie-payments, and the issue of inconvertible paper-money, in Great Britain, were fundamentally different in character from the same measure as adopted in other countries,—its only parallel, albeit upon a small scale, being the suspension of payments in coin in France during the Franco-German war of 1870.

No other event in history has more strikingly shown how disastrous may be the effects of Panic upon the financial condition of a country. Here, at a time of great national peril, was the whole banking-system of England, the Government Bank included, suddenly reduced to a state of collapse: Credit was at an end, and consequently the mainspring of trade and industry, of all commercial enterprise and industrial employment, was broken. In the course of a great war, and when the United Kingdom was actually threatened with and not secure from invasion, a national bankruptcy was all but produced; and yet, as events showed, this dire catastrophe was occasioned purely by a popular panic. A suspension of payments in coin could not have been ultimately avoided, in consequence of the progressive requirements for the export of specie; nevertheless the suspension might have been postponed for probably a dozen years, but for the artificial or exceptional demand for coin occasioned by the panic. Despite the demands of the war, there was still a sufficient stock of coin in the country for the ordinary domestic requirements. This is shown by the fact that for half-a-dozen years after the Suspension Act, gold could be obtained by those who wanted it as readily, and at the same price, as bank-notes. Our people do not want gold and silver for ordinary use or for domestic currency, except as "small change:" but the Government wanted specie for military purposes abroad. Nevertheless, for nearly four years after the Suspension Act the Government was able to obtain all the gold that it wanted at no increase upon the old and usual price.

It was not until 1801 that the price of gold in bank-notes rose to four guineas the ounce. During the Peace of Amiens, brief and imperfect as that cessation of war was, the price of gold relapsed; nor did it again exceed £4 the ounce, as measured in the inconvertible bank-notes, until the year 1810, when not only was the War waged upon a greater scale than ever, but Great Britain had begun to take an active part in the military struggle on the Continent, and Wellington had commenced the career of victory in the Peninsula which ultimately carried the British standards in triumph across the Pyrenees to the walls of Bordeaux and the banks of the Garonne. One of the many difficulties which then obstructed

our great General was a lack of specie, for the
support of his army,—a difficulty which grew more
urgent as he became separated from the British fleet
and transports, in his advance inland through Spain
and southern France.[1] The requirement of our
Continental Allies for British subsidies likewise
augmented as the contest approached its climax.
Under this increasing war-demand for specie, and
especially for gold, the price of that metal in England
rose to £4, 10s. in 1810; in 1812 the price advanced
to £4, 15s. 6d.; and finally in 1814, when the whole
of Europe was simultaneously in arms, and Great

[1] In 1814 "the difficulty of furnishing specie in sufficient quantity
for an army of such magnitude [a hundred thousand men], which paid
everything in ready money and levied no contributions upon the
conquered territory—especially at a time when the prodigious armies
on the Rhine absorbed nearly the whole circulating medium of the
Continent—had become excessive. The utmost that Government
could furnish was £100,000 in gold and silver coin a-month; but,
though this steady drain was felt as so severe at home that the Under-
Secretary of State, Colonel Bunbury, was sent out to endeavour to
reduce it, yet it was very far indeed from meeting Wellington's necessities. Some of his muleteers were two years in arrear; the soldiers,
in general, had been seven months without pay; the debt owing by
the British authorities in every part of the country was immense,
although in the last year £2,572,000 had passed in specie through the
military chest; and the creditors, long kept out of their money, were
becoming importunate." So serious was this want of specie, and so
resolute was Wellington in his heroic and self-denying war-policy—by
which, in the words of Napier, "order and tranquillity profound, on
the edge of the very battle-field, attended the march of the civilised
army which passed the Bidassoa"—that sixteen thousand Peninsular
troops could not be brought into France, and were sent back from the
Pyrenees, because Wellington had no funds either to pay or feed them.
How little would Napoleon have been restrained by such considerations,—or even the legions of Germany at the present day!—See
Alison's History, chap. lxxxvii.

Britain, in the grand crisis, wisely lavished her subsidies in support of the general uprising of the Germans and other Continental nations against the military despotism of Napoleon, the price of gold in the British Isles rose to its maximum, namely £5, 4s. the ounce, or one-third above its normal price in English bank-notes. After the Peace, with the decrease (not absolute cessation) of the war-demand, the price of gold fell proportionately,—being only £3, 19s. in 1816, and £3, 18s. 6d. in 1817.[1] Indeed for some months gold returned to

[1] PRICES OF GOLD AND SILVER BULLION IN BANK OF ENGLAND NOTES DURING THE SUSPENSION OF SPECIE-PAYMENTS:—

	Price of Gold per oz.			Ratio to former or Standard Price.			Price of Gold per oz.			Ratio to former or Standard Price	
				Gold.	Silver.					Gold.	Silver.
1798,	£3	17	10½	100	100	1810,	4	10	0	116	111
1799,	3	17	10½	100	103	1811,	4	4	6	109	118
1800,	3	17	10½	100	111	1812,	4	15	6	123	122
1801,	4	5	0	109	115	1813,	5	1	0	130	133
1802,	4	4	0	108	109	1814,	5	4	0	134	123
1803,	4	0	0	103	108	1815,	4	13	6	120	105
1804,	4	0	0	103	105	1816,	4	13	6	120	94
1805,	4	0	0	103	109	1817,	4	0	0	103	91
1806,	4	0	0	103	108	1818,	4	0	0	103	97
1807,	4	0	0	103	106	1819,	4	1	6	105	99
1808,	4	0	0	103	105	1820,	3	19	11	103	93
1809,	4	0	0	103	106	1821,	3	17	10½	100	91

—Table given by Professor Jevons, in his Paper "On the Variation of Prices and the Value of the Currency since 1782," read before Statistical Society in June 1865. Mr Jevons says that "the prices of silver probably furnish a better criterion of the value of the paper currency" during the suspension of specie-payments than the prices of gold do.

Alison, quoting from Parliamentary Tables, gives the price of gold in the years immediately following the close of the war as follows:—In 1816, £3, 19s. 0d; in 1817 and 1818, £3, 18s. 6d.; in 1819, £4, 1s. 0d. (a rise owing to the great French loan); and in 1820 (after the return to specie-payments), at £3, 17s. 10½d. In 1795 and 1796, *before* the suspension of specie-payments, the price of gold in bank-notes is given as £4, 4s.! Jacob (ii. p. 370) states the price of gold in bank-notes in the year 1814 at £5, 10s.——These are very remarkable diversities.

£3, 17s. 10½d.: in other words, its price in the inconvertible bank-notes was just the same as it had been twenty years previously in the convertible paper-money before the War, and as it bears in similar currency at the present time. Within two years after the close of the War, the Bank of England voluntarily resumed payments in specie. This step, however, was premature and had to be retraced, in consequence of a renewal of the drain of gold to the Continent, owing to the loans then being made to enable France to discharge her financial engagements to her conquerors. Although the War was at an end, the foreign expenditure connected with the War was not concluded for fully three years afterwards, owing to the Army of Occupation then maintained in France; and farther, the loans raised by the French Government, being largely subscribed by London financial firms, prolonged the demand, or rather created a new and exceptional requirement for the precious metal,—a circumstance which proved unfortunate and embarrassing as it occurred contemporaneously with the repeal of the Bank Suspension Act and the return to payments in coin throughout the United Kingdom.

To an unprejudiced student of those times—certainly to myself—it appears clearly that the true cause of the increased price of gold in bank-notes subsequent to the year 1800 was the increased value attaching to the precious metal from the new and exceptional requirements for it created by the great War. As above shown, the price of gold in bank-notes remained unchanged for several years after our bank-notes had become legally inconvertible,— a fact, also, which proved that the "suspension of cash-payments" in 1797 was somewhat premature, or at least would not have been necessary but for the serious Panic of that year,—the price of gold for some years thereafter showing that there was still enough of that metal in our country to meet not merely the ordinary requirements for it, but also the contemporaneous demand for export (not very heavy in those years) in connection with the War. Further, as above shown, gold returned to its ordinary price in bank-notes almost as soon as the War ceased, although our paper-money was still legally "inconvertible;" and thereafter the price only rose again slightly in consequence of our Capitalists subscribing (of course in specie) to the Loans raised by the French and other foreign Governments, together with a partial prolongation of our own military expenditure on the Continent. This view of the matter, I am well aware, is different from that which has been ordinarily taken by writers on the subject —who, ignoring the patent fact that the value of gold was greatly enhanced in this country by the exceptional demand for it created by the operations of the Great War, maintain that the rise in the value of that metal was merely apparent, and only occasioned by our bank-note currency becoming depreciated from excessive issues.

A great war is a greatly exceptional event, and cannot be met by the agencies and appliances of ordinary national life or social organisation. It necessitates exceptional measures; and the most common of such measures is the use of credit-money. When Hannibal and the Carthaginians were at the gates of Rome—when the flower of the Roman State had fallen in battle along with the army on the bloody field of Cannæ,—and when Rome, cut off alike from allies and from the resources of Italy, was compelled to stand at bay behind the ramparts of her capital against the menacing attack of her Semitic rival, the Senate passed a law temporarily suspending cash-payments.[1] After that crisis, the Roman State was free from deadly jeopardy until its final fall before the onset of the Northern Barbarians. During the ensuing chaos of the Dark Ages, there was so little commerce in Europe, and social life was reduced to so rudimentary a condition, that the lack of currency (although its subtly repressive action upon industry must have been evil and severe) was but little felt in a sensible form. Moreover, as Credit could hardly exist in so unsettled a state of society, credit-money for national use would have been impracticable,—indeed so obviously impracticable that even the idea of it appears never to have been entertained.

It was Great Britain, impelled thereto by a great war-necessity (in 1694) which first showed to modern

---

[1] The public creditors were paid in bonds not convertible into money until the end of the war. As Livy says, the Censors decreed that "no one was to demand coin from the Treasury until the war was finished."

Europe the vast power which can be obtained by means of a well-ordered system of paper-money and bank-credit. Banks and banking-currency mightily strengthened the State during our war with France under Louis XIV.,—permitting the greater part of the coin of the country to be employed in the support and maintenance of our army on the Continent, while the notes of our banks of issue supplied a sufficient currency for the domestic trade, industry, and production. A century later we reaped still more fully the benefits of the system first adopted in 1694. The Napoleonic War was far more severe than that of the previous century. It was the very crisis of the British Empire. It was to us what the second Punic War had been to Rome; and Napoleon in his camp at Boulogne (before Trafalgar relieved us from the contemplated invasion) was hardly less formidable than was Hannibal and his swarthy legions at the gates of the Imperial City. As the crisis was greater, so also was the extent and form of the aid which we then drew from paper-money. Paterson had established paper-money, in the form of banking-currency, or bank-notes convertible into coin on demand, as a representative of and partial substitute for the precious metals in coin; but under the greater exigencies of the Napoleonic war, our nation went further, and employed this banking-currency in complete but temporary substitution for the precious metals. And it proved the salvation of our empire, as well as upheld the safety of our shores.

It is impossible to pass by this memorable recourse

to inconvertible paper-money without some notice of the peculiar features, or conditions of issue, which rendered it so successful. The British system was widely different from and far superior to the system adopted by the Continental Powers. Indeed Great Britain had only one want to supply, while the Continental Governments had two. In War, as in ordinary trade-expenditure, the fundamental want is of Wealth, Capital, Property, to give in payment or exchange for the supplies and services of the war. But this wealth, or stock of property, is of little use of itself for expenditure. Of what service is a landed estate to a man who wishes to buy a hat or a dinner? There must also be Money, Currency, the means or medium of exchange, before the wealth can be made available for the numerous payments and purchases of various kinds. Wealth, in fact, is but the arm, with its strong motive power; and it needs some adequate currency, like its hand and fingers, before its power can be effectively utilised. The Continental Powers during the Great War were in want both of Wealth and of Money, or currency; whereas wealthy and prospering Britain lacked only currency. Accordingly, after the early years of the war, the Continental Powers issued paper-money, in the form of State-notes, chiefly as a creation of wealth. They had exhausted not only their revenues, but their power of raising loans, or of obtaining on credit the wealth of others. They issued the notes in payment to their creditors—to the soldiers, to the contractors for the supply of the army, and in all the ordinary expenditure of the Government. Hence the paper-money was issued totally irrespective of, or at least unlimited by, the wants of the public for currency. There was no limit to its issue save the needs of the State. It was, in truth, exactly equivalent to a forced loan. Each fresh issue of these State-notes, of course, produced a double evil,—it diminished the credit of the Government, and also made this currency more and more redundant,—evils perfectly distinct from one another. The currency became depreciated by the weakening of both its bases, or elements of its acceptability and value. The value of the notes, in short, fell from two causes,—namely, alike from distrust of the Government's power or willingness to redeem these notes, and also because, being issued in large excess of the currency-requirements of the public, there was no adequate demand for the notes, so that they fell in value, like all things else of which the supply is much greater than the demand.

It is hard even to conjecture the extent to which each of those two causes acted separately, or of itself, in producing a fall in the value of these Continental State paper-currencies. It cannot be determined how far it was a purely currency-question,—that is to say, how far the notes fell in value (just as coin itself does, and must do) from a sheer plethora of the means or medium of exchange;—or, secondly, how far the depreciation was owing to the financial discredit of the Governments which issued the notes, and which stood pledged to redeem them, in coin, at the close of the War, or as part of the National Debt. But it is manifest that the latter cause of the depreciation operated very powerfully. Enormous as was the amount of this forced and inconvertible paper-currency issued by Russia, Austria, and some other Continental States, it appears unquestionable that the vast payments and expenditure specially occasioned by the War were sufficient to absorb, or create an effective demand for, a remarkably large portion of these issues. This was shown in the closing period of the war, when the collective guarantee of the Allied Powers (Great Britain included) sufficed to raise the excessive and discredited paper-currency from the worthlessness into which it had fallen, and made it serviceable for prosecuting the war, and overwhelming Napoleon by sheer mass of force at Leipzic, as finally upon the bloody fields of Champagne. Of course this could not have happened had the depreciation of the Continental paper-currencies been owing simply to excess of issue.

The inconvertible British paper-currency was fundamentally different. As already said, it had not to be employed as a creation of wealth, or as a forced loan. The prosperity of the country, resting upon the command of the seas and upon an ever-increasing trade, maintained unimpaired the credit of the Government, as well as the loan-making power of the people. Immense as was the wealth required for carrying on so great a war by land and sea, the Government found no difficulty in obtaining it from the yearly revenue, supplemented by loans from its own people. Indeed, so marvellous was the credit of the Government as well as the ever-increasing reserve-wealth of the nation, that in the last years of the war, after twenty years of the severest contest ever waged in Europe, the British Government was able to borrow on as favourable terms as at the beginning of the long war-struggle,—the great loan of fifty millions sterling in 1815 having been contracted actually on more favourable terms than one for four and a half millions at the commencement of the war! A fact unparalleled in history, and which shows how, under the masterly policy of Pitt,[1] the opportunities of the contest had been made to contribute to the commercial prosperity and general wealth of the country.

Every State, whether a monarchy or a republic, which during a great war cannot procure the requisite funds or "sinews of war" from its revenue or from loans, employs paper-money as a means of paying its creditors and the expenditure of the contest,—and not purely, or even chiefly, to provide a currency for its people under the exceptional demand

---

[1] As often remarked by Napoleon, Pitt had no genius for military strategy or combinations, and his military policy was a failure. There were occasions, especially in the early years of the war, when a bolder and less scanty employment of the military power of Great Britain might have terminated the contest, thereby saving a vast sum for the British Exchequer. But no Minister ever had a greater love for the commercial interests of his country, or a shrewder discernment for upholding and fostering them by his conduct of the war,—thereby "making war maintain war," not (as Napoleon did) by the plunder of hostile populations, but by constantly recruiting the trade and augmenting the wealth of his own country.

for and consequent scarcity of the precious metals which ordinarily occurs in such emergencies. But—marvellous as the fact is—the British Government during the Great War was never reduced to this extremity; and consequently paper-money in this country was employed only as a means of supplying the nation with currency, in lieu of the gold and silver coin which had to be sent abroad in payment of the subsidies to our Allies, and for the maintenance of our army upon the Continent. This is an all-important point, and one which can be seen as determining the character of the numerous and various issues of paper-currency which have been witnessed during the present century — or indeed ever since the system of paper-money was first established by Paterson, and followed in brilliant but perilous fashion by Law of Lauriston. Indeed as "Money" is generally understood as synonymous with "Wealth," the one kind of paper-issue (that employed directly as wealth, to pay debts, &c., like the French assignats and American greenbacks) might, for popular distinction, be termed Paper-money, and the other, which acts purely as a temporary substitute for coin, as Paper-currency.

It appears probable, or wellnigh certain, that some of the best features of the system which was adopted or commenced by the Suspension of "Cash-payments" (*i.e.*, of coin-payments) were not appreciated or even perceived at the time. The liberation of the Bank from its legal—and indeed fundamental—duty, of paying both its notes and its deposits in coin of the realm, arose in one of those great exigencies which had to be met at once. Both the Ministry and Parliament saw that this was the only step to be taken to obviate a fatal catastrophe, alike political and commercial. There could be no doubt as to the correctness of, and indeed absolute necessity for this procedure. And so the step was taken,—without any scientific consideration of the distinctive working of the system thus established: apparently, without a perception even of the conditions which so widely differentiated the inconvertible bank-notes thus legalised in England from the inconvertible State-notes of the Continental Governments.

The inconvertible notes on the Continent were wanted by the Governments, as a means of paying their debts; accordingly, the notes were issued by the Government to its creditors of all kinds. In England the Government did not want the notes save as a means of supplying currency to the community, in lieu of the coin withdrawn from the banks or circulation for export under the peremptory requirements of the war. Our Government had taken the coin and bullion from the Bank of England, in Treasury-payments or in loans; and the Bank, being thus left without gold, was thereupon legally exempted from paying coin either to its depositors or note-holders; and as a necessary sequel or accompaniment to this Parliamentary enactment, the bank-notes thus rendered inconvertible were made legal tender throughout the community, or between man and man; and also were paid out like coin by the other banks in England, in the "cashing" of their own notes. This measure was a temporary one; and, as it was the War which occasioned the scarcity of gold and silver in this country, the Act was to remain in force only until the restoration of peace,—at which time, presumably, the scarcity or exceptional requirement for the precious metals would cease, and coin or bullion would flow back into the Banks as before. Nevertheless the two events—namely, the close of the war and the re-accumulation of specie in the British banks—could hardly be quite simultaneous. The latter event was a natural sequence, but could not be an actual accompaniment, of the former. It was easy to send gold in large quantity abroad: the payment of a single loan to one of the Allied Powers might carry several millions of guineas to the Continent; but, if not brought back by some similar operation, and if the specie were left to trickle back in the ordinary operations of Trade, the return of the specie would be gradual and very much slower than the export had been. It was like emptying a reservoir of water into the sea, and having to wait until the water returned to the land in fogs and rain, and, descending from the hills, accumulated anew in the reservoir.

As was natural under this arrangement, the Banks carried on their operations just as before,—with the important exception, of course, that as there was no coin to be had, the Banks, like the rest of the community, were exempt from paying their customers or depositors in the coin of the realm. The notes, after they were made inconvertible, were issued exactly in the same manner, and upon the same terms or rate of charge, as before,—namely, in repayment of deposits, or in loans and discounts; the only change being that the Banks charged a somewhat higher than its usual rate of interest. In other words, during the suspension of specie payments, the supply of currency was issued at a higher price or value than before—one-fourth higher than usual: a notable fact, little attended to. During the war, the Bank-rate, or charge for discounting bills or for making loans upon suitable securities, was never below 5 per cent during the suspension of cash-payments, whereas both before and after, the Bank's ordinary charge was 4 per cent: which was also, in those times (and until comparatively recently) the fixed or established charge of the Bank of France.[1] The notes being thus issued under the same conditions, and at a charge twenty-five per cent higher than usual, it is hard to see how this paper-currency could become depreciated owing to excessive issue. Every one who got notes from the banks had to pay for them as before, indeed at a considerably higher rate of charge. When people pay the same price for a thing as before, it means that their need for the thing is as great as previously. In such a case as this, I can think of no better proof, or indeed of any other single proof equally valid. Now, as is well

---

[1] When founding, or at least remodelling, the Bank of France, the Emperor Napoleon said:—" Write in golden letters over its doors— 'It is the function of the Bank to discount bills at *Four per cent.*'"

known and fully recognised, a mere addition to a currency does not necessarily depreciate it: an augmented currency is no more in excess than before so long as the demand or requirement for currency remains as great as before, by having increased in like proportion. Moreover, if the currency be issued at exactly the same price or value as formerly, how is it to acquire a lower value when it cannot be obtained at a lower price?

Unfortunately there are no complete records of the actual amount of gold and silver sent abroad from this country during the War, or during the suspension of payments in coin, nor do we know the amount of the previous metallic currency of the kingdom. But, if we look at the increase in the paper-currency, or bank-notes of the kingdom, and remember that the entire gold-coin, and the greater portion of the silver-coin also, were sent abroad during the war,—even were we to consider these two things alone, the increased issue of bank-notes would not appear serious. But this is a mere fragment of the case: because both the population and the trade, alike foreign and domestic, had vastly increased, producing a corresponding increase in the requirement for currency,—as consequences, creating not merely a requirement for more currency, or more coin in actual circulation, but more money in bank to represent and utilise the increased deposits of wealth, accompanying the growing prosperity. Great Britain, in fact, during the Suspension of specie-payments, carried on conjointly, and to an extent unparalleled in history, the trades of war and of peace,—engaging as leader in the gigantic war of European resistance to Napoleonic France, and simultaneously vastly extending her own trade, and acquiring the greater part of the maritime commerce of the world.

It is beyond our purpose to deal fully with the important and highly instructive monetary circumstances of that time. Our purpose is confined to exhibiting in broad scope that memorable epoch of scarcity, or entire absence, of gold-coin in the British Isles, and the character and general consequences of the suspension of coin-payments which then became necessary. It was the peremptory war-requirement for the precious metals—the imperative necessity for exporting our stock of coin to maintain the contest on the Continent—which raised the value of the precious metals in this country to an exceptional height. But, besides this purely military demand, the War created, or was attended by, another exceptional requirement for gold in the British Isles. Under the "Continental System" of Napoleon, the ports of Europe were closed against British trade, and British goods were liable to be seized and confiscated. One part of the difficulty thus astutely created for us by Napoleon was the obstruction to our obtaining food-supplies from abroad, which consequently, at times, raised the price of corn to an exorbitant point in this country. Another result of the Continental System was that, as British goods were excluded from the

Continent, our merchants had to pay in coin, or chiefly in coin, for the goods which we imported. Thus, while the British Government needed all the specie it could get for the maintenance of the War, our importing merchants were equally in want of gold wherewith to pay for the grain and other commodities of Continental produce. The ordinary conditions of Trade were forcibly suspended, occasioning a much larger demand for specie than usual. With the cessation of the War, of course, these monetary difficulties ceased, or nearly so. Indeed, when Peace came, the exceptional value of specie so quickly disappeared that the ounce of gold returned almost, if not quite, to its old and ordinary value as measured in our existing paper-money, "inconvertible" though it still was; and it was owing to a slight revival or continuance of the War-requirement for specie, and especially owing to investments in the French Loan, that the price of gold thereafter slightly rose again, prior to the passing of the Act of 1819.

But there were two other causes, beyond the actual War-requirements, which naturally enhanced the value of gold at the time when a return was made in this country to the ordinary system of payments in coin, and which alone produced the hardships occasioned by this change. First, the mere cessation of the War, and of the exceptional demand for specie created by the war, could not at once remove the difficulties attending a resumption of coin-payments by the Banks. The direct cause and sole purpose of the Suspension Act was not (although it might well have been) to save our people and Trade from a violent change in the value of the currency, unavoidably produced by the temporary enhancement of the value of gold during the War; but simply to remedy, or compensate the Banks for, the sweeping away and sending abroad of their entire reserves of coin, through the loans and general expenditure of the State. Accordingly, when Peace came, the Banks had to replenish these reserves before they could safely meet a return to coin-payments. Hence it happened that, when the War-requirements for specie had ceased, the coming of a return to coin-payments in this country of itself produced a new and exceptional demand for the precious metal. The old reservoirs had to be refilled before the old monetary system could be revived; while, owing to the vast growth of the nation in the interval, the stock of specie in the Banks required to be much larger than before, consistently with an adequate and stable monetary supply. This was something that no mere Act of Parliament could provide. The most effective course for the Banks to take would have been to sell a portion of their reserve of securities abroad, converting it into gold; and this exceptional demand would undoubtedly have kept (or raised anew) the price of gold at an exceptional height in this country. The Banking demand would have succeeded to the War-demand; thus keeping gold above its ordinary value and price. This, however, was not the operation mainly relied upon by the Banks to replenish their reserves by bringing back gold from abroad. When the Resumption of coin-payments was in progress, the Banks, as a rule, did not enter the bullion-market to buy the gold which they needed; and consequently gold stood at its ordinary value, as re-established by the cessation of the War-demand. Nevertheless the difficulty was only disguised, and the evil appeared in another form. Money, the whole currency, became dear, and a Fall in Prices ensued. The Banks contracted their issues,—lessening the amount of currency compared with the amount of exchangeable commodities: whereby, of course, the price of all commodities fell, while the value or purchasing power of money increased,—inducing an influx of specie from abroad by the general depreciation of property in the British Isles, which induced foreigners to send specie here wherewith to purchase our artificially depreciated goods — the whole products of the national labour being lowered in money-value by the contraction of the currency.

It is important to observe that, contrary to the ordinary view of the matter, the banking difficulty attending the resumption of payments in coin did not arise in connection with the Notes, but with the Deposits. Indeed it was not a cashing of notes which had produced the dilemma in 1797, necessitating the Suspension Act, but the demand for payment of the bank-deposits in specie, —partly from panic and partly for the purpose of export. In like manner, what the banks had to dread when a return to specie-payments was made in 1819 was not a cashing of notes, but a demand for payment of the deposits in specie — especially as gold was still in request for export in connection with the French loan and other purposes. Prior to the repeal of the Suspension Act, as stated in Parliament by Mr Vansittart, although specie was still in exceptional request, the difference in value between gold-coin and the inconvertible notes was only three per cent, — or 7¼d. in the pound. The notes, too, were all in the hands of the public, employed in active circulation; and also the people were perfectly content with the notes. Under such circumstances there was little or no ground for apprehending any large cashing of the notes by the note-holders; and in fact no such danger occurred. But the case stood otherwise with the Deposits,— at that time amounting to an immense sum. The French Loan, amounting to thirty millions sterling, was chiefly subscribed in London; and the subscribers or contractors for the loan had to transmit the amount to Paris in specie. Accordingly, when the banks were made liable again to pay in coin, the contractors to that and other loans demanded the specie which they wanted from the banks by calling up their deposits.

Such, then, was the real danger which beset the banks upon a return to payments in coin. To meet demands upon their Deposits, the Banks required to replenish their stock of specie, which had been wholly swept away during the progress of the War. As already said, the banks did not do this by selling their reserve of securities and thereby providing themselves with gold. They threw the burden of replenishing their stock of specie upon the public. They contracted their loans and discounts,—in other words, the supply of currency,—and simply waited until gold came back into the country, and accumulated anew in their coffers, as paid to them in the form of deposits. As needs hardly be said, every branch of Trade in this country is dependent upon, and is carried on by means of banking-accommodation, in the shape of loans and the discounting of bills. Accordingly, when the Banks largely contracted these advances, many traders had to stop payment; while the others, only less unfortunate, had to make forced sales of their goods, in order to turn them into money or currency. The result of this contraction of the currency, together with numerous bankruptcies and forced sales, was to produce a general fall of prices,—in other words, a rise in the value of money. The property of the kingdom became depreciated. The purchasing power of money was increased. Foreigners were thereby induced to buy more largely in this country than usual,—making payment, of course, in specie. And so, and in this way, gold came back, and gradually accumulated anew in the banks, in the shape of deposits: at length restoring to the banks their customary reserves of specie.

The resumption of payments in specie in 1819,

and these banking occurrences connected with it, have been regarded by not a few writers and politicians as the main cause of the terrible distress which contemporaneously occurred in this country. That the distress was aggravated by this monetary change cannot be disputed; yet it is certain that a severe crisis must have occurred, quite independently of this monetary change; and it is impossible to disentangle the effects of that change from the unavoidable consequences of the transition from the Great War (the most peculiar in its trade-circumstances of any ever waged) to the routine of peaceful industry and ordinary finance.

Great Britain, as already remarked, had occupied a peculiar position throughout the great French War, and the peculiarities were of a kind eminently favourable for our people. In previous wars, the Trade of the country had been diminished; whereas between 1792 and 1815 British trade, both foreign and domestic, had received a vast expansion, unparalleled even in the most prosperous periods of peace. The early years of the War witnessed important additions to our colonies and dependencies beyond the sea, in all quarters of the globe; commensurately augmenting our Foreign Trade and the markets for our home productions, as well as insuring a supply of raw materials for our manufactures. Thanks to the steam-engine and the achievements of mechanical invention, especially in textile machinery, the British Isles were then becoming fit to be the workshop of the world. At the same time, overleaping the resources of our own country, our population were becoming largely dependent upon other parts of the globe, alike for food and for the staples of our manufacturing industry. As Antæus renewed his strength by contact with mother Earth, so England was dependent for her power and even for existence by constantly maintaining and extending her contact and commercial relations with the world at large. Cut off her trade with the outer world, and she would quickly have been forced to succumb in the costly and gigantic contest which she had then to wage. This was the supreme object which Napoleon sought to attain; and so, while shutting the ports of Europe against her trade and shipping, he sought to overwhelm her at sea, by combining against her the navies of the Continental Powers,— so as to destroy her Foreign trade, thereby paralysing her domestic industry, while also laying open her coasts to the military Invasion which was to give the death-blow to our independence. By marvellous energy and naval genius, England shattered all those maritime confederacies against her: and, as a natural consequence of her triumphant success, she became mistress of the seas; every rival flag was swept from the ocean, and the whole carrying-trade of the world passed into her hands. As the result, the Foreign Trade of Great Britain nearly doubled during the twenty-three years of the war,— opening markets and providing a profitable demand for the fullest development of manufacturing power of which she was then capable. Thus, despite the mighty war which rolled around her, the domestic industries of Great Britain—alike in the forge and foundry, the factory and the farm—not only pursued their course as securely as if in the bosom of peace, but progressed and prospered as if by the help of beneficent magic.[1]

While commerce, shipping, and manufactures thus increased and prospered, the other great branch of national industry and resource was prosecuted with equal energy and success. Agriculture at that time still constituted at least one-half of the resources of the country, and of the employment of the people. But already in bad harvest-years our population were largely dependent for food upon supplies from abroad. Moreover, the time was still far distant when oceanic steam-navigation could bring to our shores the harvests of the New World. The only available source of grain-supply was the neighbouring region of Germany and Russia; and in those years

[1] The imports of the United Kingdom in 1792 and 1793 averaged $19\frac{1}{2}$ millions sterling (official value). In 1809 they had increased to fully 30 millions. In 1810, an exceptional year, they amounted to upwards of $37\frac{1}{2}$ millions. In the last two years of the war (1814 and 1815) they averaged $32\frac{1}{3}$ millions: or, 66 per cent larger than they were at the beginning of the war.

The total Exports (of which there is no return in the previous years) amounted to $27\frac{1}{3}$ millions, official value, in 1798. During the first eight years of this century, they averaged 32 millions. In 1809 and 1810 they averaged $44\frac{1}{2}$ millions; and in the last two years of the war they averaged 56 millions,—more than double what they had been in 1798.

Our Shipping, which had amounted to one million tons in 1792, increased to $2\frac{3}{4}$ million tons in the closing years of the War—more than $2\frac{1}{2}$ times as large as at the beginning of the War: and upon this amount there was no increase for a dozen years.

of the War when the military power of Napoleon was able to close against us the German and Baltic seaports, our people must have been starved into surrender but for the extraordinary development of Agriculture in the British Isles.[1] The expansion of grain-growing was but little due to a conversion of pasture-fields into tillage: for the existing grass-lands were needed for the flocks and herds of a rapidly increasing population. But Agriculture invaded the old waste-places. During the last ten years of the war, under the virtual food-blockade established by Napoleon's Continental System, no less than twelve hundred Enclosure bills were passed; and the extent of land thereby brought into cultivation was estimated at two million acres. In truth, as was said by Lord Brougham, Great Britain, "which foreigners are wont to taunt as a mere manufacturing and trading country, in reality became for its size by far the greatest agricultural State in the world." Marsh and fen were energetically reclaimed for agriculture; while the area of cultivation, like a golden tide, rose far up the bleak and stony hillsides, and even sought out the sheltered nooks and level spots where a scant soil was to be found amidst the moorlands. To this day the sportsman or rambling tourist, especially among the

---

[1] "Agriculture flourished beyond all former precedent, and more than kept pace with the growth of the population"—which increased from barely fourteen millions in 1793 to upwards of eighteen millions in 1813; "and the nation, for the first time for half a century, became independent of foreign supplies of food."—Alison's History, chap. xcv. § 65.

Scottish hills, comes upon smooth green spots, where perhaps the furrowing plough has still left its traces,—spots where corn was grown in that former time, and whose verdurous surface proves the strength of old cultivation by resisting any return of the wild moorland vegetation. By the peasant of a subsequent generation, not a few of these green spots—tiny oases among the hills—were named the "Fairy Knowe," or the "Fairy Ring," and their strange verdure was attributed to the midnight revels of the Elves and the light tripping of fairy feet! But in truth their origin was hardly less remarkable, and much more memorable; because these tiny oases were the hard-won outposts in the campaign of national industry which, under the necessities of the Great War, carried Agriculture into the lone wasteplaces of our Isles,—green and quiet records of the Heroic Age of the British nation,—when, more even than in the days of the Black Prince and Henry V., of Poictiers, Cressy, and Agincourt, our people could say, in the proud lines of Shakspeare,—

> "Come the three corners of the world in arms,
> And we shall shock them! Nought shall make us rue,
> If ENGLAND to itself do rest but true."[1]

Moreover, War itself is a Trade. Grim though it be, it is a branch of industry giving large employment, and calling for various productions and services, peremptorily required for the safety of the State and security of the commonwealth. The army

---

[1] *King John*, Act v. scene 7.

and navy were vastly increased, while (besides the Yeomanry and local corps) there was a Militia numbering no less than seventy-seven thousand men. More war-ships had to be built—more cannon, muskets, and other war-material manufactured; thereby creating a new branch of manufacture, while adding still more extensively to the employment of the people. The iron trade especially prospered, for England was the armoury of the world. War also—whatever be the ultimate effects of its more or less unreproductive expenditure—is mainly paid for by the wealthier classes (as by the Income and Property tax), while the employment which it gives is shared mainly by the poorer classes. The Income-tax and other War-taxes of that time—including an Income-tax yielding in 1815 fifteen millions—did not touch the common people, who meanwhile benefited by the expenditure owing to increased employment and higher wages.

But there was another, and much more powerful immediate help to the condition of the people, howsoever greatly trenching upon the resources of the future. This was the great Loans, contracted and disbursed by the State during the War. The War-taxation was, at the best, a consumption of wealth taken from one portion of the community in giving employment or higher wages to another. But the wealth obtained by means of the Loans came, as it were, from another world or a different nation—a generation, or indeed generations of Englishmen, still unborn. These Loans were like a gift to the nation from its posterity,—a gift of vast sums upon which the nation had merely to pay the interest while actually employing and enjoying the capital. For example, say that a loan of fifty millions, at 5 per cent interest, was raised and expended in a year of the war, the nation obtained the full use and consumption of this wealth merely by paying back two and a half millions out of the sum so received: in other words, the nation at the time, and while the money was being spent, got possession of 95 per cent of the borrowed sum (or forty-seven and a half millions sterling) *gratis*, as an addition to their resources during that year.

The wealth thus acquired, or placed at the disposal of the nation gratuitously during the War—that is to say, the capital sum of the Loans *minus* the current interest—amounted to a vast sum: equal to about five or six times the annual income of the country, or, in other words, to the produce of the then very heavy taxation for five or six years. Let us briefly show the facts of the case. At the close of the War, the National Debt was nearly six hundred millions sterling larger than at the commencement in 1793.[1] But as the greater portion of these Loans was contracted (in the Three-per-Cents) at £60 for each £100, the State actually received barely four hundred millions. Moreover, a very considerable portion of this money (the produce of the Loans) was spent abroad, in the victualling and maintenance of our army and navy on foreign ser-

[1] The net addition to the Debt—that is, after deducting the sums annually paid off by the Sinking Fund—amounted to £574,000,000.

vice,—their equipment and warlike munitions being supplied from home. Also at least fifty-two millions of the produce of the Loans was paid in subsidies to Foreign Powers, and was therefore, in a commercial sense, wholly lost to our people. Altogether we may conjecture that of the 400 millions sterling received by the Government as the produce of the Loans, at least 100 millions were expended abroad, —leaving about 300 millions of borrowed money expended at home during the twenty-three years of the war. This gives an average of thirteen millions a-year for the whole period; but the loans were very trifling at first, while becoming very large as the war progressed; and thus the *per se* beneficial result occurred that in proportion as the taxation and the national sacrifices increased, so also did this expenditure of borrowed wealth,—*pro tanto* helping the nation to bear its heavy burdens.

If we take the year 1813, when the military crisis and financial burdens of the War were at their height —when Napoleon, recovering from his defeat in Russia, led forth from France a new army into the heart of Germany, overthrowing the Allied armies at Lutzen and Bautzen, and finally stood at bay against the united hosts of Russia, Prussia, and Austria at Leipzic,—we find that the Revenue of Great Britain amounted to upwards of seventy-six millions, and the Loan of that year to fifty-eight millions nominally; but the money actually received from the Loan was only thirty-six millions:—making a total State expenditure for the year of 106 millions sterling,—

by far the largest in British annals. Of this vast sum, upwards of eleven millions were expended in subsidies to our Allies—an assistance without which Napoleon would have triumphed anew, and the Grand Alliance would have been broken up after the retreat from Bautzen,—and perhaps about five millions were spent abroad upon our own troops under Wellington. This would leave twenty millions of the borrowed money to be spent at home. Moreover, of the seventy-six millions of taxation, sixteen millions belonged to the Sinking Fund—a simple transference of this amount from the general public to the Fund-holders. It is easy to see how this expenditure of borrowed money, yielding extra profits and employment to the people, must have lightened the enormous burden of taxation. It was, for the time, a clear gain of thirty-six millions a-year, minus the current interest,—a calling up of resources from the future to help the nation to tide over a tremendous national crisis, wherein the commercial fortunes as well as independence of the country were at stake. It was a heavy price; but one must not forget that apart from the priceless boon of freedom, the War itself served immensely to expand our commerce and provide markets for our manufactures, with employment for the people engaged on them.

At the close of the war in 1815, there also ceased the vast war-expenditure—the money for which had been obtained partly by taxation from the wealthier classes, and partly by the loans,—an expenditure which, speaking roughly, was a diffusion of wealth from the rich among the nation at large. This expenditure had created some new branches of trade (those immediately connected with the war), and had enlarged some of the old ones; and when this amount of trade came to an end, a general hardship set in,—especially as the cessation was sudden, not permitting time for a transference of labour to other trades, even supposing that such an alternative had presented itself. But it did not. On the contrary, there was a reduction of trade all round: so that there occurred not merely a fall of wages, but an absolute lack of employment. In particular, the iron-trade suffered severely. England had become the arsenal of the world, and our iron-trade flourished exuberantly,—almost every iron-foundry in the kingdom became acquainted more or less with the manufacture of war-material;[1] and when this exceptional demand suddenly ceased—ceasing, too, when at its highest point—great hardship ensued in all branches of that important national industry.

The most natural course for a people, when passing from a state of war into peace, is literally to convert their swords into ploughshares, and find employment in the cultivation of the land. This course was taken

---

[1] In early boyhood, when playing with comrades in the workshops and "yard," or open ground, of my father's foundry at Edinburgh (the old "Edinburgh Foundry," in Leith Walk—mentioned, also, as a playground of his, in comradeship with my elder brothers, in the Memoirs of the subsequently distinguished James Nasmyth) we often came upon memorials of the old War-time, in the shape of bomb-shells and grenades—some of them charged, and occasioning dangerous explosions when heedlessly thrown into the cupolas as old iron.

in a very striking manner in the United States, at the close of the great Civil War, wherein at least a million and a half of men were engaged in active service. A similar social or industrial phenomenon was exhibited at the close of the Sikh War in India, when the brave militia of the Punjaub, under the wise administration of their British conquerors, rapidly settled down to the cultivation of the soil —happily relieving the country of the serious apprehended danger arising from a floating and discontented mass of disbanded soldiery. In 1815, unfortunately, the British Isles had no large reserves of unoccupied land; and, moreover, under the requirements of the War, Agriculture had been pursued even upon too large a scale to be profitable on the return of peace with the renewed importation of grain from the Continent.

Nor was the desired opening for the disbanded war-labour to be found in general trade or manufacturing industry. Indeed it is to be remembered that the return of Peace actually took away from our people some important commercial advantages which they had enjoyed during the War. With the Peace, the seas at once became open to the ships of all nations. The exclusive sovereignty of the ocean which had transferred to the British flag the carrying-trade of the world, had to be resigned; and Nature's great highway of trade, for civilised nations, became once more the common property of mankind. And finally, the nations of the Continent, released from the imperiously absorbing pursuits of war, began anew—albeit slowly at first—to compete with us in manufacturing industry and foreign trade.

But, most of all, did the return of peace press heavily upon British Agriculture. Not only did it suffer in common with other trades from the cessation of the extraordinary State expenditure, but—as has been stated—for the salvation of the nation, Farming had been extended and improved to the utmost limits then possible. Under the high prices for grain occasioned by the scarcity of bread-food in our Isles, when the Continental ports became closed against our shipping, even very poor soils were placed under tillage, with profit to the Farmer, and great advantage to the then food-beleaguered nation. But with the return of Peace, the Baltic and German ports were permanently reopened, while foreign Agriculture became pursued on a large scale, because free from the desolation of war, and by the vast disbanded armies of the Continent. Farm-rents, of course, had risen with the high price of grain in this country; and both landowners and farmers became the chief sufferers of the time. By extraordinary enterprise they had kept the nation supplied with food in the years of bad harvests and Continental blockade; but the very extension of their industry—the praiseworthy energy with which they had carried tillage into the poor soils and waste-places—disabled them in the competition, not only with the cheaper labour of the Continent, but with grain grown upon fertile, or at least tolerably good soil, such as was alone tilled by the farmers of countries never pinched for grain, and whose normal condition was to produce more grain than their people required.

These peculiar circumstances of Great Britain at the close of the great French War—circumstances without a parallel in history, and never likely to befall any nation again,—circumstances due, under Providence, to the heroic energy of the nation, the resolute sagacity of our statesmen, and the genius of our naval and military commanders—must be kept clearly in mind before it is possible to understand the period of distress which followed. Commercially Great Britain was actually a loser by the Peace. She had to come down from the pinnacle of war-won commercial privileges and opportunities, and had to relinquish the practical monopoly of the trade of the ocean, of which her people had so energetically availed themselves; and although she became relieved of a vast war-expenditure, that expenditure of itself had created some branches of trade and greatly stimulated others; and further, the Loans came to an end, while the annual burden of the Debt had to be borne entirely out of the annual income of the kingdom, then diminished by the commercial results of the Peace. Hence it happened that, despite the immediate abolition of £18,000,000 of taxation, the nation became distressed, and little more than fifty millions sterling of taxation proved a heavier burden than seventy or seventy-five millions had been during the height of the War. As we refer to these matters simply in order to elucidate the true character of the national circumstances which accompanied and followed the Resumption of payments in specie, and the return to the precious metals as the basis of the British currency, it is needless to give the full statistics of the vast expansion of British Trade during the War, and of the serious and sudden commercial decline which followed the restoration of peace; but we give an official statement of the "Commercial paper under discount at the Bank of England,"—which is the briefest, and one of the clearest, testimonies that can be adduced upon this subject. The picture therein presented, or reflected, of the state of British trade and industry is a most remarkable one. From the subjoined statistics[1] it appears that these trade-discounts amounted to little more than a million sterling in 1792, the year before the War; by the end of the century they had risen to six and a half millions; in the year 1805, they

[1] *Commercial Paper under Discount at the Bank of England:—*

1792, . . £1,179,641	1812, . . £14,291,600
1793, . . 1,842,781	1813, . . 12,380,200
1794, . . 2,146,671	1814, . . 13,285,800
1795, . . 2,946,500	1815, . . 14,917,000
1796, . . 3,505,000	1816, . . 11,416,400
1797, . . 5,350,000	1817, . . 3,960,600
1798, . . 4,490,600	1818, . . 4,325,200
1799, . . 5,403,900	1819, . . 6,515,000
1800, . . 6,421,900	1820, . . 3,883,600
1801, . . 7,905,100	1821, . . 2,676,700
1802, . . 7,523,300	1822, . . 3,366,700
1803, . . 10,747,600	1823, . . 3,123,800
1804, . . 9,982,400	1824, . . 2,369,800
1805, . . 11,265,500	1825, . . 4,941,500
1806, . . 12,380,100	1826, . . 4,908,300
1807, . . 13,484,600	1827, . . 1,240,400
1808, . . 12,950,100	1828, . . 1,167,400
1809, . . 15,475,700	1829, . . 2,250,700
1810, . . 20,070,600	1830, . . 919,900
1811, . . 14,355,400	1831, . . 1,585,600

See also, for exports, imports, and shipping, footnote, *supra*, p. 54.

amounted to eleven millions; in 1809 to 15½ and in 1810 to 20 millions; from thence to the end of the War, they averaged 14 millions. In the first year after the Peace (1816) these trade-discounts fell to eleven millions; during the next three years (1817-19) they averaged barely five millions; and throughout the subsequent twelve years—beginning with 1820, the first year after the Resumption of coin-payments, and ending with 1831—the average was little more than 2¼ millions; while for the last five years of the period (1827-31) the Bank-discounts had fallen back almost to their old amount before the war, forty years previous! No wonder that there was distress in the country; and remembering the contemporaneous agitation for "Parliamentary Reform," the student of politics will find here a striking instance of the truth that national distress (howsoever occasioned) is the great parent of political discontent and agitation, frequently leading to revolution.

From this brief review of the state of affairs which ensued upon the conclusion of peace in 1815, it is obvious that a considerable portion of the subsequent distress throughout our country was unavoidable. Indeed many of the circumstances which had operated so much in our favour during the War, and which, together with the energy and heroic fortitude of our people, had carried Great Britain in triumph through by far the grandest crisis and direst peril to her fortunes and independence, inevitably produced a reaction at the close of the contest. We lost the trade-advantages which we had won during the war, while the burden of the great loans remained. Nevertheless the Resumption of specie-payments, the return to a metallic currency, was a further sacrifice imposed upon the nation, aggravating all its other difficulties. We say this without any questioning of the wisdom of re-establishing the old and ordinary system of metallic currency. And the most ardent supporter of the Act of 1819 must surely admit that, since the necessary and first effect of that measure was to reduce the currency, through a restriction of banking-accommodation—that is, by a curtailment of loans and of the discounting of the bills by which Trade is carried on,—such a change (whether regarded as indispensable or not) must have restricted trade and industry; and that, too, at a time when the national industry and enterprise were checked in all directions, both at home and abroad, and required the most careful handling if the perilous transitional period was to be surmounted without great suffering.

It is true that at the time of the passing of the Act of Resumption there appeared little obvious ground for apprehension as to the effects of the change. The actual war-demand for specie had ceased; even in 1816, before any restriction of the currency, gold had fallen to, or within an insignificant fraction of its old value in our paper-money; and although the value of gold slightly rose again in connection with the maintenance of the Army of Occupation in France, the supporters of the Act, at the date of its passing, could point encouragingly to the fact that the premium upon gold was only 3 per cent. Nevertheless Parliament took a most inadequate view of the changes which it then made in the national currency, and, still more, of the circumstances of the world under which a metallic currency must be influenced in all its operations.

It is a memorable fact—and one which is generally regarded as a strange one nowadays—that at the close of the War, our people were generally content with the inconvertible currency then fully established in this country. Even Parliament showed great reluctance in making a return to the old metallic currency. Indeed, after studying the records of that time, it seems to me that the prime consideration which determined Parliament to recur to the former and ordinary system of currency— namely, as wholly based upon the precious metals— was the necessity for the State to keep faith and adhere to its pledges. And undoubtedly Parliament deserves great credit for its self-denial upon this point; because, in exact proportion to the correctness of the prime view upon which a resumption of specie-payments was advocated — namely, that the currency had become depreciated,—the change involved a great gain to the national creditors, with a corresponding loss to the nation, owing to the repayment of loans in a more valuable currency than that in which these loans had been contracted. But the age was a heroic one; and our people, as represented by the aristocratic form of Government of that day, and by the classes most chiefly interested in the permanent condition of the country, shrank from no sacrifices called for by the honour of the State and the independence of the country.

Nevertheless, in re-establishing the old form of currency, several important changes in the state of the country and of the world at large were overlooked, and which, had they been observed and appreciated, would have seriously swelled the tide of opposition to the monetary legislation which followed the return of peace. Happy would it have been for the nation if Parliament had taken a fuller view of the whole matter; and if, thus quickened and enlightened, its intelligence had been equal to the devising of a monetary system as adequate for the new times as the old system had been for the condition of our country in the previous century! At the close of the seventeenth century, under the monetary pressure of a Continental war, England had shot ahead of the rest of the world by adopting paper-money issued on a basis of the precious metals. At the beginning of the present century, Great Britain was under a similar but much heavier pressure; but instead of taking another step in advance, her legislators merely recurred to the old system, while actually aggravating it by restricting the metallic basis of the currency to gold alone—instead of gold and silver conjointly.

During the eventful years of the long War, a great change had come over British Trade, and the general relations of the world. This change was the growth of INTERNATIONALISM. It is a remarkable fact that War is the greatest popular teacher of geography, and brings into common knowledge both foreign places and foreign peoples. Every war in a new or comparatively little known locality makes the public familiar with the features of the country which is the seat of war; and considerable towns and places which previously were either wholly unknown, or which were mere names, "airy nothings," acquire a correctly distinct localisation, and even a vivid portrayal by the pen of the War-correspondents. To take one of the most recent examples of this fact,—the Civil War in the United States literally unveiled to the British public a large portion of North America. In three years' time, the war increased our geographical knowledge of that region to an extent far surpassing the results of any scholastic tuition which even the best educated classes amongst us had then received. Not less so did the Civil War extend our acquaintance with the character and sentiments of the American people. Albeit they are of our own blood and kinship, and despite the intimate relations which by trade and emigration had subsisted between us and them, unquestionably it was their great Civil War which first enabled us to know and understand the Americans and their country with the happily full knowledge of the present day. And—need it be said?— with fuller knowledge comes greater sympathy and respect. Second only to self-interest—to an antagonism of personal or national interests in actual conflict—the greatest begetter of Prejudice is Ignorance. Nations are too much alike in the main to remain aloof from one another, in suspicion or distaste, when they meet on common ground, as in the pursuits of trade and commerce; and commercial relations once established tend to bring the trading nations together, more and more closely, in the other and various relations of national life.

The Great War had brought about a vast extension of British Trade; and the War itself had brought us into new and comparatively close contact with the other nations of Europe, most of whom had been our Allies in the war; and not less, or indeed even more, had our relations been improved with our great enemy, France. Even in "high politics," it was the British Diplomatists who had done most to obtain good terms for the French King and nation at the Peace; and Wellington employed his glorious reputation, and the high regard in which he was held by the Allied monarchs, in successfully repelling at the Congress of Vienna, as previously in the march to Paris after Waterloo, the revengeful and spoliatory conditions which some of our Allies were eager to impose upon conquered France. At the close of the War, also, well-to-do Englishmen of all classes hastened to revisit the Continent; the "grand tour" became more popular than ever; and the barriers of old prejudice and dislike which had so long separated the nations began to give way in all directions.

Most conspicuously, Great Britain became united

to the Continent in the bonds of commerce and
finance. The Trade-fabric overspread Europe with
its manifold ramifications, and network of mutual
interests; while the Money-market acquired the consolidation which is one of the marvels of present
times. The conjoined and interlacing system of
trade and finance thereafter bound together the
various countries of Europe; and every change in
one of those countries became felt for good or evil by
the others. Just as the web of the spider is of such
delicate structure that the slightest touch or vibration, even at the farthest verge, thrills throughout
the whole fabric, and arouses to action the watching
author of it in his central lair; so, nowadays, does
the slightest change in the value of money in any
part of the world arouse the capitalist or money-dealer,—ready either to send or to withdraw the precious metals according to the nature of each momentary change, and with the view to profit from each
passing difficulty. The new period in the movements
of the precious metals was as different from the old
as is the wellnigh tideless expanse of the Mediterranean Sea from the ceaseless alternation of high and
low water upon the coasts of the British Isles.

This was a great change from the state of Europe
in the previous century, and prior to the French
war. Especially was the change a great and serious
one with reference to State Loans and international
lending. The Hebrew capitalists, it is true, had
never allowed the prejudices of country, or the
common international hates of Europe, to interfere

with their trade in money; but what Englishman, Frenchman, or Prussian of last century would have thought of investing his wealth in Foreign Loans? More natural would it have seemed to him to regard any such lending of his money to another Government as an act of treason to his own,—or at least as an act for which the jealous patriotism of that time would blush. Perhaps still closer to the truth would it be to say, that, under the very limited knowledge of foreign countries, the idea of investing money upon the Continent appeared as absurd to an Englishman as an investment in the Moon; and to entrust a portion of his wealth to a foreign Government would have seemed as mad-like as to put his head in a lion's mouth, or to trust his person and fortunes within the fabled castle of Giant Despair.

On the other hand, during the Great War, Great Britain came into the closest relations with the Continental Powers. Our people became familiar with the making of loans, in the form of war-subsidies, to most of the Continental Governments; and so widely had their knowledge and sympathies been extended during the contest, that, on the restoration of Peace, the large loan required by France to discharge the war-indemnities quite fairly imposed upon her, and thereby to get rid of the foreign Army of Occupation, found its chief subscribers on this side the Channel,—about three-fourths of the required money having been subscribed in London. And this, as we shall see, was but the beginning of such lendings and investments of British capital abroad.

to the Continent in the bonds of commerce and finance. The Trade-fabric overspread Europe with its manifold ramifications, and network of mutual interests; while the Money-market acquired the consolidation which is one of the marvels of present times. The conjoined and interlacing system of trade and finance thereafter bound together the various countries of Europe; and every change in one of those countries became felt for good or evil by the others. Just as the web of the spider is of such delicate structure that the slightest touch or vibration, even at the farthest verge, thrills throughout the whole fabric, and arouses to action the watching author of it in his central lair; so, nowadays, does the slightest change in the value of money in any part of the world arouse the capitalist or money-dealer,—ready either to send or to withdraw the precious metals according to the nature of each momentary change, and with the view to profit from each passing difficulty. The new period in the movements of the precious metals was as different from the old as is the wellnigh tideless expanse of the Mediterranean Sea from the ceaseless alternation of high and low water upon the coasts of the British Isles.

This was a great change from the state of Europe in the previous century, and prior to the French war. Especially was the change a great and serious one with reference to State Loans and international lending. The Hebrew capitalists, it is true, had never allowed the prejudices of country, or the common international hates of Europe, to interfere with their trade in money; but what Englishman, Frenchman, or Prussian of last century would have thought of investing his wealth in Foreign Loans? More natural would it have seemed to him to regard any such lending of his money to another Government as an act of treason to his own,—or at least as an act for which the jealous patriotism of that time would blush. Perhaps still closer to the truth would it be to say, that, under the very limited knowledge of foreign countries, the idea of investing money upon the Continent appeared as absurd to an Englishman as an investment in the Moon; and to entrust a portion of his wealth to a foreign Government would have seemed as mad-like as to put his head in a lion's mouth, or to trust his person and fortunes within the fabled castle of Giant Despair.

On the other hand, during the Great War, Great Britain came into the closest relations with the Continental Powers. Our people became familiar with the making of loans, in the form of war-subsidies, to most of the Continental Governments; and so widely had their knowledge and sympathies been extended during the contest, that, on the restoration of Peace, the large loan required by France to discharge the war-indemnities quite fairly imposed upon her, and thereby to get rid of the foreign Army of Occupation, found its chief subscribers on this side the Channel,—about three-fourths of the required money having been subscribed in London. And this, as we shall see, was but the beginning of such lendings and investments of British capital abroad.

opinion of the country. Indeed, as a matter of fact, (and for reasons which need not here be discussed), a currency-system, which is always more or less based upon credit and mutual confidence, often lags behind the requirements of the time, and cannot possibly be in advance of them. It is rarely that the world changes so fast, or that a country progresses so vastly as Great Britain did, in so short a period as that between 1797 and 1815: yet, such being the changes, there was certainly no security that the monetary system which had served so well down to the beginning of the Great War would prove adequate for the wider and multiplied requirements of the country on the return of peace. England and her trade and population had grown largely, while the supply of the precious metals had sunk to one-half, when the Act of 1819 was passed. The stripling had become a full-grown man, while his old vestments, put upon him anew, had wofully shrunk in the interval. For a metallic currency, the supply from the Mines is a matter of supreme importance: and hence, in truth, one may praise our monetary system of the last century, and even praise it as it exists now by the aid of California and Australia, and yet see many a contemporaneous drawback upon the legislation of 1816 and 1819.

Moreover, the monetary legislation of Parliament which followed the Peace of 1815, was not a mere return to the previous metallic currency of the kingdom. On the contrary, it effected a fundamental change in that currency; it revolutionised the British monetary system, and tended greatly to enhance the value of money. This was done by the Act of 1816, whereby silver was demonetised, and all payments beyond £2 were required to be made, and debts discharged, only in gold-money. Until then, both silver and gold had been Money in this country. Indeed in the British Isles, as throughout modern Europe, Silver had originally been the standard-money, and formed the bulk of the currency; but during the eighteenth century gold had become the chief money in this country; and Parliament had enacted that payments in silver should not be legal tender for sums above £40. By the Act of 1816, silver ceased to be legal tender for sums above forty shillings, and the silver-coin was ordered to be so much mixed with alloy that thenceforth it has been little else than token-money: that is, our silver coins now bear a value greatly exceeding what attaches to them as bullion. Thus Great Britain led the way in the demonetisation of silver—thereby reducing by one-half the stock of the precious metals available as the money of the world:—setting an example which, greatly to her own disadvantage, other nations have recently followed.

That this curtailment of the basis of our currency should have been adopted in 1816 is one of the most striking proofs how little the general question was then understood. It may perhaps have been thought that a return to metallic currency furnished a highly suitable occasion for making such a change. When (speaking roundly) there was no gold or silver coin in the country, the demonetisation of the latter metal could not be a loss to coin-holders. On the other hand, when the nation had, by purchase from abroad, to supply itself with a new metallic currency—with specie sufficient not merely for the requisite amount of circulating coin, but also to replenish the coffers and tills of every bank in the kingdom, so as to provide for a return to specie-payments,—surely no season could be more inopportune for a legal enactment which more than doubled the national difficulty, by demonetising, and rendering unavailable for our wants, one-half (or indeed by far the larger portion) of the world's stock of the precious metals, from whence our new currency must be drawn. This, too, at the very time when the annual supply of the precious metals had fallen to less than a half of its old amount!

"There is no royal road to knowledge." Nations and Governments have to learn from experience, like humble individuals. Doubtless the *Assignats* of Revolutionary France constituted a warning to the British Government, strengthening its resolve to abstain from any similar course in our own national emergency. In like manner, unquestionably, the experience of Great Britain in suspending and resuming a metallic currency was profitably studied by the American statesmen who conducted with masterly ability the similar crisis imposed upon them by the Civil War of 1862-6. Nor was the lesson lost upon the Bank of France, in 1870, when a suspension and resumption of specie-payments was accomplished without the slightest hardship either to the Bank or the country, or indeed without even a tremor of disquietude on the part of either.

Unlike these two recent instances, the monetary crisis in this country, occasioned by the French War, did not terminate without inflicting much hardship upon the nation. The Act of 1816 severely increased the difficulty of re-acquiring a metallic currency, while the subsequent Act for abolishing the small bank-notes was premature; and although the latter Act was, from sheer necessity, suspended again and again, this by no means prevented its effect being injurious and restrictive upon the currency prior to its coming into final operation,—the Banks preparing for this impending contraction of the currency by further contraction of their loans and discounts. The monetary change then desired by Parliament was twofold: first, (and this was the really important point) to return to specie-payments, which required that the banks should resume the ordinary system of paying their depositors in specie, on demand; secondly, the re-establishment of a metallic currency. Neither of these objects could be attained in a moment or without much difficulty; and, obviously, it would have been better that the imported gold should go into bank, thereby enabling a return to specie-payments in its most useful and needful form, before requiring that it should be absorbed in the active circulation. Further, it may be questioned whether the price of gold in the inconvertible bank-notes, which was only 3 per cent below par before the Act of 1819 was passed, was a reliable criterion of the value of gold or of the consequent pressure upon the industrial classes in the process of returning to specie-payments, when the demand for gold came actually and fully into play. True, as a return to payments in gold was then certain, and in near prospect, this consideration must have affected the price of gold even prior to the Act: nevertheless, it is questionable whether 3 per cent fully represented the premium upon gold after the demand for that metal became general and imperative. Of course, as soon as the Act of 1819 came into operation, the premium upon gold necessarily disappeared: but the monetary difficulty remained, and instead of a higher price for gold, the effect of the difficulty was seen in the restriction of discounts and contraction of the currency, requisite (according to the policy then adopted) to attract the needed supply of gold from abroad—albeit at the expense of our own producers. By these monetary restrictions a Fall of Prices was produced, not only in consequence of a reduction of the circulating medium, but also from the bankruptcies and depression of trade occasioned by the withdrawal from the commercial and industrial community of the banking accommodation, in the form of discounts and loans, by which almost every branch of trade is carried on.

"The fall of prices," said Mr Attwood, M.P., in 1822, "has been uniform and progressive since the Monetary Act of 1819 was passed, embracing all commodities, extending over the whole period. Wheat, which in the year 1818 was 84s., is now selling at 47s.,—showing a reduction of 45 per cent. Iron, in 1818, was £13 the ton; it is now £8,—a fall of 40 per cent. Cotton, in 1818, was 1s. the pound; it is now 6d.—a fall of 50 per cent. Wool, which in 1818 was selling at 2s. 1d., now sells for 1s. 1d.—a reduction of 50 per cent. These are the great articles of commerce, and the average of the fall upon them is 45 per cent—being exactly the reduction on the price of grain. Mr Tooke has compiled a table exhibiting the fall of prices between May 1818 and May 1822, and the fall is the same on all the articles, with the exception of indigo. The fall, therefore, is not peculiar to agriculture: it is universal, and has embraced every article of industry, every branch of commerce." Lord Londonderry expressed the simple truth when he said, in 1822, "The currency of the country is too contracted for its wants."

It was the obvious necessity (so emphatically declared by the Bullion Committee) for such measures of monetary contraction, in order to provide sufficient gold from abroad, which constituted the great ground of opposition to the Act of 1819. The mercantile and producing classes, in the main, were perfectly content with the inconvertible bank-currency which had prevailed, and under which the nation undoubtedly had greatly prospered, since 1797; and they protested in advance against the hardships which they foresaw must be inflicted upon the national trade and industry by the adoption of the Act of 1819. The Bank of England, foreseeing the disastrous consequences of the measure, recorded their protest against it in serious and emphatic terms. It was allowed on all hands—by the Bullion Committee and the warmest supporters of the Act of 1819—that the Directors of the Bank had always placed the interests of the State paramount in their regard, as a guide to their management of the Bank; and, while expressing their readiness as Bank officials to return to specie-payments, the Directors refused to take upon themselves any responsibility for the measures of monetary restriction, with their perilous consequences to the "universal interests of the empire, in all the relations of agriculture, manufactures, commerce, and revenue," which the contemplated legislation would render necessary on their part.[1]

---

[1] "The proposal of the Committee is that the Bank shall be obliged, from 1st May 1821, to discharge their notes in standard gold bullion at Mint price, when demanded, in sums not amounting to less than thirty ounces; and that from 1st February 1820 the Bank should pay their notes in bullion, if demanded, in sums not less than sixty ounces, at the rate of £4, 1s. per ounce; and from 1st October 1820 to 1st May 1821, at £3, 19s. 6d. per ounce. . . . When the Bank Directors are now to be called upon, in the new situation in which they are placed by the Restriction Act, to procure a fund for supporting the whole national currency either in bullion or coin; and when it is proposed that they should effect this measure within a given period, by regulating [*i.e.* reducing] the market-price of gold by a limitation of the amount of the issue of bank-notes, with whatever distress such limitation may be attended to individuals or the community at large, they feel it their bounden and imperious duty to state their sentiments thus explicitly in the first instance to his Majesty's Ministers. . . . The Directors have already submitted to the House of Lords the ex-

Despite the hopeful anticipations confidently entertained by the Bullionist party in Parliament, the feeling of serious apprehension, if not of positive antagonism to the Resumption Act, appears to have largely preponderated throughout the country; and, undiscriminating as this feeling for the most part was, it seems doubtful if the Act would have been passed at all but for the sake of maintaining the "good faith" of the State, which was pledged to the resumption of specie-payments on the return of peace. The elder Sir Robert Peel, the founder of the family, as an experienced trader and manufacturer, was so convinced of the disasters which must accompany the resumption of specie-payments in that position and condition of the national affairs, that he felt compelled to take part in the debate in opposition to his own son, who was chairman of the committee which recommended an immediate return to a metallic currency. It is also worthy of

pediency of the Bank paying its notes *in bullion at the market-price of the day*, with a view of seeing how far favourable commercial balances may operate in restoring the former order of things, of which they might take advantage; and with a similar view they have proposed that Government should repay the Bank a considerable part of the sums that have been advanced upon Exchequer bills. These two measures would allow time for a correct judgment to be formed upon the state of the bullion-market, and upon the real result of those changes which the late War may have produced, in all its consequences, of increased public debt, increased taxes, and increased prices, and altered relations as to interest, capital, and commercial dealings with the Continent." The Petition (dated 20th May 1819) closes with the Directors protesting against assuming responsibility for "a measure in which the whole community is so deeply involved, and which may possibly compromise the universal interests of the Empire, in all the relations of agriculture, manufactures, commerce, and revenue."

mention that Mr Cobbett — a shrewd observer of affairs — who was then in the United States, no sooner (as he tells us) heard of the passing of the Act of 1819 than he resolved to return to England, confident that the national distress which must ensue would make the people ripe for those schemes of Parliamentary Reform which previously he had advocated in vain. We repeat, it was acknowledged by the supporters of the Act—nay, it was the very result which they desired to attain by it—that the currency of the country would be contracted, by means of contracting the banking loans and discounts; and it was obvious that a contraction of the banking accommodation must produce proportionate suffering and industrial distress. The best that the supporters of the Act could say upon this point was that the monetary contraction would be slight, and that it was better to incur some degree of hardship at once than to postpone the return to specie-payments to which the Government stood pledged. "Wait until the Exchanges become favourable," pleaded the opponents of the Act, who pointed to the loans and current expenditure abroad as formidable transient obstacles to the proposed change. "Not so," replied the supporters of the Act: "the Banks can at any time turn the Exchanges in our favour by restricting their discounts and contracting the currency; and it is absurd to allow the foreign investments of our merchants and financiers to stand in the way of a great act of State policy and duty." Yes!—but so to "turn the exchanges" meant ruin to the great body of our people. And the Directors of the Bank of England told Parliament so.

The necessities of Great Britain as a food-importing country at that time (as far more so subsequently) constituted a great difficulty relative to the maintenance or reacquisition of an adequate stock of gold for the currency and banking purposes. But the Bullionist party pleaded that further delay in the resumption of a metallic currency and specie-payments would render such a measure still more difficult; and doubtless, also, they felt that delay would only add to the manifest reluctance with which the change was regarded by a very large section of the nation. On the other hand, the opposition to the measure was bound to fail. Had the opponents of the Act of 1819 been able to propose a well-considered counter project — some definite system, in place of the old one which it was proposed to revive—they would have found public opinion in a mood remarkably favourable for the consideration of such a project, — more favourable, indeed, than it has ever since been. But it was hopeless to expect that matters could continue simply as they were. The change made in 1797 was the suspension of an old system, not the adoption of a new one; and, vastly as the country had benefited from the change under the exceptional circumstances of the War, the monetary arrangements thereby put in operation were too crude and defective to find acceptance as a permanent system.

Accordingly, in so far as the opponents of the Act of 1819 not merely objected to the measure as premature, but desired (as not a few of them did) to retain as permanent the currency-arrangements adopted provisionally in 1797, they were fighting a hopeless battle. The disasters which they apprehended from a return to a metallic monetary system, in the novel and restricted form of a single gold-standard, under the then greatly altered conditions of British trade and finance, along with a greatly diminished supply of the precious metals, were in the main well-founded; but they ought to have directed their efforts to the attainment of a new and better monetary system than that contained in the Act of 1819 — one more in accord with the changed conditions of our trade and of the world at large, — rather than wasted their strength in seeking to uphold the arrangements then existing, which were too crude for permanent adoption even if the nation had then been ready and willing for a system of inconvertible paper-money.

For a full hundred years, the monetary system admirably established in 1694, and which gradually expanded with the progress of the kingdom, had proved amply sufficient for the national wants; but, on the so-called resumption (but actual contraction) of that system by the Act of 1819, the country had not long to wait for sad proofs of the inadequacy of the system in its really novel and restricted form, in the midst of a new world—a greatly diminished production of the precious metals,[1] contemporaneous with a world of trade and finance, and of far-reaching international arrangements alike of peace and war, not only widely different from what had existed in 1694, but which had vastly changed even during the last memorable quarter of a century.

It is indispensable, in considering this matter, to observe the exact sequence of events. The difficult period of transition from a great and long war to profound peace had been seriously aggravated by the bad harvest-year of 1816, and also by the exaggerated expectations of trade with the Continent now that Peace had reopened the long-closed ports of Europe to British merchandise. To our merchants and manufacturers, who shared largely in the general elation of spirits, it seemed that the Continental nations must be starving for British merchandise; and a remarkably large export of manufactures took place from our shores to the northern ports of Europe. Indeed the expectations of new trade were exuberant, and similar exportations were made to South America and other parts of the world. But this venture, in the main, proved a disastrous failure. The peoples of the Continent were still exhausted by the burdens and devastation of the Napoleonic wars, while the exportations from this country were on a scale of excessive magnitude even for ordinary times. The

---

[1] As previously stated (p. 25) Mr Jacob reckons that of the 1497 millions sterling of gold and silver produced between 1492 and 1830, only 380 millions remained as coin in Europe and America in 1810; and only 313 millions (a reduction of one-sixth) at the end of 1829.

result was that British goods became like a drug in most foreign markets, and for the time they could actually be purchased at a lower price in Northern Europe and at Buenos Ayres than in our own markets! The failure of these commercial ventures necessarily added greatly to the distress at home, occasioned by the cessation of an immense Government expenditure, largely supported by Loans, together with a disbanding of labour from the military and naval services, the Militia included (nearly a million of men in the prime of life), and a total stoppage in the production of the munitions of war. Indeed the very depression of the Home market, during this period of transition, had largely promoted the large exportation of manufactures : goods were sent abroad owing to the temporary decline of the customary demand for them at home. And when these speculative exportations proved ruinous, the distress pressed heavily upon the manufacturing industries. By an unfortunate conjuncture, the harvest of this critical year of transition proved one of the worst on record; and as the consequent imports of grain had to be paid for largely in specie, a new difficulty was raised to the resumption of specie-payments,—a difficulty quickly added to by the great French Loans of 1818 (amounting to £30,000,000) which began to be subscribed in this country. Under these influences, the price of gold, as already mentioned, rose again; and the Bank of England, which had voluntarily commenced to pay in specie, had soon to abandon this course as premature; while the contraction of discounts contributed considerably to the general depression.

Nevertheless, by the year 1822 the nation had got through all these difficulties, and was at the outset of a new and vigorous prosperity. The Transition-period was passed: the war-industries and other employment connected with the war had become things of the past; and trade and production had settled anew on a basis of securely established peace. Indeed Great Britain was then without an enemy; while the triumphant part which she had played in the Napoleonic wars, alike by her policy and her victories, and her crowning magnanimity, had placed her at the head of Europe. Never before, nor since, has any State attained the position of paramount influence which was then held by Great Britain. In truth, while fighting for her own existence, she had been the saviour of the liberties and independence of Europe, and the faithful and powerful ally of the Continental nations; while her successes in the war —the marvellous career of Wellington in the Peninsula, and, still more, the brilliant victories of Trafalgar and Waterloo, the one battle as decisive of the empire of the seas as the other was of the dominion of Europe—not only surrounded her name with a halo of glory, but won for her a deference and respect as a fighting power which proved a "cheap defence,"—securing her not merely from attack but even from conflict, for forty years: and even then, in 1854, she would have had no war if her antagonist Russia had not been led to believe that England would not engage in the contest. Together with this peerless position, and this cheapest security for a nation—namely, the knowledge that it can triumphantly repel attack,—Britain also found herself in possession of a splendid war-won colonial empire, together with a world-wide Foreign Trade, and an unapproachably vast mercantile navy, the natural outcome of twenty years' possession of the dominion of the seas and of the maritime carrying-trade of the world. Such was England at the close of the Great War. Never has any State in the modern world held so proud a position, nor any nation enjoyed such peerless opportunities for profitable employment of its energies in commerce and production. The only drawback, and a heavy one, was the vast Debt contracted during the War; yet even the annual burden of the Debt, owing to the increase of the national wealth, was not proportionably heavier than the similar charge had been at the outset of the great European conflict.

Before the close of 1822, also, the transitory difficulties attending the Resumption of specie-payments had been surmounted, or at least passed through; so that, except the increased charge for the Debt, all the difficulties connected with the Great War had become things of the Past; and, while the security for a long peace permitted a minimum establishment of the military and naval services, the vast colonial resources and a large portion of the commercial advantages obtained by the War remained for the benefit of the nation, as a splendid open field for the national enterprise in the arts and industries of peace. And so there came three years of remarkable prosperity. The prosperity, too, was universal throughout the kingdom. The complaints of the agricultural classes, and the depression in the manufacturing industries, had alike ceased; while the shipping interest prospered from the activity of the Foreign trade. The national wealth, too, had so largely increased by successive accumulation that, for the first time in our history, British capital became in excess of the means of employing it upon the limited resources of our small islands. This general prosperity, beginning in 1822 and lasting to the close of 1825, is amply vouched for in the annals of the time. "The trade and manufactures of the country," said Tooke, " had never before been in a more regular, sound, and satisfactory state than from the end of 1821 to the end of 1824." "The narrative of the years 1823 and 1824," says Alison, "exhibits an unbroken stream of prosperity, and of the financial [fiscal?] reductions consequent on such an auspicious state of things." The year 1825 opened not less auspiciously. "Our present prosperity," said Lord Dudley and Ward, when moving the address of the House of Lords to the King's Speech (Feb. 3), " is a prosperity extending to all orders, all professions, and all districts; and the public contentment is on a level with the public prosperity." The *Annual Register* and the *Quarterly Review* strikingly corroborate these statements of the general prosperity.[1] Both of these

[1] The *Annual Register* said: — "Agricultural distress has disap-

publications make especial mention of the growth of wealth in the country, and the low rate of interest; and the *Review* refers to the "enormous" increase of the money-balances lying in bank, and the consequent "avidity with which any opening for capital is sought after." As a result of this abundance of wealth, combined with assured peace and general prosperity, the Funds stood in the summer of 1825 at 96,—only four per cent below par, and higher than at any time since 1792, despite the trebling of the amount of the Debt in the interval.

peared; the persons engaged in the cotton and woollen manufactures are in full employment; the various branches of the Iron trade are in a state of activity: on all sides new buildings are in progress of erection; and Money is so abundant that men of enterprise, though without capital, find no difficulty in commanding funds for any plausible undertaking."

The *Quarterly Review* said:—"The increased wealth of the middle classes is so obvious that we can neither walk the fields, visit the shops, nor examine the workshops and storehouses, without being deeply impressed with the changes which a few years have produced. We see the fields better cultivated, the barns and stackyards more fully stored; the horses, cows, and sheep more abundant and in better condition; and all the implements of husbandry improved in their order, their construction, and their value. In the cities, towns, and villages we find shops more numerous, and better in their appearance, and the several goods more separated from each other,—a division that is the infallible token of increased sales. The increase of goods thus universally diffused is an indication and exhibition of flourishing circumstances. The accounts of the Bankers in the metropolis and provincial towns, small as well as large, with the balances of money resting with them, ready to embrace favourable changes in the price of any commodity, or to be placed at interest as beneficial securities present themselves, are increased to an enormous amount. This, indeed, is evident from the low rate of interest which can be got in the public securities, and the avidity with which any opening for capital is sought after."—Quoted from Alison's History, 1815-52, chap. xix. § 62-63.

Elated by the national advantages and opportunities of that time—of which the peerless world-position of Great Britain was alike a cause and a patent symbol,—eagerly longing, too, for outlets alike for their capital and their industrial and commercial energies,—feeling also, for the first time, that their own country had become too small for their energetic enterprise, our people threw themselves with their characteristic vigour, but with less than their customary prudence, into foreign ventures, alike commercial and financial. Especially were they attracted to the countries which were the gold-and-silver-bearing regions—the home of the precious metals. It was in deference mainly to the impulse of our people towards acquiring the old lucrative trade with the Spanish dominions in the New World that the British Government had broken the laws of neutrality by aiding, first permissively and then openly, the American colonies against the rule of Spain. The coveted outlet was thus attained, and British money and British enterprise rushed in an impetuous stream towards South America and its new Republics. The very fact that the mines had been so long neglected gave zest and hopefulness to this new enterprise; while the scarcity of the precious metals promised to render the enterprise as profitable to the adventurers as useful to the world, and especially to our own country, with its new gold-needing monetary system. Hence our Banks looked with favour, if not with direct encouragement, upon the then popular schemes for regenerating

Spanish America and for working the treasure-bearing mines from Mexico to Peru. The hardships experienced in connection with the return to a metallic currency had attracted general attention to the importance of an ample supply of the precious metals; and the confident expectations that such a supply was henceforth assured, by the application of British energy and capital to the working of the Mines, hopefully affected Credit in general, and induced the Banks to make liberal advances not only to the ordinary trade of the kingdom, but to many of the new industrial enterprises and speculative projects, which multiplied under the existing wealth and prosperity combined with the prevalent enthusiasm. This hopefulness quickly rose to fever-heat under the influence of the large but delusive gains which at first attended some of the speculative undertakings. "The gain made on the shares of some of the South American companies," says Alison, "in a few months, exceeded 1500 per cent." Of course this immense profit was not owing to actual returns, but merely to Stock Exchange operations: the price of the shares being "rushed up" by the competition of the public, who, as already said, were flush of money, and who also entertained the most extravagant ideas as to the profits to be obtained from these enterprises. Still more numerous were the joint-stock enterprises for domestic purposes, including the new Gaslight companies; and at the beginning of the year 1825, the number of joint-stock companies in Great Britain amounted to two hundred and seventy-six, with a subscribed capital amounting to £174,000,000.

While money thus became in unusual demand, for carrying on this host of new enterprises, a serious drain of gold from the banks set in. This drain was occasioned, in the first place, by the numerous loans and mining investments in South America and Mexico, the capital for which had to be exported in specie; and the exportation of gold was augmented in consequence of the large increase of the national imports, owing to the prosperity which had prevailed throughout the three previous years. Twenty millions sterling had been subscribed for mining ventures in the New World; and between July 1824 and October 1825 twelve millions sterling in specie were exported from this country. In consequence, the coin and bullion in the Bank of England diminished rapidly,—falling from £12,658,000 on 31st August 1825 to only £1,027,000 in December 1826. Meanwhile banking-accommodation had been in unusual demand throughout the country, in order to carry on the extensive industrial operations then in progress, and to meet the calls of the numerous new joint-stock companies. A large portion of this demand upon the banks, whether in the shape of loans and discounts or by the calling up of deposits, was made for gold,—then so greatly required for export, in connection with the foreign enterprises and speculations. Unable to support these demands upon them, the provincial banks, cashing their reserve of negotiable securities, applied for coin from the Bank of England, which in turn contracted its loans and discounts, and therewith also the supply of currency. Under this combined dearth of banking accommodation to companies and individual traders, and of currency in the hands of the public, a general crash began. The Plymouth Bank was the first to close its doors at the end of November; and in the first week of December, the important London banking-house of Sir Peter Pole & Co. suspended payment; and as this house kept the accounts of forty provincial banks, a panic and disastrous banking crisis ensued. In the next three weeks, no less than seventy banks closed their doors. The London banks were besieged by depositors demanding payment in coin,—a demand which, if carried far, it is impossible for any bank to meet. The Bank of England itself, already in straits, and knowing the impossibility of withstanding such a "run" for specie, made urgent applications to Government for an Order in Council temporarily suspending payments in coin. But the Government refused to interfere as long as the Bank had a guinea left. After having re-established a metallic currency so recently, and with so much difficulty in Parliament and not a little distress to the country, the Government was naturally reluctant to undo its own work, especially as such a step would appear like an acknowledgment of a grave mistake. "Meanwhile," says the historian Alison, a contemporary of that time, "the consternation throughout the whole country reached the highest point. Every creditor [himself in want of money] pressed his debtor, who sought in vain for money to discharge his debts,"—the banks refusing (and indeed being unable under the Act of 1819) to make advances even upon the best kind of securities, while sales of goods and property of all kinds were for the moment impossible. "The bankers, themselves on the verge of insolvency, sternly refused accommodation even to their most approved customers: persons worth £100,000 could not command £100 to save themselves from ruin:" in short, said Mr Huskisson in Parliament, "we were within twenty-four hours of barter." The Funds, which a few months previously had stood at 96, fell in December 1825 to 76!

In this extremity, the Government wisely gave way. Despite their strong faith in the gold-currency, they saw that any longer adhesion to the legally established system would leave the nation without currency at all. Accordingly they resolved to meet the obvious requirement of the case by authorising a suspension of the Act of 1819, and an expansion of the currency, irrespective of the drain of gold,—namely, in the old form of bank-notes inconvertible into coin. Also, as the kind of money most imperatively needed was that required for actual circulation, the Government ordered that the addition to the currency should be made in small notes, for one and two pounds sterling. Huskisson's statement that the nation was on the brink of Barter, was no exaggeration,—owing to the void in the circulating medium occasioned by the failure of so many banks of issue, and of the general discredit which attached to the notes of the provincial banks; and the Government found extreme difficulty in its measures for relieving the embarrassment. In 1825 and 1826 there were seventy-seven country banks, and of these sixty-three had stopped payment. Nevertheless, as one-third of this number immediately resumed payment, and as on the average those who failed paid 17s. 6d. in the pound, despite the enormous fall of prices (even the Funds fell more than 20 per cent!), it is evident that the country banks, like the Bank of England itself, would have remained solvent but for the drain of gold and the panic and "run" for deposits.

Such was the period of monetary dearth, which, far beyond any other in modern Europe, exhibits the evil influence upon national affairs of a temporary absence or inadequate supply of the precious metals. In this aspect the first quarter of the present century was as remarkable as the third quarter has been in the opposite respect. The scarcity was owing first to War, with its imperative demands for payments in coin; and secondly, and more lastingly, to a falling-off by one-half, and for several years by three-fourths, in the yield of the American gold and silver mines.[1] Both of these disastrous changes fell most heavily upon our own country; during the war, because of

[1] The effect of the diminished production of the precious metals in the early part of the present century (1810-30) in reducing the world's stock of money is exhibited in the following statistics,—showing the

the peculiarly large amount of foreign expenditure, in subsidies and military expenses, which was incumbent upon the British Government; and after the war, because of the re-establishment of a metallic currency being made in the restricted form of monometallism. This was the first act in the perilous policy of demonetising one of the precious metals: a policy of real, although doubtless unmeditated selfishness, by which a nation seeks to gain an advantage for itself at the expense of the civilised community of the world, and which, as adopted in turn by other nations in recent years, occasions much monetary perplexity and commercial embarrassment at the present time. Further, although unobjected to and hardly even noticed by the public at the time, this act of demonetising silver, in 1816, was singularly inopportune,—the yield of the American mines being then at its lowest point; while our country was entering upon the always difficult task of returning to specie-payments: so that, by this act of demonetisation, the new British currency and entire monetary system were made to rest upon only one-third part of the current supply of the precious

total stock of gold and silver coin existing in the world (Asia excepted), at successive periods, as given by Jacob (and by Tooke, vi. 363):—

	Stock of Coin.	
In 1492,	£33 Millions	= 1
,, 1600,	130 ,,	= 4
,, 1700,	297 ,,	= 9
,, 1810,	380 ,,	= 11½
,, 1830,	313 ,,	= 9½

Thus the stock of gold and silver coin in 1830 was only a fraction larger than it had been nearly a century and a half before.

metals, and upon merely one-sixth part of the metallic basis (both gold and silver) upon which our monetary system had previously been based during the full hundred years of its existence subsequent to its foundation in 1694. And this, too—as we have shown—when both the Trade and the Finance of the world at large, and especially of our own country, had passed onward into an entirely new epoch, of Internationalism and vast expansion. No wonder that "hard times" came in train; and that, even when the transient difficulties of the Resumption had been suffered and surmounted, the nation felt little relief under the new and arbitrarily restricted currency thereby established,—an insidious monetary incubus and distress, only made tolerable twenty years afterwards, when the Ural and Siberian mines began to bring to our shores a new supply of gold.

Two memorable commercial and financial events, connected with the precious metals, marked the latter portion of this period of peculiar scarcity. First, although "Manias" in commercial or industrial enterprise were not unknown before—as, notably, the "Canal Mania" of the previous century,—the speculative outburst which ended in the Crisis of 1826 was entirely new alike in its magnitude and in its leading features. It belonged to a new age—the age of Internationalism, both in Trade and Finance,—as well as to a new stage in the progress of the nation: that of accumulated capital. The national wealth had been greatly augmented, by the trade of the world, since the close of the preceding century;

and the moneyed classes eagerly cast their eyes abroad in search of profitable investments, while they were also ready to welcome any new outlets for financial enterprise at home. Hence the twofold aspect of the speculative outburst which ensued,—namely, investments in State Loans and mining enterprise in the New World, along with a host of industrial joint-stock projects at home. In truth the speculation which culminated in the years 1825 and 1826 is memorable as the first of the great "Company Manias," on the joint-stock system, which have characterised the present century; and it also paralleled, and anticipated by half a century, the Foreign Loan mania of 1872-4. On the former as on the latter of these occasions, it was lamentable to reflect upon the vast amount of wealth squandered and utterly lost in foreign countries, but which, if judiciously expended at home, would have added so greatly to the permanent resources of our own country. A domestic enterprise may fail, bringing ruin upon its projectors, but the money so expended at least gives profitable employment to our people; whereas in an abortive foreign enterprise the money is lost to us entirely. The difference between the two kinds of investment in a national point of view is enormous. A hundred millions, if invested abroad, at best yields a fair rate of interest—say 5 to 10 per cent—to its owners; but, if spent successfully at home, besides the interest to the owner, there will be a hundred millions of money spent among our own people—added to the pay of labour and the profits of trade. The most stable and permanently beneficial results of wealth obtained from foreign trade arise when that wealth is invested in developing and fully utilising the resources of the Land,—rendering the father-land more productive alike in food for the sustenance and in raw materials for the employment of its population: thereby placing its power and prosperity on a stabler basis than the fickle fortunes of ever-shifting Commerce, and endowing it with natural resources which often survive in usefulness when the more alluring gains of foreign trade are over, and Commerce has flowed away into other channels.[1]

The Crisis of 1826, in which this wild speculation ended, was likewise an event significant of the times. It was the first of those Crises, since become lamentably frequent, which, although various in their origin, are always monetary in their culminating and most prominent features,—and purely monetary also in their most pernicious operations and effects upon the general community. Reckless and misguided as were many of the commercial ventures then undertaken in this country—in which, be it remembered, the new Gas-industry played, on a small scale, the

---

[1] In the early part of the present century, especially during the War, one of the benefits which Great Britain derived from her splendid colonial possessions, was the amount of wealth obtained from colonial trade and property which was invested in our own soil. Landed estates were purchased by retired Planters and merchants, who frequently (especially in Scotland) gave to their estates or farms names taken from places in the East or West Indies,—such as Berbice, Surinam, Portobello, or the like.

same part as Railways did twenty years afterwards, and as the grander illuminant and new motive force, Electricity, may do now—and heavy as were the losses of the moneyed class who had lent large sums to the insolvent new Republics of South America, the most direct and imperious cause of the Crisis, and one which of itself would have produced a severe distress, was the *export of gold*, which necessarily accompanied the various investments of capital in foreign countries, alike in State-loans and in mining enterprise. Such investments, as already stated, were a new feature of the times,—creating a trial to our monetary system unknown throughout the previous century; a trial which always must be perilous, and restrictive of enterprise, to a largely trading country with a metallic currency; and which was not only a new state of affairs, but which was necessarily much more perilous to the national well-being under the mono-metallic currency established after the War, than it would have been under the old monetary system of the kingdom, which was based on the entire stock of the precious metals, instead of merely upon one of them, and that the more mobile and difficult to retain.

All institutions, whether of Trade or of general Society, are defective: they are and must be designed for ordinary circumstances, and are liable to operate badly, or it may be unjustly, when the circumstances happen to be abnormal and exceptional. Wellington modestly said that the greatest general was merely the one who committed the fewest mistakes; and with equal truth it may be said that the best of institutions are simply those which least frequently prove defective in their operation. Whether or not the monetary system established by the Acts of 1816 and 1819 was the best possible, at least for that time, is a question upon which opinions may and do differ: nor do we here discuss the subject,—beyond pointing out the unwisdom of then altering and narrowing the basis of the national currency at a time when the precious metals had become unusually scarce, while the world, and especially our own country, had moved onward into a vastly expanded system alike of commerce and finance. But even the most confident advocates of the change must admit, as a fact beyond questioning, that the Monetary System then established (really a new one) occasioned a great aggravation of the commercial and financial disasters which brought to a speedy and lamentable close the re-established prosperity which pervaded all branches of the national industry, both agricultural and manufacturing, in the years 1822–5; disasters which threw the nation back into hard times, reviving the distress and discontent which had temporarily passed off.

The Monetary system established in 1819 would of itself—owing to the scarcity both of gold and silver which then and subsequently prevailed—have brought ruin in connection with the large investments of British wealth in foreign countries, even if those investments, both financial and industrial, had been in other respects judicious. It was the large export of gold which was the direct cause of the Crisis of 1826, — producing a curtailment, or indeed actual stoppage, of the discounts and loans indispensable to all Trade. Under the drain of gold, the Banks deemed it necessary for their own safety to refuse discounts not only to the speculative companies and other parties whose ventures were perilous, but to the public at large. Thus the whole community was compelled to suffer from an export of the metal which had been made the sole basis of our currency. This, in truth, is an evil, a working defect, of our Monetary system which has been exhibited many times since 1826. What the nation has to experience under commercial Crises even so severe as that of 1826, is not merely the loss of wealth from the failure of Trade or of speculative enterprise; but also the twofold hardship, first, that the monetary contraction, or withdrawal by the Banks of their customary loans and discounts, converts into failure many an enterprise which, but for that contraction, might have proved perfectly successful and profitable; and, secondly, that the inability of the Banks, under a drain of gold, to continue their customary accommodation to the public—which is alike their prime business and source of profit—extends the commercial disaster from the speculating firms and companies (always but a small portion of the population) to all kinds of trade and to all classes of the community. Thus, we repeat, in whatsoever shape the crisis originates, it always assumes a monetary character when at its height; and it is the monetary restriction thus occasioned which (with the consequent fall of prices, bankruptcies, &c.) always produces the largest portion of the national disaster.

Hopelessly ruinous as were nearly all the foreign investments of that time—whether in State-loans or in mining speculations,—a large portion of the domestic enterprises which broke down in 1826 were really of a permanently useful character, calculated to increase the comforts of life, and add lastingly to the property and producing power of the kingdom. Such, for example, were the numerous Gaslight Companies, and not a few other enterprises of that time—viz., canals, docks, and railways. With respect to these, the mistake committed (in so far as there was a mistake) was that the projects were, either in their character or in their extent, in advance of the existing wants and requirements of the time. Too long a time was requisite before they could become remunerative: so that the investors got no interest on their money, while their capital was locked up in an unsaleable and unnegotiable kind of property—in property quite unsuitable for banks to make loans upon, and for which it was impossible to find purchasers, at least without a ruinous loss. Under such circumstances, the majority of the investors, and all of them who are not great capitalists, become unable (in homely phrase) to "pay their way"—to pay debts or meet their ordinary expenditure: they become bankrupt, and Credit becomes contracted owing to a general feeling of distrust. This, indeed, is the commonest of all causes of failure in commercial or industrial enterprise. The project may, in itself, be highly useful and advantageous for the community; but if it takes too long (as measured by the means or wealth of the investors) to ripen and yield fruit, in the shape of pecuniary returns, the enterprise fails as regards its undertakers; yet their work may ultimately become profitable in other hands, and permanently serviceable to the community at large. It is upon this class of enterprises—of which there were then not a few—that an export of gold, like that which originated the Crisis of 1826, proves most lamentably disastrous; because such an event—or any drain of gold from the banks, however occasioned—causes the banks to contract or entirely stop their customary advances, thereby imposing failure upon enterprises which are then immature,—unless indeed (which can be, or at least is, but rarely the case) these enterprises are conducted by great capitalists who can dispense with banking accommodation.

The Crisis of 1826 was the last striking incident connected with the scarcity of the precious metals, during the period when that scarcity was at its height. And it is noteworthy in this respect, that it came at the close of that period, and when the supreme difficulties attendant upon the scarcity of specie had been surmounted successfully (as during the War), without hardship to our people, as without the least restriction upon the expanding commerce of the kingdom. For grand and obvious dangers, men energetically prepare: hence, occasionally, comparatively small difficulties produce worse results, because preparation has been neglected. For several years previous to the Crisis of 1826 the precious metals had become almost plentiful in England; and heavy as was the export of gold in 1825-6, the scarcity so produced was quite insignificant compared with what had existed during the War. Indeed this monetary collapse came like the foundering of a ship in quiet waters after it has passed through the storm-belt of a cyclone; or like the ill-fated *Eurydice* which, after voyaging upon the ocean, went suddenly to the bottom off the Isle of Wight, struck by a passing blast, when, with open port-holes, all on board were rejoicing over the ending voyage and the sight of home.

As already shown, the scarcity of the precious metals began, in the closing years of last century, entirely in consequence of the specie-requirements of the great European War; and in 1810 it became aggravated, as well as perpetuated beyond the close of the war, by the failure of the American mines, which at that time were wellnigh the sole source of the world's supply both of gold and silver. We have briefly shown the disastrous effects and embarrassing dilemma produced by that scarcity in the British Isles, where the scarcity was experienced with peculiar severity. And if any one reflects upon the history of those years, he will come to see how largely the hardships occasioned by the dearth of specie after the Peace tended to create, and profoundly aggravated, the political discontent which was so lamentably prevalent at that time; and which, as revived by the acute suffering produced by the Crisis of 1826, and the suppression of small bank-notes in England in 1829, imparted so much bitterness and turbulence to the agitation in favour of Parliamentary Reform. In the debate on the Address in 1830, Earl Stanhope, referring to the prevalent distress, said:—" It is not confined to Agriculture; it has extended to manufactures, to trade, and to commerce. All these great interests have never before, at one time, been at so low an ebb. The depression has been continuous and universal ever since the Bank Restriction Act was passed, and especially since the suppression of small notes took effect in the beginning of last year. . . . The fall of prices has been so great that in the last ten years [since 1819] it has amounted to 68 per cent. Such a universal and continued depression can be ascribed only to some cause pressing alike upon *all* branches of industry; and that cause is to be found in the enormous contraction of the currency. When we recollect that the Bank of England notes in circulation have been reduced from £30,000,000 to £20,000,000, and the country bankers' in a still greater proportion, it is easy to see whence the evil has arisen, and where a remedy is to be found."

Distress is the grand generator of political discontent. Cobbett was right when he predicted that the contraction of the currency, by producing wide distress, would quicken the popular discontent, and fan into a flame the then smouldering desire for a revolution in the system of Government. Napoleon maintained that "every man has his price," and that if a bribe does not succeed, it is only because it is not large enough. It seems certainly true that there is no class of men, howsoever loyal and politically contented, who will not become Radical Reformers under prolonged suffering in their business and worldly affairs. It was the long Agricultural distress which, by producing discontent among both farmers and landowners, carried the Reform Bill of 1831, in a Legislature in which the Land-interest predominated. As Alison, then a youth at college, put the matter, "Given the Toryism of a landed proprietor, how many years of want of rents will reduce him to a Radical Reformer!" A somewhat parallel phenomenon is apparent at the present time, when the distress produced by a long series of bad harvests has largely converted the farmers to the side of Innovation, especially as regards the Land-laws, and has raised opposition to Primogeniture, &c., among the class who hitherto have been most favourable to that law of inheritance. When such is the potent influence of Distress upon the agricultural classes, who in all countries are the stablest supporters of old institutions, it is needless to speak of the impulse which Distress gives to political innovation on the part of the more mobile and excitable manufacturing classes. The passion for political change may readily assume a dangerous and noxious form, under the pressure of hardship and suffering, even though it be occasioned simply by the course of the seasons and influence of the weather: and certainly it behoves statesmen, entrusted with the welfare of their country, to guard well that periods of national distress are not aggravated, or even created (as has sometimes happened), by the operation of the Monetary system, which more than any other is the product of pure legislative enactment, and which, as shown abundantly in history, and not least so in our own annals, is one of the most powerful agents for weal or woe upon the condition of a nation,—especially of a nation like our own, whose needs alike of sustenance, industry, and enterprise far transcend the limits and resources of our own islands; and whose very existence is dependent upon a world-wide commerce and foreign financial investments, necessarily full of vicissitudes, and with ceaseless ebb and flow of the precious metal which has been made by law the sole basis of our currency and entire banking system, which in turn is the indispensable support of the whole trade of the kingdom and employment of the people.

CHAPTER XIV.

THE SCARCITY LESSENS.—BEGINNINGS OF A NEW GOLD-SUPPLY.

WE now enter upon a period, of nearly twenty years, during which the annual supply of the precious metals gradually increased, until it became fully one-half larger than it had been at the beginning of the century, and more than three times as large as it was at the outset of this period, viz., in 1829. Contemporaneously—although it was in great part a period of stagnation in the British Isles—there was a considerable increase of general production and trade throughout the world: an increase of domestic production and trade in each of the leading countries of the globe, and also of international trade, or the general commerce of the world. The accumulation of wealth, too, progressed. And in consequence of this progress in material civilisation, the requirement for money increased, in its twofold shape,—namely, alike as actual currency, for effecting exchanges of property in its various forms, labour included; and also as a means of storing wealth, in a condensed and

BEGINNINGS OF A NEW GOLD-SUPPLY. 113

most readily available shape. Hence, as will be shown, despite the increase in the annual supply of the precious metals, the period of scarcity did not come to an end.

Happily, there was in one respect a most favourable difference between the twenty years immediately antecedent to 1848 and the first quarter of the century, when the dearth of the precious metals was at its height. That dearth had been aggravated and intensified by the contemporaneous course of the longest and most terrible war which Europe has witnessed. But thereafter, as a sequel to that great war, a long period of international peace ensued,— the famous Forty Years' Peace, which followed the victory of Waterloo, and to the attainment of which the noble efforts, the indomitable valour and energies, of our own nation had so largely contributed. Industry and enterprise — with their results, production and trade — advanced considerably in all countries during the period at which we are now arrived; but happily the increased requirement for the precious metals thereby occasioned was not added to by the imperious specie-demands of War. Every Treaty of Peace is perishable: the wisest and most perfect Treaty can do no more than attain what is possible in the world, or among the rival nations, at the date of its framing. It cannot meet unknown or undeveloped requirements, nor satisfy opinions and sentiments of future growth or predominance. Indeed it is such changes of views and sentiments which ere long antiquate and destroy all treaties. And, whatever defects may now be attributed to the territorial arrangements made by the Congress of Vienna, the Treaties of 1815 at least gave to Europe the longest period of repose from international combat which our Continent has enjoyed; while the fame of Waterloo, and of the redoubtable part played by Great Britain throughout the War, secured for our country not only immunity from attack, but a peerless position of power in the international politics of Europe.

The period now in question, 1830-48 (or indeed the somewhat longer period between 1810 and 1848) may be regarded as an Interregnum between the Silver and Golden Ages of the world,—a transitional period in the history of the precious metals, during which Silver was gradually losing its old supremacy, alike as regards the amount of supply and its use and acceptability as Money, the circulating medium of the civilised world.

The Great Silver Age of the world came to a close with the outbreak of the Revolutions in Spanish America, which produced a neglect and partial abandonment of the Mines of the New World,—some of which, like those of Potosi, had been worked continuously and profitably for upwards of two centuries and a half. Thereafter the American production of the precious metals, in which Silver predominated, declined greatly; and even when the new American republics had become established, the Mines of those countries never regained anything like their old productiveness. On the other hand, a notable increase ere long began in the production of the precious metals in the Old World, where Gold predominated. And so it happened that, in course of the forty years subsequent to 1810, a remarkable revolution (and Revolutions were the order of the day in that period!) occurred in the supply of the precious metals,—the regal predominance of silver giving place to a not less remarkable predominance of gold.

At the beginning of the century, and down to the year 1810, the total annual production of gold and silver throughout the world, according to Humboldt, was a little more than ten millions sterling; of which amount £7,732,976 was silver, and £2,634,137 was gold,—the quantities in weight being 19,126 kilogrammes in gold, and 869,960 kilogrammes in silver. Throughout the next twenty years, according to Jacob, the total annual production of the precious metals averaged five and a quarter millions sterling, or only one-half of the previous production; the production being below this average in the latter years of the period, and at its lowest (viz., 4¼ millions sterling) between the years 1815 and 1820—so critical in the currency annals of Great Britain. During this period of scarcity, the average annual production of silver was £3,639,000, and of gold, £1,598,000: of which amount four-fifths came from America,—namely, £3,109,000 in silver, and £878,000 in gold; and the annual produce of the Old World being rather more than half a million sterling in silver, and not quite three-quarters of a million in gold. Thus, while the production of silver in the New World was fourfold that of gold, in the Old

World the production of gold was in excess of that of silver. It will also be noticed that already, during that period (A.D. 1810-30), the ratio of the production of silver to that of gold had somewhat declined,—falling from fully 3 to 1 in 1810 and previously, to 2.3 to 1 on the average of the twenty years following.

By this time, some new sources of gold had been discovered in the Old World—namely, the gold-mines of Russia and Siberia—which came to play an important part in the monetary history of the next twenty years, and saved the civilised world from a continuance and even aggravation of the severe dearth of the precious metals, in the generation immediately anterior to the great discovery of the Californian gold-fields. It was in the year 1819—contemporaneous with the Resumption of specie-payments in Great Britain—that the first discovery was made of the existence of gold in the Russian Empire. In that year, particles of gold were found by some peasants in the sands of streamlets in the Ural Mountains. But a good many years elapsed before the supply of gold from this new source became of any notable magnitude. At first, the annual production was less than £100,000; but it increased steadily, and amounted to two-thirds of a million sterling in 1829,—the total yield of the Ural gold-deposits during these eleven years (1819-29) having been £3,500,000. In 1829 gold was also discovered in Siberia, and in larger quantity; and in 1842 the aggregate annual production of gold in the

Russian Empire amounted to two millions sterling. In the next three years (1843-5), the annual production averaged about £2,650,000; and in 1845 it rose to three and a half—or, according to M. Chevalier, upwards of four millions sterling. The total produce of the Russian gold-mines, from the outset in 1819 down to the close of 1846, amounted to close upon thirty millions sterling; and between 1829 and 1847 the total production was nearly twenty-six millions sterling, or about one and a half million a-year. This was a notable and highly important addition (nearly one-third) to the annual supply of the precious metals, which, as above stated, amounted in 1829 to little more than five millions sterling.

At the close of the period now in question (1829-47)—in other words, in the year immediately antecedent to the discovery of the Californian gold-fields—the annual production of the precious metals, gold and silver alike, had become larger than it had ever been before. In the course of the eighteen years subsequent to 1829, the annual production of gold and silver throughout the world fully trebled,—increasing from little more than five millions sterling (according to Mr Jacob, £5,237,000) in 1829, to about seventeen millions in 1847. M. Chevalier, indeed—who is the only author who gives a detailed estimate, or an estimate of the production of each continent or region of the world separately—reckons the total yearly production of the precious metals in 1847 at almost nineteen millions sterling. His estimate is as follows:—

	Gold.	Silver.
North and South America,	£2,100,000	£6,200,000
Europe, exclusive of Russia,	360,000	1,320,000
Russia (European and Asiatic),	4,100,000	200,000
Africa,	550,000	—
Archipelago of Asia, and other Sources,	3,000,000	1,000,000
Total, £18,830,000 :—consisting of	£10,110,000	£8,720,000

The production as here estimated for the American continent, Europe, and the Russian Empire, may be accepted as substantially correct; but the available information with respect to the production of the precious metals in Africa and in the Asiatic Archipelago, or the Islands of the Pacific Ocean (notably Borneo and Japan), is very vague, scanty, and unreliable; and M. Chevalier's estimate for these latter countries is held by all other authorities to be much in excess of the facts or probabilities of the case. When the Japanese empire first became open to European trade and mercantile settlers, in 1858, a remarkable difference in the relative value of gold and silver was found to exist in that country compared with the rest of the world; and it may be inferred from that difference that gold existed in Japan in much larger proportion to silver than has ever been known elsewhere, even from the earliest times of the world. But a recent Consular report states that, "whatever may have been the case in former times, the production both of gold and silver in Japan is at present very small." Also, whatever may be the latent mineral wealth of the immense and little explored island of Borneo, neither from that country, nor Java, nor any other part of the Archipelago, is any considerable amount of the precious metals known to be received into the markets of the world. Accordingly, in the present state of knowledge upon this matter, we incline (albeit merely conjecturally) to assign two millions sterling at most as the annual production of gold and silver in the Asiatic Archipelago, instead of the four millions assigned in M. Chevalier's estimate. This large deduction, if accepted, brings the total annual production of the gold and silver mines throughout the world in the year 1847, or just before the gold-discoveries in California, to about seventeen millions sterling (rather a high estimate, as seems to me),—which amount is considerably more than one-half larger than the annual supply of the precious metals had been in 1810, when the old supply was at its maximum; fully three times as large as the supply had been in 1829; and more than five times as great as in 1815, when the old supply was at its lowest point, and the dearth of the precious metals, so far as regards supply, was most severe.

Three important monetary events checkered, with various influence, this period of eighteen years immediately prior to the great Gold-discoveries. The period included two of those monetary crises in the British Isles, which, although unknown before, have so peculiarly characterised the middle period, or the second and third quarters of the present century. As previously remarked, these Crises are, in most cases, mainly a consequence of that Internationalism of Trade and Finance which sprang up after, and had been powerfully promoted by the events of the great European War, and in which the British nation have taken and still maintain the lead. The year 1826 had witnessed the first Crisis of this new kind,—the first, also, of a series which has marked our commercial annals with "black days," and measures the progress of British Trade as gloomily as if every ninth or tenth year were marked by a gallows instead of a milestone.

It was in the year 1837 that the second of those Crises occurred; produced by a brief and transient drain of gold from England,—owing to the precious metals having suddenly become in exceptional demand in the United States. There had been a highly prosperous state of trade in Great Britain. The political turmoil which had preceded and attended the passing of the Reform Bill of 1832, and the paralysing political disquietude which had prevailed for some time after that constitutional revolution, had passed off; and throughout the whole of the year 1835 and the first half of 1836, every branch of industry in the British Isles revived and became flourishing. Although the Crisis of 1826 was still fresh in men's minds, it was hopefully said that the circumstances of the country were now quite different: that vast sums of money were not, as in 1825-6, being sent abroad in wild speculations or in perilous loans; that prices were not forced up by extravagant hopefulness and speculation; and that the commercial orders and commissions were solid and rational,—coming from all quarters, and for ready-money or bills at short dates, based on the firm foundation of increased opulence among the consumers in all parts of the world. Prices, too, as usual in times of prosperity, were high and remunerative,—so that almost all the undertakings were proving advantageous; and the amount of profits made in every department of business during these eighteen months was (says Alison) "probably unparalleled, and beyond the experience of that generation, in any country."

The depressed state of trade consequent upon the Crisis of December 1826 was prolonged in varying degree for half a dozen years owing to political agitation and the shock which that and other circumstances gave to credit. But with the year 1832 there commenced a series of four unusually fine harvests, producing general prosperity throughout the kingdom. As a consequence of this prosperity, people had more to spend, and the consumption of the comforts and luxuries of life increased. Moreover, the imports increased to a greater extent than the exports, because a considerable portion of our population had come to consist of non-producers, whereas the entire population, of course, continued to be consumers: and the consumption of all classes increased so much that in the year 1837 the Board of Trade returns showed a then unprecedented excess of twelve millions sterling of imports over exports. In the same year the seasons entered upon a new cycle; and to the series of good harvests which the British Isles had enjoyed, there ensued a series of bad ones, which lasted until the year 1842. The harvest of 1838 was the worst which had occurred since 1816; and the quantity of grain imported during the following twelve months (the harvest-year 1838-9) amounted in value to about ten millions sterling,—nearly the whole of which sum had to be paid for in gold.

Simultaneously, some memorable events were occurring in the United States which of themselves occasioned a serious drain of gold from this country. General Jackson, the leader of the democratic party, had been elected to the Presidency: and a great agitation pervaded the Union against the "mercantile aristocracy" and the "plutocracy," or moneyed power, of the Banks—particularly the Bank of the United States, which was charged with using its power in opposition to the democratic Government. Indeed so exaggerated and foolish was a great part of this movement that the organs of the democratic party charged the Bank with the desire to usurp the supreme authority of the State, with "Biddle (the chairman of the Bank) for King." The charter of the Bank, which then expired, was renewed by a large majority in Congress; and it was said that the members who voted for the renewal, had they apprehended what was coming, could have passed the measure by a majority of two-thirds, which would have secured the measure against any veto on the part of the President. But General Jackson waited until the Session was over, and then put his veto upon the renewal of the Bank's charter. In like manner, upon his own responsibility, the President withdrew the Government moneys from the Bank, distributing them among the small local banks; and finally (July 11, 1836), he issued an order—as despotic as the ukase of a Czar — forbidding bank-notes to be recognised as legal money by the State, and requiring that all payments to the Government (taxes, customs-duties, the purchase-money for Government lands, &c.) must be made in gold or silver coin.

It was by means of paper-currency, in the form of bank-notes, that the United States had been enabled to carry on its remarkable progress, alike in trade and in the settlement and cultivation of the vast unoccupied territories beyond the Mississippi. General Jackson's crusade against the banks severely checked this prosperity; and also it rendered necessary a great addition to the stock of specie in the country. Owing to the succession of fine harvests (1832-35) in this country, which rendered unnecessary any export of gold in the purchase of wheat, the stock of gold in the Bank of England had reached an unprecedentedly large amount (£12,000,000); and it was upon this stock of gold that the American banks set their eyes, with a view to supply their own wants. In the preceding year the directors of the Bank of England, embarrassed by the large amount of unprofitable or non-interest-bearing bullion in their vaults, and also desirous of giving relief to a country so closely connected in trade with our own, had made a loan of £1,000,000 in gold to the embarrassed banks of the United States. But this supply was quite inadequate to meet the new demands for coin created by President Jackson's ukase, so much so that it was publicly stated by Mr Biddle that "in November 1836 the interest of money had risen to 24 per cent: merchants were struggling to preserve their credit by various sacrifices; and it cost six times as much to transmit funds from the West and the South-west as it had done in 1832, 1834, or 1835." Yet at this time, he added, "the exchanges with all the world are in our favour!" In consequence of this dearth of specie (then made the sole legal money of the United States), the American banks, especially the Bank of the United States, acting in concert with the merchants, engaged in an extensive system of operations for the purpose of drawing gold from England. The cotton-crop in the United States had been deficient, and the Bank made large advances to the cotton-growers or their brokers for the purpose of enabling them to hold back the cotton until they could extort a famine-price for it from the English manufacturers. This scheme, however, was hardly successful; because (as again happened at the outset of the Cotton Famine of 1864) our cotton-factories had previously been in such brisk employment that the stock of cotton-goods had become in excess of the demand for them, and the foreign markets were temporarily glutted. Accordingly, when this exorbitant price for cotton was demanded by the

American merchants, our manufacturers were able to resist, by delaying their purchases, and waiting until the price of the raw material was reduced. The general plan of operations adopted in the United States, to procure specie, was to draw long-dated bills payable in England, and thereupon to discount these bills at the Bank of England, and withdraw the amount in gold. In these operations they were assisted by some of the leading mercantile firms in England.

The result of these operations, combined with other causes productive of a drain of gold from this country, seriously affected the Bank of England; and its stock of the precious metals, which had been above ten millions sterling in April 1838, began rapidly to decline. In July 1839 the Bank took the hitherto unprecedented step of raising its rate of discount above five per cent, — a procedure which greatly startled the commercial classes; and when, soon after, the Bank-rate was raised to six per cent, the public disquietude wellnigh amounted to panic. At the same time the Bank began resolutely to throw out, or refused to discount, the bills of the American firms. Nevertheless so serious was the drain that in the middle of October 1839, the Bank's stock of gold had fallen to only £2,522,000. In this emergency, the Directors applied for assistance in specie from the Bank of France, and obtained a timely loan of two millions sterling from twelve of the principal bankers of Paris. By these means the crisis in England was surmounted, but not without sharp suffering among the mercantile and industrial classes, who for a time were unable to procure their usual banking accommodation. In the United States the results of this struggle for gold were far more disastrous. The Bank of the United States finally collapsed and ceased to exist, while a suspension of payments in coin became universal among the banks throughout the Union. Thus, the results of the despotic procedure of President Jackson towards the banks of his country were, first, to produce a deadly struggle for gold between the American banks and the Bank of England, and finally to cause a universal suspension of payments in coin on the part of the banks throughout the United States, as well as a great collapse of industry and general depression, in place of the previous prosperity.

During this memorable international struggle for gold, public feeling became greatly excited on the subject in the United States. The democratic party, proud of their triumph over the Bank of the United States, also boasted that they would bring the moneyed power of England to its knees. Happily the large resources and resolute policy of the Bank of England successfully resisted the attack; and on the opening of Congress in December 1839, President Jackson had to confess that the moneyed power of Great Britain was too strong for them. This international struggle for possession of the precious metals is a memorable one, and happily it is as yet the only one of its kind,—that is to say, it is the only one in which national feeling has been enlisted, and in which the attack has been carried out in a hostile spirit, and on a deliberate and systematic plan. On the other hand, the system of competing for the possession of gold—not offensively, or as an act of hostility, but simply by each Bank raising its discount-rate on its own account—thenceforward became an established usage alike in this and in other countries,— giving rise to a frequent War of the Banks, of doubtful advantage to those establishments as against one another, and, by their increase of charges and contraction of discounts, creating ever and anon havoc and disaster in the trade of their own countries. Like autocrats, the Banks proclaim this war as they please, each fighting for its own hand; and truly, it may be said of these contests, "*Quicquid delirant Reges, plectuntur Achivi!*" Whether or not the Banks gain, the community suffer.

The commercial disasters and general contraction of business produced by this monetary crisis of 1839 contributed in a serious degree to aggravate the prevalent distress in the British Isles, primarily occasioned by the series of bad harvests,—a distress which, with the consequent political discontent, mainly produced the downfall of Lord John Russell's Ministry, and brought back to office the Conservative party, for the first time since the old aristocratic form of Government was overthrown by the Reform Bill. But the cycle of the seasons was even then on the change; and had the Whigs remained a few months longer in office, it is probable that, owing to a return of fine seasons, their downfall might have been prevented or postponed for some years,—thereby altering one of the most momentous epochs alike in British legislation and in the history of Political Parties. A new series of fine harvests began with the year 1842, and, together with another happy event, which was equally beyond the control of statesmen, greatly contributed to the national prosperity, and to the remarkable popularity of the Administration of Sir Robert Peel.

By this time the gold from the Ural and Siberian mines had accumulated to a large amount in the Bank of St Petersburg, where it had been kept by the Government as a security for the note-circulation of the imperial Bank. But in 1840 the Russian Government resolved to utilise a large portion of the new gold in an interest-bearing form. Government bonds were to be deposited in the Bank for much the larger portion of the requisite securities, and the gold thus set free was invested in the Government stocks of Western Europe, and especially in the British Funds. This was the first time that the produce of the new Russian gold-mines (which were the exclusive property of the State) came into the markets of Europe; and this addition to the scanty stock of international money proved highly beneficial to trade and industry. In our own country, to which the greater portion of the gold came, its beneficial influence in facilitating trade

BEGINNINGS OF A NEW GOLD-SUPPLY.

and production became peculiarly manifest; and, co-operating with the still more powerful influence of a series of fine harvests, it contributed to produce a memorable although shortlived period of prosperity, in happy contrast to the long and gloomy depression which had prevailed with only two short breaks (viz., in 1823-5 and in 1833-6) since the close of the Great War. But for this sudden and unexpected addition to our stock of gold, it would have been impossible for our monetary resources to have sustained, even in its solid and healthy form, the outburst of industrial enterprise which gave prosperity to our people in the immediately subsequent years.[1] The stock of coin and bullion in the Bank of England in the year 1843 rose to sixteen millions sterling,—an amount fully twice as large as the average stock had been since the resumption of specie-payments in 1819, and fourfold what the average had been since the crisis in 1839.

Unfortunately, by a great change in our Monetary Laws, this welcome addition to the stock of gold was speedily robbed of its beneficial power. Originating with the Bullion Committee of 1810, and profoundly impressed by the " depreciation of the note-circula-

---

[1] The gold and silver held by the Bank of England, which in April 1838 had been above £10,000,000, sank on 15th October 1839 to £2,522,000; and even in February 1842 it had only risen to £5,600,000. Naturally, there was a contemporaneous decrease of the note-circulation,—which in August 1818 had amounted to £26,212,150, and in 1835 and '36 had been rather more than £18,000,000, but which at the end of 1839 was only £16,732,000, and in February 1842 was £17,500,000: one-third less than it had been in 1818.

tion" during the Suspension of specie-payments, there arose a sect of monetary authorities who adopted the "Currency Theory,"—the main feature or basis of which was the paramount influence upon Prices, or the value of money, of each increase or decrease in the amount of bank-notes at any particular time in circulation. Every million sterling, or so, of more notes in circulation was regarded as a depreciation of the currency, for which the Banks were responsible. To such inadequate, or indeed wholly erroneous, causes these monetary authorities attributed the drains of gold and silver to which our country had been, and was yearly becoming more and more, subjected. Consequently, these writers were ceaseless in their complaints against the Bank of England,—almost every increase of its note-circulation being regarded as a proof of depreciation of the currency: and further, when, as sometimes happened, during a drain of gold, it could be shown that there had been no increase in the note-circulation of the Bank of England, a depreciation of the currency was still believed to be the cause of the export of specie, albeit the blame was then thrown upon the other banks of the kingdom. In truth, the provincial banks were made the scapegoat whenever it was impossible to lay the blame of this fancied depreciation upon the Bank of England.[1]

[1] This utterly mistaken charge was made in a notable manner so recently as during the Crisis of 1866,—although in that case, as in many previous ones, the complaint against the English provincial banks was wholly unfounded.—See Appendix to my *Science of Finance*, where the statistics and other circumstances of the case are given.

Moreover, the English banking-system was undoubtedly in a very unsatisfactory condition. To begin with, it was a chaos. There were three different kinds or classes of banks in England. First, there was the Bank of England; secondly, there was a new class of banks, just beginning—namely, joint-stock banks which had not the power to issue notes; and thirdly, there was the great mass of the provincial banks, issuing notes, but forbidden to have more than six partners. Thus the entire body of English banks out of London were merely private firms, devoid of the large resources available under the joint-stock system; yet these non-metropolitan banks were usually, or universally, banks of issue: indeed the issue of notes had been regarded, ever since 1694, as a natural or inseparable function of Banking, these notes being to Banks precisely what Bills are to trade and the commercial classes—that is to say, the means of employing their Credit. Accordingly it happened, as a consequence of the weakness imposed by law upon these provincial banks in England, that failures were frequent among them in times of crisis and panic; whereby extensive embarrassment was occasioned to the community from the lack of currency at such times, when the notes of the fallen or suspended banks of course became useless.

These evils were directly traceable to the vicious legislative policy of the State, which, in return for loans received, had conferred upon the Bank of England a monopoly of joint-stock banking—at least so far as regards banks of issue;[1] whereby all the other banks of issue throughout England were compelled to be merely private establishments,—too weak to withstand stormy times, and also, very limited in their operations, owing to their credit being merely local. The true remedy would have been to get strong and securely solvent banks, on the joint-stock principle, as in Scotland: in which case the bank-notes likewise would have been solvent and safe. But the Government took a different view of the matter. The abolition of small notes in England—notes under £5—(made final in 1829) was adopted not so much, or not at all, for the useful and important purpose of maintaining a permanent stock of coin in the country, but in order to patch up some of the defects of the existing currency-system in England, by preventing the frequent bank-failures from pressing severely upon the poorer classes, into whose hands the £1 notes largely came in payment of wages. And it is a noteworthy fact that the chief object stated by Sir R. Peel in his monetary legislation of 1844-5 was to obviate this hardship to the working-classes by securing a sound currency. In his own words, Sir R. Peel's animating motive was "to ensure the just reward of Industry and the legitimate profit of commercial enterprise."

[1] It was believed for more than a century that the Bank of England's monopoly of the joint-stock system applied to banking of all kinds; but just about the time of which I here write, it was found that the monopoly extended only to banks of issue—that is, banks which issued notes of their own. Hence the establishment of the London and Westminster and other new joint-stock banks in London.

A wise and noble object—the true aim of monetary legislation! But alas! how mistakenly it was pursued!

What here concerns us, in the new or greatly altered monetary system established by the Act of 1844, is solely the character of that measure as affecting the influence of the precious metals upon trade and industry, and thereby upon the general wellbeing of the nation. The Bank Act of 1844 was really a Currency Restriction Act of a severe kind. Thereafter, no new bank of issue was to be allowed; and except in Scotland (which would not submit to much interference with its banking system), no existing bank of issue, except the Bank of England, was allowed upon any terms to extend its note-circulation beyond its recent average amount; and in Scotland any extension of note-issues was only permitted under the condition that gold should be kept in the banks to an equal amount,—thereby leaving no profit upon the further issue of notes. In short, the Bank of England was treated as the sole source from whence any addition to the currency should be obtainable; while a new and severe restriction was placed upon its issue of notes. Fourteen millions (now fifteen millions) of its note-circulation were deemed to be issued upon the security of an equal amount of Government securities which had long been held by the Bank, while the remainder of its circulation was required to be issued upon, and strictly limited in amount by, the varying amount of gold in the Bank.[1] And to emphasise this

[1] The Act of 1844 permits silver to form one-fourth of the stock of

arrangement, the Bank was divided into two Departments: in one of which the discounting and other ordinary operations of banking are carried on, while in the other, or Issue Department, were placed the Government Stock and gold held in security for the issued notes. As the ordinary note-circulation of the Bank at that time, and for twenty years thereafter (since which time it has largely increased), averaged about twenty-one millions sterling, it became necessary for the Bank to hold at all times in the Issue Office about seven millions of gold (in addition to the fourteen millions of Government Securities), if the currency was to be kept at its ordinary amount; and no increase of note-issues was allowed unless the Bank stock of coin and bullion exceeded in amount these six or seven millions.

This was a great and most restrictive change in our currency system. Previous to that Act, the banks of the United Kingdom, subject to maintaining "convertibility," could issue as much currency, in the form of bank-notes, as was required by the ever-varying wants of the public; while no one called for more notes than he could profitably employ, seeing that every one had to pay for the notes (in discounts) at the current rate of interest, or price of money on loan. But now, not only was the Bank of England made the only source from whence (or rather through which) additional currency could

coin and bullion against which the Bank is allowed to issue notes: but the Directors have hitherto preferred to keep all their stock of specie in gold.

CONTRACTION OF THE BRITISH CURRENCY. 135

be obtained, but, as above described, nearly seven millions of its gold were immobilised, permanently locked up in the Issue Office, in connection with the ordinary circulation of the country, and virtually unusable except in the wellnigh impossible event of the Bank's insolvency,—whereupon these six or seven millions would be divided among the creditors, as an ordinary part of the ordinary assets of the Bank.[1] The whole amount of the new supply of gold from Russia was at that time four millions sterling a-year, and no sooner did this new gold begin to reach Western Europe than British statesmanship proceeded to permanently lock up and practically nullify six or seven millions of the gold held by the Bank of England,—an amount actually as large as the average stock of coin and bullion which the Bank had held since the resumption of specie-payments in the year 1819!

The Act of 1844 was a strange abuse, or practical nullification, of what may truly be called a gift of Providence—namely, the discovery of the Russian gold-mines; and further, it was a most perilous restriction upon the supply of currency to the British nation,—perilous to the Bank of England, which, under its new fetters, became exposed to artificial bankruptcy, while still holding seven millions of

---

[1] It is commonly supposed that the gold in the Issue Office of the Bank of England would, in the event of insolvency, belong to the note-holders; but the Act of 1844 contains no such enactment, and accordingly the gold, in the case of bankruptcy, must be treated in the same way as the other effects, and belong to the general body of creditors, whether note-holders or depositors.

gold; and perilous to the nation, by creating frequent dearths of currency and banking-accommodation, for which there may be no real or natural cause. The Act, also, was a strange preparation for the subsequent and already anticipated outburst of industrial enterprise in the British Isles. In 1844 the Government was already engaged upon legislative measures which, when in operation, would certainly require more currency at home, while almost certainly necessitating the employment and export of more gold than usual in our Foreign trade. These measures were the numerous Railway Bills, together with the adoption of Free Trade; and, finally, the recurrence of bad harvest-years and an actual Famine in Ireland led to the abolition of the Corn-laws, and increased purchases of grain from abroad. The Railway Mania, which produced a purely domestic demand for currency, was surmounted; but the large importations of grain in 1847, and the consequent export of gold in payment thereof, at once created dire monetary embarrassments; and the Bank of England, under its new fetters, was saved from insolvency only by the suspension of the Act of 1844. So speedy a falsification of the views and expectations of Sir Robert Peel and the "Currency School" created astonishment even among the supporters of the Act of 1844; and both Houses of Parliament appointed Committees to inquire into the character and causes of this third disastrous Crisis since the Act of 1819. The Committee of the House of Lords reported explicitly against the Act of 1844, blaming it as an aggravating cause of the crisis; and a report to the same effect, submitted to the Committee of the House of Commons, was rejected only by a majority of two,—in the unavoidable absence of two members whose opinions were avowedly hostile to the Act. Thereupon the Act of 1844 was set on its legs again, and the Bank of England went on anew, as before,— Parliament could do that: but who could set up again the numerous fallen firms and ruined individuals who had perished during the Crisis, and many of whom would have retained their credit and their fortunes but for the currency-contraction and wide refusal of banking accommodation occasioned by the export of gold and the operation of the new Bank Act?

The contemporaneousness of the abolition of the old Corn-law with the first break-down of the new Bank Act is not the only ground for here placing these two Legislative measures in juxtaposition, for illustrative comparison. In truth, these two Acts may be classed together as regards fundamental spirit and underlying motive; and the fall of the former soon after, and wellnigh contemporaneously with, the adoption of the latter was strikingly significant of the changed centre of political power in this country. In so regarding the matter, we have no desire—nay, as will be seen, we deliberately abjure—to impute unworthy motives to the political parties which in turn have possessed a predominance in the State, and consequently in the making of laws for the nation. It is a mean and ignoble feature in political contests (albeit by no means peculiar or confined to them)—and especially in such contests where an appeal is made to the passions of the multitude —that the most exciting argument which can be addressed to the masses, or lower classes, proceeds on the imputation of class-selfishness to the party in power, the supporters of the laws against which the political agitation is directed. At the same time it is idle to ignore the influence of self-interest—the most universal and reasonable of all human motives or sentiments,—which, although in myriads of cases triumphed over, tends to affect the judgment even when its operation is insensible. Self-interest, especially in a hereditary form, like that of classes, surrounding a man like the atmosphere from his cradle to the grave, colours his sentiments and soaks into the habits of thought, to an extent none the less powerful because it may be insensible. Unless there is a philanthropic and generously sympathetic heart, it needs a very clear brain and cold passionless nature—a temperament indifferent to the attractions of worldly power and the pleasures of life—to disentangle the threads of selfishness from the web of Thought, and to perceive clearly and acknowledge equally the common rights of the community, and the respective duties of each separate class, as these are or ought to be reflected in the national legislation.

Excepting this insensible influence of class-interest upon the judgment and actions of mankind—an influence to which, from their superior training and wider views of life and policy, the upper classes, in this country at least, are the least subject,—I feel assured that the old Corn-law, alike in its origin and in its long-continued maintenance, was as much the product of national duty and of statesmanlike considerations as the most democratic measure—Reform Bills or the rest—which have ever been made law by Act of Parliament. To the same extent, but no more, I feel assured that our Currency-legislation has been framed with a sincere and anxious desire for the good of the nation. Yet the so-called Bank Acts of 1844-5 are as distinctly favourable to the interests of Capital and the moneyed classes as the Corn-law ever was to the interests of Agriculture and the landowners. And if the subject-matter of the Corn-law (viz., bread) was more vitally important, or indispensable, to the community than the subject-matter of the Bank Acts (viz., money), the privileges or special advantages established by the latter measure are in other respects the more invidious, and confined to a smaller class or section of our people. The Corn-law expired with the overthrow or downfall of the old landed aristocracy as the predominant power in the State. After 1832 there arose the middle-class Government, the most powerful section of which were the Moneyed and Manufacturing classes; and the large manufacturers being capitalists, in common with Banks and pure capitalists, desired that their property, their moneyed wealth, should lose none of its value, or should increase it. Hence a cry for low

Prices at home, permitting a smaller increase of wages than would otherwise be possible. Nor is there, in reality, much to choose between the two measures as regards the peculiarly objectionable character, as subjects of a monopoly, of the two commodities with which these Legislative measures respectively deal. Second only to Food itself, Money is the supreme necessity of existence to a civilised people, and especially to a predominantly trading and commercial nation like our own. Indeed there are cases on record—Famines, for example, like those in India—where Money (actually mere money, or currency—not Property, but the means of Purchase, by exchange of property) has, from its want, occasioned starvation to a degree only inferior to the scarcity of Food itself. But, apart from such highly exceptional cases, is it not a truism to say that a restriction or temporary dearth or diminution of the supply of currency, by restricting all the operations of trade, and consequently employment, produces Poverty, which is the *dura mater* of all Want—starvation itself included?

It is somewhat curious, and perhaps not devoid of significance, that in 1844-5, the serious changes made in our monetary system should be brought before Parliament, and enacted by the Legislature, under the inappropriate and illusive title of "Bank Acts." The title suggests changes and improvements in Banking proper,—such as better security for Deposits—security to the public for the moneys entrusted to the keeping of banks; possibly, also, regulations of the banking-charges, or in regard to the Rate of Interest, which is one of the most important agents or factors affecting the prosperity of a trading community. But the Acts of 1844-5 were purely Currency Acts, introducing severe restrictions not merely upon the manner, but also upon the power, of supplying currency to the nation. It was essentially legislation in restriction of the currency. As already described, six or seven millions of gold—an amount equivalent to what had been the entire average stock of coin and bullion held by the Bank—were by the Act locked up permanently in the Bank, and rendered useless, or unuseable either for export or for domestic circulation, as acting currency. Thanks to the Russian gold-mines and to the large purchases made by the Russian Government of the State-bonds of Western Europe, the stock of gold in the Bank of England became much larger after 1842 than it had ever been previously; but at the same time, in consequence of Peel's Act, the Bank became checkmated and powerless when its stock of coin and bullion still amounted to seven millions sterling quite as thoroughly as if, in previous times, its stock of specie had been exhausted. Indeed, as the amount of gold thus permanently locked up in the vaults of the Bank is, as already said, as large as the whole previous average stock of coin and Bullion held by the Bank, it is no exaggeration to say that after 1844 the Bank has been kept agoing only by the new or extra supply of gold which became available in Europe,—and which to this extent became diverted from general use. Thenceforth, also, the Bank-rate had to be raised as high when there were ten millions of gold in the Bank as used to be previously when there were only three! Thus the Acts of 1844-5—the changes made with respect to the British currency—nullified the new supply of gold, as affecting the British nation, as effectually as if such nullification had been the special object of these legislative changes. And not only was Money thus rendered as scarce and dear as ever, but the direr calamity was also induced that the fostered and expanding Trade of the kingdom became subject, artificially or by Act of Parliament, to constantly recurring Crises and widespread disasters, which under a wiser and less fettered currency-system would in all cases have been greatly mitigated, while some of them would not have occurred at all. It was as if a fathom deep of water were withdrawn from beneath a ship sailing among shoals, thereby exposing it to more frequent foundering and its crew to ruinous shipwreck.

It is a remarkable fact that the twenty-five years which followed the close of the Great War was a dreary time of commercial adversity and general suffering in this country,—broken only by transient prosperity in the years 1823-4, 1835-6, and 1843-5; and yet this was the period of the Long Peace, when the armaments and military taxation of Europe were at a singularly low point compared either with the previous or the subsequent periods; and when, as a consequence of the War, our country had made the most remarkable strides in foreign and colonial commerce that the world had ever seen. A curious fact, and not of easy explanation! Some writers of unquestionable ability have ascribed this general suffering in our own country to the depressing effect of the contraction of the currency in consequence of the return to a metallic monetary standard in 1819, aggravated by the subsequent restrictive changes in 1844,—the new state of matters being (as these writers maintain) very inferior to what prevailed during the War, and unsuitable to a country like ours, which was becoming more and more dependent for its wealth and prosperity upon Foreign Trade, which to a peculiar extent creates frequent drains of the precious metals. That these writers exaggerate the effects immediately produced by the Act of 1819 seems to me certain. Nevertheless there is a very serious aspect of the case, which appears to have been overlooked, at least in that entirety and cumulative action which, as seems to me, give to it its peculiar importance. There are few things more inscrutable than some of the influences exerted upon a nation's condition by changes in the currency or circulating medium. All men know that money or currency is as indispensable to civilised Trade as the circulation of the blood is to the human frame; and further, we know in a general way that an abundance of the circulating medium facilitates Trade and promotes industry and production, while a dearth of currency checks or stops Trade—as much as a want of roads, or a sudden snowfall or freezing of the canals, stops traffic and locomotion. Nevertheless, unless the case be an extreme one, it is singularly difficult to trace home to the currency changes in the national condition which may really be due to that cause, and to it alone. But, considering how close is the connection between the currency and Trade, and also between the state of trade and the condition of a people, the following series of monetary changes in Great Britain can hardly be passed in review without begetting a reasonable conjecture that their effects must have been more or less detrimental to the national wellbeing,—especially to the trading and industrial classes, both agricultural and manufacturing, who constitute the general community.

Ever since the currency or monetary system of this country was established on the principles and in the form devised by the Founder of the Bank of England in 1694—a currency suitable to civilisation, as well as capable of meeting the national emergencies of that time,—there has occurred a series of alterations in that system, every one of which has been (not a development, but) an encroachment upon Paterson's plan, and restrictive of the supply of currency to the nation. Paterson was the first—apparently in any age of the world—to devise a monetary system worthy of civilisation, and partially ridding human industry from the barbaric tyranny of gold and silver. Truly discerning between the fundamental and the merely accessory or accidental qualities of Money, he saw that an intrinsically valueless thing like paper could be made into a circulating medium, representative of Property and Value, within the limits of any civilised country, so as to compensate a deficiency of the precious metals; and still more advantageous in this respect, that this new currency could be readily increased when wanted, so as to obviate the disasters produced in civilised and trading communities by any diminution in the supply, arising from that ceaseless ebb and flow of gold and silver which every expansion of the bounds of commerce tends to intensify. This new monetary system, also, was peculiarly needful at that time, owing to the drain of specie to the Continent, to carry on war against the Grand Monarch of France, —a circumstance which, despite its exceeding gravity at the time, may justly be regarded as a "happy accident" for human progress; for, judging by all subsequent experience, and not least from that of the present generation, it seems manifest that nothing short of such a perilous exigency of the State would have sufficed to secure the adoption of Paterson's ideas and their embodiment in the Bank of England.

The currency or monetary system thus established in Great Britain in 1694 was briefly this,—that power to issue paper-currency[1] was given to large

---

[1] As stated by Mr Dunning Macleod in his admirable recent treatise on *Credit and Banking*, p. 110, the right of issuing promissory notes—notes payable on demand—was a common-law right recognised from Edward III. downwards; the issue of bank-notes being a means of utilising the credit of banking establishments substantially similar to the issue of bills by other individuals or companies. In 1692 this old common-law right was challenged and annulled by a decision of

and wealthy establishments or corporations (joint-stock banks), whose subscribed capital and the resources of a numerous and wealthy proprietary or partnership, would enable them to meet the frequent and severe strains to which every monetary system is occasionally exposed; and this note-circulation, or supply of currency, was to be regulated in amount only by the effective demand for it on the part of the public (it being issued in the discount of bills and upon other suitable securities, for which the public had to pay from 4 to 5 per cent), and by the power of the banks to maintain the convertibility of their notes into coin of the realm on demand. In the case of the Bank of England, which was established purely on Paterson's principles, the note-circulation (besides the fundamental requirement of convertibility) was based upon an equal amount of Government securities; but the Bank of Scotland and other Scotch banks were established under what may be called the

the Law Courts, which maintained that valid promissory notes could not be issued without an express Act of Parliament—a piece of that "Judge-made law" from which our community suffers so much, and which runs counter to the national will as expressed by Act of Parliament. But in 1875 the whole subject was thoroughly discussed (Goodwin v. Robarts), when the Court of Exchequer Chamber unanimously reversed the decision of Lord Holt in 1692,—the Lord Chief Justice of England declaring that the series of cases decided by Lord Holt and adhered to ever since was *a blot on our judicial history:* it was a most culpable and mischievous curtailment of individual freedom and the interests of trade. It is most incumbent upon our people to keep jealous watch upon this "Judge-made" Law, which by accumulation (each Judge accepting the decision of his predecessor) now so extensively prevails, and which not seldom renders of none effect the true Law of the country—namely, Acts of Parliament, discussed and approved by the National Representatives.

general principle then recognised by Parliament—namely, that convertibility into coin of the realm was the only indispensable requirement for the issue of bank-notes.

This original currency-system of Paterson's, although neglected and again and again departed from in the interval, is now recognised as the best, both as regards safety and suitableness, and as such has recently been adopted by the United States Government. It combines State-security for the notes, as much as if the notes were issued directly by the Government; while the functions of issue and convertibility—the former utterly impossible, and the latter nearly so, for any Government—are entrusted to powerful trading or commercial companies constituted on the joint-stock principle. With so admirable a system placed in their hands, it is lamentable to know what a mess subsequent Parliaments and Ministries made of the English monetary system!

But, hardly had this valuable currency-system been established, and its success demonstrated, than the retrograde work of contraction began. Indeed it was the very success of the system which led to the first disastrous retrogression. Paterson had been essentially opposed to any monopoly in the supply of currency,—which supply he justly regarded as hardly less necessary to a trading or civilised community than Food itself. But only fourteen years after its establishment, the Bank of England in 1708, as a condition in making a loan to the

Government, demanded and obtained a monopoly of joint-stock banking in England. It obtained an Act of Parliament forbidding the issue of notes by any bank in England which should have more than six partners. In those days this was really (as we have called it) a monopoly of joint-stock banking; for, all through last century deposit-banking was of little account: there was little spare money to deposit in bank, and banks had to trade almost solely with the money of their proprietors and the issue of notes. This monopoly, and first act of contraction, did not primarily or ostensibly affect the amount of currency; yet it did so indirectly, by weakening the credit of all English notes save those of the Bank of England, and also by confining the circulation of all the other English banks (mere private firms) to their own locality. The monopoly thus granted in 1708 was the offspring of pure selfishness on the part of the Bank of England; but it exercised a most disastrous influence upon both banking and currency throughout England, in sad contrast to the opposite regime of freedom, and consequently of powerful joint-stock banks, in Scotland.

The second contraction of the British currency was of an entirely different kind,—namely, the partial demonetisation of silver. By an Act of Parliament in the middle of last century, silver coin was rendered a legal payment only to the amount of £40. Next, at the close of the great war with France under Napoleon (in 1816), silver was wholly demonetised. The silver coinage was debased, mixed with alloy, so as to render it little else than "token-money;" and silver-money ceased to be a legal tender except in payments not exceeding forty shillings.

Consider how severe these restrictive measures were. The first—namely, the monopoly of joint-stock banking for the issue of notes, conferred upon the Bank of England—did not deprive the public of any actually existing source of currency; but it vastly narrowed the rights and latent power of supply, as established by Paterson's scheme and principles, and as fully carried out in Scotland,—cramping our original currency-system, and preventing it from expanding, at least in a safe form and effective manner, with the population and trade of England. The two subsequent restrictive measures amounted to the entire demonetisation of one of the precious metals, and, moreover, of that one which then constituted by far the larger amount of the existing stock of specie in the world. Thus, as we have previously said, although nominally the Act of 1819 was merely a resumption of specie-payments, and of the convertibility of our paper-currency into coin of the realm on demand, such as had existed down to 1797, the Act was in reality a severe contraction of the former currency-system of the country, by narrowing the stock of metallic money and, therewith, the basis of the bank-note currency to only gold, instead of both gold and silver. Hence, whatever may have been the immediate hardship to the community of the return to specie-payments and convertibility of the paper-currency in 1819—which some authorities hold to have been very severe,—this immediate and necessarily transient hardship was really the very smallest part of the public injury; by far the larger part of the hardship being the permanent effects—not of the mere act of resumption, but of the new and vastly contracted monetary system established conjointly by the Acts of 1816 and 1819, whereby, while population and trade had greatly increased, the stock of legal metallic money was reduced by more than one-half, and the difficulty of issuing paper-currency, in the form of bank-notes, was proportionately increased.

Consider, too, that this great reduction upon the amount of legal metallic money, and the consequent restriction upon the power of issuing paper-currency based upon or convertible into that metallic money, were enacted by Parliament at a time when the supply both of gold and silver from the Mines had diminished by one-half since the beginning of the century, while the annual supply of gold to the whole world had sunk to barely two and a half millions sterling,—in lieu of the previous annual supply of more than ten millions of gold and silver, (which were legal money in this country, as throughout the world,) at the beginning of the century: Consider these things, and it will become manifest that the monetary changes made by legislation immediately after the close of the Great War could not possibly fail to produce lasting effects of a very important kind upon the commercial and industrial population of Great Britain, and also that these effects must have been injurious in character. Thus, while I differ considerably from those writers—Alison and others—who attribute most disastrous consequences to the mere transition from inconvertible to convertible currency in 1819, I cannot help thinking that their mistake lies not in exaggerating the connection between the national distress and the currency, but in attributing the distress chiefly to the mere act of transition, instead of to the fact that the monetary system then established was widely different even in form, and far inferior in suitableness to the national wants, from that which had existed throughout the previous century, down to 1797. The Act of 1819 was not—as its authors alleged—a mere return to the old currency or monetary system of the kingdom: It was a great change, a new system—a most notable and severe contraction of the currency, and of the power of supplying it, and consequently of banking accommodation in the shape of loans and discounts,—although the need of such accommodation had increased with the growth of trade and population since 1797. And if these changes did not alter the value of money in this country, by making money dearer and more difficult to get—thereby artificially, or by legislation, adding to the wealth of the rich and the moneyed classes, while aggravating the poverty of the poor,—then, cause and consequence, as it appears to me, must in this case be divorced.

The Act of 1844—the so-called Bank Act—was another and highly notable step in the same direction. Sir Robert Peel, with his wonted plausible adroitness, represented the measure as simply "the complement" of the Act of 1819,—very much in the same spirit as, a quarter of a century before, he and the other Bullionists (Ricardo and others) had represented the Act of 1819 as a mere return to the old currency-system of the kingdom. In 1844, as in 1819, there was illusion, if not delusion. From 1694, down to 1844, despite the demonetisation of silver and other restrictive measures in the interval, paper-money, which had originally been devised and adopted expressly to take the place of gold and silver coin during a severe temporary drain of those metals from England, continued for a century and a half to be employed in the same manner and with the same function—namely, in partial (or, as between 1797 and 1819, in complete) substitution for the precious metals,—the only limitation upon its issue and amount being its convertibility, originally into gold or silver, and latterly into gold only. But the Bullionists—whose opinions were adopted by Sir R. Peel, and which were embodied, so far as he could then go, in the Acts of 1844-5—maintained that the proper function of paper-currency was merely to *represent* the precious metals, not to act in substitution for them, even though the substitution were but temporary; while after 1816 they had, by demonetising silver, rendered useless for our monetary purposes fully two-thirds of the existing stock of the precious metals, and narrowed the basis of our monetary system to gold alone. Even with the help of the new Russian mines, the stock of gold held in this country was not large enough to enable this Bullionist principle to be rigidly applied to the paper-currency. Accordingly, under the Acts of 1844-5, a certain portion of the note-circulation was allowed, as hitherto, to be issued simply under the condition of convertibility into gold-coin on demand; but the remainder, including any extension of the note-circulation, was imperatively required to be issued only against an equal amount of gold in the banks: so that, thenceforth, the only use or economy to be further obtained from paper-money in this kingdom was reduced to the mere saving of the gold from abrasion in the hands of the public! Thus a principle became established which, had it been acknowledged in 1694, would have rendered paper-money unavailable, save for an utterly insignificant purpose, not worth adopting by itself, and would have left the nation as completely dependent upon gold as if such a Substitute as paper-money had never been devised or thought of.

The adoption of such a principle as this in the middle of the nineteenth century, after the incalculable advantages of paper-money had been recognised by every civilised people, was really a marvellous occurrence,—proving how little the British Parliament understood currency-matters, or the momentous influence which the currency exerts upon the fortunes and condition of a nation. Members of

Parliament did not understand the matter, and they placed great faith in the authority of Sir R. Peel. It is a matter of history that this most perilous, obnoxious, and in some respects even absurd measure passed through both Houses of Parliament with an unexampled unanimity. Yet to the eye of competent observers — the ablest of whom was the sagacious author of the 'History of Prices'—the vicious character of the Bank Act was as manifest in 1844 as it is now, after nearly forty years of its pernicious operation.

The defectiveness of this new currency-system was soon manifested. The Act of 1844 was hardly three years old when, despite the continued influx of gold from Russia, together with a general increase in the produce of the gold-mines of the world, the Peel currency-system broke down, in 1847, producing widespread distress throughout the community; and the Bank of England itself was only saved from bankruptcy by the intervention of the Government by means of an Order in Council, summarily annulling for a time the fetters placed upon the issue of its notes by the Act of 1844.

Such was the first break-down of the Bank of England, and with it of banking-accommodation throughout the country, under the Act of 1844,—a measure which, together with that of 1845, was as purely a Capitalists' Act as ever the Corn-law was a Landowners' Act; and with this mighty difference, that the Corn-law directly tended to maintain a home-supply of food for our people, together with employment for our rural population, and also to uphold the value of the Land (the main and only abiding source of the national wealth), and while the advantage conferred on landowners by the Act had been from the first counterbalanced, and appropriated to the nation, by the special fiscal burdens which the Land had to bear; whereas in the case of the so-called Bank Acts there is not only no attendant advantage to the nation, but a frequent check upon industry, and ever and anon widespread bankruptcies and ruin: the sole winners being the Capitalists and moneyed classes, and also, but for the peril which the Act creates for them, the Banks, whose profits increase with every monetary scarcity and rise of the Bank-rate.

Thus, for exactly a century and a half, the supply of the circulating medium, or the power of issuing currency, had been undergoing a series of contractions; until the monetary system of 1844 became little more than the mere husk of the old and original currency-system of the kingdom. Moreover almost the whole of those contractions had been enacted since the close of the Great War in 1815, when the produce of the American mines was reduced by one-half; and the rich fruits of the splendid triumphs of Britain during that war—the vast accession of foreign and colonial trade then opened to our people, together with (for the first time) our dominion of the seas in peaceful commerce, as previously also in war, were greatly shorn of their benefits to us, alike in wealth-making and employment, by the successive contractions thereafter imposed upon the national supply of Money, which is as truly the sinews of Trade as it is of War. First, by the demonetisation of silver, fully two-thirds of the existing stock of the precious metals, the money of the world, was rendered useless to our nation, either as money or as a basis of our paper-currency; then the £1-notes were abolished in England, creating a new demand for, and large absorption in daily use of, the precious metal then alone left to us, viz. gold; and lastly, when a new yet small supply of gold began to reach us, Paper-money in this country was degraded from the position which it had held amongst us for a century and a half as, more or less, a substitute for metallic money, and, so far as legislation could venture, rendered a mere representative of an equal amount of gold stored immovably in a few favoured banks. And these changes and severe contractions upon the currency-system of the kingdom were made at a time—between 1815 and 1847—when not only had the Trade and population of Great Britain rapidly increased, but when, as already remarked, the new spirit and system of Internationalism had come into operation, alike in Trade and Finance, creating great and previously unknown requirements for the precious metals, and especially for gold.

We cannot help thinking that these currency-restrictions — these successive contractions of the medium and means of exchange, which is indispensable to the operations of all trade and industry—

exerted a baneful influence upon the condition of our people, and produced some while aggravating all of the adversity which so strangely befell our nation after the close of a war which had given to Great Britain the headship of the nations in commerce as well as in political influence. The harvest of commercial power and opportunities which had been won for us by Pitt, Nelson, and Wellington, subsequent Ministers prevented us from reaping. And so the rich fruits of the Great War were turned into Dead Sea apples! Never before, since Imperial Rome was absolute mistress of the world, has any State or nation held so peerless a position, not merely in arms and political influence, but in commercial power and dominion and abounding opportunities and facilities for Trade, as was held by Great Britain at the Peace of 1815. Her colonies and dependencies overspread the globe, and dotted the oceans, while her new empire in India gave to her the wealth-making trade of the East. She was mistress of the seas, with trading settlements all over the world. She was Queen of Commerce,—a Tyre and Sidon swelled to a more than Roman magnitude— to that of "an empire upon which the sun never sets." Yet what came of it all?—and why was so splendid an opportunity shorn of its natural results? And why did nearly forty years elapse ere Great Britain rose anew into a position of prosperity—yet one which, even commercially, was inferior, relatively to the rest of the world, to that which she held potentially, or indeed actually, in 1815? Unusual though such a case be, the Great War was so conducted by Pitt, and so successfully waged by Nelson on the seas, that British Commerce actually grew more rapidly in the bosom of war and within sound of the cannon, than it had ever done before, or than it did for a generation afterwards. Incredible as it may seem, the foreign trade of Great Britain in the year 1841 was no larger than it had been in the year of Waterloo and the Peace!

It is a mere truism to say that a greatly expanding trade, especially in the form of international commerce, demands an increase of currency,—or at least an increase in the power or potentiality of the supply of currency. And it is an exceeding great marvel that our statesmen should have been so blind to this fact, or so repugnant to practically recognising it. What had been the history and the domestic progress of this country for more than half a century prior to the Currency Restriction Acts (called the Bank Acts) of 1844-5 ? During all that period, the British Isles had been becoming too small for the energetic race to which they had given birth. Great Britain had ceased to be a self-sufficing country. The external world had become necessary to us,—first, to furnish employment for the increase of our population, and, secondly, to provide that new portion of our population with food; and thirdly, even to furnish employment for the growth, or steady increments, of our accumulating capital: and the successful conduct of the recent War had opened vast opportunities for the national energies in all these directions. Indeed, as Professor Jevons remarks, "the very foundations of our Home industries were being energetically laid throughout the period from 1782 to 1815."

Thus our population, obtaining profitable employment beyond what our own Islands could supply, simultaneously became dependent upon other countries for the raw material of a large portion of our manufactures; and this new employment sufficed to absorb and maintain the new additions which each year made to the population. The growth of population had become independent of the Land; and, naturally, the produce of the Land began to be inadequate for the food-supply of the nation. During bad harvest-years this inadequacy became felt at times even during the Great War; and, as previously remarked, it was only by the energy of our farmers and the enterprise of the landowners that, under the Napoleonic Continental blockade against us, the nation escaped being starved into surrender, as truly as Paris was in 1870 under the blockade of the German army. And still, Foreign Trade found expanding employment for our people; so supported, the growth of population progressed; until at length the foreign food-supply, which had been necessary only in bad harvest-years, became an enduring and fully recognised necessity. The fine seasons of the years 1833-6 was the last time when the British Isles were self-supporting (or almost so) as regards the necessaries of life. Then the end came; and the Famine of 1847 sufficed to establish the free import of corn and other necessaries of life, far more than all the arguments of political or commercial economy. Free Trade, to its fullest attainable extent, had become a national necessity, if the country was to retain its increasing population.

Since then, the annual growth of population (minus Emigration) has found employment solely by means of Foreign trade; the agricultural population remains stationary, or indeed is greatly decreasing; and Great Britain, almost by necessity, has chosen for her lot to be the workshop of the world. A remarkable position, unparalleled in history save by the smaller, yet hardly less famous, cases of Tyre, Carthage, Venice: a lucrative and lively, yet most unstable, form of prosperity. Exempt, in all probability, from the fate of Venice, which fell from greatness mainly from a mere shifting of the channels of Trade, England may well ponder the fate of Carthage; for her position must be maintained by arms, while the commercial spirit, combined with the rich gains of Trade, are eminently adverse to military aptitude, repugnant to imperial foresight, and intolerant of sacrifices when a peril is still in a remediable form—at a distance! A nation, too, which depends for existence upon Foreign trade is peculiarly dependent also upon arms; because its interests being world-wide, its policy comes in contact with an unusual number and variety of foreign Powers; and the whole fabric of its own greatness and wellbeing must fall as soon as it ceases to be an Empire and is reduced to its own limits.

A nation which has an ample territory, and thereby is enabled to root itself in the Land, is indestructible; wave after wave even of foreign conquest may roll over it, and yet as soon as the earthquake-wave of war recedes, the nation and its industry reappear. So rooted in its native soil, a nation, escaping destruction, can take lesson from its disasters, and regain under the bracing influence of adversity the manly virtues which are prone to disappear under the relaxing luxury of an advanced civilisation. Look at China, as an example of this, and there behold a people again and again losing its pristine vigour in the lap of material comfort and the pursuits of peace, and again and again reviving, renewing its national spirit under conquest and adversity, and so attaining to what may be called an eternity of national existence, while all the other old monarchies of the world have crumbled into the dust. Look even at France, and note how the nation quickly revived from the utter exhaustion produced alike by the bloodshed, social chaos, and exhaustion of its realised wealth by the *assignats*, at the first Revolution; as again, in our own day, from the Germanic invasion, conquest, and extortionate war-indemnity: yet France still lives, and reacquires the frugality of life and the manly virtues,—like a second youth, preparing for another and not less powerful stage in its national career. Antæus-like, such a nation, when beaten and overthrown, finds new strength in its contact with the soil. But a people dependent upon Commerce—like Tyre or Carthage—perishes utterly, rapidly declining and dropping out of the world, whenever naval or military defeat breaks off from it its colonies and settlements, or sweeps its navy from the seas. And so must it be with England,—whose greatness is that of an Empire (an aggregation of different countries and peoples); and which can only exist as the head of a vast dominion to be maintained by far-seeing policy and arms. Democracy never yet created such an empire, nor has long maintained one; nor is the new democracy of England likely to prove an exception.

While Great Britain—wasting or abusing the windfall from the Ural and Siberian mines, by further restrictions upon her contracted and mono-metallic currency-system—arrayed herself in a golden net, whose meshes cover and overlay her whole national industry, and which necessarily contract to the point of strangulation whenever even a small portion of the precious metal (the mere reserve-stock of gold in Bank) is withdrawn from the country, nay, even from the Bank, however transiently and briefly,—how fared the rest of the world at this period, as regards the precious metals and money, immediately antecedent to the great Gold-discoveries which were destined so happily to revolutionise the monetary world, to set free from its metallic fetters the industrial enterprise of mankind, and to render tolerable the restrictive monetary legislation, a despotism of Gold, established in our own country in 1844?

CHAPTER XV.

GENERAL DISTRESS BEFORE THE GOLD-DISCOVERIES.

We now come to the years immediately previous to the great Gold-discoveries,—years so disastrous in their events, alike industrial, social, and political, that for the time they seemed almost to forebode a cataclysm in the fortunes of our continent. It was a dark hour in the history of the modern world,— forming a striking background for the epoch of golden prosperity which, with almost magical swiftness, succeeded to it. The civilised world was outgrowing its supply of Money, and that want operated seriously in aggravating all the other calamities— famine, bad trade, and political troubles and revolution — which, closely interwoven, then formed a Nessus-robe of torture for Europe and its peoples.

At first sight, it is true, it may seem that the condition of the world with respect to the precious metals was highly satisfactory during the years immediately prior to 1848. The major, or at least the primary and most obvious elements of the case were distinctly favourable; inasmuch as both the annual supply from the Mines, and the existing stock of gold and silver, had become larger than at any previous period in history. On the other hand, there were elements of the case, less noticeable, but not less important, which went far to alter, or indeed actually reversed, these favourable influences. Of the two grand elements or factors of Value—namely, Supply and Demand — the latter is unquestionably the more important; inasmuch as it is the Demand, the desire to possess, which is the active and indispensable source or creative cause, of Value. Demand may be called the male element of Value, and Supply the female. Nothing possesses, or can possess, value unless there be a demand for it, a desire to acquire or possess it. Now, the demand or requirement for the precious metals had never before been so great throughout the modern world.

In the first place, there was the growth of Population in all the civilised countries. This growth of itself produces an increased requirement for the precious metals. Unless mankind are to retrograde gradually into barbarism, each successive and more numerous generation, each increment of the population, must work, produce, and make exchanges of their produce, to the same extent as their fathers, in order merely to retain the social condition which had previously been reached by the communities to which they belong. And if any one considers how great in modern times is this growth of population in civilised countries, it will be seen that the increased requirement for the precious metals occasioned by this single fact is serious and considerable. Yet this is but one-half, or merely a fraction, of the influence of increasing population upon the demand for the precious metals. Most happily, it has for long been the normal course of events that population not only increases in numbers, but also in the comforts of life. In other words, there is larger production and augmented commerce, or exchanges of produce, among the same number of people. Also, in modern times, there is a steady growth of moneyed wealth: which requires additional gold and silver for the storing of it in a convenient and instantaneously available form; and the possession of which engenders a taste for the arts and luxurious ornament, such as plate, gilding, and ornaments of the person. It is true that, under the present forms of industry and society, this growth of wealth and of material comforts or wellbeing is by no means equably diffused in any nation or community. Unfortunately there is a constant tendency towards the creation of very wealthy classes in each community, along with masses of indigence, and side by side with classes whose condition (although unquestionably improving) is far from keeping pace with the improvement in the condition of the more fortunate classes. But this circumstance rather augments than impedes the requirement for the precious metals, whether for purposes of luxury or for the storing of reserve-wealth, inasmuch as it is the possession of large fortunes which tends most to the absorption of gold and silver for these purposes. Accordingly, as the growth of population, production, commerce, and wealth with luxury, had been great since the beginning of the century, it is manifest that the demand or requirement for gold and silver during the same period must also have very considerably increased; although whether or not this increase in the demand equalled or exceeded the increase in the annual supply of the precious metals subsequent to the year 1840, or thereabouts, is beyond the possibility of correct estimate.

But there remains to be considered another element of the question, which, although readily intelligible when described, is apt to be overlooked by the public at large, or even in the estimates and conclusions of ordinary politicians. In the years immediately prior to 1848, it was easy to recognise the fact that the annual supply of the precious metals, and especially of gold, had reached an amount largely in excess of what had been the annual produce of the Mines at the beginning of the century. The severe dearth of gold and silver which began in 1810, owing to the revolt and revolutionary troubles in Spanish America, and which had prevailed with severity down to 1830, and in lesser degree for a dozen years thereafter, had been succeeded by a period of comparative abundance,—so that, as already stated, the annual produce of the world's Mines had become about three-fourths, or 75 per cent, larger than in the early years of the century. The existing stock of the precious metals had likewise, by accumulation, become larger than it had ever previously been.

So regarded, the position of the world with respect to the precious metals appeared eminently satisfactory. The chief cause of the suitableness of gold and silver as Money is their normal steadiness in value; and it is obvious that the larger the amount of the existing stock of those metals, the more stable becomes their value,—because the less can it be affected by any change, whether of increase or of decrease, in the amount of the annual supply. And as, in the ordinary course of human existence, and excepting great cataclysms, such as the fall of the Roman Empire, the stock of gold and silver becomes larger and larger, this primary element of their suitableness as the world's money —namely, their stability of value—tends to improve with the progress of mankind: which is undoubtedly an advantage for the world's currency.

Nevertheless this state of matters has an inevitable drawback, inasmuch as it renders necessary an ever-increasing annual supply of gold and silver. In exact proportion as stability of monetary value is enhanced by the growing magnitude of the existing stock of the precious metals by annual accumulation, the less efficacious for human use becomes any given amount of annual supply. The main explanation of this fact is the unavoidable diminution of the existing stock owing to loss from wear or abrasion of coins and ornaments, as well as from casualties of various kinds, of which the most ordinary, and perhaps also the most serious, is shipwrecks. The annual loss of gold and silver from abrasion and casualties has been estimated by Jacob, and accepted by Tooke and other authorities, at a quarter of a per cent of the existing stock, or one per cent every four years, and twenty-five per cent in each century. Thus, in order that an existing stock of 400 millions sterling may be maintained undiminished throughout a century, there must be an annual supply of one million merely to replace the wear of the coin; and consequently an absorption and consumption of 100 millions throughout the century, — this vast sum being no available addition to the existing stock, and entirely useless save for the maintenance of that stock, by replacement of the unavoidable loss upon it by abrasion and casualties. Accordingly, in estimating the condition of the world with respect to the precious metals —or the monetary condition of the world at large— at any particular period, the annual produce of the Mines, whether large or small, goes for little: the correct criterion being (speaking roundly) the proportion which the annual supply bears to the amount of the existing stock. This statement, it will be observed, is made in addition to the considerations which have been stated in the previous paragraph,— namely, the growth of population, trade, and production, and also of wealth (which, I repeat, needs more of the precious metals to store it), and of the absorption of gold and silver in ornaments and the arts—the latter of which requirements for the precious metals varies greatly with the wealth and tastes of each age and country. But beyond or in addition to these considerations, and with respect to the condition of mankind in relation to the precious metals as money, the amount of the existing stock of these metals is at least of equal importance in the calculation as the annual supply, or yearly produce of the Mines.

Let us, then, glance for a moment at the position of the world, from this point of view, at successive periods since the discovery of the American continent came to the aid of mankind by furnishing a supply of the world's money, and thereby facilitated and quickened the progress of civilisation, launching modern Europe upon its illustrious career. At the close of the fifteenth century, when the New World was discovered by Columbus, the entire amount of the precious metals in Europe is conjecturally estimated at less than forty millions sterling; and the annual supply, chiefly from mines in Hungary, was about £100,000. Throughout the latter half of the following century—say, from 1546, two years after the discovery of the rich Potosi silver-mines, to A.D. 1600—the existing stock of the precious metals in Europe and America is estimated to have averaged 80 millions sterling, with an average annual supply of two millions. Throughout the next half-century —say from 1601 to 1646 A.D.—when Prices reached their maximum, the existing stock averaged about 155 millions sterling, with an annual supply of about three and one-third millions. Throughout the remaining half of that century (1646-1700), the existing stock averaged 220 millions, the annual supply continuing at 3½ millions. During the next hundred and nine years—from 1701 to 1810 A.D., in which latter year the revolutions in Spanish America began,—the existing stock of gold and silver, in all forms, averaged 700 millions sterling, and the annual supply contemporaneously averaged eight millions. Then began the period of dearth, when for twenty years (1810-1830) the annual supply of gold and silver averaged only five millions sterling, although, from accumulation, the total existing stock of these metals in all forms amounted to about 800 millions.[1]

Thus, bearing in mind the importance of the magnitude of the existing stock, it will be seen that the more obvious and striking element of the case, namely, the amount of the annual supply of the precious metals, is quite delusive as regards the monetary condition of the world during the greater part of this long period—viz., from the discovery of

[1] The following Table shows how the enlarging stock of the precious metals absorbed a correspondingly increasing portion of the annual supply in merely replacing the loss by wear or abrasion: thereby reducing the portion available for other purposes. The figures represent averages, in Millions sterling:—

Periods.	Existing Stock.	Annual Supply.	Annual Loss by Wear.	Surplus, available for Coinage, Ornaments, &c.		
				Annual Amount.	Proportion to Stock.	Proportion of Annual Supply.
1546-1600	80	2	·2	1·8	2·25 p. c.	Nearly all.
1601-1646	155	3·3	·4	2·9	1·87 ,,	
1641-1700	220	3·3	·5	2·8	1·27 ,,	
1701-1809	700	8	1·7	6·3	·90 ,,	⅘
1809-1830	800	5	2·	3·	·37 ,,	⅗

America down to the early years of the present century. The annual produce of the Mines increased progressively and to a large extent during that period,—rising from two millions in 1550 to four times that amount throughout the whole of last century, and to upwards of ten millions sterling at the close of the period, or beginning of the present century. Nevertheless, entirely apart from increase of population and trade, the monetary condition of the world, if measured by the ratio of the available supply of the precious metals (*i.e.*, the surplus after replacing loss) to the existing stock, was declining throughout the entire period subsequent to A.D. 1650, when the rise of prices stopped. Deducting the constant loss on the existing stock, the portion of the annual supply of gold and silver which constituted a real addition—available for use, after replacing the annual loss and maintaining the existing stock—averaged two and a quarter (2·25) per cent of the entire stock during the latter half of the sixteenth century (1546-1600 A.D.) During the latter half of the following century (1651-1700 A.D.), the portion of the annual supply available for new uses averaged only one and a quarter per cent of the contemporaneously existing stock. During last century, and down to 1810, the available portion of the annual supply (that is, after simply replacing the loss upon the existing stock) averaged less than one per cent of the contemporaneous stock. And finally, during the twenty years when the production of the precious metals was at its lowest (1810-1830), the available portion of the annual supply (the portion available to meet the new or growing requirements of increasing population, trade, &c.) was equal only to one-third of a per cent upon the existing stock,—little more than one-sixth of what the proportion had been between 1540 and 1600 A.D.; while the total annual supply between 1810 and 1830 was not more than two and a half times as large as it was during the latter half of the sixteenth century. And yet, how much vaster was the yearly addition to population and trade during the latter period than it had been more than two centuries previous, when modern Europe was still in its infancy! In truth, so severe was the scarcity in the years 1828 and 1830 (the epoch of the Reform agitation in this country), that for the first and only time at least in modern history, the flow of specie from Europe to the East not only ceased, but was *reversed!*

Again, dealing simply with the entire annual supply, as compared with the entire contemporaneously existing stock of the precious metals in all forms within the realms of Christendom (Asia being excluded), the estimates of the accepted authorities show that the proportion which the annual supply bore to the existing stock in the latter half of the sixteenth century (1546-1600) was 2·5 per cent; during the following half-century (1600-1646), it was 2 per cent; from 1646 to 1700, it was only 1·5 per cent; from 1701 to 1809, it averaged only 1·14 (1¼) per cent, and at the beginning of the present century the proportion of the annual supply to the existing stock was ·8, or four-fifths of a per cent; from 1810 to 1830, it fell still lower, viz. to ·62, or three-fifths of a per cent; and in 1847 it had risen to 1·43, or nearly 1½ per cent,—the gold-supply in that year amounting to 1·78 per cent of the existing stock of gold, and the silver-supply in the same year (1847) amounting to 1·09 per cent of the then existing stock of silver. Thus, at the beginning of the memorable year 1848, the proportion which the annual supply of gold and silver, taken together, bore to the then existing stock of these metals in all forms, amounted to little more than one-half of what the ratio of annual supply to existing stock had been during the latter half of the sixteenth century, two hundred and fifty years previously.

Finally, if we regard the same facts in a narrower and more definite shape—that is, if instead of dealing with the stock of gold and silver existing in all forms, alike as money, plate, ornaments, &c., we take into account only the portion which is reckoned to have existed at successive periods in the form of Money, or as Coin,—the statistics point equally to a gradual decline in the world's monetary supply, or stock of coin. Starting with the conjectural estimate of 33 millions sterling of coin in what may be styled "the ancient world," in 1492, we find (according to Jacob's estimate) that in 1550 the stock of coin in Europe and America had increased to 50 millions; in the year 1600, it was 130 millions; in 1700, it had risen to 297 millions; in 1810, it was 380 millions; and in 1830, only 313 millions.

Thus, the stock of coin in Christendom, or in the world exclusive of Asia, became quadrupled during the century after the discovery of America; at the close of another century, viz. in the year 1700, the stock of coin had become nine times as large as it was in 1492; and at the beginning of the present century (in 1810) it had become nearly twelve times as large as the original stock. Thus it appears that the rate of increase in the stock of coin was by far the most rapid at the outset,—having been fourfold at the end of the sixteenth century; whereas, thereafter, the stock increased barely threefold during the next 210 years,—an increase which appears to have been barely adequate to keep pace with the growth of population and trade. In 1830, after the stoppage of the American mines, the stock of coin was one-sixth part less than in 1810, and only a fraction larger than it had been a century and a half previous.[1] No wonder, then, that there should have then occurred that marvel, and unique event in history, a reversal of the eastward flow of the precious metals!

All the estimates of the amount of the precious

[1] Mr Jacob (vol. ii. p. 348) says:—"The consumption of gold and silver, and the application of these metals to other purposes than the fabrication of coin, has in the last twenty years (1810-29) exceeded that supply of them which the Mines have afforded." In other words, the loss upon the stock of the precious metals by abrasion and casualties, and the quantity of these metals converted into ornaments, was larger than the entire contemporaneous produce of the Mines: the result being a serious reduction in the stock of Coin,—namely, to the amount of nearly seventy millions sterling, or upwards of one-sixth of the previously existing stock.

metals in the world, or within Christendom, are, it must be confessed, highly conjectural; the only sure portion of the basis for such calculations being the annual supply, and the aggregate produce of the Mines. Nevertheless these estimates have engaged the laborious attention of some eminent men, and, being the best which are attainable, are accepted more or less by all writers upon this subject. But, granting the dubiety which must attach to these statistics, and making the largest allowance for their defectiveness, the conclusion to which they point, and which I have brought out—namely, the lesser plenty of the precious metals which began to prevail in the closing years of the seventeenth century (or, just before the founding of the Bank of England, and the wise adoption of a supplementary paper-currency in this country), and also the actual dearth which began by the interruption in the working of the American mines in 1810—is clearly manifest from the simpler and entirely unquestionable facts of the case.

Thanks to her Banking-system—with its original paper-currency, ever free to expand with the requirements of the nation—Great Britain doubtless entirely escaped the effects of the slightly tightening money-market (as it would now be called) throughout last century; and her subsequent adoption of inconvertible paper-currency—of paper-money in complete although temporary substitution for coin—carried her commerce and industry unscathed through the severe dearth of the precious metals in this country at the beginning of the present century, occasioned by the operations of a great war and the contemporaneous failure of the Mines. The export by England of nearly the whole of her metallic currency, to maintain the war, constituted a temporary addition to the stock of specie on the Continent; and the vast amount of inconvertible paper-currency issued by Austria and most of the other Powers engaged in resisting France under Napoleon—and which was ultimately replaced by the paper-currency issued by the Allied Powers collectively, under a guarantee from Great Britain—likewise contributed to conceal the falling off in the produce of the Mines. Further, the War on the Continent was an actual displacement of pacific industry,—the trade of war largely took the place of ordinary trade in the belligerent countries; whereas, as already pointed out, this was not the case in the British Isles, where, made secure by our "wooden walls," the nation continued to prosecute its trade and industry, and on a greatly increased scale, in consequence of our dominion of the seas and ever-growing colonial empire. Nevertheless, when the War came to a close, and the guaranteed Allied paper-currency was gradually withdrawn from circulation, while the contraction of State-loans became necessary—and when Great Britain, too, began to collect gold for her revived metallic currency,—the Continental peoples began to suffer severely from the effects of the dearth of the precious metals.[1]

[1] "In a Memorandum furnished to Parliament by the Bank Directors in 1832, they give twenty millions as the aggregate amount which they were obliged to obtain from foreign countries; and, as they say, this great supply of gold 'could only be purchased by re-

A monetary dearth is necessarily felt in very different degrees in different countries: the dearth being most severely felt in those countries which trade most, and especially in those whose industrial enterprise is most connected with Foreign trade, wherein the payments or trade-balances must necessarily be settled in gold or silver. Accordingly, when Great Britain — doffing her war-panoply of paper-money, and arraying herself in a golden robe ever-fluctuating in its dimensions with the variations of the gold-supply — became for the first time exposed to the brunt of the world-wide dearth of specie, in 1819, — especially since, by the decree of Parliament, she had restricted her legal currency to gold, and thereby rendered unavailable for her use the silver which then constituted nearly three-fourths of the world's stock of money, — the dearth broke in upon her like a destroying flood, and smote with paralysis the magnificent fabric of her commerce and industry. What heightens the marvel is, that this establishment, by Act of Parliament, of a currency restricted to gold was adopted at the very time when the produce of the gold-mines had sunk to its lowest point, — the total production of gold in the year 1816, according to Soetbeer, being

duced prices of commodities in Great Britain.' Thus it is seen that the Bank of England in taking, in 1816-20, out of the stock of gold of the civilised nations, £20,000,000, was in fact absorbing for England alone a sum equivalent to fifteen times the annual production of gold which was at the time, according to M. Soetbeer, worth £1,320,000." — *International Bimetallism.* By Emile de Laveleye. English translation, 1881, — p. 44.

less than one million and a half sterling. And so it had happened that the happy occurrence of Peace, so triumphantly won, by bringing preparations for returning to a metallic currency in this new and contracted form, at once brought in a flood of national distress, with its natural concomitants, social troubles and political discontent and agitation.

Lord Bacon, who had witnessed the remarkable monetary events of the sixteenth century — the sudden change from dearth to abundance in the supply of the precious metals, which contributed so much to the splendour of the Elizabethan age—saw clearly the woful influence of a scarcity of money; and upon this ground he urgently exhorted his countrymen to the promotion of Agriculture, in order to render unnecessary the importation of Food, which in his time was almost the only, as it still is ordinarily the chief, cause of the drains or exportation of the precious metals. Locke, writing upon the same subject, remarked that when such a scarcity occurs, " people, not perceiving the money to be gone, are apt to be jealous one of another ; and, each suspecting another's inequality of gain [*i.e.*, that some classes are prosperous while other classes are suffering], every one will be employing his skill and power, the best he can, to bring money into his pocket in the same plenty as formerly. But this," he adds, " is but scrambling among ourselves, and helps no more against our wants than the pulling of a short coverlet will, amongst children that lie together, preserve them all from the cold : some will starve, unless the father of the family provide better, and enlarge the scanty covering." Malthus, writing of the fall of prices to be expected from the monetary legislation of 1816 and 1819, remarked that, "if we completely succeed in the reduction of the price of corn and labour, the pressure of the taxes will appear to be absolutely intolerable." The taxation in connection with the National Debt of itself amounted to thirty millions, and its weight or pressure increased with every rise in the value of the currency. "Indeed," adds Malthus, "if the measure of value were really to fall as we have supposed [that is, to such an extent that the price of wheat would fall to 50s. the quarter], there is great reason to fear that the country will be absolutely unable to continue the payment of the present interest of the National Debt." Postponing an exposition of the actual mode in which a dearth or abundance of money affects trade and enterprise, and consequently the prosperity and wellbeing of a nation,—and also without seeking to determine the precise extent of the connection betwixt the dearth of specie and the long distress of nations, extending from 1815 to 1851, and pre-eminently severe in bad harvest-years, when the national loss from diminished crops was aggravated by the export of specie to pay for the importations of corn,—we may at least note the contemporaneous occurrence of these things, as well as the mysterious character of the distress, which was too widespread to be explainable by local or political causes, and so significant of that insidious monetary malady which may be likened to the blood-poisoning in the human frame from the unconscious breathing of a polluted atmosphere,—or at least to the insensible wasting which occurs under several hidden forms of disease.

We have already described the Crisis of 1826 and some other of the earlier events of this woful period of depression in the British Isles; and thereafter it continued unbroken, save by the two passing gleams of prosperity, in 1834-6 and 1844-6, down to about 1852. Political administration, or the constitution of the Government, had nothing to do with it: indeed it is merely as a concession to the ridiculous prejudices of Party-strife that we even interject this remark. The Distress swelled the agitation in favour of the great Reform Bill, but Parliamentary Reform did nothing to lessen the general stagnation of industrial enterprise, or the sufferings alike of our agricultural and manufacturing classes; indeed, owing to the political disquietude, for a while it aggravated them.

The contemporary historian Alison says:—"The whole period from 1819 to 1829 had been one of incessant fall of prices. The chief articles of commerce during that time had declined in money-value fifty per cent,—many much more. Such a long-continued and prodigious fall of prices filled all classes living on the sale of commodities with despair. True, they bought everything cheaper, but what did this cheapness avail them when the wages of labour came down in a still greater proportion; when two millions of destitute paupers in Ireland were at every moment ready to inundate the labour-market of England; and employment even on the lowest rates was often not to be had, from the discouragement to speculation of every kind which the continual fall of prices occasioned? The only thing which rendered this fall tolerable to the working-classes in towns and the manufacturing districts was the extremely low price of the necessaries of life which the magnificent harvests from 1832 to 1836 occasioned; but this reduced the agricultural classes to despair, and the table of the House of Commons groaned during these years under petitions which set forth with truth that under existing prices cultivation of any kind could be carried on only at a loss. And when the bad seasons began in 1837, and five cold and wet autumns in succession raised the cost of food again to the War-rates [which then were felt as famine-prices], a still more general and acute suffering was experienced by the manufacturing classes; for in proportion to the decline of their wages, from the contraction of the currency and consequent commercial distress, was the rise in the cost of the necessaries of life from the badness of the seasons."

As a natural result of this unparalleled series of internal disasters, pauperism increased to such an extent as (through the Poor-rates) to threaten to swallow up the profits of trade, and especially the income from land, upon which these rates were chiefly levied. Lord Brougham, in the House of Lords, said, "If something is not done *to stop relief being given*, your lordships' estates will be swallowed up, and I myself, Lord Brougham, will become a Westmoreland pauper." The Liberal Ministry of the day, taking this view of the matter, had brought forward a new Poor Law Act; the object of which, while correcting abuses in the administration of the poor-laws, was to prevent the widespread pauperism of the times from impoverishing the entire community. And so, in the middle of this period of national distress, the lower classes were partially deprived of the relief which for centuries they had been legally entitled to from the more fortunate classes. No wonder that the same epoch of hard times witnessed the birth of Chartism.[1] Neverthe-

[1] Writing of this change in the Poor-Law, which he heartily condemned, Sir Archibald Alison says:—"The intention of its authors" (the Reform Ministry) "was to go a great deal further, and to put an end altogether to parochial relief, unless in such cases of extreme destitution or incapacity for labour as induced the applicants for relief to go into the Workhouse rather than forego it. The *workhouse test* was the great discovery of the Economists which was to distinguish real distress from that which was assumed, and thereby to bring down the burden of poor-rates to the lowest point consistent with the prevention of actual death by famine. This purpose, carefully concealed from the public, was not disguised in the private instructions of the Commissioners to the boards of guardians. With this view the regulation was made that husband was to be separated from wife, parent from child; that the inmates of all workhouses should wear workhouse dresses; and the fare was to be regulated in such a manner as to be the most economical which was consistent with the support of life. Relief was to be sternly denied to all who declined to enter these gloomy abodes; and to render them capable of containing the multitudes who might be expected to apply for admission, huge Union workhouses were erected in most places, called by the people 'Bastilles'— the very sight of which, it was trusted, would deter any one from seeking admission."—*History of Europe*, 1815 to 1852, chap. xliii. § 47.

less, when the bad harvests of 1838 and 1839 came to aggravate the prevalent distress, it became utterly impossible to carry out the principle of the Act and the instructions of the Poor-law Commissioners. At Nottingham the crowd of applicants was so great that there was no building which could hold a fifth part of them, and outdoor relief or serious rioting was the only alternative. In Lancashire similar scenes occurred; and in all the manufacturing counties the pressure was so immense that a general relaxation of the system, in favour of outdoor relief, took place. A wise and merciful change, which has been continued to the present time, yet is (I think) by no means an adequate one.[1]

The condition of the country in 1843, at the end of the ten years of Whig rule which followed the passing of the Reform Bill (when the bad state of the national revenue, shown by a succession of deficits amounting in the aggregate to upwards of ten millions sterling, gave rise to the then popular saying that "the Whigs are always bad financiers"), has thus been described by Miss Martineau, an ardent Liberal and contemporary observer, whose statements have recently been adopted as correct by an independent Liberal of the present day (Mr Fawcett):—"The distress had now so deepened in the manufacturing districts as to render it clearly inevitable that many must die, and a multitude lowered to a state of sickness

---

[1] I have expressed my opinions on this (I confess most difficult) subject in my book on *The State, the Poor, and the Country*.

and irritability from want of food; while there seemed no chance of any member of the manufacturing classes coming out of the struggle at last with a vestige of property wherewith to begin the world again. The pressure had long extended beyond the interests first affected; and when the new Ministry came into power, there seemed to be *no class* that was not threatened with ruin. In Carlisle, the Committee of Inquiry reported that a fourth of the population was in a state bordering on starvation,—actually certain to die of famine, unless relieved by extraordinary exertions. In the woollen districts of Wiltshire, the allowance to the independent labourer was not two-thirds of the *minimum* in the workhouse. . . . In Stockport, more than half the master-spinners had failed before the close of 1842; dwelling-houses, to the number of 3000, were shut up; and the occupiers of many hundreds more were unable to pay rates at all. Five thousand persons were walking the streets in compulsory idleness; and the Burnley Guardians wrote to the Secretary of State that the distress was far beyond their management; so that a Government Commission and Government funds were sent down without delay."[1]

Next let us take the remaining portion of this disastrous period,—from 1842 to 1852. The Peel Administration with which those years opened is commonly looked back to as the ablest and brightest within the memory of the present generation; and

[1] Miss Martineau's *History of the Peace*, vol. ii. pp. 520, 521.

the three years, 1843-5, were the most prosperous in the domestic history of our country during the first half of the century. Yet, wise and beneficial as was the fiscal legislation of Sir Robert Peel, no competent judge will hesitate to regard the prosperity which accompanied the first part of his Administration as mainly owing to a succession of fine harvests, together with the accession of gold from the new Russian mines into the Bank of England, whereby commercial credit was greatly strengthened, and trade was promoted by an unusually plentiful supply of money. The stock of gold in the Bank rose, for the first time on record, to sixteen millions sterling, or about threefold its previous amount; while Consols rose above par,— for the first time in the present century, standing at $101\frac{1}{4}$. But the series of fine harvests soon came to an end, giving place to the famine-year of 1847; while the Bank Acts of 1844-5 greatly nullified the recent influx of Russian gold, and rendered the British currency more than ever dependent upon the inadequate gold-supply of the world. Moreover, when the Revolutions broke out in Western Europe in 1848, the Czar forbade any further issue of the new Russian gold, keeping it locked up in the fortresses at St Petersburg, as the sinews of war for Russia herself,—which doubtless served to equip the Muscovite army which soon afterwards crossed the Carpathians to suppress the gallant revolt of the Hungarians, and probably also the grander invasion of Turkey, which led to the Crimean War.

These "hard times" in our own country — and indeed in other countries likewise — grew to their worst in 1848 and 1849, just as the gold-discoveries in distant California were about to bring not merely an alleviation, but an unparalleled career of new prosperity for the nations, throughout the entire civilised world. The night was at its darkest when the dawn was at hand—nay, even when sunrise was already appearing in a distant part of the earth. By that time Free Trade in England was complete, —even the Navigation Laws, so long regarded as the palladium of our national safety and independence, had been abolished. Yet our manufacturing towns were in a state of the deepest prostration. Even in orderly Scotland, not merely destitution but very serious disturbances prevailed, in Glasgow and the manufacturing districts; while agricultural bankruptcies became unwontedly numerous. Trade was paralysed in all directions; and the railway-traffic, which in 1845 had amounted to £2640 per mile, and which naturally was expected rapidly to increase, sank in 1849 to only £1780 per mile,—a decline which, as the *Times* remarked, was "alarming, and which looks like a sinking to zero." Two-thirds of a million (666,338) of able-bodied men were in receipt of public relief in England and Wales; while a host of two million Irish paupers were ever ready to invade and flood the already depressed labour-markets of Scotland and England. In the summer and autumn of 1847-8-9, the waters of the Clyde and the Mersey hardly bore up the crowded steamboats which, sunk to their paddle-boxes with crowded decks, brought over the starving swarms from the Emerald Isle; while during the weeks of harvest, the quiet country-roads were rendered unsafe and the farm-houses in many parts of England and Scotland were besieged by roving bands of sturdy but tattered Irishmen, driven forth by actual famine into the "fat lands" of the Sassenach.

For the first time within the range of authentic records, the growth of population of the British Isles ceased; and in one year at least, the numbers of our people actually diminished, owing to the Emigration exceeding the annual increase, which at that time used to amount to about 230,000. At the end of the five years from 1847 to 1851, our population fell short by nearly a million, certainly by 860,000, of what their number would have been under ordinary circumstances,—this remarkable decline of growth being occasioned partly by actual deaths from famine, and partly by compulsory emigration, the result not of hope but of despair. Still worse, despite this diminished growth of population, both crime and pauperism immensely increased. "Crime, that sure index of straitened circumstances among the working-classes," said Alison, "increased so rapidly between 1845 and 1848 that it advanced in that short period above 70 per cent: it had swelled from 44,000 committals to 74,000." In England, the committments upon criminal charges, which had numbered 7818 in 1815, the last year of the War, had risen to about 17,000 in the years 1826-7; and to upwards of 31,000 in 1842. In October 1848, the *Edinburgh Review*, referring to official statistics, stated that "every ninth person in England is now a pauper!" In Lanarkshire, including Glasgow, "one-fifth of the population," said Alison, were in receipt of public charity. In the ten years then ending, the amount of the Poor-rates trebled in Scotland; and it is needless to do more than mention the case of Ireland, where, besides the charity of the landowners, the Government had to interpose, with a State-loan, to prevent large masses of the population from dying from sheer starvation, and where Famine nevertheless killed numbers hardly inferior to those who sought refuge in emigration. In England and Wales, in the quarters ending July 1847 and 1848, the numbers of the poor in receipt of relief rose to the wellnigh incredible amount of 1,721,350 and 1,876,541 respectively,—of whom no less than 480,584 in the former year, and 577,445 in the latter, were *able-bodied*. In Scotland, the paupers in receipt of relief, including the casual poor, rose to 204,416 in 1848; while in Ireland, in the same year, the number of persons relieved by public charity, aided by the loan of £8,000,000 from the Government, amounted to no less than 2,177,651. Thus, in the British Isles, the persons in receipt of public charity in that one year amounted to the enormous number of four and a quarter millions (4,258,609), or more than one in seven of the entire population!![1]

[1] For these and other facts of those disastrous years, see Alison's *History of Europe*, 1815-52, chap. lxiii.

Throughout this long period of almost unbroken adversity, from 1815 to 1851—in other words, all but conterminous with the Long Peace which followed the crowning victory of Waterloo,—political discontent had been unwontedly rife in the British Isles, together with a continuous cry for Retrenchment of the national expenditure. Impressed by the strange but widely prevalent poverty of the times—so contrary to all natural and reasonable expectation,—the Duke of Wellington during his brief Premiership had introduced the severest economy into all departments of the public service—so much so as afterwards to win from Cobden the title of the most economical Administration which he had ever known; yet it is a well-known fact that the attainment of further retrenchment, and a reduction of the Government taxation, was looked forward to as the most desired consequence of Parliamentary Reform. Yet in vain did successive Whig Ministries study retrenchment; in vain did Sir Robert Peel reform the commercial tariff and abolish the Corn-law; and in vain did his Whig successors in office complete the new Free Trade system, by abolishing the Navigation Laws, and sweeping away the remains of the Differential tariffs by which Pitt, strengthening the empire on the basis of self-interest, had sought to unite the Colonies with the Mother country in a commercial union. All these changes and abolitions were made under the pressure of the prevailing adversity. Not merely Protection for British Agriculture, but the traditional policy of maintaining England and her colonies in an imperial zollverein or customs-union, was abolished in order to attain a present cheapness at home, and thereby render tolerable the inadequate wages of our people.

Nothing could stop the dreary continuance of hard times. Besides agrarian outrages, incendiarism, and disturbances in the manufacturing districts—including violent outbreaks of Trade-Unionism, of which the Glasgow Cotton-spinners' strike, with its murderous conspiracy, was a memorable outcome,—Chartism, or veiled rebellion in one form or another, was rampant throughout the entire period; finally breaking into its crowning effort in April 1848, nearly simultaneous with the outburst of an equally abortive rebellion in Ireland. The Ministerial Budgets were perpetually breaking down in consequence of the disappointing yield of the taxes; and, at the close of the period, Sir Charles Wood proved so unlucky in his financial schemes as to expose him to Mr Disraeli's memorable taunt at his budgets, "withdrawn, and re-withdrawn, and withdrawn again!" Yet, throughout the greater, and all the latter part of this unhappy period, economy had been so loudly demanded, and so severely practised, in the Government expenditure, that the national armaments and defences had been perilously reduced and neglected, so that the country would have been actually helpless against an invader. The contrast betwixt then and now, in this respect, is so great as to seem wellnigh incredible to the present generation. No fortifications!—Chatham, Portsmouth, Plymouth, all our arsenals and dock-

yards, wholly unprotected: no Militia, no Volunteers, not even a Channel Fleet! As for an army,—
"I tell you," said the Duke of Wellington, so late as the spring of 1852, "for the last ten years, you have not had more men in your armies than are sufficient to relieve your sentries in the different parts of the world." And when Lord Hardinge became head of the War-department under the Conservative Ministry in that same year, he found only forty guns in the United Kingdom capable of service; and most of them, he stated, "would have gone to pieces the first time they got into a clay field!"

Such, in the years 1847-51, was the England of Pitt, Nelson, and Wellington. Such, after full thirty years of Peace, was the matchless Power which had worsted Napoleonic France wielding the resources of the greater part of Europe! Such was the nation which had so grandly prospered during the War,—which, while winning naval and military victories in all parts of the world, had led an even more triumphant career in the domain of peace; —which, while with one hand overthrowing the greatest military Power which the modern world had ever beheld, with the other so industriously plied the enginery of trade and production that, with an increasing and prospering population, the exports had more than doubled and the commercial shipping nearly trebled during the course of the contest; and Britain became Queen of Commerce and mistress of the seas while the thunders of a mighty war rolled loudly but harmlessly around her. In the latter years of the war, when she led the grand effort of Europe for the overthrow of its military tyrant and conqueror, the national expenditure of Britain rose to £110,000,000; the people poured about seventy millions sterling of taxation yearly into the Exchequer, besides thirty or forty millions of readily subscribed loans; while a Sinking Fund was maintained for the Debt, besides the payment of a larger amount of interest on the Debt than was ever after chargeable. Yet hardly had the rejoicings at the Peace, and the Io Pæans for the peace-giving victory of Waterloo, ceased throughout the British Isles, than national suffering began, lasting for a generation; so that, thirty-five years after the Peace, Great Britain had neither an army nor a navy fit for war, or even for the defence of the country; and although the weight of taxation was little more than one-half (having diminished from £4, 14s. per head in 1817, to £2, 11s. 9d. in 1842), bankruptcies and pauperism, together with acute and riotous political discontent, were the order of the day; and Chartism or veiled rebellion in one form or another was rampant.

Indeed, as already stated, the very growth of population had stopped; and the largest and most profitable business for our shipping was in conveying pauperised myriads who were forced to flee from their country as from a sinking ship! The decline in the growth of our population in the five years from 1847 to 1851—the most remarkable upon record —was owing, as need hardly be said, partly to actual deaths from famine, especially in Ireland, and partly to emigration. The emigration in those years was produced entirely by famine and dearth of employment, and was thus quite different in character from the emigration which occurred in 1852-4, in connection with the new gold-mines. Nevertheless, despite this great weeding out of the poorer and feebler classes, pauperism existed in most appalling proportions. Despite the augmented stringency of the new Poor-law, the number of paupers relieved in one year was no less than four and a quarter millions! Everything that popular demand or Ministerial wisdom could devise to revive the old prosperity, or alleviate the prevalent distress and stagnation of trade, had been tried. Public expenditure had been curtailed until the country was defenceless against attack; and the rise and doctrines of the Peace Party were partly an outcome of the inability of the country to bear the costs of maintaining the Empire by war. Public economy, even in domestic matters, was carried to the length of a mean parsimony, while the Revenue (which broke the financial reputation of successive Ministers) was eked out by such miserable expedients as the sale of the Crown-rights over Epping Forest! Free Trade had been fully adopted, the Navigation Laws had been sacrificed, together with the Differential duties in favour of our Colonial produce (established by Pitt as the germ of an imperial British zollverein), and everything had been done to make things cheap to the suffering masses. Yet all was in vain. The brief heyday produced by some good harvests and the Railway mania quickly gave place to a still deeper gloom than before; and the period closed with Chartist riots and a fresh series of disastrous Budgets. And all this national distress—stagnant trade, prevalent poverty, and declining population—happened at the close of the longest Peace, won by the grandest triumphs, in British annals: a Peace as famous in modern Europe as was the closing of the Temple of Janus by Augustus in the heyday of the Roman Empire!

There must have been a cause or causes for such a change; and, obviously, the cause must have been of a character and influence adequate to produce so marvellous a transition from the pinnacle of power, progress, and prosperity to this low abasement and widespread national suffering. What was it? The annual interest on the Debt was less in amount than it had been in 1816; and, apart from this diminished charge, the Government expenditure was vastly reduced, and the taxation was a bagatelle compared with what it had been in the latter years of the war. Further, while the population by slow growth had much increased since 1815, the number of men withdrawn from industrial pursuits for the defence of the country was a mere fraction of those who had been enrolled in army, navy, and militia—not to speak of yeomanry and volunteers—during the previous period of war. Was it Politics?—had the political condition of the nation become worse, or more repressive of national industry and enterprise?

The question needs not be asked, save to be at once put aside. It is rarely that even a pernicious despotism seriously affects the industrial condition of a European people; and in this country the nation moulds its Government to its liking; the national will has been acknowledged as supreme; and the keenest political contests have turned upon no graver constitutional questions than as to whether, or how far, the power of Numbers is to be tempered by the influence of Property, and guided or checked by Intelligence. Parliamentary Reform had been established for a score of years; Free Trade had been made complete by the abolition of the Navigation Laws; and yet the national suffering, nay, even the popular discontent, were as great at this period, on the eve of the Gold-discoveries, as they had previously been.

What, then, was the cause or causes which had so blasted the prospect and natural expectations of a splendid prosperity from the Peace, and which rendered the nation suffering and discontented, although the annual burdens of the State had been largely reduced in amount, besides being borne by a doubled population? Doubtless we shall see this problem more clearly when we turn over a leaf of history, and behold how quickly this long and weary period of suffering gave place to a glowing prosperity—as soon as Earth poured forth new and unexpected metallic treasures, and the world escaped from the dearth of the precious metals which, after the lapse of three centuries, had been slowly settling down like an Arctic winter upon the new world of civilisation which had sprung into existence from the discoveries of Columbus and Vasco de Gama—discoveries which had made little Europe the busy heart of the globe, by placing her in commercial contact alike with the old world of the East and the new continent beyond the Atlantic.

While endeavouring, in the course of this history, to exhibit the powerful influence which the precious metals, as the Money of the world, exercise upon trade and industry, and thereby upon the wellbeing of civilised mankind, I have no desire to exaggerate that influence, nor dogmatically to trace its effects upon the condition of nations under circumstances where that condition must obviously have been affected by numerous and highly complicated causes. But that the dearth of the precious metals, during the forty years subsequent to 1810, did operate most injuriously, and, together with our monetary legislation, mainly robbed the British nation of the splendid prosperity which would otherwise have followed the Peace of 1815, I entertain no doubt. Mr Jacob—an author most cautious and ungiven to theorising—bears explicit testimony to the monetary dearth which prevailed between 1810 and 1830 (at which latter date he wrote), and also as to the contemporaneous general suffering, both in Europe and in America. As already stated, he computed that the amount of gold and silver coin in these continents during that period had considerably diminished,—namely, from 380 millions sterling to 313 millions. He then takes into account the nominally very large amount of paper-money contemporaneously issued in Europe and America, to meet the war-requirements and the diminished production of the precious metals. "From this review," he says, "it is seen that there has been no such alteration of the paper-money in those twenty years [1810-30] as could affect the value of commodities when measured by the precious metals. The paper-money [between 1810 and 1830] has fluctuated in its nominal value, but the whole quantity of it has been able to exchange for nearly the same weight of gold or silver, whatever those fluctuations [in its nominal amount] may have been. For example, our bank and other bills in 1810 would buy a little more than ten million ounces of gold when they amounted to forty-eight millions nominally; they would purchase nearly the same weight of gold in 1814, when they had reached sixty millions; and almost as much when, in 1829, they had sunk to forty millions. And the same effect may be traced in the other countries where paper-money was issued." The total gold-value of this paper-money—or the amount to which it acted as an auxiliary to the metallic money, he states at about "one hundred and twenty millions sterling during the whole period." But of this amount, he reckons that only two-thirds were a real and effective addition to the stock of currency; because coin to the extent of one-third the amount of paper-money must have been kept in reserve, retained in deposit,

" as a resource to meet unforeseen demands, or as a preparation for that which was looked forward to, with different degrees of intensity at different periods —namely, a return to cash-payments. Thus only two-thirds, or eighty millions of paper-money, were available to the currency, for the general purpose of the interchange of commodities." Adding these eighty millions to the metallic currency, or stock of coin, it results that there was "a circulating medium in 1810 of four hundred and sixty millions, and in 1830 of four hundred millions sterling,"—a decline of nearly one-eighth, or 13 per cent. In fact the amount of coin was considerably less, and the total circulating medium only a little more, than the stock of coin in the Roman empire during the reign of Augustus.

Next, as to the effect upon prices. While this decrease occurred in the amount of money, both population and commodities had considerably increased; so that there would be an additional decline in prices, and rise in the value of money, beyond the thirteen per cent due to the diminished circulating medium. Mr Jacob reckoned the increase of population in Europe and America, between the years 1810 and 1830, "at about thirty-two per cent; which, added to thirteen per cent diminished in the mass of money, would cause a natural decline in prices at the rate of forty-five per cent." In this estimate no allowance is made for increase of wealth and commodities per head of population; on the other hand, allowance has to be made for the more rapid circulation and greater potency (so to call it) of money in times of peace, compared with wartimes when " a large quantity of money is in a state of inactivity." Such were the computations of Mr Jacob in 1830; and he concluded his work by warning his readers that apparently the world was about to undergo a reversal of the happy monetary condition which was experienced between 1490 and 1590.[1]

As has been repeatedly stated, it is exceedingly difficult to show direct and positive proofs of any current change in the value of money, occasioned purely by changes in its amount. Mr Jacob purposed compiling a Table of Prices with this object in view, but he felt compelled to abandon the attempt. In lieu of this criterion of change in the value of the precious metals, he set himself to examine the change indirectly, by observing the condition of the various "classes of society in the different countries:" the result being to show, during this period of monetary scarcity, a great dete-

[1] The average annual production of gold and silver during the sixty years ending in 1840 is stated by M. Soetbeer as follows:—

	Kilos silver.	Kilos. gold	Total value in million francs.
1781-1800,	879,060	17,790	259·7
1801-1810,	894,150	17,778	265·7
1811-1820,	540,770	11,445	161·8
1821-1830,	460,560	14,216	153·2
1831-1840,	596,440	20,289	205·0

Thus the annual production, which had exceeded ten and a half millions sterling in the first ten years of the century, averaged only six millions in the second decade (1811-20), and less than six and a half millions sterling in the third decade (1820-30). The fall of prices, or rise in the value of money, which occurred between 1810 and 1840 is estimated by Professor Jevons at 30 per cent at least.

rioration, and widespread suffering, of a kind such as a monetary dearth would naturally produce. In this inquiry, Mr Jacob deals especially with the Agricultural class, "the cultivators of the soil:" both because they constituted the most numerous part of the community, and "because their products are the least complicated in their origin and the most simple in their distribution, and therefore are likely to be the first affected by any increase in the value of the precious metals. They would be the first to experience the difficulty of obtaining the usual weight of gold and silver, if those metals became more rare, for the usual measure of corn, of meat, of cotton, of wool, of sugar, or other agricultural products;" and they would experience a corresponding difficulty in paying their rent and other fixed annual charges.

What, then, was the condition of this numerous and preponderating class in Europe and America during this period of monetary scarcity? Writing in 1830 Mr Jacob said:—"In this country, where the cultivators of the soil are a class of capitalists distinct from the proprietors, their capitals have generally been diminishing; whilst the decline of the Mines has been proceeding, and whilst the application of their produce to other purposes than that of coin has been increasing." He adds, "It certainly does not follow from these two courses having been in simultaneous progression that one is the cause of the other." But, he continues, "the same has been the condition of the cultivators of the soil in every other country also, so far as it is accurately known. In every part of the continent of Europe the same complaints are heard, however various may be the tenures by which land is held." The same distress, he states, prevailed beyond the Atlantic. "Such complaints are not bounded by the limits of Europe. The cultivators in North America assert that the prices of their productions yield them no profit, especially those of corn, cotton, tobacco, and rice. The same "—he goes on to say— "is the case in the West India Islands, and also, according to the common reports, in South America and in India." Reviewing this picture of wellnigh universal distress — prevalent alike in Europe, all over the New World and its Islands, and also in India — Mr Jacob remarks, "There must be some general cause producing such extensive effects,— which are thus felt alike where taxation is high or low; under despotic and free governments; and whether the land is cultivated by slaves, by serfs, by hired labourers, or by proprietors." And what conceivable cause is there, operating so universally and under the most various and opposite circumstances, save that "decline of the Mines and increased application of their produce to other purposes than coin" which, as he says, then "proceeded in simultaneous progression,"—uncompensated, too, by any real increase of the paper-currency?

Prices fell continuously and severely throughout the entire period from 1810 down to 1852, in which latter year the New Gold came to terminate the dearth, and to happily reverse the monetary position of the world. "For about twenty years prior to 1848," says Mr Newmarch,[1] "the annual supplies of gold had been insufficient to meet the wear and tear of the coin in use, together with the requirements of the Arts, and the needs of enlarging industry, commerce, and population. There had been a slow but steady and progressive tendency towards lower prices; and therefore towards a discouragement of enterprises in which lapse of time and the state of distant markets had to be considered." This is merely a statement of the general inadequacy of the gold-supply; but in another part of the same Paper he goes further, and states that, "prior to 1848, the annual supplies of gold were barely sufficient even to meet the wear and tear of the coins in use:" and this appears to be the now prevalent estimate of the case. More specifically and decisively, Professor Jevons says:—" Between 1809 and 1849 prices fell in the ratio of 100 to 41 "—a rise in the value of money, and consequent depreciation of Labour and its produce, to the extent of 59 per cent, or about three-fifths. And the last years of the dearth were the worst of all: Professor Jevons adding, "in 1849-52 prices were *unprecedentedly* low."[2]

Alison, in his great History, dwells emphatically

---

[1] "On the Foreign Trade of the United Kingdom." Paper read before the Statistical Society in June 1878.

[2] "On the Variation of Prices and the Value of the Currency since 1782." Paper read by Professor Jevons before the Statistical Society in June 1865.

upon the evil results of the diminished supply of the American mines of the precious metals, combined with the contraction of the currency in our own country; and in quite a recent publication, the well-known French economist, M. de Laveleye, unhesitatingly attributes to this monetary dearth, exclusively, the long-continued and apparently mysterious adversity which befell Europe, and in some degree America also, for a dozen years after the resumption of specie-payments, and the demonetisation of silver, in Great Britain. Of our own country, M. de Laveleye says:—" This period of 1820 to 1830, which should have been one of unparalleled prosperity, was characterised, on the contrary, by cruel distress. The fall of prices [consequent upon the monetary dearth] was so severe that Brougham proposed to reduce taxation proportionately; and in 1822 the idea was even put forward of reducing the sovereign from twenty shillings to fourteen. Agriculture and general industry suffered alike. The distress of the labouring class was manifested in England by bread-riots, by threatening Chartist processions, and by demands for help addressed to Parliament. Armed repression had repeatedly, as now in Ireland, to be resorted to." It is a curious matter that the great decline in the yield of the American Mines should have almost entirely escaped contemporary notice; but, judging from the startling change in prices, and rise in the value of money, Mr Attwood (one of the best-informed men of his day upon such subjects) and some other members of Parliament called attention to the fact that Money must have become unusually scarce. On 10th July 1822, Mr Attwood, referring to a list of prices prepared by Mr Tooke, called attention to the fact that thirty of the most important articles of commerce and manufacture showed a fall of prices to the extent of £40 in the £100. And, replying to the assertion that a similar state of things prevailed in other countries, he remarked that since, obviously and admittedly, the proportion between money and commodities had been altered, it followed of necessity "either that all the productions of all industry, all climates, and all countries had suddenly increased"—an hypothesis which he could not accept—"or, otherwise, from whatever cause, a reduction in the amount of money generally in circulation has taken place."

Speaking of the contemporaneous condition of Europe and America, or at least of the chief commercial countries, M. de Laveleye[1] says:—"From 1817 to 1827, such were the economic sufferings in the United States, that an increase of customs' duties was demanded as a remedy." And he refers to the reports of Mr Fearon—who, he says, was "sent by the English to America to study the situation"—for an account of "the details of this persistent crisis" in that part of the world. "In France," continues M. de Laveleye, "there was the same pressure, and the same demand for the protec-

[1] See his Treatise on *International Bimetallism*, (English edition) pp. 44-56.

tionist system. In the address of the Chamber of Deputies, of 26th November 1821, 'the complaints of Agriculture, that nursing-mother of France, were laid at the foot of the Throne.'" Complaints from all quarters of France (especially from the eastern, western, and southern departments) were made as to the insufficiency of the measures taken against the importation of foreign corn; and the wide prevalence of the distress was acknowledged by the King in his reply to the Chamber in 1822. From Italy, Germany, and the trading cities of northern Europe, came the same complaint of falling prices. "In Piedmont the landowners complained that the prices of agricultural produce had fallen more than one-half. According to the testimony of Dutch farmers, the rent of land had fallen more than one-third. The reports of the British consuls of the time are full of details as to the fall of prices." Commerce suffered as well as Agriculture. In 1819 a series of bankruptcies occurred at Stockholm, Stralsund, Stettin, and Riga; and in the following year a severe crisis, consequent upon the fall of prices, occurred at Hamburg, where "the premium on gold mounted to nearly 10 per cent, while the rate of interest remained extremely low,—discount falling to only $1\frac{1}{2}$ per cent per annum: a proof of the extreme stagnation of business."

Although the fall of prices and consequent depression extended to the industrial classes generally, it is a noteworthy fact that the change attracted most attention in the case of Agriculture. And, apart from the important fact that Agriculture was still the primary industry in Great Britain, and much more so in France and other countries of the Continent, there was an obvious cause why a change in the value of money should be most clearly seen, and also most severely felt, in the produce of the soil. Corn, especially wheat, has been accepted as by far the best standard by which to judge of variations in the value of money. Unlike manufactured goods, where a change of machinery may suddenly alter the cost of production, corn needs in each country — in other words, under similar conditions of soil and climate—a nearly equal amount of labour for its production. Corn, too, as "the staff of life," is a commodity for which there is always an urgent demand; and that demand remains exceedingly steady, or actually invariable with a given amount of population,—there being nothing which can take the place of bread or cereal food; whereas in the case of manufactures and most other commodities, great fluctuations in value are possible, due merely to one kind of manufacture taking the place of another, owing to changes in the channels of trade, or even at the mere dictate of transient fashion. Accordingly a great fall in the value of corn was, *à priori*, the most striking indication that money was changing in value, and growing unusually scarce. Further, it was only natural that this change should be felt with peculiar severity by the classes connected with the Land,—partly, owing to the permanent money-charges (whether public or private, whether taxes, or mortgages, family-settlements, &c.) connected with its possession; and partly with the long leases, or agreements as to rent, connected with its occupancy. A manufacturer or merchant has his trade much more in hand than an owner or cultivator of the land has; and therefore a manufacturer can contract or expand his business, or otherwise modify it, so as to suit changes in the value of money, with less difficulty or embarrassment than is possible for the agricultural classes, whose business is expected to run in the same groove, and be prosecuted to a fixed extent, for comparatively long periods.

Another circumstance in the preceding account of the widespread distress of that time, and which will probably be deemed a curious one, was that the cause of disaster—namely, falling prices, owing to the prevalent scarcity of money—led in all the suffering countries to a similar cry for remedy, in the shape of Protection for the native industries, by fiscal charges upon imported foreign goods. If the cry was loudest from the agricultural classes, this, doubtless, was owing to the causes above-mentioned, backed by the fact that the Land is obviously the most important, certainly the stablest and most reliable source of national wealth; and every diminution in its value, or in the value of its produce, is *per se* (although in some countries, perhaps, the loss may be compensated) an undoubted loss of the national wealth. Probably, if not certainly, the main cause of the universal demand (both in Europe and in the United States) that a remedy for the distress should take the form of Protection to native industry, was of a twofold character. The predominant aspect of this period of distress was that of a universal glut; and the direct agency in producing the distress was the Fall of Prices: but the monetary cause of this calamitous change is one which constantly eludes popular observation and recognition; and as the fact of falling prices and reduced money-payment for labour was obvious, and must be owing to some cause or other, it was not unnatural, especially in those times of jealous international rivalry, that it should be ascribed to the importation of foreign produce; which, since the advent of Peace, and in consequence of the increase of navigation, was becoming much larger than in former times. Hence the general complaint against foreign competition —that foreign goods were either underselling the productions of native industry, or at least were surfeiting the home-markets, and thereby lowering prices. But there was another, and probably more general, motive for this universal cry for Protection: namely, that, owing to the rise in the value of money, the taxation became more onerous, really heavier than before,—while it was impossible suddenly to reduce the charges of government in proportion, and wholly impossible to do so with respect to the interest payable on the National Debts. Under such circumstances it seemed the best remedy to raise a larger portion of the revenue by means of Customs-duties—taxes which, in the first place at least, are paid by the foreigner; and which at the same time served to carry out the popular demand for Protection for the native industry. Taxation of this kind, also—namely, "indirect" taxes—is much less felt, and is paid less reluctantly, than taxation in its other and "direct" forms.

Yet another point, and one which is of permanent significance, deserves to be noticed:—namely, that the distress extended even to the capitalists or moneyed class. In most cases, a rise in the value of money benefits capitalists just as a rise in the value of his goods benefits an ordinary tradesman. The wealth of a capitalist consists largely, and of a money-dealer entirely, in the form of money (which is property in its most mobilised form); and every scarcity and rise in the value of money proportionately adds to the amount—the exchangeable value or purchasing power—of the capitalist's property. But in order that this gain may be fully reaped, it is requisite that the demand for money on loan remains at its previous amount. In ordinary times of monetary scarcity—like those transient monetary or banking crises so common in this country—the demand for money on loan not merely remains at its ordinary amount, but for the time vastly augments, and the value of money in both its forms—both its loanable value and its purchasing power—rises to a famine-price: each reduction in the supply of money (as of Food) below the previous and ordinary amount, causing its value to rise in a geometrical ratio. Accordingly, during such brief periods of monetary scarcity, the moneyed classes can profit enormously—at the expense (speaking roundly) of the industrial and producing classes; who must either pay a famine-price, in the shape of interest or discount, upon the customary loans or advances of money by which nearly all business is nowadays carried on, or who otherwise have to procure the indispensably required cash by selling their goods at the ruinously low prices at such times current. But the case becomes greatly altered as soon as the monetary dearth proves long-continued, and has produced its ultimate effects in numerous bankruptcies and a consequent stoppage or severe contraction of Trade, whereby the ordinary demand for money on loan ceases. When this point is reached, the Bank-rate falls rapidly; loanable money, like the wealth of capitalists, becomes "a drug," because no one can employ it profitably in business. The purchasing power of money, it is true, remains high; and capitalists who desire to convert their moneyed wealth into what may be styled property in a fixed form, such as goods or land, or wealthy traders who desire to extend their business by profitable purchases, continue to benefit by the enhanced exchangeable value of money. But for capital as capital, or the reserve-stock of money, the demand greatly ceases. Trade contracts not only into the limits imposed upon it by the scarcity of the medium of exchange and of loans, but to a still greater extent in consequence of the ruin, and disablement for further enterprise, which have so widely befallen the community. Hence the commercial demand for Capital, and money on loan, almost ceases: the only field for investment is in fixed securities (*de tout repos*, as the French style them) such as the Funds,—the rate of interest upon which, of course, falls in consequence of the competition of the capitalist purchasers. And thus, as Alison remarks with reference to the effects of the resumption of specie-payments in England in 1819, "there is no doubt that the reduction of the rate of interest inflicted upon holders of capital as great a loss, in many cases, as that undergone by the producing classes through the fall in the prices of merchandise."

Perhaps the most impressive testimony to the strange widespread distress which then lay like a nightmare upon Europe, or indeed upon the whole civilised world, is that borne contemporaneously by the calm-minded philosophic historian Sismondi, who wrote as follows (in 1827) of what he justly called this "great European calamity:"—"A cry of distress is raised from all the manufacturing towns of the Old World, and all the fields of the New World re-echo it. Everywhere Commerce is struck with the same languor; everywhere it encounters the same difficulty of selling. It is five years, at least, since the suffering began; far from being allayed, it seems increasing with time. The distress of the manufacturers is the most severe, because, unlike agriculturists, their entire livelihood depends upon making exchanges. The 'Patriotic Societies' which are being formed in Belgium and Germany to keep out foreign merchandise are, also, a grievous symptom of this *universal suffering*. The [protective] system now predominant in the public mind has been produced by the distress everywhere visible." Those persons at the present day who so keenly condemn the renewal or extension of the Protective system in this country after the close of the Great War, may find in these sentences some ground for tempering their vituperation of the landowners as the authors of Protection to native industry,—for the cry came from the producing classes generally, and was a popular demand in other countries as well as here. After speaking of the distress of the manufacturers and artisans, Sismondi says:—"At the same time, farmers and landlords complain of being ruined. They loudly cry for protective laws, for monopolies; they declare they cannot stand foreign competition: and in truth, many farmers have become bankrupt, while many landowners voluntarily give up a quarter or a third of their rents. Lastly, the frequent incendiarism of crops and farm-houses bespeaks the irritation and fermentation of the farm-labourers, and the *precarious condition of all Society*."[1]

Thus, after three hundred years of steady and rapid progress, Christendom, conterminous with the civilised world, was settling back into a dearth of

[1] Sismondi's *Studies in Political Economy*, vol. ii. p. 226. Published in 1827.

the precious metals, the world's money, together with the mysterious or wellnigh unsearchable distress which inevitably attends such a dearth in trading and civilised communities. A dearth which was to Trade and industry what a dearth of Food is to Life,—and, thereby, itself an indirect Famine —a Famine certain, although one step removed— because diminishing the means of Employment and the remuneration of Industry, by whose money-profits alone, under the established system of subdivided labour, individual members of a community can obtain the means of existence. And so this period of distress went on, lightening merely for passing moments; until suddenly, in 1848, the apprehension of Sismondi was realised. "All Society" was shaken to its foundations; Governments were overthrown by a wild impulse, a groping after some better order of things; and wars and revolutions rolled over Europe, from the Baltic to the Adriatic, and from the Bay of Biscay to the Euxine. The Danube and the Rhine, the Seine and the Po, rolled in blood to the surrounding ocean. Paris stood trembling on the brink of destruction while a three days' battle was waged in her streets, —recalling to memory the horrors of "the Terror" fifty-five years agone, and preluding the still fiercer outburst of the Commune in our own day. These convulsions aggravated, and to a frightful degree, the European distress out of which, to some extent at least, they sprang. Even the wisest of Revolutions is destructive to Trade, and thereby to the contemporaneous wellbeing of the people : because all Trade depends upon Credit and Capital; and when Revolution is abroad, Credit collapses like a pricked balloon, and Capital shuts its purse, and makes sure of its cash, until Law and Order are firmly re-established. Moreover there was the desolation of War, far and wide, destructive of property, and impeding agriculture; while many myriads of able-bodied men were enrolled in the various armies, or had to shut their shops, shoulder the musket, and join the civic forces in support of order. Even the close of that revolutionary tempest brought a new kind of distress, and prepared a host of exiles among the beaten ranks, who became proscribed, whether legally or socially, as political offenders in their native country.

The period of this "great European calamity," as Sismondi called it, which began soon after the Peace of Waterloo, and which (whether as a culmination or not) ended in the wars and revolutions of 1848, seemed to threaten the very existence of the prosperous Modern Europe which had grown to manhood — or as it momentarily seemed, to old age — after and largely in consequence of the twin discoveries of Columbus and Vasco de Gama, which simultaneously opened for Europe a New World in the West while reopening the Old World of Asia in the East. And yet, the underlying cause of this modern distress and apparent decay was wholly a mystery at the time,—as to some extent, perhaps, it still remains. In its strangeness and universality, it seemed to resemble one of those cataclysmal changes which, as we of the present generation have come to know, the Earth itself is liable to, and has experienced in far past ages. We know—from the wonderful hieroglyphic records of the rocks—that there was once a time when all Northern Europe basked in what is now called a Tropical sunshine,— when the land was covered with forests of the Palm and the estuaries with luxuriant jungles, where roamed the hippopotamus, elephant, tiger, rhinoceros, and other mighty wild-beasts of the Lands of the Sun. Then slowly the scene changed. The sunshine began to wane; the Arctic frost came down from the Pole; and snow and ice, creeping slowly downward, gradually covered with a winding-sheet the once luxuriant region southward to the Pyrenees; and indeed (as moraines in the Sierra Morena show) the glaciers rolled down their icy masses even to within sight of the blue waters of the Mediterranean Sea. Then man and animal life drooped and perished under the mysterious cold, or withdrew in flight, if they could, to other lands where the sun still shone brightly, as erst in their ancient homes. The wise and happy Hyperboreans, remembered in the verse of Homer (if ever such there were), gradually became extinct, along with the mammoths and the palm-trees. The inhabitants knew not why they should thus suffer: only, the sun seemed dying; and, in their hearts at least, they raised a wailing cry far more bitter and despairing than ever rose in lyric lamentation from the maidens who, in less ancient times, wailed for the beautiful Adonai, the Lord of Day, by the rivers of Syria.

In 1848, under the pressure of suffering, Europe entered upon her new period of Emigration. The peoples who long ago, in the dawn of the world, had strayed in adventurous bands from Asia into Europe (*Irrib*, or "the West," as our continent is named in Babylonian tablets) had explored and settled over the "dark continent," which spread out as a westward prolongation of Asia; and now, in the middle of this nineteenth century—by a strange distress, rather than by mere growth of population—finding themselves too many for the land, the European Aryans swarmed forth anew in search of other homes. Western, even Southern Europe sent forth myriads of fugitives and wanderers. The energetic Teuton, and especially the more adventurous, roving, and sea-loving section of the same race—the Norsemen of Scandinavia, whose blue blood circulates so widely among the northern and eastern portion of our own nation—took the lead in the migration of hopeful adventure; while the Hibernian Celts swarmed forth in despairing flight, driven out by Famine and Pestilence, as tumultuously in helpless crowds as in ancient times whole tribes and peoples had fled before some new wave of conquering population coming from the wilds of Upper Asia.

Then it was that the name of Columbus might have arisen, with grateful blessings, in the thoughts of millions, alike of those who fled and of those who remained, and who found new elbow-room in the old country. Then, and not till then, did the gift of a New World to mankind reveal itself in its full bountifulness. True, at the outset, it was no longer treasures of silver and gold that attracted this European Exodus. The numerous Mines of the Andes had been greatly on the wane for a generation past: some of them, exhausted by three centuries of working, had become barren,—all of them showed diminished productiveness; and the mining towns planted far up among the mountains had, like Potosi, shrunk into mere hamlets, or had been abandoned, and their crumbling walls, alongside of vast mounds of mineral dross, alone remained to mark the old prosperity and the sites of once famous mines whose produce had freighted many a stately Spanish galleon in the earlier times. But the New World possessed a far more splendid and more useful gift for mankind, in its LAND—its vacant regions of still virgin soil, which the unassisted fertility of Nature rendered crop-yielding for one or more generations of human life. There, beyond the Atlantic, lay the boundless Prairies and the rich Savannahs, virgin, and yet ready for the hand of the rudest cultivator; and there, too, where the strong arm must first wield freely the woodman's axe, were the still wider regions of the primeval forest, where the soil underneath, as fertile and far deeper than any garden-mould, had been enriched by the yearly fall of the leaf through immemorial ages,—raising and deepening the soil inch by inch through countless centuries, like to the fertilising inundations of the Nile, and in happy contrast to the yearly deposits of the never-melting snow on the summits of the Andes and Himalaya.

It was amidst a very similar epoch of general distress in ancient Italy, nineteen centuries ago—at the height of the bloody and devastating Civil War which preceded the reign of Augustus—that Horace, the sweetest and most lovable of Roman lyrists, composed one of his finest and gravest Odes, in which, unwitting of the golden peace that was near at hand under the beneficent sway of the " great Emperor," and despairing of a land and society which seemed in the agonies of dissolution from effeteness and corruption, he exhorted the people of Rome— " this city's doomed inhabitants," or at least " those that rise above the herd, the few of nobler soul"—to do like the men of Phocæa when attacked by Cyrus, and, leaving their doomed city after swearing an oath never to return, together seek the " Happy Islands" in the West which lay in some yet undiscovered seas. Leaving "the craven and the hopeless here, on their ill-starred beds to loll," the Poet cries :—

" Ye who can feel and act like men, this woman's wail give o'er,
And fly to regions far away beyond the Etruscan shore !
The circling Ocean waits us : then away, where Nature smiles,
To those fair lands, those blissful lands, the rich and happy Isles !
Where Ceres year by year crowns all the untilled land with sheaves,
And the vine with purple clusters droops, though unpruned all her
    leaves ;
Where honey from the hollow oaks doth ooze, and crystal rills
Come dancing down with tinkling feet from the sky-piercing hills.

> That shore the Argonautic bark's stout rowers never gained,
> Nor the wily maid of Colchis with step unchaste profaned;
> The sails of Sidon's galleys ne'er were wafted to that strand,
> Nor ever rested on its slopes Ulysses' toilworn band;—
> For Jupiter, when he with brass the Golden Age alloyed,
> That blissful region set apart by the good to be enjoyed;
> With brass and then with iron he the Ages seared,—but ye,
> Good men and true! to that bright home arise and follow me!"[1]

In reading these verses of the Roman poet, one is struck by the strange aptness of almost every word to the modern occasion of which I here write. If ever there was a prototype or counterpart of the Atlantis, the Gardens of the Hesperides, and the Happy Isles in the West, of Greek and Roman legend, it might well be the luxuriant Islands of the Gulf of Mexico, floating like baskets of flowers upon the sunny sea, and whose exceeding loveliness has awakened rapture in every beholder, from their discoverer Columbus to Humboldt and Kingsley in our own times. Or what land could be blessed by Ceres more bountifully than this New Continent, which, besides the delicate fruitage and vegetation of its Tropical region, was rich with the grape-vine, growing in wild festoons amid the luxuriant solitudes or climbing the crags on the rocky Sierras; and with honey so abundant in the hollow trees as to give rise to the trade of the bee-hunter, who with keen eye learned to track the flight of the roving bee through the clear air home to its honey-nest in some tree of the primeval forest? A land, too, still more rich in

---

[1] Extract from Sir Theodore Martin's admirable translation,—with two trivial changes (I hardly dare call them amendments) in the sixth and eighth lines, for which I am responsible.

the maize-plant, most prolific of the cereals, whose heavy golden-tasselled head makes the finest wheat-ears of Europe look ragged and poor. There, too, in parts, were the crystal streams descending from the sky-piercing hills, as the Roman poet saw in his yearning vision; and the search for which (as already told) drew the Swiss exile, Johan Sutter, onward and onward across the continent, and over the great mountain-chain to the sunny slopes of the Pacific, until he found the dream of his heart realised on the banks of the Sacramento river,—building his hut and stocking his hacienda with cattle upon a verdurous meadow-land, teeming beneath with the yet unknown treasure-beds of gold.

Much has been said of the occasional truthfulness of dreams, and of the correctness of world-wide instincts and beliefs of the human heart,—and is not the mind of man, as a part of intelligent Nature, a feeble reflex or index of the great world amidst which he exists? But surely no dream or vision of the human soul was ever so strangely realised as that old belief in a Happy Land far-off in the bosom of the Atlantic,—" Isles of the Blest," believed in alike by the cultured Greek and by the rude Bretons of wild Wales, and which some favoured mortals had at times actually beheld. And what more curious than the belief expressed by the Roman poet that mankind would go seek and find that visionary Land in the latter days,—when the golden youth of the world was long past; when the Age of Brass had given place to that last and worst, the Iron Age (the precise equivalent of the Kali-yug or Black Age of the Hindoos); and that then, amid their sufferings, the better part of mankind should there find a haven and home, and literally, as Horace says, "a new Golden Age"—which Jupiter, the Supreme, had kept in reserve for them from the beginning of Time!

And so, while the gloom of deep distress, a night of trouble and woe, lay upon Europe, and bands of people from all quarters—from the Seine and the Spree, from the Scottish highlands and the Norwegian mountains—the pale sickly families from the Lancashire mills, and the stout plaided shepherds from the Scottish Borders—were hastening to the seaports and gathering on the western shores of the Old World, or standing on crowded ship-decks, eager to be off in search of a new home, anywhere out of this rotting old world! anywhere that room was to be found for them!—lo! in the quarter of the heavens to which they looked, yet far beyond the horizon of their sight, suddenly, as out of its course, there was a sunrise in the Far West! A golden light, at first half-hidden behind the long dark chain of the Rocky Mountains, rose up into the sky, darting its gladdening beams eastward across the great Prairies, startling the cities of the Pilgrim Fathers, crossing as with a golden pathway the waters of the Atlantic, and then, like a cry of joy, illuminating the myriads of anxious and careworn faces of the crowds standing gathered on the Old World shores. Then there came a sound as of many waters—the glad roar of peoples, re-echoing the cry, "Gold!

Gold!" All doubt was past. Gold in abundance, for the gathering! Gold everywhere—far beyond the flats of the Sacramento,—the whole Californian soil teeming with it! Nay more (men asked), were not even the great mountains which blocked the way a vast treasure-house of the precious ore?

The Old World sent forth its now elated swarms into the New,—rushing westward to the Land of Gold. It was a tumultuous rush of peoples: each man thought only of himself. The very name of the discoverer, Johan Sutter, was unheeded in the jubilee and the crush. Nay, worse—as too often has happened in the stern tale of human life, the benefactor became a victim—and the first!—all but literally trampled down, himself and his prosperous farm, by the eager and self-absorbed crowds of men whom his discovery had attracted thither from the ends of the earth. Poor Sutter! gallant captain of the Royal Body-Guard of France! dreamy wanderer after an Arcadian Utopia! is there no statue or memorial pillar to him in the market-place of Sacramento town,—upon the ruins of the rural estate, rich with flocks and herds, where he had so long lived peacefully and patriarchally as Lord of the wide Manor?

So the new Golden Age began; and the long distress—which was such a satire upon the Long Peace!—quickly came to an end, and thereafter was well-nigh as much forgotten as if it had never existed. More's the pity!—for it is by a study of that time that we may best learn to avoid, at no distant date, a recurrence of the same evil anti-industrial and anti-commercial influences. Then might it be said of a truth, and with wider and grander meaning than Canning had dreamt of, the "New World came to redress the balance of the Old,"—maintaining the existing fabric of Government and Society, by carrying off in hopefulness the masses of Poverty and Discontent which grow up under all old Societies of the present type. The Gold-mines for a while made Europe young again. At the outset of the discovery of the New World, the very thought that had risen exultingly in the imagination of Horace found a counterpart in the mind of Columbus himself, who believed that Paradise (the Golden Age of Christendom) might be found still existing, preserved by the Maker of the worlds, upon some of the sun-kissed uplands of the new Continent. And more alluring still, and more confidently believed, were the tales of the Indians of the Fountains of Youth existing in the lovely woodlands of Florida, —the search for which attracted Ponce de Leon and other cavaliers even from the search for gold and the spoils of conquest. America was traversed, but the adventurers never came upon the Garden of Eden, and no lip had tasted nor any eye beheld the sparkling waters of Immortal Youth. Yet now at last, in the fulness of time, and when Man's needs were at the sorest, the auriferous gravel-beds of California, open to all, and where the yellow metal lay thick and pure on the surface, needing only to be gathered, proved a veritable Paradise for the Poor; while the masses of treasure, annually adding millions and millions to the world's stock of money, rejuvenated ageing Europe, and launched her upon a new and brilliant career, in which prosperity and contentment at home were happily combined with a vast extension of the area of Civilisation into the outlying regions of barbarism.

Thus, too, opened the Pacific Age of the world,—as if completing the cycle of human development. When the grand isolated civilisations of the primeval historic world—the monarchies of Babylon, Nineveh, Persia, Egypt—had passed away, there arose the Mediterranean Epoch, which appears to us as the flowering-time of past mankind. Next, with the discoveries of Columbus, the Atlantic Epoch commenced; and Spain, France, Holland, Britain, became the leading Powers, alike in arms, in commerce, and in the arts. It was around the stormy ocean of the Atlantic that mankind then prospered, as previously around the shores of the Inland Sea of the Old World. At last, with the discovery of gold in California and Australia, the Pacific Epoch has begun; and the European race—'the *audax Japeti genus*—is being drawn farther westward, to settle upon the strip of land, fertile as a garden, which fringes the Pacific along the base of the great Cordillera of the Andes; still more, to colonise the thousand isles, each lovely as a dream, of the Archipelago of the Pacific—where Cybele still sits crowned in the green sunny solitudes. A Venice-like world for Commerce! Let us hope, also, that the epoch which will take its name from the calmest, as well as vastest, of oceans, may be, in fact not less than in name, an epoch of Peace; and that the new and probably crowning world of human civilisation may be as much in contrast with the warring and socially jarring worlds of the Past as the narrow and stormy islandless ocean-trough of the Atlantic falls short of the broad and calm island-dotted expanse of the Pacific. There, too—strange meeting and reunion of the human Family!—the youngest and oldest of civilised peoples are coming together; and the European race, whose civilisation is as but of yesterday, and which has taken its newest form in its westward course across the New World, will come in contact with the most ancient alike of Empires and of civilisations—with the population, usages, and political system of China,—the apparently indestructible Nation and Monarchy; the one sole surviving Empire of the Primeval world, which has existed unbroken and undestroyed from the earliest times, from the dim dawn of oldest history; and to which now belongs nearly one-half of the civilised population of the globe![1] Drawn by the spells of Commerce, and aided by the almost magical agencies of still-improving locomotion, alike by sea and land, the many peoples and races of the Old World and

[1] Mr E. A. Freeman, writing of the various races in the United States, quotes the following remark of "an acute American:"—"The Indian dies out. The Negro is very far from dying out; but if he cannot be assimilated by the White man, he, at least, imitates him. But the Chinaman does not die out; he is not assimilated; he does not imitate; he is too fully convinced of the superiority of his own ways to have the least thought of copying ours."

the New, pushing forth from the shores of the surrounding continents, will meet and gather in the midst of the Pacific Ocean. And there, untrammelled by old influences, and amidst a region where Nature by climate and fertility makes existence peerlessly easy, human society and civilisation may assume new and higher forms, worthy of this Eden of the earth which Providence has hitherto kept in reserve, only to be reached in the latter days, after mankind has had a millennial experience of life while traversing the whole globe on their way to this lovely and long-secluded meeting-place and reunion of the Human Family.

BOOK FOURTH

"CHEAP" AND "DEAR" MONEY

CHAPTER XVI.

ON THE EFFECTS OF CHANGES IN THE QUANTITY AND VALUE OF MONEY.

The suffering peoples of Europe rushed forth to new homes in new or hitherto sequestered regions of America and Australasia: all of them in eager search for employment and comfortable maintenance, while some sought also for that political freedom and repose from social troubles which were contemporaneously wanting in Europe. In these great objects of the Exodus the fugitive adventurers were wholly successful. If they did not find what some of their more ardent predecessors of the sixteenth century had expected or imagined—if they did not arrive at the long-lost terrestrial Paradise, nor stumbled upon the Golden Age of paganism still surviving as a solace for humanity in a New World,—they at least found beyond the Rocky Mountains, and also in the heart of the Southern Pacific, veritable Gold-countries—each a Chosen Land, "flowing with milk and honey," and paved with the most precious of metals. The very soil of California, and also of inland Australia—the plains over which the newcomers wandered, or upon which their flocks browsed, were (to use the new phrase) "mineralised," teeming with gold. The history of California and Australia is a romantic record of rapid progress and human prosperity; and the present condition of these two regions is of itself a proof how splendidly the European Exodus prospered, and how happy was the change then made from an old world to a new. But what here concerns us most is the benefit which this change, with its monetary results, arising from the Gold-discoveries, conferred upon the general fortunes of mankind.

Accordingly, in the present chapter we shall briefly set forth the effects of changes in the quantity and value of Money—in common phrase, of "cheap" and "dear" money,—which will reflect a light upon the course of affairs described in some of the preceding chapters, and also, I hope, serve as a useful study preliminary to the concluding portion of the work.

In disregard of History, which tells that every great discovery of gold and silver mines, or easy and ample acquisition of these precious metals by any civilised nation, has been an epoch of prosperity,—that a dearth of money means calamity, and that monetary abundance is an element of commercial progress and general prosperity,—the doctrine still exists, and is frequently met with, that an abundance or scarcity of Money is an illusion, and that it does not matter a straw whether the currency or medium of exchange in any country be changed from 100 millions of coin to only 50, or enlarged from 50 millions to 100 : because, it is said, in the former case the 50 millions will suffice to buy just as much as the 100 millions did previously, while, in the latter case, the 100 millions will buy no more than the previous 50 millions did. And hence it is maintained that the discovery of new gold or silver mines, and a more abundant or cheaper supply of those metals, is, to say the least, of no benefit to mankind.

In one respect this doctrine is obviously and totally wrong; but in another respect, at first sight, it appears perfectly true. The point in which the doctrine is obviously, and even at first sight, wrong, is this,—that all production of things desired by mankind is in itself beneficial; and that, within the limits of human desire (and no production will go beyond that, except accidentally and momentarily), an increased abundance of such things, as a result of cheapness or diminished cost of production, is alike desirable and beneficial. From this point of view, gold and silver are regarded chiefly in their native qualities—as attractive commodities which have been desired by mankind, both savage and civilised, from the earliest times. But the case is undoubtedly altered when these metals are regarded as Money,—as the sole medium by which other kinds of commodities, Labour, and Property of all kinds, are rendered readily exchangeable. It is quite true that a currency of 50 millions in a given country will buy as much property, or have the same value, as a currency of 100 millions would: because the total amount of exchangeable property and labour remaining the same, while the coins are reduced by one-half, then each coin will exchange for twice as much property as before. Hence, we repeat, the doctrine that it matters nothing if the currency of a country be halved or doubled, enlarged or contracted, may appear at first sight correct—nay, even an axiom. Nevertheless, the portion of truth which it contains is entirely inapplicable to, indeed becomes positive falsehood in, practical affairs. The doctrine is a mere figment of abstract thought,—it is only conceivable within the realm of speculative and unconditioned reasoning, and has as little counterpart in the world of real life as the analogous axiom of pure geometry that a line is a something which has "length without breadth."

In truth, the doctrine that it matters nothing whether the currency of a country, or of the world, be doubled or halved—100 millions or 50—could only be correct if all, or nearly all, the circumstances of a country and condition of the people necessarily changed *pari passu*, contemporaneously, and exactly to the same extent as the currency; as if the whole machinery of the world, the whole circumstances of human life, were like an orrery revolving around Money as its centre, and all parts of which change together with the changes in Money. *Given* Time, and then, no doubt, the doctrine might be perfectly correct; for 50 coins will serve the same purposes as 100, as soon as the monetary revolution has been accomplished, and affairs have accommodated themselves to the change. To a community starting *de novo*, and existing by itself, fifty coins might (although less conveniently) do as much as a hundred; but even in such an independent community, after a generation or two, to change the amount of coins from 100 to 50, or from 50 to 100, would make a severe commercial and industrial disturbance, at the same time producing an unfair transference of wealth from some members or classes to others. Such a change, in short, could be a matter of indifference, or void of practical consequences, only upon one or other of these two impossibilities,—namely, either that the Past, with all monetary contracts and usages, were obliterated; or else that a slice of time were to be cut out of the Future, and that the new course of affairs were to start in a moment from germ into consequence and maturity,—like the seed which an Indian juggler plants in a flower-pot, and then, after covering it for an instant with a handkerchief, exhibits it to the startled onlookers in full growth and flower! A change in the amount of money, we repeat, could be devoid of important consequences only if the other circumstances or conditions were or could be changed simultaneously and to an equal extent: which is impossible. Therefore, we repeat, the above-mentioned doctrine is really a misuse of the reasoning faculty: for what else can be said of such unconditioned thinking—of reasoning which takes no account of the necessary irremovable conditions of human life and affairs,—which ignores Time and Circumstance, the most potent elements of existence,—and which is as devoid of actuality as the theorem which views a line as a thing of length without breadth, and a point as destitute of both! Such a doctrine, in truth, is as absurd, and far more mischievous, a waste of reasoning as the problem of the Schoolmen as to how many angels, as incorporeal beings, could dance (were they inclined to such a frolic) upon the point of a needle!

Let us, then, consider this currency-question as it presents itself in practical affairs—in the world of reality. And first, consider the effects of a reduced currency, a scarcity of money, in the case of a State or Government,—in other words, how it operates upon national expenditure and taxation. By far the larger portion of Government expenditure is of a routine and more or less permanent character: it consists of salaries, or fixed annual payments, of interest upon Debt, and of contracts for the supply of materials, chiefly for the army and navy. The whole Civil Service, from the Judges down to door-keepers and tide-waiters, is paid by fixed salaries; so are the Army and Navy, from the Field-Marshals and Admirals down to the private soldier or sailor; and so also is usually the Church, although in England and Scotland these ecclesiastical salaries do not come out of the Exchequer or national purse. At the time of which we now write (about 1850, when the interest on the National Debt amounted to about £30,000,000), these fixed and more or less permanent charges constituted fully five-sevenths of the Government expenditure; and, with the exception of this amount, hardly any portion could be altered under less than a lifetime, as by the death of the existing generation of the many thousands of persons (Army and Navy included) in the service of the Government,—a reduction of whose pay would be a violation of the covenant or understanding under which they entered the service.

Farther, consider other difficulties connected with this matter. Before even the difficulty of remedying a monetary change like this, there is the difficulty of perceiving it.[1] There is nothing less recognised, or more difficult to discern and ascertain, than a change

---

[1] Striking instances of this kind are on record. Gibbon, when describing the desolating effects of the taxation in Italy in the times of Constantine, attributes it entirely to the defects of the Imperial administration; whereas, as Mr Jacob sees and shows plainly, the oppressiveness of the taxation was due to the growing scarcity of the precious metals and rapid rise in the value of the currency. Mr Jacob himself, while clearly discerning the effects of monetary scarcity in past and immediately previous times, remarks that the usual signs of such a dearth were not visible (although a dearth was obviously impending) when he finished his book, in 1830—a date at which, according to subsequent authorities (Mr Tooke included), "dear money" with its disastrous effects was wellnigh at its worst. Finally, Mr Tooke himself, or Messrs Tooke and Newmarch, thought that in 1848-50 and thereabouts there were no signs of money having become dear; whereas twenty years afterwards Mr Newmarch spoke in the strongest terms with respect to the dire monetary dearth in the years immediately prior to the gold-discoveries; and Professor Jevons states that in those years (1845-50) prices were at their very lowest point. (See *supra*, pp. 202-4). So difficult is it for even the most eminent authorities on the subject to discern a change in the value of money when in progress; or for the public to discern and appreciate such changes at any time!

in the value of money produced by purely monetary causes, as by a change in the quantity or supply of money. Accordingly, such a state of affairs being unrecognised, its evil consequences are likely to last even longer than they must necessarily do; while any steps taken by the Government towards a remedy, as by reducing salaries in correspondence with the increased value of money, are sure to excite opposition and create discontent,—the reason and the equity of the reduction not being perceived by the general public. The result, however, in such cases, of a scarcity of money and rise in its value, is that the same amount of taxation weighs much more heavily upon the nation. If the amount of money, or the currency, be reduced one-half, as from 100 to 50—which the above-mentioned doctrinnaires hold to be a matter of indifference—the hardship will be as great, and the burden upon trade and industry as onerous, as if the taxation of the country were doubled.

The result differs considerably according to the kind of taxation, or fiscal system, which prevails in each country: and it is worthy of note that if the whole taxation were levied in the form of Customs-duties, the hardship would be least, and if by an Income-tax, or by direct money-payments, the hardship would be greatest. Let us illustrate the heavy burdens imposed upon a country or community through Taxation, at times when money is growing scarce, and consequently is rising in value. A very notable instance of this kind occurred in Italy under the later Emperors, when the vast stock of gold and silver which had accumulated in the Augustan epoch had become dispersed, and reduced by wear and loss; while the mines in Greece, Spain, and Hungary, if not exhausted, had ceased to be worked owing to the irruptions of the Barbarians and the weakened power of the Imperial Government. The most natural or the easiest form of taxation or revenue-raising under an Empire — a Government ruling over different countries and peoples—is the exaction of annual tribute-money, payable by countries or prefectures as a whole, and levied in assigned portions from the various townships or districts of each country or prefecture. A revenue-system of this kind was fully established by Darius (if not earlier) for the Persian Empire,—the whole empire, from the Mediterranean and Ægean Seas to the Punjaub, being classed under six great fiscal divisions, each paying a fixed tribute in money to the central Government. A similar revenue-system prevailed under the Roman empire, —each province contributing an allotted sum to the imperial exchequer. The Turks, who were a conquering race of soldiers (among the bravest and finest in the world) holding in subjection what was at first an alien world, adopted nearly the same system, —the Ottoman empire being divided into Pashaliks, each yielding a certain tribute, the amount of which was raised from the separate vilayets, townships, &c., comprised in the Pashalik. So also with the Mogul Empire in India, where not a few of the chief Nawabs and Princes of the present day are simply descendants of Prefects of the Mogul Emperors who made themselves independent in the decay of the empire; while the zemindars, whom the English mistook for large landowners, were merely revenue-collectors (or responsible revenue-officers) of the villages over which, a century ago, we inadvertently made them lords and proprietors.

The disastrous effects of a rise in the value of money, in connection with Taxation of this kind, is strikingly illustrated by what occurred in Italy under the later Emperors. Gibbon thus describes the system of direct taxation as existing in the reign of Constantine—an impost which partook of the nature of a tax upon property and a capitation tax,—and which was imposed "in addition to the taxes on articles of consumption," or indirect taxes, to use the modern phrase:—"This was not a fixed impost, but varied in amount according to the wants or the will of the reigning emperor. A regular survey was made of the value of the property every fifteen years. The lands were measured by surveyors, who were sent into the provinces: their nature, whether arable or pasture, or vineyards or woods, was distinctly reported, and an estimate made of their common value from the average produce of five years. The numbers of slaves and cattle constituted an essential part of the report. An oath was administered to the proprietors, which bound them to disclose the true state of their affairs; and their attempts to prevaricate, or elude the intention of the legislator, were severely watched, and punished as a capital offence, which included the double crime of treason and sacrilege."

Owing to the loss or exhaustion of the mines of the precious metals which had previously supplied the Roman world, the value of money was yearly rising—as had been the case ever since the time of Augustus[1]—and the effects of this direct taxation are thus described by Gibbon:—"The taxes at length evidently produced a general and increasing distress in every province of the dominion. The agriculture of the Roman provinces was insensibly ruined; and the emperors were obliged to derive some merit from the forgiveness of debts, or the remission of tributes, which their subjects were utterly incapable of paying. The fertile and happy province of Campania, the scene of the early victories and of the delicious retirements of the citizens of Rome, extended between the sea and the Apennine, from the Tyber to the Silarus. Within sixty years after the death of Constantine, and on the evidence of an actual survey, an exemption was granted in favour of 330,000 English acres of desert and uncultivated land, which amounted to one-eighth of the

---

[1] See *supra*, vol. i. p. 311. As a remedy for this growing dearness of money, the Emperors made successive reductions in the weight of the coins, and latterly, with the same object, the purity of the coin was debased with alloy. "The *aureus* (says Jacob) in the time of Augustus, was the fortieth part of a pound of gold, and consequently was equivalent to 20 shillings of our present money." "In the reign of Nero, 70 or 80 years later, the *aureus* was only the forty-fifth part of a pound [of gold] = 17s. 6d.; but in the reign of Constantine (270 or 280 years after) it diminished to a 72d part of a pound = 11s. or 12s. of our money. Between Augustus and Constantine the coin had frequently been debased with alloy—a fact which in some measure accounts for the increase of pay to the soldiers whilst the consumption of the precious metals was proceeding."

whole surface of the province." And, as Gibbon adds, "this amazing desolation" occurred before the footsteps of the Barbarians had been seen in Italy.

Gibbon, as was natural in his day, ascribes this desolation to the defects of the Imperial administration; but, says Jacob, "another cause had been operating, which from its secrecy, or its almost imperceptible progress, may have equally escaped the observation of the Government and the notice of the historians. While the production of the mines had ceased, there would be a consumption, a decay, of the quantity of gold and silver in constant progress, which by lowering the metallic [money] price of all other commodities, would check that industry by which alone a country can continue to prosper. This cause it is indeed difficult to weigh, yet in the period now under review it must have operated with prodigious force."[1]

For modern times, let us take the case of our own Government and revenue-system, as represented alike in a European and Asiatic form. First, let us consider how a monetary dearth, and rise in the value of money, would operate through taxation in our Indian empire. There, in accordance with the immemorial usage of Eastern nations—and in all cases where manufacturing industry and foreign trade engage but a small portion of the population —the Land is the great national property; and it is the land, through its cultivators, which furnishes

[1] See Jacob, vol. i. pp. 217-21.

THE VALUE OF MONEY. 241

the chief portion of the public revenue. In India, according to the present system, the land is inspected and revalued at intervals of thirty years; and each occupier or cultivator has to pay annually a fixed sum in money for his portion of ground. Suppose, then, that during one of these periods of thirty years, the currency or stock of money were to be reduced until the exchangeable value or purchasing-power of money in India were to become twice as much as previously. Then, money would be twice as difficult to get: in order to procure the rent, or Land-tax, payable to the Government, the cultivators or peasantry would have to sell twice as large a portion of their produce as formerly. Their labour and the productiveness of the soil would go only half as far as before to procure the money which they have to pay to the Government,—while, as already explained (viz., owing to nearly the whole of the Government expenditure being in the form of salaries and other fixed payments), the Government itself would be no better off than before. In truth—as always happens—the Government would be the most prominent sufferer: inasmuch as the peasantry to a large extent would be ruined, and unable to pay the Land-tax; while the general impoverishment, by reducing consumption, and expenditure of every kind on the part of the population, would tend to render unproductive the other and subsidiary taxes—such as customs or excise-duties. While the Government suffered most prominently, the people would suffer still more cruelly. In India, as in most Asiatic countries, the bulk of the population are very poor,—living from hand-to-mouth, and in a style which is no more than a bare maintenance of life. Accordingly a monetary scarcity, and rise in the value of money —by rendering it necessary for them to sell a larger portion of their means, or agricultural produce, in order to procure the money payable as rent or Land-tax to the Government—would subject them to a crushing degree of poverty and misery. The cause of this change would not be discerned: the taxes would nominally remain as before,—doubtless even large remissions of taxation would have to be made by the Government: but the people would find themselves growing poorer and poorer, down to actual starvation. Yet the cause of their misery would be a mystery to them, and as much beyond their control as an extraordinary run of bad harvests.

As regards the case at home, the effects of a scarcity of money operating upon a country through Government expenditure and taxation, would be more various, inasmuch as our taxes are more varied; but it would be substantially the same in the suffering occasioned to the people, and in the embarrassment of the Government. Although the taxes remained the same, fifty millions would weigh almost as heavily and injuriously upon the nation as a hundred millions prior to the monetary change. Indeed, as regards the further effects of such a change, upon the trade and industry of the people, these effects would be still more prejudicial than they would be in an agricultural country like India: first, because Trade is more quickly sensitive to (although less profoundly affected by) monetary changes than Agriculture; and, secondly, because actual want and starvation come less readily (barring bad harvests) to a people cultivating and firmly planted upon the land, as under the Land System of India, than to a population almost entirely dependent upon Employment in hired labour, and who consequently lose their entire means of subsistence when thrown out of employment by a depression of Trade, alike agricultural and manufacturing. The most obvious injury to a country like ours, from such a change in the value of money, is that which arises in connection with the National Debt: a matter so well understood that, vastly important though it is, it hardly needs any explanatory or illustrative remarks. Obviously, if the value of the currency rose one-half—as it wellnigh did between 1810 and 1830,—the thirty or more millions sterling annually payable as interest would become equal in purchasing-power, and as onerous to the nation, as forty-five or fifty millions: while the taxation would remain nominally, and to appearance, merely the same as before.

Next, turn from Government taxation, or the public monetary obligations of a community, to the wider and general effects of a scarcity of the circulating medium,—namely, upon classes and individuals in the ordinary transactions of civilised life. Money, as already said, has a twofold quality: it serves to store wealth, as well as to circulate it by exchanges of property. Taxation is an annual draft upon the wealth of the community, payable or transferred in money; and consequently any scarcity, and rise in the value, of money proportionately augments this draft and increases the burdens of the people. But in the case to which we now come — namely, the effects of a monetary dearth, or reduction in the amount of money, upon what may be called the ordinary transactions and social relations of a civilised community—the change operates through money in both its qualities: alike as realised or accumulated wealth, and also as the means by which exchanges of property are facilitated, and in civilised countries effected.

For example, the most obvious manner in which a reduction in the quantity, and consequently in the value, of money affects the condition of a people is to augment the weight of all monetary contracts and obligations, — in just the same way as the burden of taxation is augmented. The monetary contracts—notably, leases and mortgages, but also including all the ordinary kinds of debt — remain nominally of the same amount, but their real amount or value is raised (*cæteris paribus*) in proportion with the extent of the reduction of the quantity and rise in the value of money. As needs hardly be said, these monetary obligations—such as leases, trade-contracts, mortgages—pervade all classes of society, especially the middle and upper classes; and the general result of a rise in the value of money is, to unfairly enrich the wealthy at the expense and to the detriment of the poor, or less wealthy; and also, among the wealthy themselves, to give a great advantage to capitalists and the moneyed class over those who hold their property in the form of land, houses, and general commodities. From the various causes and through the various agencies above-mentioned—especially in consequence of the wide prevalence of Debt in its manifold forms in civilised communities, and the existence of leases and money-contracts,—the effect of a reduction in the quantity of money has always proved highly injurious to the commonwealth, or general interests of a community: in the first place, because such a change operates most unfairly, or unjustly,—taking wealth from some individuals or classes, and giving that wealth to others, in mere consequence of a change in the value of money—owing entirely to what is admittedly a defect and fault in the standard of value. It is in fact a transfer of property for which the gainers and losers are not responsible,—which the former have done nothing to earn, and for which the latter have done nothing to suffer. It is an act of robbery (so to speak) due to the Law itself,—a suffering inflicted upon individuals or upon whole classes owing to the defective system of Civilisation under which they live,—and which, though no single nation can alter as the law of the world, each community has it in its power to remedy within its own bounds, for its own commonwealth.

A change in the productiveness of the mines of

gold and silver has hardly ever lasted for less than a lifetime, and more usually it continues for a century or centuries. When the supply falls short—whether by a diminished production of the precious metals, or owing to that production being outstripped by the growth of human requirements,—the broad result is that every one finds his property falling in price or money-value, except the capitalists who hold their wealth chiefly in the form of money itself. There begins a universal, or all but universal, fall in the price of commodities, the produce and outcome of labour: and this change proves injurious very much in proportion to the length of time that commodities remain in stock, or in the trader's hands. For example, the merchant who imports cotton, rice, grain, &c., from distant parts of the world, or who exports coal, iron, or manufactured goods to distant countries, finds his stocks steadily falling in value. He is an intermediary between the producers and the consumers; and his usual custom is to keep in his warehouses, or "in bond," a stock of various commodities, which he ships now to one quarter, now to another, wherever he finds the market barest. In many cases he makes a contract in advance for the supply of the goods in which he trades. He may, in his usual course of business, contract for the purchase of cotton or grain even at the time of sowing or planting, or for railway-iron while the metal is still in the ore; and, likewise in ordinary course, his warehouses may be filled with merchandise which cannot be distributed and sold until after a very considerable interval of time. This may be, and frequently is, the merchant's ordinary course of business. But in times when money is becoming scarce, the merchant finds that he cannot sell at the old prices, upon which his profits have been estimated; the margin of value between the price at which he purchased and the price at which he can sell grows small,— reducing his profits, or, it may be, merely covering his expenses, or even involving him in ruinous losses. Yet he is conscious of no diminution of his industry or of his commercial skill. It seems as if the markets were everywhere becoming glutted. Indeed, all the readily observable phenomena point to this conclusion. The dilemma or " depression" wears the semblance of a universal glut. The merchant knows from experience that if, from miscalculation, or by the chapter of accidents, the market to which he has sent grain, cotton-goods, &c., happens to be overstocked with these goods, he gets, and can get, only a comparatively low price for them. And he is quite familiar with the fact that such over-supply, or overstocking of markets, is constantly happening in some part of the world or other. He knows this,—it is one of the first things he has been taught to consider; but he also knows that in previous times his commercial knowledge and skill enabled him ordinarily to escape such difficulties. But now, the glut seems to be universal. He turns from one country or market, only to find the others similarly circumstanced. The sign of a glut is low prices: and low prices meet him in all quarters. It is a truth that a change in the value of money due to a change in its quantity, is most difficult to ascertain—owing, chiefly, to the circumstances and influences which affect Prices being so numerous and multiform. Although such a change may become plain in retrospect, it is hardly possible to discern it clearly and surely when in progress, or at least in its early progress. Nevertheless there is the woful fact for the merchant that prices are falling, and that his profits are falling with them. It seems to him that, somehow or other, there is a universal glut. Sometimes men call it a Depression of Trade, and, having given it a name, they think they know all about it!

The Home trade suffers in much the same way; the general, if not universal phenomenon being that stocks of merchandise, in common with property of all kinds, are constantly losing their former value or money-price. The home merchant, who distributes the produce of labour in his own country—just as the foreign merchant distributes over the world the produce of the world's labour—like his foreign compeer, finds his trade becoming unprofitable. With falling prices, the prospect of profits disappears; the inducement to enterprise and speculation (and all Trade is more or less speculative) ceases; and the natural result of the "universal glut" (as it appears to be) is a diminution of production, and consequently a widespread reduction of employment. Beginning with the produce of labour, the fall in value quickly extends to Labour itself. It is needless to say how much suffering is thereby occasioned, especially in a highly commercial country. The calamity is intensified by the fact that the suffering goes all round. As already said, farmers and others, who are under leases, find that they cannot get the old or ordinary price for their produce, so that they become impoverished, and cannot pay their rent: then the landowners suffer in turn, and a cycle of misfortune quickly goes round the whole nation. While the merchant and manufacturer are hard pressed by the fall of prices, due to the change in the value of money, their difficulties are multiplied by an actual diminution of the number of purchasers. The home market becomes contracted; the farmers and landowners, indeed the whole agricultural and rural population, are unable to make their usual purchases of manufactured goods; in consequence, the manufacturing classes suffer; so also do the importing merchants; while the intermediate class of the retail merchants and shopkeepers likewise find their sales diminishing, not merely in price but also in number or quantity. Lastly, not necessarily in time, but in the grades of society, the labouring classes suffer, as the depression extends from one industrial section of the nation to another. True, the working-classes are wellnigh exempt from those money-contracts of various kind which operate so disastrously upon the middle and upper classes; also, everything is cheap at such times—so that equal wages would go further than usual: but, like everything else, Labour itself is cheap (the demand for it being reduced), and wages fall; while the contraction of trade and industrial enterprise leaves a large portion of the lower classes without employment, and consequently without wages, which is their sole means of subsistence. In not a few cases of trade-depression, the working-classes suffer in much lesser proportion than their employers: nevertheless, owing to their having no reserves to fall back upon, and as the margin between comfort and indigence is in their case extremely narrow, it is upon the labouring class, on the whole, that a depression of trade weighs most heavily. The natural consequence of suffering is discontent; and usually the masses complain of the Government, or break out into political or social disturbance. In former times such outbreaks took the form of the wars of the Jacquerie, and were sternly crushed by the military power of the feudal system. At the present day, any prevalence of popular distress breeds Communism, and suchlike revolts of Poverty, in which Ignorance and Want are prone to the perpetration of violence and bloodshed, and of which modern Europe has already witnessed not a few deplorable examples,—and seemingly bids fair to see more.

Although a monetary dearth, when occasioned by an inadequate production of the precious metals, usually operates very slowly, and more or less imperceptibly to common intelligence, yet, from its very duration, producing a most serious revolution in the condition of society, in which the moneyed class obtain an unfair advantage over the rest of the community—a circumstance which has contributed to engender those cruel persecutions and general hatred of the Jews (who choose to trade chiefly in Money) during the Dark and Middle Ages of Europe, when the precious metals were gradually growing scarcer and scarcer, and which doubtless contributes to the *Juden-hetze* of the present day,—there is another and very brief kind of monetary dearth, of which the present generation has witnessed not a few instances, and which serves to exhibit the fundamental phenomena of such times in a narrower and limited form, but in a manner unusually striking. Such monetary dearths are occasioned—not by any lack of the precious metals throughout the world, but simply by a slight and temporary shifting of coin or bullion from one country to another: just as the volume of the ocean remains the same while ships become stranded in some places, although there is high water elsewhere. In a short time high water will return; so likewise will the precious metals, in the course of Trade: and undoubtedly it is a disgrace to Legislation that such natural and almost periodically recurrent movements of gold and silver should be allowed to operate disastrously upon a civilised community. From one or other of many various causes, the precious metals (in their character as Money) have at times to be sent in more than the usual quantity from some one country to another: all that is needful is to compensate their temporary and partial absence,—for the brief period of a few months to find a substitute for a few millions sterling of gold. Such is the problem, especially in our own country, where the commercial system and the powers of Credit are most fully developed, and where a breakdown of that system is most widely and severely disastrous; yet also where the system of paper-money, as a partial substitute for the precious metals, has been firmly and successfully established for nigh two hundred years, and which is ready at hand to entirely compensate those transient drains of gold, if only Legislation did not prohibit this means of remedy.

To complete, then, our brief and doubtless inadequate exposition of the injurious effects, alike to individuals and to nations, of a scarcity of money, let us describe the effects of such a scarcity, in its narrowest and briefest form, as it is presented during one of those monetary, banking, or commercial Crises, which have become normally recurrent in the history of this country.

Money has two separate kinds of value: namely, (1) its value in exchange, or its purchasing power, which is represented by Price; and (2) its value on loan, or the Rate of Interest—especially in that form of it which is called the Bank-rate, or the charge which banks make for supplying currency in exchange for property—chiefly by the discount (really, purchase) of bills. It is upon this second value, or the Bank-rate, that sudden changes in the supply of money primarily operate. Money, or the circulating medium of civilised countries, in its relation to Trade, is like water proceeding from a reservoir (the banks), and drawn off and employed in a thousand fertilising rills. However much water may proceed from the reservoir, it will not become redundant, or overflow its channels, so long as the irrigating rills are open in sufficient number and area to diffuse and absorb the water in the work of irrigation. Also, as no water is delivered from the reservoir without being paid for, no more water is taken out than the cultivators or applicants believe they can profitably employ. But, of course, if the charge is reduced (owing to abundance of water in the reservoir), the cultivators usually take more of it,—because they can obtain a higher profit upon its use,—or can employ it upon poorer soils, or in ways which, in themselves, yield a smaller profit than usual, yet which profit becomes to the cultivator as large as usual in consequence of his getting the water at a lower price or charge. But say that the Bank-rate (or water-charge) stands at its ordinary amount, say 4 or 5 per cent; and that, as is the normal fact, the traders or cultivators engage in operations which, under such a charge, are profitable to them. Next suppose that, from any cause, the water in the reservoir—the money in the banks—falls below its ordinary level: or, dropping the simile, suppose that a drain of gold takes place from our own country, thereby reducing the amount of money in bank, which, speaking roundly, constitutes the amount of loanable money in the country. Thereupon, the banks raise their charge for discounting the bills by which all trade is more or less carried on. This rise proportionately curtails the profits of the traders, and may entirely absorb it: in which case, traders have no longer any motive for continuing their operations, except to avoid the serious injury to themselves from a discontinuance of business, together with an actual loss upon the capital invested in their "plant"—it may be, in costly factories, or in mines or blast-furnaces, any stoppage and reopening of which necessitates a large and entirely profitless expenditure. Thus, under a high Bank-rate, there must be (except where profits are exceptionally large) either a cessation of industrial and commercial business, or a profitless continuance of it: the result being a contraction of trade, and "hard times" for the population at large,—besides a diminished revenue for the State.

But suppose—as too often happens—that a drain of gold reduces the stock of money in the banks to such an extent that, besides an exorbitant Bank-rate, they must contract the amount of their loans and discounts: that is, refuse to discount the bills of their customers to the ordinary extent. The very approach of such a position of affairs shakes Credit to its foundations; at the same time, capitalists, seeing money rapidly rising in value, are disposed to hold back, for higher terms, or for further and better opportunities of employing their stock of money. Under such circumstances, bills which would have been readily discounted in ordinary times, or a few weeks previously, are rejected by the banks,—partly because these establishments have little money to lend, and partly because the weakening of credit and the fall of prices (a fall which always occurs at such times, and alike creates and is then aggravated by the general distrust) make the banks doubtful as to the continued solvency of the holders or givers of the bills. In this way, some of the weaker firms—or even wealthy firms whose money is locked up in enterprises not immediately profitable — may be forced to suspend payment. Then, other firms, connected in business-transactions with the suspended firms—holding their bills, or entitled to remittances from them—are likewise forced to suspend. And so a Panic arises: the banks themselves are called upon to pay an unusually large portion of their deposits; while some of them which are known to be connected with fallen firms, are subjected to an actual "run,"—depositors calling up their money merely out of apprehension, and without any immediate intention of employing it. Indeed this hoarding takes place largely at such times even without any dread of a bank's insolvency; and, at the very time when the stock of money in bank is extremely reduced, a larger number of bills than usual are presented for discount, owing to the holders of these bills desiring to forestall their wants,—being apprehensive that if they do not get these bills discounted at once, they will have to pay a higher rate of discount afterwards, or possibly fail to get their bills discounted at all. In fact, the very apprehension of a scarcity of loanable money precipitates and aggravates the scarcity, — by an increased demand alike for discounts and for cashing or repayment of deposits. And also, besides the effect of apprehension or panic, there is a solid and most reasonable ground for this domestic drain, or increased demand for money from the banks; because, owing to the fall of prices, and difficulty of making the ordinary sales of goods, traders make every possible effort to avoid the loss inseparable from forcing the sale of their goods upon a falling market, by calling up whatever money they possess or can command,— in order to tide over the bad time, and keep back their goods for better times with a better or less unprofitable market. Indeed by far the most disastrous effect of a very high Bank-rate, and its usual concomitant a contraction of credit, is a severe fall of Prices. The effect of a high Bank-rate, pure and simple, is *pro tanto* to destroy a trader's profit on the borrowed portion of his capital, including the amount of the bills which he discounts in the ordinary course of business. But a fall of Prices is a far more serious calamity: for, thereby, the entire products or outcome both of a trader's labour and of his capital (whether borrowed or not) are diminished in value, or rendered wholly profitless. And such changes frequently come with great suddenness, and accordingly act with peculiar severity upon traders whose operations extend over a considerable length of time. For example, a merchant who orders goods from India or China may find, not only that he has to pay double the ordinary Bank-rate on the bills representing those transactions, but also that the fall of prices in the interval between the giving of the order and the arrival of the goods is so great as wholly to destroy his expected profit, or even to render the goods unsaleable in England. Hence the phenomenon, occasionally witnessed, of goods selling cheaper in the country into which they are imported than in the distant country where they are produced. The conclusion of a monetary dearth of this kind is, a severe fall of prices, numerous bankruptcies, and a general contraction of trade and loss of employment: whereupon the Bank-rate, or the value of money on loan, falls as rapidly as it rose — frequently to only 2 per cent, and still lower in the open market; because there is little business and few bills, — consequently little or no demand for loans or banking-accommodation. The crisis has swept over Trade like a tornado, — levelling with the ground many a goodly firm or establishment, and throwing thousands of the poorer classes out of employment,—presenting a brief time of exorbitant gains to capitalists and the moneyed class, — and finally begetting a general prostration of Trade and enterprise, during which all classes suffer — the industrial and producing classes from impoverishment or want of employment, and the State from a diminished revenue; while even the capitalists, together with the banks, find their previous gains largely neutralised by the subsequent cessation of even the ordinary demand for loans and advances, in consequence of the difficulty of employing capital in a reproductive and profitable manner.

Such is the kind of monetary dearth with which people are most acquainted, and which, in our own country especially, may be witnessed several times in the course of a single lifetime. But this sudden, violent, and transient form of the calamity, although it serves to exhibit in vivid colours the evils arising from a monetary dearth, differs widely, in all but its general effect, from those great monetary dearths which are produced by a failure or inadequate production of the gold and silver mines, and which tend to affect and oppress the civilised world at large. The Monetary Crisis as above-described, and which rarely affects more than one or two countries at a time (seeing that the drain of specie which creates the crisis in one country tends to make specie plentiful in others), differs as greatly from the other kind, or great world-famines of the precious metals, as the rapid bleeding to death from a gunshot or sword-wound differs from the decease from anæmia produced by the slow operation of deficient food and unhealthy surroundings.

During several centuries after the fall of the Roman empire, as also during the comparatively short period between the years 1810 and 1830, and indeed onward till 1850, the diminished or inadequate production of the precious metals weighed like an incubus upon the trade and industry of the world.

As if cramped and fettered by invisible bonds, a slow decay overtook the energies of mankind. Previous to the discovery of the New World, productive enterprise languished, from lack of capital to put it in motion and support it when in operation. Of fixed property, no doubt, there was much, but of loanable wealth there was very little. The Land, at least, remained as extensive as of yore, with its fields, forests, and minerals; there were houses and towns, whose structures lasted more or less enduringly; also herds and flocks, supported by the vegetation of bountiful Nature: and, further, much of this kind of property existed as reserve-wealth,— that is, in greater quantity than the owners required for current use. But such wealth is of but little use for the promotion and prosecution of commercial or industrial enterprise. What is requisite for such a purpose is capital, or reserve-wealth, in a readily loanable form,—mobile, and (like money) exchangeable for the various commodities requisite for the maintenance of life and the operations of trade. And Money was wanting. Commerce is simply and entirely the exchanging of merchandise; and even the common industry or day-labour of civilisation involves a ceaseless exchange of property for Labour, in wages, &c. But the medium of exchange (money) was scarce. In Commerce, as in a lesser degree in general industry, this want of an efficient medium of exchange proportionately obstructed exchange in all forms. A merchant might export his wares to some distant market or foreign country; but when he sought to sell his wares, he had to encounter the obstacles of the barter-system: the produce of that country might be of little value in his own country, or in the other ports and marts with which he traded; and moreover, in most cases he desired, and necessarily preferred, to obtain the produce of his sales in money, in a form or medium which he could employ equally well in all places.

Thus, there occurred a serious break and obstruction in the course of mercantile transactions. The obstruction was much the same as if there were a want of roads, ships, or other means of conveying merchandise, or from the frequent occurrence of locks in a canal: only, the obstruction arose not, perhaps, so much in course of transit or conveyance, but at the last stage of the operation, in the process of actual exchange. The actual and immediate means of making exchanges being lacking, exchanges of all kinds were proportionately hindered; the circulating medium being deficient, the circulation of commodities was correspondingly impeded. Thus Trade of all kinds languished, and both commercial and industrial or productive employment became contracted, with a commensurate impoverishment and gradual decline or degradation in the conditions of life and society. Wealth might and to some extent did exist—in the hands of a few; but very little of it existed in the form of money, so as to be available to set in motion the wheels of Trade, and to promote and sustain industry and production, —by which means alone wealth, while becoming reproductive, is distributed among the population in the process of profitable employment, in the shape of salaries and wages,—the many being benefited, with equal advantage to the wealthy few. In short, a deficiency of money is a retrogressive approach to Barter,—a backward step from civilisation, a reduction in the productive and trading powers, with consequently loss alike of employment for the labour of the many and of profitable investment for the wealth of the few,—a general reduction of material wellbeing. And further, by increasing the weight or value of debts, and of all monetary contracts such as leases of farms or factories, a dearth and rise in the value of money operates unfairly in favour of the wealthy classes,—aggravating that clamant and perilous evil of old societies, whereby the rich grow richer and the poor poorer; tending to split the commonwealth into two distinct and more or less hostile classes,—a conflict between which, like a wider French Revolution, may ere long temporarily destroy Civilisation itself, and bring to an end the existing form and system of Society, as gradually evolved in the progress of modern Europe.

Having exhibited the iron side of the money-question, let us now turn to the golden one, and observe the happy contrast which is presented under an ample and expanding currency, or enlarged stock of money, compared with a monetary scarcity. This side of the question may be dealt with more briefly than the other, inasmuch as the operation and effects of a dearth of the circulating medium obviously suggest, and by implication indicate, the operation and effects of an opposite condition of affairs. These latter effects may be of two kinds, according to the extent to which the increase of the stock of money proceeds. The increase may simply suffice to promote and support—or allow of—a profitable expansion of human industry and enterprise, of production and trade; or it may proceed further, and occasion a gradual change and fall in the value of money. In both cases alike, there is or tends to be an increase of production, upon profitable terms for the producers,—a vast boon to the world, inasmuch as, under such conditions, there cannot possibly be too large a supply of any of the commodities and appliances of life desired by mankind; and along with this increase of profitable production, and partly preceding it, there goes an increase of profitable employment,—the wages or money-pay for which enables the industrial classes to purchase and consume or enjoy the commodities and comforts of life so produced or otherwise called into existence.

The first result of the discovery of new mines, or an increased production of the precious metals, is an increase in the amount of loanable capital,—the most efficient, or in civilised times the only efficient, form of which is Money. But, as each addition to the circulating medium, if so large as to exceed or outstrip the demand, lessens the value alike of the currency as a whole, and also of each particular coin, —and as, when the supply of money has reached this point, the gold-miner or other possessor of the precious ore knows that each new coin which he gets from the Mint is becoming of lesser and lesser value, —the question arises, and has puzzled some able writers on such subjects, Why should these additions to the circulating medium continue to take place —seeing that each new ounce of gold minted continuously reduces the value of money, and of the gold still unminted, or still in the mines upon the working of which the gold-diggers depend for their profits and subsistence? M. Chevalier appears to have been much struck by this circumstance, at a time when (as he believed) the value of gold was undergoing, or about to undergo, an enormous fall in value in consequence of the New Gold of California and Australia which was pouring into the markets of the world. He speaks of the circulating medium of the world as an insatiable undiscriminating whirlpool which absorbs the precious ores into its vortex, even although the wants of mankind are fully satisfied, and when these additions to the circulating medium are (as it seemed to him) a waste and an evil. But the mystery vanishes when the true and plain facts of the case are observed. The common, at least what is held to be the established doctrine is, that gold or silver money derives its value simply from the value of the metal of which it consists. But this is a great mistake, leading in practical affairs to a serious error. Gold and silver as money possess a value beyond that of the mere metal. That this fact is lost sight of is mainly owing to the circumstance that nowadays there is an " open

Mint," and no charge or royalty upon coining; and hence it may seem that the precious metal cannot acquire value by being subjected to a costless process. But the fact remains that coined gold, or gold as money, does possess a value beyond that of an equal weight or quantity of the precious metal.

In truth, this extra value of minted gold or silver is of a twofold character, or at least of two degrees. In the first place, the mere assaying and stamping of the precious metals—the official stamping of bars or ingots—gives to these pieces of metal a wider value than that possessed by common bullion: it gives them a wider market and enlarged demand, and consequently a greater value: because the purity and weight of these portions of metal thus become known to all men, instead of being known or knowable only to a few individuals, such as gold-merchants and chemists. Indeed this mere stamping of the ingots suffices to render them international currency—a means or medium by which the merchants of one country can make purchases or discharge their debts in another country. But the minting or coining into Money adds somewhat further to this value; because the process renders these pieces of metal a legal tender in all payments and purchases, besides putting the precious metal into the most convenient form for circulation, and for everyday use. Hence it is that the miner, or the trader who supplies the miners' wants, hastens to send the gold-dust or the silver ingots to the Mint, thereby adding its amount to the currency or stock of money. Though Money be falling in value, what then? Fall as it may, the coin is more valuable than the mere metal. This, then, is the mystery (if so it may be called)—this is the reason why, when new mines are discovered, additions of gold and silver continue ceaselessly, unpausingly, to be made to the stock of money, although each addition may successively reduce the value of the whole stock, and of each particular coin. The attractive force by which, as M. Chevalier said, the circulating medium ceaselessly absorbs new supplies of the precious metals, as into an insatiable vortex, is simply the additional value which the precious metals acquire as Money, or when minted into coin: a value beyond that of the mere metal, which, though it is ignored and denied by the "established doctrine," is nevertheless real and true, besides being a most important factor in all correct reasoning upon money, or the circulating medium. Thus it was that during the century and a half after the discovery of America, the gold and silver from the New World was added year by year to the circulating medium despite the correspondingly continuous fall of the value of money; and even when money had sunk to less than one-third of its former value, the precious metals were poured into the Mints as readily as ever. Again we say, the motive was simply the new or extra value which is acquired by the precious metals when converted into coin—legal money, a valid tender alike in discharge of debts and in payment of purchases.

Continuing the exposition, let us observe the next step towards that increase of loanable capital which, we have said, is usually the first change or agency through which an addition to the stock of money operates, and diffuses its beneficial effects. The New Gold, either after being minted into coin, or in the form of assayed ingots, is deposited in bank—just as other spare money is: whereupon the banks have more money to lend; and in consequence they can either discount the same amount of bills as before at a lower charge (which is usually the first event)—or, as the demand increases (which usually follows under such circumstances), the banks can increase their discounts and advances while charging no higher than the ordinary Bank-rate.

Now, what is this process of discounting bills and making loans or advances, which constitutes the chief business of Banks? It is substantially this, to give Money in exchange for Property. Banks trade in money, just as a merchant may trade in corn or cotton: and in both cases the object is the same,—namely, to make a profit upon the commodity dealt in. The merchant, or general trader, obtains his profit through Price, by selling his goods for more money than he gave for them. The banker makes his profit through the rate of interest: by issuing his stock of money at such a rate of interest as will be profitable to him. He sells his wares (so to speak) only for a short time,—not absolutely and altogether, like the ordinary tradesman. As the banker trades more or less in other people's money—temporarily deposited with him, and liable to be called up or withdrawn—he makes his loans for short periods, and also upon the most marketable or realisable kinds of property: for, otherwise, if the banker were to make loans upon land or merchandise, and if the borrowers could not repay the loans at date, the banker would be compelled to sell or realise these forfeited securities, and in so doing would have to go beyond his own trade and become a merchant,—doing so, also, under highly unfavourable circumstances; for the banks would have goods left on their hands at the very times when goods are least readily saleable. Accordingly, banks deal almost exclusively in short loans — made chiefly upon commercial bills, which are payable from one to six months after date. The banker discounts such bills—that is, he pays the amount of the bill to its owner, minus interest (ordinarily at the rate of 4 or 5 per cent per annum), for the period which must elapse before the bill becomes payable,—the amount of this discount, the sum deducted from the amount of the bill, being the price, including the profit, which the bank makes on the transaction —*i.e.*, for converting the bill into ready money. Thus, men who are in want of money (or general currency, as trade-bills are commercial currency) take commercial bills or other suitable securities to the banks, and obtain in exchange the currency which they require. The transaction, we repeat, is substantially a conversion of Property (of various suitable kinds) into Money. This, in truth, was the prime purpose for which banking in this country was established—viz., as banks of issue; and, subject to the condition of paying coin for the notes on demand, this conversion of Property into currency may be carried to any extent required by the community and profitable to the banks,—an almost inestimable advantage to nations, for the promotion of trade and production, and consequently of industrial employment of all kinds. Banking, also, as is well known, multiplies the power of wealth and the means of production through the Credit system; because a comparatively small quantity of coin suffices to enable a bank to meet a large amount of liabilities, whether for the cashing of its notes or for repayment of the money entrusted to its keeping. To increase the value, or multiply the effective power, of anything, is in effect the same as to multiply the quantity of the thing,—because any given portion of it becomes more powerful or valuable than before. This is what Banking does for general Property: and consequently every increase of banking, or of banking power, augments the means of employment and production in exactly the same way as if the loanable capital of a country were increased.[1]

Accordingly when, owing to the discovery of new mines, or from any other cause, there is a large influx of the precious metals into a country (and the same is true of the world at large), the banks

---

[1] A full exposition of these matters is given in my *Science of Finance*, chiefly in chaps. vii. and viii., on "the Potency of Capital" and "Negotiability of Value."

are enabled to lend, or issue to the public, a larger amount of currency than before. In other words, a much larger amount of the Property or wealth of the country can be converted, or exchanged, into Money,—which is wealth or property in its most potent form, especially for the promotion of trade and production. In this way the loanable capital of a country can be vastly increased; thereby supplying the means of carrying on a variety of industrial and commercial enterprises which otherwise without money or currency would be impracticable. In truth, the mere amount of Property—even of surplus property, or reserve-wealth—is no measure of the national power or capacity for trade and industrial production, and consequently for the profitable employment of the population. All, or nearly all, depends upon the form in which this surplus wealth or property exists. For example, herds and flocks, or agricultural produce, may exist to an extent far exceeding the current wants of the population; but, save in the very limited operations of Barter, such surplus property is of no use for the support of enterprises of trade and production. Property, or wealth, becomes effective for such enterprises, and for giving employment, in exact proportion as that wealth or property acquires, or can at pleasure acquire, or be invested with, the quality of Negotiability, and of being converted into currency. Wealth, in short, must be *mobilised*, rendered capable of acting as the circulating medium —the completest and most perfect and potent form of which is Money. And, as already said, it is the special function of Banking to mobilise wealth, by converting into money, or general currency, such suitable portions of the wealth of a country as may be desired or required,—issuing currency (whether in the form of coin, bank-notes, or even cheques) in exchange for trade-bills and other kinds of suitable, or readily negotiable, property. Thus the introduction of Banking, acting through the Credit-system, adds immensely to the effective wealth and productive power of a nation: but thereafter (so long as the present order of monetary affairs exists), the power of the banks in this respect is limited or expanded in proportion to their stock of the precious metals, which must contract or expand (speaking roundly) in proportion to the abundance or scarcity of the world's stock of gold and silver,—which, of course, depends chiefly upon the produce of the Mines.

Such considerations exhibit clearly the importance and benefit to mankind of the discovery of rich gold-mines, like those of California and Australia. At all times in the history of the world there has been, as there still is, an abundance of natural resources in every country ready to be developed or utilised by human skill and labour. The greatest feature of material civilisation is the Conquest of Nature by Man. By obtaining a knowledge of the elements, qualities, and processes of Nature—that is, of the world in which we live,—mankind come to know how to turn these things more fully to human use, and even to master and usefully employ natural forces which previously had been an obstacle or a terror. By such knowledge, Man has not only rendered the soil and surface of the earth more fertile and productive, but he has penetrated deep, even for miles, through subterranean regions, ransacking them, and bringing to the surface the various mineral treasures of the earth. He bridges the seas by navigation, and turns to his own use the animal population of the ocean. Most of all, by chemical and mechanical Invention, he constantly increases his powers of producing the multiform and infinitely varied commodities necessary for the comfortable maintenance and fuller enjoyment of human life and society. It is this circumstance—this steady growth and increase of human power—this gradual advance in the conquest of Nature by Man—which happily vitiates the once famous Malthusian doctrine, that the growth of population must necessarily abridge the comforts and lower the condition of mankind, inasmuch as population tends to increase faster than the necessaries of life,—a theory, no doubt, partially correct, but shorn of its worst and most despairing inference and result by the constant increase of man's power of production, through his progressive control and utilisation of the elements and forces of Nature.

At all times there is an abundance of profitable enterprise, of the most varied kind, for men to undertake. The future value of these enterprises, when completed, may be reasonably certain; but a considerable expenditure is requisite for their execution and accomplishment; and to meet this expenditure the projectors must possess, or be able to command or obtain, a corresponding amount of wealth or property in a form suitable for defraying this expenditure, whether in payment of labour or in purchase of machinery and other commodities. In other words, Money is wanted. The future value of the enterprise may be widely recognised; and there may be an abundance of surplus property in the community — property which the community does not require for immediate or current use, and which therefore can be spared for the purposes of the enterprise, and to cover the protracted expenditure requisite before the enterprise can be completed and become profitable. In faith of this future value, others than the projectors may be willing to advance or invest capital in the undertaking. But if property in a loanable form be wanting — if there be a scarcity of loanable capital in the form of money, — the enterprise becomes, according to the degree of that scarcity, either wholly impracticable, or else devoid of profit, owing to the excessive charge to be paid for the temporary use of the money. On the other hand, when money is plentiful, enterprises become more profitable, and more easy of execution. Thus the Rate of Interest, which in its commonest form is the Rate of Discount or Bank-rate, is a potent promoter or restrainer of national industry, and of the reproduction of wealth. With an abundance of money, the undertaking of industrial and commercial enterprises becomes easy, because then there is a large amount of available capital ready for investment at a low rate of charge; and at the same time, Prices tend to rise,—thereby adding a further inducement to industrial enterprise, inasmuch as the future value of each enterprise tends to increase, ensuring to the projectors increased profits, or a higher value than otherwise for the product of their labour when completed. Rising prices, in fact, are a constant and the highest inducement alike to trade and to production, seeing that the commodities produced or traded in are constantly increasing in value: so that by the mere lapse of time, the cotton which a man plants will bear a higher price by the time it is ready for gathering; the metal in the ironstone which the ironfounder throws into his furnaces will advance in price ere it can be brought to market; while the factory-owner, in like manner, when he sets his mills agoing upon some venture in textile fabrics, is cheered by the expectation that by the time the venture is complete there will be an upward movement of prices in the market for which his goods are designed. All industry, at such times, flourishes. As the historian Hume remarks, in his Essay on Money, "we find that in every kingdom into which money begins to flow in greater abundance than formerly, everything takes a new face; the merchant becomes more enterprising, the manufacturer more diligent and skilful, and even the farmer follows his plough with greater alacrity and attention. An increase of money, in its progress through the whole community, must first quicken the diligence of every individual, before it increases the price of labour,"—in other words, before it begins to raise prices, or fall in value. And so highly advantageous is such a condition of affairs for mankind, that Hume goes so far as to maintain that "the good policy of the magistrate [in such matters] consists only in keeping the stock of money, if possible, still increasing. . . . The interval is as pernicious to Industry, when gold and silver are diminishing, as it is advantageous when these metals are increasing."[1]

So wide and various is the field of industrial and commercial enterprise open to mankind, provided there be an adequate supply of the requisite auxiliaries of trade and production, especially in the form of a low Bank-rate, that a vast addition may be made to the stock of money—new Mines may yearly pour forth many millions sterling of gold and silver—without occasioning any fall in the value of money: in consequence of the demand for money keeping pace with the supply,—the demand for money expanding *pari passu* with the opportunities for its profitable employment. Hence the saying of the late Mr Newmarch, at a time (1853) when most people were frightened by the productiveness of the new Gold-mines, that instead of there being ground for alarm, he believed it would be a good thing for the world were a new gold-mine to be discovered every ten years.

[1] *Hume's Philosophical Works* (edit. 1826), vol. iii. p. 325, &c.

But, lastly, even supposing that the supply of the precious metals were to become so large as considerably to lower the value of money. Even then, how small, if any, would be the evil or mischief so occasioned compared to the general benefit derived! If viewed along with the contemporaneous, and largely precedent, benefits arising from the brilliant expansion of Trade which inseparably attends an abundant or ultimately superabundant supply of money, and the general prosperity thereby created, the evil effects of a fall in the value of money are hardly worthy of notice. As already shown, Trade, national industry, increases with the increased facilities for carrying it on which an abundance of the precious metals affords; and with more Trade there is more employment, and consequently augmented prosperity among the working classes. Nor among these alone: for even annuitants and others who derive their income from fixed payments benefit likewise — as regards themselves, and still more as regards their families—from the increasing abundance of employment; so much so that in most cases this cause will actually compensate them for the loss which they experience upon the fixed portion of their income.

But even if, for the sake of exposition, we do what is impossible in reality, and consider the effects of a fall in the value of money *per se*, entirely irrespective of the universal benefits necessarily attending such a plethora of circulating medium, it must at the least be allowed that if *any* change of monetary value is to happen, it is the change to a fall that must rightly be preferred. Nay more: it may even be maintained that in the latter stages of civilised Society (at least as hitherto constituted, on the competitive and belligerent or anti-coöperative system of industry), a fall in the value of money, in consequence of a largely increased production of the precious metals, is in some degree to be recurrently desired by philanthropy, or even for the very maintenance of Civilisation, by alleviating smoothly, without violence, and by wellnigh imperceptible stages, certain evils hitherto found inseparable from organised society. For what feature is more striking and hitherto inevitable in the conditions of matured Society than the tendency of the rich to grow richer, and the poor poorer? Happily, this progressive change is not an absolute, but only a relative one: it is not true that the poor retrograde in condition, but their advance is small, and is apt to be hidden from notice and appreciation in consequence of the relatively rapid improvement and enrichment of the classes above them. Moreover the superiority of the upper classes, at any particular time, is mainly owing to the Past. It is the accumulated wealth of generations, operating in favour of the wealthy, which so greatly stereotypes the distinction of classes, and generates the in some respects valuable, but undoubtedly invidious system of Caste. Mankind are no more equal, nor will ever be so, than are the trees of the forest as regards height, foliage, or fruit: and hitherto, considering the general poverty or narrow circumstances of the mass of mankind, it has been a distinct advantage, beneficial for general progress in knowledge and civilisation, that there have been classes hereditarily possessing wealth, and thereby enjoying that leisure and intellectual culture which are indispensable for the guidance of nations, and also for the gradual acquisition of that mastery over the powers or forces of Nature which can alone permanently improve the wellbeing and exalt the material condition of mankind at large.

Obviously, however, this state and stage of society is but a means to an end, and is destined to gradually disappear in proportion as that end is attained, by a wider and, comparatively speaking, full or matured development of the intellectual powers of the community. Indeed human passion, in the form of the desire for Equality—supported only too largely by Envy and jealousy—is only too prone to anticipate the results of actual progress; and already the existence of Caste, so far as it still exists, and of hereditary classes of all kinds, has become invidious, and is threatened with precipitate or even revolutionary overthrow. The distinction of hereditary Nobility, by the blare of titles and the possession of land, doubtless attracts the largest degree of hostility; but the same passion for equality extends its levelling influence to hereditary Wealth also. And, we repeat, although some men will be superior and others greatly inferior, so long as the human race exists—and although this difference or inequality will show, and more or less assert itself, even in each single successive generation,—nevertheless, under the existing social system, the superiority of classes in any generation depends largely, nay, mainly, upon the Past—upon the legacy of wealth and of position inherited from ancestors. *This* is the kind of distinction most attractive of envy, and most likely to be first assailed. Love of distinction among one's fellows is too natural and healthy a passion to be obliterated; but, on this very account, the passion for equality is peculiarly intolerant of the power of the Past, as dominating the Present, and obstructing the rise of personal merit by the existence of hereditary and merely transmitted advantages.

Moreover, if instead of thus looking ahead, into a future which the keenest eye cannot pierce, nor the most prescient intellect forecast,—if we simply look backward upon the course of human affairs, and observe the tendency of the human mind in the affairs of society and national life, one of the most prominent facts so exhibited is the desire to guard against the despotism of accumulating wealth, and to modify the proverbial tendency of wealth to grow and of poverty to deepen. Hence the Usury-Laws—the establishment of (so to speak) a fixed value for the use of wealth on loan, and the prohibition against exacting higher rates from the necessities of the borrower: Laws still existing in not a few countries, and only recently abolished in our own—not so much from censure of the principle, as because the application of the principle was found impracticable among us, to such a degree that it was thought better for the borrower that he should openly pay a usurious rate of interest than be compelled to do so in evasive forms which would be still more burdensome to him. Among the Jews, restrictions of this kind were peculiarly peremptory,—for example, "the Lord's release," or annulment of debts in every third year; and also that grand provision of the Mosaic Code—the Jubilee—whereby, at the end of each fifty years (an average lifetime), the land was restored to the family and the Tribe, together with a release from all debts: an announcement of great joy, proclaimed from the hills and mountain-tops of Palestine by sound of the silver trumpets of the priesthood. At morn, as each new half-century began, "beautiful upon the mountains were the feet of those who brought the glad tidings!"—and the silvery notes of the priestly clarions awoke the land from Dan to Beersheba with the news that the year of jubilee had begun. The grim power of the Past was lifted off the fortunes of the Present; and the nation, in its individual members, started afresh,—the burden of past failure or mischance fell off from the bowed shoulders of the poor and unfortunate; the career of wellbeing or of social ambition was thrown open afresh to all; and each new generation, inspired with new hope, bounded forward untrammelled by the Past, —while the realised wealth of the nation, the result of the labour of past generations, remained intact, merely undergoing a partial redistribution of its surplus portion, for the benefit of the many, while reducing only the surplus wealth of the prosperous few.

Such was a fundamental condition of ancient Hebrew society, as established by the great Lawgiver, "learned in all the [wellnigh lost] wisdom" of the far older civilised people of Egypt. A joyous usage of national life, such as the later world of Aryan civilisation has never known; and it is one which, if the Better Time (when the Conquest of Nature shall place a comfortable livelihood within the easy reach of all) be long of coming, may yet be found an elixir of Society, not less than glad tidings of great joy to the myriads or millions of the unfortunate classes, at present bowed down ever more and more by the cumulative burden and despotism of an unlucky or untoward Past. And although this Mosaic legislation had a local object (namely, that of preserving each Tribe in the possession of its own originally assigned territory) which has utterly disappeared by course of time in Europe, and which has never had a place among the European population of the New World; still, it is well to remember that the social organisation of Christendom, with all its philanthropy and beneficence, does not even yet approach the realisation of some of the most fundamental principles of human conduct enunciated and reiterated by the Founder of Christianity. True, these principles seem to us too exalted to be the basis of Society and national life: yet who can doubt that such lofty dreams or aspirations of human brotherhood, with equality, and the devotion of surplus wealth to the general good — principles embodied honestly and devotedly, albeit in narrow scope, in the Christian communism of the Monks—may yet become realised in secular Society as the world grows older? What is Civilisation, and what ought it to be, but the realisation of Utopias, —the Present and the Future gradually making possible and attainable the aspirations of the Past!

To conclude. Under all conditions of existing civilisation, the discovery of rich mines of gold or silver, and a large production and supply of the precious metals, is a most powerful means of augmenting the profitable employment of human labour, with its natural outcome of increased Production, and the diffusion of this produce by means of Trade. The world's stock of useful commodities available for human wants becomes thereby increased to comparative plenty or abundance; while the means of obtaining or purchasing those commodities, on the part of classes who do not produce them, or who are the mere hands of production, become widely diffused in the form of money, through the extension as well as elevation of wages and salaries. Moreover, as we have endeavoured to show, even a comparative excess in the supply of the canonised metals which constitute Money—a supply of gold or silver so large as to produce a gradual fall in the value of money—necessarily produces all the above-described advantages in the first place; and thereafter, gradually and by a slow operation, tends to mitigate the pressure of Debt; and, while all classes are benefited more or less, the change yields a peculiar benefit to the poor or less fortunate classes, which constitute the more numerous portion of each nation or community. In the sixteenth century, when this rare event in human affairs occurred in the most striking form or degree which the world has ever witnessed, the result was the birth of Modern Europe, and the first giant-like stride forward to an improved condition of Society, with a renewal of the long-interrupted work of developing and utilising the resources of Earth[1]—the conquest of Nature by Man—which has constituted the grandest feature and triumphs of subsequent Civilisation: a work, and an achievement, which is the fundamental mission of mankind, and to the further development and gradual completion of which we may hopefully look for the higher material condition and general wellbeing of the nations in the Future.

In the age of Columbus, a New World was revealed to the sight and opened to the enterprise and occupation of the youthful peoples of Europe, as also by-and-by to the Old World at large; and, fortunately, in its abounding mines of the precious metals, the New World at once supplied, through the circulating medium, the most potent (and previ-

---

[1] " It is certain," says Hume, " that since the discovery of the Mines in America, Industry has increased in all the nations of Europe; and this may be justly ascribed, amongst other reasons, to the increase of gold and silver."—*Philosophical Works*, vol. iii. p. 323.

ously most lacking) means or agency for its own conquest and development at the hands of its civilised discoverers.

No equal splendour of events ushered in the Golden Age of the present century. By that time the earth had been fully unveiled. Magellan and Drake, Cook, Hudson, and others, had explored the mighty expanse of ocean, northward and southward, up to the impenetrable ice-fields of the Poles. By land, adventurers and merchants had followed Marco Polo across the vast regions of Asia; while the "dark continent" of Africa had yielded to human knowledge all but its last secrets, under the explorations of Bruce, Ledyard, and their compeers. Instead of the discovery of a new hemisphere comprising two continents, which so grandly preluded the Silver Age, it was but two countries, already known and sparsely settled by the European race, which were directly added to civilisation, and opened to European settlement, under the attraction of the great gold-discoveries which made famous the middle of the present century. It is true that the New Gold immensely exceeded, in annual yield and supply, the production of both gold and silver in the sixteenth century, and at first even trebled the annual amount of the old supply of the precious metals in 1810, after that supply had been steadily progressing throughout three centuries. But the Golden Age has witnessed no such revolution in the value of money as was caused by the Silver Age: and whatever may have been the transient decline in the value of money, it has already become a thing of the past,—a pleasant remembrance compared with the opposite prospect now rising into view.

Such a result, it is true, seems strange, considering the vast masses of crude money, in the form of gold and silver, which began so suddenly to pour into the world thirty years ago,—masses enormous beyond all precedent, and which, while filling even clear-sighted men with dismay at the prospect of an unparalleled Monetary Revolution, in dim fashion cheered the heart of dumb millions with an instinct of coming prosperity.[1] Nor has the benefit fallen short of this dim anticipation, even although it may have assumed a different form than was expected. If there was no new world in geography to be discovered, for human use and to supply employment for the new gold, a far wider world was then being opened for human enterprise, by human Invention, than really existed four centuries ago, when the twin continents of America were added to the known world by the

---

[1] Writing of a fall in the value of money, Professor Jevons says truly:—"No one can feel much commiseration for the richer classes of the community even when their expenditure presses close upon their income. A footman, a horse, a ball, or a shooting excursion retrenched during the year, will restore the balance without inflicting any very great hardship." Further, he says:—"To the mass of persons [of small fixed incomes] an alteration of ten, fifteen, or even thirty per cent is almost swallowed up and rendered inconsiderable among the many improvements and ameliorations, and the general increase of industry, profit, and general prosperity which then takes place."—*A Serious Fall in the Value of Gold considered*, p. 59.

adventurous explorations of Columbus. The conquest of Nature by Man had proceeded far in the interval; and the new powers then springing into existence—and all the old ones too—at once obtained golden wings, gifting them with wider range and higher capabilities of usefulness. Enough has been said in this chapter—and has been exhibited in the prior review of the Past—to demonstrate, or at least to indicate, the benefits to mankind at large, and not least to the poorer and dependent classes, of an ample supply of the precious metals which mankind have accepted as the measure of value, and as the means by which wealth becomes most potent and efficient for the civilised work of production and trade, through the profitable employment of human labour, and consequently for the comfortable maintenance of those classes whose labour is their only property. In the chapters on California and Australia, together with the two chapters next following, we show how strikingly and potently the New Gold operated in the gold-countries, which it served so rapidly to populate and develop, and also in its first great impulse upon the British Isles, to which country the New Gold chiefly and most directly flowed. It only remains to show how the benefits of expanded commerce, and of increased employment and production, were realised, under the influence of the rich mines of California and Australia, during that bright quarter of a century which—I hope fitly—is here designated the New Golden Age.

BOOK FIFTH

THE NEW GOLDEN AGE

CHAPTER XVII.

FIRST GETTING OF THE NEW GOLD.

In the work of gold-finding as prosecuted in modern times, in California and Australia, there were two circumstances which are unique, whether regarded universally, as a matter of fact, or in Economical Science. Of these circumstances I shall begin with the secondary one, because it can be the more briefly treated. It relates to the primal acquisition of Wealth in this peculiar branch of industry,—that is, from the gold-mines.

Under ordinary circumstances, in all branches of Trade and Production the profits and increase of wealth go first to the Capitalist—to the Manufacturer, Merchant, or Farmer; not to the Labourer, but to the Employer of labour. It is in the hands of the masters and capitalists that wealth begins to accumulate; and it is through and from their hands, and usually as a consequence of an extension of their business, that new wealth ultimately reaches the labouring class. At the Gold-fields the case was quite different. The ordinary course or flow of wealth was reversed. The New Gold came first to the Labourers. It was the labouring class which first grew rich: it was the broad lower stratum of Society which was primarily benefited. In these Gold-countries, in effect, Wealth, instead of descending from the pinnacles, first of all covered with prosperity the broad plains. Instead of, like the beams of the rising sun, first bathing in gold the mountain-tops, the new wealth from the Mines rose like a rising sea over the lowlands. The new wealth, in fact, instead of being created by Capital acting through many-handed Labour, and accruing to the Employer of this capital and labour, was won by rude Labour itself, and was thence diffused upwards through the community.

This reversal of the ordinary acquisition and course of Wealth, in the new Gold-countries, was owing to a combination of peculiar circumstances. In the first place, the gold-fields were open to all comers at a merely nominal cost; also, thereafter, no Rent was payable. Secondly, the golden ore lay upon the surface, and required no capital or machinery to work it. Thirdly, the labour required was of the commonest kind—as rude and simple as that of the ordinary navvy or agricultural labourer; so that the penniless masses could effectively engage in it. Fourthly, the commodity produced was immediately exchangeable or negotiable — it was disposable without the help of intermediate persons or agencies. The commodity, Gold, was ready for the market the moment it left the sieve or "cradle" of the Miner. Further, the work of gold-digging was of a kind least of all suitable for, or agreeable to the better classes. In this way rude Labour, the masses who constitute the lowest stratum of society, could engage in gold-finding as freely as the greatest capitalist, and more successfully even than the middle classes. No capital was needed—either to win the gold, or to dispose of it when got. By-and-by, as has been shown, Capital became requisite for the working of the gold-mines; and, thereafter, wealth-making followed pretty nearly the same course in the Gold-countries as elsewhere. But in the earlier years, we repeat—in the first stages of gold-finding, which were also by far most profitable,—the vast wealth reaped in these new regions was obtained and accumulated by the Labourers themselves, and, through them, diffused itself among the other classes.

The peculiarity of the conditions here presented, and which so strikingly reversed the ordinary course of Wealth, are readily intelligible. But we may illustrate the case by referring to another branch of industry which, in its economic as well as general character, is perhaps the most kindred to that pursued in the Gold-countries,—namely, Coal-mining. Unlike Iron-mining, where costly furnaces and skilful appliances are required before the raw commodity assumes a commercial form available for human wants, the product of the coal-pit is, like gold, immediately marketable. But, unlike the working of the gold-fields, coal-mining requires a vast amount of capital, such as places the work, however profitable it may be, beyond the enterprise of all but wealthy individuals. Usually a large sum has, first of all, to be spent in the acquisition of the land; another large expenditure has next to be made in exploratory borings and in constructing the pit. All this has to be done before the coal is reached. And even when the pit is in full working order, individual labour is helpless. Suppose that some large coal-pit, fully excavated, were thrown open to all comers (like the gold-fields), the Labourer would be unable to avail himself of it. Even if, unlike the free individual working at the gold-fields, the mass of labourers were to combine and organise themselves for the working of the coal-pit, the absence of Capital, of previously accumulated wealth, would be fatal to the scheme,—owing to the large outlay required for putting and keeping the machinery in motion, and especially to meet those accidental damages and mishaps, which, if not immediately repaired, soon render a coal-mine unworkable. Coal, as we have said, like gold, is immediately marketable: but even if we suppose another important point of resemblance —by assuming that our coal-mine exists, as the gold-fields did, in "no man's land," or in some region where the ground can be obtained at a merely nominal price,—let us assume, too, as is sometimes the case, that the value of the coal-seam is as great as that of a gold-bed: still, the necessity for capital would place the richest of coal-beds entirely beyond the sphere of unsupported Labour. Untold wealth in coal-beds may co-exist with a vast mass of Labourers, and yet be as entirely profitless to them as if these mineral treasures were non-existent. Coal, also, is so bulky, costing so much for freight, that coal-mining is rarely carried on save in populous countries where the demand is surrounding and immediate. In the rare cases, as in some parts of India, where coal-mining is pursued at a distance from seats of trade and population, this can only be done after railways or canal traffic have greatly reduced the ordinary costs of conveyance. It was steam-power, in Watt's engine, which first rendered available our deep-lying coal-beds a century ago; and it is steam-power, in Stephenson's locomotive, which by cheapening conveyance now provides profitable markets for the produce of many a coal-bed which otherwise would remain unworked and worthless. The bulky produce of the coal-pit could not be carried far to market until our own time, when railways and steam navigation, while themselves creating a demand for coal, have marvellously cheapened all forms of conveyance. Gold, on the other hand, at the new gold-fields, could be got simply by Labour—the profitable return being immediate; and no intermediate agents were needed to render the commodity marketable, possessed of exchangeable value—in short, convertible into money; the commodity, or produce of this labour, being Money itself, or at least the raw material of it. A peculiar state of matters, this: one, indeed, which may be said to apply to gold, and gold only; not even to silver,—

which, although it likewise is Money, is found under circumstances widely different from the commoner forms of gold-finding, and in which mere labour is impotent without the aid of scientific skill and capital.

So it happened that the new treasures in the gold-countries came first into the hands of Labour—of the poor, the many: and, after enriching them, it passed upwards with its trade-supporting and wealth-making power, into the hands of the other classes in those countries. On the other hand, as we shall see by-and-by, as soon as the new treasure passed from the Gold-countries, its diffusion followed the ordinary course of wealth—coming first into the possession of employers and capitalists, and then spreading downwards to the labouring classes—in the chief trading and exporting countries throughout the world.

But how came it that the discovery of these Gold-fields should produce, as it certainly did, a much vaster prosperity than any other kind of discovery has yet done? In considering this question—to which the remainder of this work gives an explanation in full—we come in contact with a host of theories, not a few of which are directly antagonistic to some of those which I shall submit to the reader, not only here but in subsequent parts of this work. The primary answer is, because Gold is the only substance the production of which can be largely increased, and at reduced cost, without the product falling in price. If gold had been like other things, the gold-beds, owing to the very richness of their yield, would have become unprofitable long before anything like the actual produce had been turned out, or before Labour had reaped half its actual profits.

The gold-fields, it is agreed, were a part of the earth's surface, suddenly discovered, where human labour could exert itself far more profitably than elsewhere. In the early times of gold-finding, of which we now speak, the diggers frequently earned (*i.e.*, found gold to the amount of) no less than £4, £6, and occasionally even £10 a-day!—and it is an estimate below the fact to say that the gold-diggers for several years earned four or five times as much as the wages of skilled labour in the richest and most advanced countries of the Old World. But how came it that this was possible? *It could not have happened in any other branch of production.* Food is the only commodity which is equally, or so widely or universally, desired and required by mankind as gold is; but had as great an increase occurred in the production of Food as did then occur in that of gold, the earnings of the persons who engaged in that production could not possibly have amounted to anything like those of the gold-diggers. A superabundance of the commodity produced, by lessening its price, would, from the outset, have rendered such a rise of wages or earnings impossible.

In truth Gold, even less from its own remarkable qualities as a metal than from the functions arbitrarily but universally assigned to it by civilised mankind, occupies a very peculiar and (except silver) an entirely exceptional position among the products of the earth or of man's industrial skill. Especially, it is the only commodity which, however abundantly produced, has never failed to find a market. And in explaining this matter as a whole, we come upon facts and theories which are hardly less interesting in themselves than important from their bearings upon economical science and the material wellbeing of communities.

Generally, if not universally, writers upon Political Economy have likened the benefit to mankind from a new gold-mine to that of the discovery of some peculiarly fertile portion of the earth's surface. And they have done so not merely as a literary illustration, but to define, and restrict to this character and proportion, the benefit which in their opinion is actually obtained from new mines of the precious metals. They hold that the benefit from a new mine to the world is no more than that obtained by the gold-miners, and is exhausted by what is termed the "first exchange." In other words, the prevalent opinion has been that just as the profit upon corn is summed up and exhausted in the price given to the grower by the purchaser, so the increase of wealth to the world from a new gold-mine is exactly measured by, or at least is included in, the so many pounds sterling, or their equivalent in goods, paid to the miners for their nuggets or gold-dust.

Now, this doctrine of valuing and limiting all increase of Wealth from production by the "first exchange," is in my opinion a very inadequate one, and entirely erroneous as applied to the produce and effects of the Gold-mines. Indeed, even in the case of corn, the doctrine only holds good when the "first exchange" immediately adjoins Production and is immediately followed by the consumption of the corn: for example, when the first buyer of the wheat or rice himself consumes it. The doctrine becomes inadequate whenever the corn is further traded with; for, in this case, the first price paid, or the amount of the "first exchange," must be so much less than the ultimate market-price, or full value of the commodity to the world, as to allow a profit upon each subsequent trading operation, or stage of the grain up to the moment when it is consumed. For example, take the splendid crops of wheat in California, which in July are waving like gold for miles along the banks of the Sacramento River, and in a few weeks thereafter are sold for consumption in the English markets. The "first exchange," say on the Bourse of San Francisco, gives a profit, a portion of new wealth, to the grower sufficient to satisfy him as a return upon his capital and labour expended upon the production of the grain. Thereafter the wheat (let us say) is sent across the Continent by railway to New York, and thence by ship to Liverpool; and both the railway and the shipowner must have a profit out of the freights or charges for conveyance,—so also must the original purchaser, or merchant, who thus sends the grain to market, have a profit. The intermediates may be more numerous than this: the grain may, and usually does, pass through other hands than those of the corn-merchant who originally purchased it. But this much is certain, that the additional world-value created on the banks of the Sacramento is not limited to the profit obtained by the Californian farmer—or the "first exchange"—but includes also the profit to the second purchaser and to every railway, ship, or carrier who conveys the wheat to the place where it is consumed. Indeed, the profit might be carried further than this: because the wheat, when consumed, is transmitted into so much vital human Force, supporting so much Labour, presumably of a profitable (and conceivably in some cases of an immeasurably profitable) kind, and which constitutes or is included in the profit which the actual consumer makes upon his purchase of the food.

Thus, even in the shape of Food, which is one of the most quickly perishable of commodities, an increase of wealth, in the form of increased profitable production, is not exhausted by the "first exchange." And I have chosen this illustration because, as seems to me, the doctrine of the "first exchange" fails in exact proportion with the enduring character of the commodity, and the length of time it remains in profitable use, or in trade, without being consumed. Now, that Gold is the least perishable of substances is well known and unquestioned. But the next point may really be called the "Mystery of Money;" inasmuch as it is a strange thing of itself, and, still more, because it has given rise to some of the greatest perplexities or discords in monetary science. The general use of things is to be consumed: apart from consumption, they have no value. The sole use of Food is to be eaten, of clothes to be worn, of machinery to be kept at work and consequently wearing. This is what may be called their "commercial consumption"—the object which creates the Demand for the commodities: and this object is, absolutely, Destruction, whether gradual or instantaneous. The value, therefore, of general commodities is only obtained from them when and in proportion as they are destroyed, or are ceasing to exist.

But Gold, as Money, stands in quite a different category. Unlike all other things, the prime and chief use of Money—and of Gold as the chief form of Money—is to be *exchanged*,—to pass from hand to hand, obtaining other kinds of things in return for it. And, however numerous these exchanges may be—in other words, however much the Gold is used, or "commercially consumed"—this circumstance of itself produces no diminution of its value. The gold-coin which has travelled across the globe, passing through a thousand hands, may and usually does possess the same value or purchasing-power at Calcutta as it did when fresh from the Californian Mint. It may lose value by abrasion, but not from the mere fact of its being employed, however long and extensively, as Money. Moreover the material is almost as imperishable as its value,— Gold being the least perishable of substances. Thus, comparatively imperishable in itself, Gold is actually indestructible in its value by any amount of mere using,—which means, presumably, profitable employment. Its destruction, in short—slight and slow in the course of centuries—is merely an accident of its use or employment; not, as with other commodities, a purposed consequence, and indispensable requisite of its usefulness and value.

This brief statement, I think, will at once awaken the most ordinary intellectual apprehension to the vast influence which the new Gold-mines must have exerted upon the world. The mere first value of the gold—the new wealth or profits obtained by the Miners—as indicated by the "first exchange," has been but a fraction, indeed even an insignificant part, of the value of the New Gold to the world. Gold, when it leaves the hands of the Miner is only at the outset, on the threshold of its career; and its value at that stage no more represents its cumulative and aggregate value to the world than the present value of an infant represents the productive power of his future life. True, an infant may prove to be a "cumberer of the ground"—at best, merely enjoying life for himself; and Gold, in like manner, may be employed wholly in gilding and decoration (which gives pleasure, but neither produces nor helps to produce anything, except the single work of thus employing the metal in the arts), instead of as Money, which is perpetually doing things both useful and profitable.

The important influence upon the value of a commodity, and upon the doctrine of the "first exchange," arising from whether the commodity is destined for immediate or deferred "consumption" (that is, destruction), and from its capacity for being variously or at least successively employed by mankind, has not hitherto been properly recognised. If a man buys and eats in an orchard some peaches —for which from their perishableness, from lack of the means of transport, or other cause, there happens to be no demand elsewhere,— this eating of the fruit (which gives some pleasure and a little sustenance), and the price paid to the producer, fully exhaust whatever value the commodity possesses. In this case, the "first exchange" adequately represents the value of the production. But the doctrine fails in exact proportion as the commodity can be, and is, variously or successively employed before it is finally consumed. It is the *final* value of any commodity, before it is consumed, that represents its complete or *world-value;* just as the price paid on its first exchange represents its value to the individual producer. In the illustrative case of the peaches, the first price is also the final value: and accordingly the doctrine of the "first exchange" here holds good. But such a case is the exception, not the rule. Indeed almost every marketable commodity may have, and to some extent generally has, a *world-value* as well as what may be called an *individual value*—or the value to the individual producer. Even the peaches, readily perishable though they be, would have some portion of world-value if they were traded in,—giving profit in conveyance to ships or railways, and also to the merchant who purchases them from the producer, and to the retail-dealers through whom the fruit is distributed to its final purchasers and consumers.

I conjecture that the origin of the doctrine of the "first exchange," with its subsequent application to the value of the new gold-mines, was influenced and promoted by the circumstance that Grain has been the favourite standard of value with writers on economical science. Grain like vegetable produce generally belongs to the perishable class of commodities; it is only susceptible of the simplest kind of manufacture—such as baking, a mere form of cooking; and, further, alike from its being easily damaged, and from its bulkiness relative to its value, cereal produce is not a favourable commodity for much transmission by conveyance, and was usually consumed in the locality of its production. Indeed, until the present generation of mankind began— which was contemporaneous with the introduction of railways and oceanic steam-navigation—it is the fact that the quantity of grain transmitted from one country to another was exceedingly small; and the practice of growing the cereals for exportation was hardly known in Modern Europe until quite recent times—indeed except to the British Isles there was no such Trade at all. Food, too, was generally scarce, and therefore (upon that account alone) consumed immediately; and even at the present day, owing to the pressure of increasing population, overtaking the food-supply, the cereal crop is as a rule entirely consumed within the year. Under these circumstances, it was approximately correct to measure the value of the grain-crop by the "first exchange," or the price paid to the Producer. And as Grain has been the favourite standard of value with Economists—as was also the case in old times, for many centuries, when Money had not displaced "payments in kind,"—the economical reasoning which, roundly, held good with respect to grain became inadvertently and incorrectly applied to the value of other produce of human labour, and recently to the produce of the Miners in the new Gold-countries,—although, as I have shown, there is really so vast and substantial a difference betwixt Gold and other commodities that the economical reasoning or maxims which may suit the one must be seriously inadequate, or totally erroneous, with respect to the other.

Nevertheless, even taking agricultural production in illustration of value, it is not difficult to find instances which alike illustrate and demonstrate the case as I desire to put it, and which will prepare the reader not merely for opinions which I shall express in the sequel, but for what I regard as the main historic truths with which this work has to deal. Suppose, for example—and the supposition appears commonplace compared with the actual Gold-discoveries—that a region or locality was discovered, or otherwise became suddenly available for human industry, where Cotton could be produced in fourfold abundance; or, which comes to the same thing, where Cotton could be produced at only one-fourth of the ordinary cost. What would be the value, or economic results, of the opening up of such a new and rich field for the operations of human industry? In the first place, since it is a new region, not previously available to human industry—and as there is always a surplus of idle or very poorly employed Labour, and in lesser degree a surplus of Capital also,—this new field for industry would be highly beneficial to the world if it merely supplied an opening or new field for Labour and Capital at the *ordinary* rate of wages and profits. But, owing to the singular productiveness of this new cotton-region, both the Labour and Capital employed upon it obtain collectively, although it may be in different degrees, not merely ordinary earnings and profits, but a fourfold profit compared with labour and capital similarly employed previously and elsewhere. And this would be indicated by the "first exchange," or the price paid to the Producers. But, while yielding this high profit, the Cotton is merely at the outset of its career. After the first sale, or exchange—*i.e.*, after the first purchase of the cotton, presumably by some merchant or speculator,—the cotton is conveyed by land or sea, or both, to the chief centres of the cotton-trade (say New York or Liverpool), where it is bought by cotton-manufacturers, who then convey it to their mills. Here it becomes the staple of a great industry. Factories have been built, and fitted with costly machinery, after giving profitable employment to thousands of workmen; and thereafter thousands of workpeople are employed at fair wages (supporting themselves and families) in working those mills and manufacturing the cotton into clothing and other fabrics. Then the cotton, in its finished state, is sent on its travels again — perhaps by long voyage to most distant countries, such as India; where it is consigned to retail-traders, and is finally purchased and consumed — that is, destroyed. And the final price of the cotton-goods is of necessity (barring accidents) sufficient not merely to pay the original Producer, but to give wages and profits at every successive stage of its career, — on its conveyance by ship or railway; on the erection of the factories, which has given profitable employment to many people; on the working of these factories, or the manufacture of the cotton, thereby employing many people, and yielding a profit on the capital, labour, and skill of the manufacturer; yielding also a profit, or "commission," to the wholesale merchants, and last of all to the retail-dealers, who supply the cotton-goods at the place of their consumption.

Of course this "world-value" of the cotton affects or even creates the first value of the commodity, as paid to the Producer; and the greater this world-value of the commodity (which at this first stage may be called its potential and prospective value), the larger will be the first value, paid to the Producer, and represented by the "first exchange." But, certainly, this world-value is not all *included* in the "first exchange," or the price paid to the Producer. In fact, the price paid at each exchange simply represents the value of the commodity at that particular stage of its existence. Accordingly, in the here-supposed case of the discovery of a rich new cotton-region, it is not the amount of the "first exchange," or the price paid to, or profit obtained by the Producers, but the final price of the manufactured article—of the cotton sold by the retail-dealer at the point where its consumption and immediate or approximate destruction occurs,—that represents the full value of the new cotton-region to the world. *That* must be adequate to cover all the wages of labour and the profits on capital and on trading industry, on freights and mercantile commissions, throughout the whole career of the cotton, from its birth to its death—from its production to its destruction. If this were not so, the cotton would not be grown, or at least its production would promptly cease. And how many thousands of mankind, and also how much capital, have been profitably employed, all in consequence of the discovery of this new cotton-region! This aggregate of wages and profits, and not the mere "first exchange," would be the real value to the world of the discovery of the supposed new cotton-region.

This illustrative instance of a new cotton-region shows clearly enough that the value of such a discovery is not confined to the mere addition thereby made to the world's stock of commodities—to the raw cotton produced on this new and fertile area of the earth,—but is dependent upon the *succession of* USES *to which the commodity can be and is profit-*

ably put without being destroyed, and which, accordingly, varies in different epochs of the world and different stages of industrial power and skill. But such an illustration fails in a very important point to illustrate the world-value of a new gold-mine; because the imperishableness of this metal, as well as the altogether peculiar use to which it is put (viz., as Money), make it impossible to find any real parallel to the case. For example, the cotton acquires new value in exchange (a higher price is paid for it) at each successive stage of its career, until it is sold as a manufactured article for immediate consumption. On the other hand, gold may, and frequently does, carry as high a price when it leaves the hands of the Miner as it possesses or acquires at any subsequent point of its existence. This is owing to the fact that (*e.g.*, at the British Mint) each ounce of the metal can, by coinage, be invested with its highest value, readily and free of cost; and this circumstance being universally known, the prospective value which so certainly awaits the metal, and which can be obtained for it freely by any one, is (so to speak) reflected back upon the thing at its source. Or, to put the same fact in another way, the first owners of and dealers in the precious metal anticipate — or in Stock Exchange phrase, "discount" — this future value which so indefeasibly belongs to it. Thus, Gold may (although it does not always, or necessarily) carry as high a value in exchange at the Mines as it does at any point of its long career or existence; and it always did so in California and Australia as soon as Mints were established in those countries. Accordingly it may be said that, the final price or exchangeable value of the gold being no greater than its first price, at the Mines, the value of New Gold to the world is no greater than that which is paid to the Producer, and which is represented by the "first exchange."

But any one who so reasons forgets—not perhaps that the prime use of gold, and its greatest source of value, is as Money—but the peculiar and altogether singular uses and functions of Gold as Money. The use of Cotton, and the source or cause of its value, is to be manufactured and thereafter employed and consumed—worn out and destroyed—as clothing. The commodity is destroyed in the using,—or rather, in its final using; (for in the process of manufacture, while giving profitable employment to many people, itself augments in value). The prime usefulness of cotton is as clothing; in which form, and stage of its existence, it perishes in exact proportion as it is used,—in other words, as its chief value is developed, manifested, and realised. On the other hand, as already said, the usefulness or value of gold as Money is totally independent of its destruction: its destruction in using, or in the process of exchange, is (unlike Food) merely an accident, and (unlike clothing) one which happens very slowly, or only in a very trivial extent. The usefulness and value of gold as Money lies simply in its exchange-ableness — or as a medium of exchange; and its aggregate or world-value is determined by the number and value of the exchanges which it serves to make—or, more correctly, upon the profits made upon these exchanges. Each of these exchanges is presumably a profitable one; each exchange gives a profit; and the value of the gold-money to the world—its aggregate final value—is (not equal to but) dependent upon the sum of all the profits on the exchanges which it has facilitated or served to effect before the coined metal is destroyed by abrasion and ceases to exist. In fact the world-value of the gold is substantially the same as if a particle of the precious metal adhered to the hand at each exchange, while the coin itself remained undiminished, circulating as freely and at the same value as before! This, we have called the Mystery of Money.

In opposition to the views here expressed (namely, that the value of the new gold-mines to the world is not represented by, or all included in, the original price paid to the Miners, and the profit acquired by the Producers), and in favour of the current doctrine of the "first exchange," it may be said that the further and frequently progressive value of the article produced, say Cotton, is not any real profit to the world, inasmuch as this further, or "world-value" of the article, is the result of *further labour;* which must be compensated by an enhanced price, or else the world would be actually a loser. The enhanced value acquired by the cotton or such-like article, in consequence of its being manufactured or traded in, does not (it may be argued) give anything to the world, but merely prevents the world incurring a loss from such transactions. And that, in fact, so far from this enhanced value being something in addition to the producers' profit, or the gain upon the first exchange, if this enhancement of value did not occur, the labour in manufacturing or trading in the article, before it attained its full use and value to mankind, would act in nullifying the producer's profit and the amount of the first exchange,—or, as the case would actually be, the subsequent labour upon the article, being (*ex hypothesi*) unremunerated by an enhanced price, would necessarily reduce the first value of the production, and the profits of the producer. So stated, this is quite true. Undoubtedly the enhanced value of the cotton, when traded in and manufactured, is a direct and necessary consequence of the skill and labour employed upon it. But it is something more than (so to call it) a mere equivalent for that labour; because the price paid for labour, under normal circumstances, is of such amount that the labourer is left in a better position than before. In short, the price of labour normally includes a profit to the workman. After doing a piece of work, the labourer is ordinarily not merely in the same position as before, but is bettered: his work has yielded a profit. This is the normal state of things as regards the employment either of Labour or of Capital. And the consideration of this fact at once nullifies the argument here adduced against my own views, and once more brings into light the full gain accruing to the world from the gold-discoveries.

At present, as in every previous age of the world, there is always a lamentably large portion of Labour which is unemployed, and also a portion which is very poorly paid, from lack of employment for it upon work of an ordinarily profitable kind. When there is an insufficiency of ordinarily profitable employment, many men must either remain idle (as is too much the case), or, if all are employed, not a few of them must be very poorly paid. Open a new field of work, and even though the work be not more profitable than it was before, this mere extension of employment will serve to raise wages, and thereby render every man's labour more profitable to himself; while the Capitalists or employers will take good care that they do not extend their own operations unprofitably. Indeed exactly the same may be said with respect to Capital as has just been said with respect to Labour. Thus everything which serves to increase or extend the area of Employment—which, of course, normally means profitable employment—benefits mankind, by giving a profit to the labourers so employed. And on this ground alone, the discovery of the new gold-mines directly and very widely benefited the world.

Had the discovery been that of a new area of cotton-growing, the effect in principle would have been the same. But even if the demand for cotton and for gold had been alike, there would have been a superiority in the case of the Gold. And for this reason:—As shown, and as is obvious, the world-value of the cotton, or its gain to mankind beyond that of the profit to the Producers, must be attained by the employment of labour, a consumption of human force,—which but for this might have remained inert or unemployed. But the useful career of Gold involves or requires no such additional labour. Once produced, gold continues to do its work, useful and profitable to mankind, *without any further and progressive consumption of Labour*,—except the cost of Minting, which usually does not fall upon its possessors. The continued usefulness or world-value of gold consists simply in its employment as Money—in passing from hand to hand, or in being employed to store wealth,—so that, owing to its lastingness, the profits which it yields to mankind in effecting and facilitating exchanges (every exchange being presumably, or in the gross, profitable to those who make it) are accompanied by no consumption of labour upon it. Here, then, there is another and very remarkable difference between the discovery, or the becoming available to human industry, of a new cotton-region and a new gold-mine. Provided there is an equal demand for the gold and for the cotton—and the former is more widely and readily marketable than the latter,—the gold not merely attains, but continues to distribute or expend its usefulness and world-value, without any further or successive consumption of labour upon it; whereas the cotton distributes its world-value (its value beyond and in excess of the profit upon its production) only by fresh consumption of labour, or expenditure of human force, at every stage of its existence or career of usefulness. And further, there is the difference—or indeed further contrast—between the gold and the cotton, that the latter perishes quickly in its consumption, or final stage of using, as clothing (for the sake of which all its previous stages have been operated or undergone); whereas the gold not only attains its complete usefulness and value almost at once, but continues in this complete stage of usefulness even for several generations of mankind,—only ceasing to exist, or diminishing in usefulness and value, under the slow and slight effects of abrasion as it passes from hand to hand in the profit-yielding process of exchange.

CHAPTER XVIII.

FIRST DIFFUSION OF THE NEW GOLD.

The new Gold-countries, both California and Australia, were remarkably and exceptionally circumstanced for promoting a rapid diffusion of the treasures from their gold-fields, whereby the gold-discoveries were turned to the best account, and speedily yielded their full value to the world at large. Had the gold-mines been found in some old and fully settled country, sufficiently peopled to supply Labour for the Mines, without curtailing the supply of food and other necessaries and comforts of life, both Immigration and mercantile Importation would have been little profitable, and therefore would have occurred only to a trifling extent,—on a scale in no way comparable with the influx of population and of merchandise which occurred both in California and Australia. In consequence, the New Gold would have been very slowly diffused: indeed the only cause or source of the diffusion would have been owing merely to an increased demand for foreign commodities on the part of the ordinary population, who, albeit not increased (or but little increased) in numbers, would naturally augment their purchases and consumption owing to their enlarged wealth and purchasing-power accruing to them from the rich new gold-mines which a happy discovery had rendered available to their industry.

On the other hand, California and Australia were new countries, in the fullest sense of the term. Both of them lacked even a population; and each of them (besides their gold-beds) possessed a virgin territory which, both as regards soil and climate, presented a profitable field and vast scope for human labour and enterprise,—for a profitable investment both of Labour and of Capital. Accordingly an influx of population, from other and chiefly distant countries, was indispensable for the working of the gold-fields. Not less indispensable was a vast importation of food and merchandise, for the support of this additional and suddenly augmented population. Not only did the original population of California and Australia become enriched and their purchasing-power greatly augmented, but the larger portion of the population, consisting of the new comers, became equally capable of and prone to increased consumption and expenditure. In truth, not only is a Gold-mine the most potent magnet or attraction of population, but gold-seeking is also, of all industrial pursuits, the one whose votaries are most tempted to profuse and luxurious expenditure. It is no exaggeration to say that if, by some miracle, an equal amount of wealth had been obtained from Agriculture or any other common industry, the expenditure of the *nouveaux riches* in California and Australia would not have been one-half of that which actually occurred under the feverous excitement of the gold-hunt; and although this difference might have been highly in favour of the population of these two countries, it is certain that the Foreign Trade would have been small compared with what it actually was, and the world would have had to wait long for that Diffusion of the precious metal, which was so desirable for the monetary wants of mankind, as well as preventive of a plethora in the Gold-countries, which would have diminished the profits of the miners and the entire value of the gold-fields themselves. Thus, while one must condemn the extravagant consumption of the Miners— their indulgence in high-priced wines and costly dainties of food and other kinds of consumption,— it must not be forgotten that a Spartan-like regime of life and expenditure would certainly have tended to create a perilous accumulation of gold in the gold-countries. It was the singularly rapid Diffusion of the precious metal which kept the price of gold unimpaired even at its source—at the Mines—and thereby maintained the value of mining labour continuously at its full and original amount. The miners spent their new wealth wastefully, extravagantly; but, after all, had they been more parsimonious (*cæteris paribus*) they might have got considerably less for their money. Doubtless the case would have stood otherwise if the Miners, while restricting their expenditure to useful objects, had devoted their thereby-increased savings to reproductive industry, such as agricultural investments. But this economical employment of their savings, by a class of men like the gold-seekers, was hardly within the nature of things; and certainly, it did not take place.

The First Diffusion of the New Gold—namely, within and from the Gold-countries themselves—was of a twofold character. It comprised two parts or stages: first, there was a diffusion of the precious metal, in the course of exchanges, from the population of the Gold-fields to the general community or population of the country; and, secondly, there was the Foreign diffusion, or export of the gold to other countries, the world at large. But, let it first be observed that even if the condition of the Gold-countries had not been exceptionally favourable for this second stage, or diffusion of the gold by exportation, there were circumstances in the condition both of California and Australia which, of themselves, operated powerfully against a depreciation of the produce of the mines, and consequently of the earnings and profits of the miners.

The opening of the gold-fields suddenly created an increased Demand, a new and better market, for the general productions of the gold-countries; thereby increasing the profits and wealth of the community at large,—all of whom were Producers. The first result and chief phenomenon of the times was a general increase of Wealth, which was stored largely in the form of gold,—and also a great addition to the available amount of currency, or potential supply of Money. Fortunately, there likewise occurred new requirements for Gold both as Capital and as Money. Apart from the increased expenditure which usually attends the acquisition of new Wealth, the increase of production and consequently of Trade throughout the country furnished ample and profitable investments for Capital, both in California and Australia, and also, indeed consequently, produced an increased requirement for currency. More houses had to be built, and houses of a costlier kind; harbours and warehouses had to be constructed and shipbuilding commenced, for the new Trade; while a great expansion of agricultural production became necessary, and was highly profitable. Moreover, the very opening and working of the gold-fields themselves absorbed a considerable amount of wealth—at the outset, for supplying the wants of the labourers so employed, and also thereafter, when costly machinery and engineering operations became necessary for working the gold-beds; while the general expansion both of production and of trade throughout the country—which the gold-mines created, whether directly or indirectly—gave ample scope for the employment of gold in the form of Capital; whose operations, in turn, produced a great additional requirement for gold in the form of Money. In short, while Wealth increased in the Gold-countries, there was simultaneously an enlargement of the field for investments of surplus or reserve-wealth; while the increased employment of Labour, and multiplication of produce or commodities, led to a vast increase of exchanges (buying and selling) and also of wage-payments, each of which things required a commensurate increase in the amount of Money,—the chief and almost sole form of which, in those countries, was Gold.

In this way, a large quantity of the New Gold was needed, and found full employment, in the Gold-countries themselves,—*pro tanto* preventing any depreciation of the precious metal, even although there had been little or no diffusion of the New Gold by exportation, or through Foreign trade. Indeed it is a remarkable reflection that had the newly discovered treasures been in any other form than gold, the reaping or development of those treasures must have proceeded very slowly and slightly. Whence was the money (both Capital and currency) to come from for the working or development of the new treasures in those remote and desert countries? For example, say that the new wealth, or source of wealth, then discovered had been a miraculously productive cotton-region, extremely valuable coal-seams, or unusually rich tin or copper mines. Where was the Capital or spare wealth to be got, in these distant regions, for supporting this industry until its produce had become marketable, recouping or replacing the original expenditure? Nay, where even was the Currency to come from, for the payment of wages to myriads of labourers? The difficulty here indicated is not merely of theoretic character, but one of actual and indeed constant recurrence in human affairs. It is not enough that men should discover a treasure; if it is to become available, there must also be the means of reaping or developing it. There are many singularly fertile parts of the earth's surface which still lie fallow, untouched by the hand of man. Or, take the case of the coal-seams recently discovered in the Nizam's territories, in Central India—some of them thirty feet in thickness! Their existence is well known; the Nizam would be delighted if so valuable a source of wealth could be utilised; indeed our Indian Government, for the sake of its railways, would be well pleased to see those rich coal-beds worked. Yet they are not,—because capitalists are not under present circumstances willing to lock up so large a portion of their wealth in this undertaking. But if those coal-seams were gold-beds, how different would be the case! Gold-fields, like those of California and Australia, *pay on the spot for their own working*—for the labour bestowed upon them. Day by day, the gathered ore pays for all the wages and other current expenses, besides yielding a surplus of profit. If hired labour were employed in the gold-field, the workmen would daily gather from the soil *their own wages*, and a good deal more. In truth we shall miss a remarkable feature and advantage of the case, unless we observe that the *New gold-mines created a self-supporting industry*. During the first and best years of the gold-finding, as we have seen, the gold-fields constituted (so to speak) a great industry which supplied both the Capital and the Currency requisite for carrying it on, by the labour of myriads of men. This, then, was one, and perhaps the chief, as it was the most singular, of the many peculiarities which enhanced the value of the Gold-discoveries. Unlike all the other treasures of the earth, available to mankind, the "Gold-fields," or surface-deposits of gold, needed no capitalists, nor even currency. Capital was not needed; and the Money, which was needed largely, was turned up in spadefuls from the auriferous soil.

Thus, then, the Gold-fields themselves—or rather, their working—caused the absorption of a large quantity of the New Gold. The eighty or a hundred thousand men, in each of the two Gold-countries, who found new and profitable employment on the gold-fields, supplied themselves with their "wages" and profits from the soil upon which they worked,—absorbing upon the spot a corresponding amount of the New Gold, which thus supported of itself the vast new and highly profitable Industry which suddenly arose in those secluded regions. And the expenditure of this wealthy, and also luxurious or extravagant, large body of new population created a great expansion of equally profitable and wealth-making production and trade throughout all the other sections of the population in the Gold-countries,—requiring more gold as currency in the making of the vastly multiplied exchanges and transactions of the domestic trade, as well as a means or medium of storing the new profits and additional wealth of these communities.

Owing to those various circumstances, acting together, it is obvious that these new requirements for gold would of themselves, by absorbing a large portion of the produce of the Mines, have sufficed to a great extent to ward off a depreciation of the New Gold. The gold did not drop from heaven into men's pockets, but was won by labour, in an entirely new branch of industry, the costs and expenditure connected with which had to be deducted from the produce of the mines before the New Gold could possibly have any depreciating effects upon the world-value of that metal; while the spending of the new Wealth created requirements for its constituent (gold) as currency.

Moreover, had the condition of the Gold-countries been much less favourable than it was for the foreign diffusion, or export, of the New Gold in exchange for the necessaries of life and suchlike merchandise, the Diffusion would undoubtedly have occurred in another but less fortunate form. The efflux would have been of gold *plus* men, attended by a declining population—instead of gold alone, in return for the merchandise and supplies. When the precious metal, owing to a plethora or excessive accumulation of it, began to fall in value in the Gold-countries, the gold-gatherers, instead of settling and turning to new pursuits, would have betaken themselves in successive relays to other countries,—each carrying with him his stock of gold. Indeed, it is a general rule of conduct — practicable in these new times of cheap and rapid conveyance — that while the countries where Money is most plentiful, where wages and prices are highest, are those where wealth can be most readily acquired, they are the worst for the spending or enjoyment of wealth — and consequently for mere consumers or non-producers. It was best to make money in the Gold-countries, and thereafter to return home, or settle in some country where Money was scarcer and comparatively dear. As a fact, this was the prevalent, and almost universal, original intention and purpose among the miners. Few or none of them purposed a permanent residence in the Gold-countries;—and although it was a love of home and kindred which chiefly influenced them, and not any considerations of economic science, still it was the almost universal purpose of the gold-seekers simply to make a "pile," or "pot of money," and thereafter return home. It is a curious proof of the attractiveness of the gold-hunt, and also of the power of habits and immediately surrounding circumstances, that so very few of the Miners did actually return to their old homes or otherwise abandon the Gold-country, carrying with them their "pile" to support in comfort the remainder of their life under other skies. But had a Depreciation of gold occurred in California or Australia, undoubtedly each miner would have left the gold-country as soon as his "pile" was made; and, instead of a rapid and steady increase of population on the originally desert plains and valleys of these new regions, as soon as Depreciation set in, an outflow of gold-laden miners would have formed a "return-current" to the influx of immigrants hungering in their poverty after the gains which awaited them in the Golden Land. Thus a diffusion of the New Gold would have come *ex necessitate*, —owing to the natural instinct of men to carry their property to the best markets, and to resist spending their gains at a loss in a country where gold has become depreciated, while the precious metal still bears its full or original value in all the world beside. But such a form of Diffusion would have been much less favourable or fortunate, alike to the World and to the Gold-countries, than that which actually occurred,—namely, through the wide and manifold operations of mercantile exchange; whereby the Gold-countries were enabled to rise from barren solitudes into productiveness and civilisation, and have continued to be havens of comfort to many myriads of the unfortunate classes, who otherwise would have remained in their old countries, a misery to themselves and a cost and peril to Society and the State.

But for the New Gold, it would have been impracticable, save slowly and scantily, to turn to account the latent resources of California and Australia, howsoever rich those resources might be. And in turn the development of these latent resources— nay, the working of the gold-beds themselves—provided employment for a very considerable amount of the New Gold. Together with the foreign Diffusion of the gold, necessitated by these industrial operations and growth of population, this circumstance prevented a Depreciation of the precious metal in the Gold-countries, and thereby maintained without diminution the profits of the large mining population. The new gold-wealth accruing from the mines diffused itself (in the expenditure of the miners) from the gold-fields as a centre over the whole of the Gold-countries,—like fertilising streams from a golden fountain,—promoting production and quickening industry in all its branches. And this first result of the Diffusion tended, in another way, to maintain the prosperity of the gold-producers. There were two embarrassments which might beset them,— namely, a plethora of Gold, and a plethora of Labour. The first of these,—viz., Depreciation of the gold,—would have been a fatal and permanent difficulty, *pro tanto* leading to the abandonment of the gold-fields owing to the decrease of the profits arising from working them. Secondly, there might have been an excessive influx of workers on the gold-fields, which, although not diminishing the output of gold, or the world's benefit from the Mines, would have lowered the earnings and diminished the prosperity of the individual miners: the mining population would have been increased in numbers, but would have suffered a loss of individual prosperity. But, as has been said, the new wealth accruing from the mines was to a large extent profitably absorbed in the Gold-countries themselves, creating new industry, and rendering employment of all kinds highly profitable. The value of Labour rose almost commensurately with the new and additional kinds of work, throughout the Gold-countries. In fact, the earnings of the Miners regulated the value of labour, and rate of wages, throughout the gold-countries. Accordingly, a large portion of the immigrants did not go to the mines,—preferring to engage in agriculture, or in mercantile, urban, or other kinds of work. Further, when the memorable crisis in gold-finding occurred, and machinery had to be employed, incapacitating and displacing much human labour, the widespread industry by that time established in the Gold-countries, and the brisk demand for all kinds of Home production, supplied openings for the surplus labour at the Mines. In this way, as a natural effect of the New Gold, Labour never became plethoric at the Mines; there was always other employment of a profitable kind in the country. And thus, the product of their labour (*i.e.* gold) maintaining its value, despite its vast production, while there was an increase of employment in all directions, Labour never became so plethoric at the gold-fields as to seriously reduce the miner's profits; and the result was that the large mining population (which varied from seventy to a hundred and twenty thousand, alike in California and Australia) continued in a state of prosperity, amply compensating them for their labour, which meanwhile was so valuable in its results to mankind at large.

Such was the first Diffusion of the New Gold, viz., within the Gold-countries,—when the New

Gold acted like a golden fountain, flowing in diverse streams over the countries where it was found, creating new Production and new Trade. Before coming to the next stage of the New Gold—namely, its export from the Gold-countries and its world-wide diffusion,—let us make some preliminary remarks. The New Gold, like commodities in general, was most prone to become superabundant in quantity and depreciated in value within the country of its production; because the *whole* of the gold, or other commodity largely produced, must, of course, first exist, and at least momentarily accumulate in the country of its production,—that is to say, within a comparatively small area, and among a comparatively small population. And, despite the new investments and other requirements for it (created, so to speak, by the New Gold itself), it is undoubtedly true that the New Gold was produced and existed both in California and Australia in a redundant or superabundant quantity relative to the local requirements for it: so that, if the case had stopped here, a serious depreciation of gold must have occurred both in California and Australia. Indeed it may be said that at any time, from the first discovery of the new gold-fields down to the present day, had the New Gold, or the greater part of it, remained in the countries of its production, the precious metal would have so greatly fallen in value that long ere this the working of the gold-beds would have been abandoned, and the most immediately valuable of the natural resources of those countries would have been proportionately nullified.

We all know how such a result, which would have been calamitous alike to the Gold-countries and to the world at large, was prevented,—namely, by the rapid exportation of the New Gold from the countries where it was produced. Nevertheless, the circumstances of the case are well worthy of a passing notice and consideration. What finally prevented a vast depreciation of gold in California and Australia was a Distant Demand—a demand coming from the furthest parts of the globe, operating at a distance of many thousand miles. Yet, by this Distant Demand the price of gold was kept at its maximum point in the Gold-countries, despite the fact that the precious metal was vastly, indeed enormously, redundant in those countries. Doubtless this is a matter which readers will take for granted. Yet really it is little short of a marvel. Its accomplishment requires three things :—namely, first, the wellnigh universal or world-wide requirement for gold as Money. Secondly, a rapid and efficient conduit, or means of conveyance, over thousands of miles by land or sea, between the secluded Gold-countries and the other parts of the globe where the Demand exists, and from which it operates. And, thirdly, it requires that the commodity which is thus in demand is capable of being readily and without damage conveyed to many and widely distant quarters of the globe. The first of these elements in the Distant Demand — namely, the wellnigh universal acceptance of gold as Money—is well understood: it is a fact of the most ancient standing: the use of gold as money has existed, and extended over the earth, almost *pari passu* with the spread of Civilisation. The third element or factor in the case—namely, the suitableness of the commodity for cheap and safe conveyance by long journeys or voyages—likewise needs only to be mentioned; namely, that gold possesses pre-eminently the two most requisite qualities, in its imperishableness and in its smallness of bulk compared to its value. But the second or intermediate element requisite to give potency to this Distant Demand is of quite recent origin. In truth, it had only just come into existence when the New Gold-Mines were discovered. This factor of the case—namely, the newly invented powers of the Railway and of oceanic steam-navigation—was perhaps the most important of all in promoting the Diffusion of the New Gold; and as it has been, in truth, coequal with the Gold-mines in producing the remarkable prosperity of the immediately subsequent or Golden Age of modern times, we shall have occasion to speak of it in the sequel.

It was owing to these three things, acting in combination, that the Distant requirement for Gold became an effective demand; so that, although the yield of the new mines was far in excess of the requirements of the Gold-countries, the marvel was accomplished that the value of the gold was as great in the countries of its production—nay, at the Gold-fields themselves—where it existed in a vast superabundance, as in the far-off countries from whence came this Distant Demand. To take the case of England alone. There, in London, was the British Mint, ready to coin the gold — in other words, to give £3, 17s. 10½d. of British money[1] for each ounce of the gold dug out of the Californian and Australian soil; and, owing to the circumstances above stated, this far-off value attached to the gold as produced, on the very gold-fields of distant California and Australia. The British Mint, as need hardly be said, was but one of the sources of value for the New Gold: more or less, a similar demand for it prevailed throughout the world at large. As a rough illustration, we may liken this Distant Demand, the requirement for gold among the leading countries of the world, to a large empty Reservoir in a locality where Water was largely needed; while the gold-miners were like men digging abundant wells in localities far-off (like California and Australia). The yield of these newly-opened springs was far in excess of the wants of the adjoining and surrounding population, and therefore the labour of the diggers would have been almost valueless, but for the existence of a large and readily available conduit, connecting the springs with the distant empty Reservoir, and which at once conveyed the water to a profitable market: and thus, the water,

---

[1] As a matter of fact, the bringer of gold to the Bank of England gets only £3, 17s. 9d. per ounce : but the trifling difference is not a charge for coining, but merely represents the Bank's loss of interest on the money for the time employed in the operation of coining.

although superabundant and wellnigh valueless at the springs, became, owing to its ready conveyance to the Reservoir, as valuable at its superabundant sources as in the distant locality where it was much needed.

Finally, as to the actual processes of Diffusion of the New Gold, by export from the Gold-countries. These have been described, or at least clearly indicated, in the preceding chapters which narrate the settlement and early events in California and Australia. In both of the Gold-countries there was a vast flood of Immigration,—into countries which previously had been wellnigh uncultivated solitudes. And this rapidly-augmented population became suddenly prosperous, actually wealthy relative to their previous condition. And thus they became lavish consumers not only of the necessaries but of the luxuries of life; while in California, and to some extent in Australia, even Food had to be imported, and the comforts and luxuries of living were absolutely wanting. Clothing and manufactures of every kind, for the new population, were likewise non-existent in the Gold-countries. Accordingly, speaking roundly, *the entire wants of the new population had to be supplied from abroad*, from great distances, and as regards Australia, almost entirely in British vessels. Wheat and tobacco were brought from the United States, tea and rice from China and India,—clothing, wine and spirits, and manufactured articles generally, from the British Isles. To bring these supplies, long lines of shipping were ceaselessly traversing the ocean; each day ten or a dozen vessels arrived at Melbourne or passed through the Golden Gate, and the previously solitary waters of Port Philip and of San Francisco Bay became dotted with the ships and gay with the flags of all nations,—a crowd of merchant-vessels which struggled and jostled among themselves for a place alongside the then rude jetties and wholly inadequate wharfage of what are now two of the finest harbours and greatest commercial seaport cities of the world.

CHAPTER XIX.

INDUSTRIAL ENTERPRISE IN EUROPE.—VAST EXPANSION OF TRADE WITH THE EAST (A.D. 1855-75).

DIFFUSED from California and Australia, in exchange for necessary importations of goods, the New Gold next arrived in Europe and the Atlantic States of America—the heart and home of the trade as well as civilisation of the globe. It was Europe which had chiefly furnished the things needful for the Gold Countries; and it was European shipping which chiefly had conveyed those commodities to the new countries. Also, it was to Europe, as the best market for gold, that the bullion-merchants of California and Australia despatched the precious commodity in which they dealt; and it was in European property and securities — State Funds, and stocks of various kinds—that wealthy Australians and Californians largely invested their reserve-wealth. Accordingly, next to the Gold Countries themselves, it was in Europe that a plethora of the precious metal was most likely to occur, with a consequent rise of prices, or fall in the value of money. Fortunately, it was in Europe also that a rapid expansion of Trade and Production —in other words, an increased requirement for the precious metals as money—was to be looked for on the largest scale. But the New Gold was so marvellously abundant. And if a plethora were to arise, it would be in the main so much loss to the world of, or reduction upon the possible benefit which Nature then presented to mankind in the Mines— in the sudden unveiling of the vast stores of glittering treasure which had so long remained hidden from the sight and search of man.

Happily, the Gold-discoveries came at a peculiar and very notable phase of the social and political life of the nations. For some years previous, there had been a remarkable ferment of the human intellect, and of the popular spirit and ideas. The student of history cannot fail to be struck with the fact that in the mental and moral, as well as in the physical life of mankind, or of some large group of nations, there occur at intervals epidemic waves of excitement —stirrings and uprousings of the heart and mind, of exceedingly various kinds. A strong breath, or spirit-wind comes, we know not how or whence,— like the breathing of the Spirit of Life which the Hebrew Prophet beheld upon the valley of dry bones. Just as there are epochs of Plague and of Famine—dreadful visitations of the Cholera, the Sweating Sickness, the Black Death,—times when the Earth seems to sicken, breathing forth noxious gases; when the very air thickens at times with fungoid life, and the Plague-cloud comes darkening the sun at noonday; when a blight falls upon vegetation, upon the corn or the vine, and a murrain upon cattle,—times when even the true bubo-plague of the Orient travels far into the regions of the West :—so are there strange " in-comes "[1] of the human spirit, various as human nature itself, rising from the Dancing Mania to the ecstasy of the Crusades and the contagious ferment of social or political Revolution. The wave of life or sentiment does not merely ruffle the surface of Society as the wind of autumn throws into long billows the surface of the golden corn; rather, it springs up mysteriously within,—like as a submarine volcano first agitates the depths of the ocean, and is only revealed by the huge waves which flow outwards from the spot, or roll in engulfing masses high up upon the adjacent coasts.

Just before the Gold-discoveries, among the nations of Europe, a passion for freedom from foreign rule and for political and social liberty was accompanied by a new fervour in Religion, and higher ideals in Fine Art, as well as by an outburst of mechanical invention and financial enterprise. Italy and Hungary—the oppressed nationalities—fought for

[1] The word "in-come" used to be in common use in Scotland (if not also in England) to designate a bodily ailment (especially a swelling or suchlike local ailment) arising from some unknown cause or influence; and in the learned form of "influenza" it became adopted by medical men in 1832, to designate a peculiar kind of lingering feverish "cold," widely attacking the mucous membranes, which became severely epidemic in sequel to the first visitation of the Indian Cholera to the British Isles.

independence; the German race, temporarily ousting their petty princes, became inspired by the desire for national unity; France made her third Revolution, which she desired to be social as well as political,—starting the new *couches sociales*, which were destined to reappear in more terrible form amid the petroleum-fires and bloodshed of the Commune of 1871. In the British Isles—apart from the impotent outbreak of long-smouldering Chartism, and of an abortive Irish Rebellion,—the wave of excitement had previously been manifested in spiritual form, in "Puseyism," the beginning of the High Church movement in England, and by the analogous Free Kirk movement in Scotland; while in Fine Art it appeared in pre-Raphaelitism—a revolt against the conventionalism which had grown like a film over the eye of Art, obscuring the great fountain of truth and beauty in Nature; and even the "Spasmodic" school of poetry was an ambitious insurrection against the world-old canons, and a feverous attempt to establish a new style, and import into the domain of poetry the effects of rhapsody, an analysis of morbid sentiment, and a display of egotistic personality.

More worthy of notice in these pages—more useful to the world at large, and hardly less remarkable than even the Gold-discoveries themselves, was the contemporaneous outburst of scientific invention applied to the common and universal wants of mankind. Some five-and-twenty years had elapsed since Fulton's first steamboat, on the Clyde, had shown how the motive power of the steam-engine could be extended from the land to the river and the sea; and a shorter time had passed since the opening of the first public Railway (between Liverpool and Manchester) had been made sadly memorable by the accidental killing of England's most promising statesman, Huskisson. But now there came a great development of joint-stock enterprise, —a financial enginery which had been well known in this country ever since Paterson's application of it in founding the Bank of England; but whose gigantic powers now began to be applied to every branch of industrial enterprise. The vast and almost illimitable power of associated capital, whose greatest recent achievement had been to enliven our cities and dwellings with the brilliant and cheerful illumination of coal-gas — supplying Light in pipes, like water,—now found a new and grander channel, lending its gigantic force to the construction of Railways; and with such energy and promptitude, albeit the enthusiasm was somewhat reckless, that in a few years—indeed one may say, by a stroke—all the main lines of travel and traffic in our Islands were fitted with the iron road, the rapid steam-car, and the comfortable railway-train.

Hardly less striking and not less useful was the progress of traffic and locomotion upon the world of waters. While not a few men of science were still teaching and ridiculing the impossibility of such an attempt, Steam-navigation crossed the broad and stormy Atlantic,—thereafter bridging the oceans, even as the Railway traversed and connected countries and continents. Engineering science, in its newly acquired strength, became ambitious and boastful. Nimrod-like, it set itself to tasks more vain-glorious than useful,—tasks which, from their daring or ostentatious magnitude, were designed rather to glorify the new Science than to satisfy then-existing wants. The Thames Tunnel was constructed, and the *Great Eastern* steamship was built. And these great works of Brunel and Scott Russell became idols of the hour,—to which the people paid homage as exulting as had greeted of old the grand tower of the Cushite conqueror upon the Plain of Shinar. Simple as the matter was to the educated mind, the news that the ocean was being safely traversed in buoyant ships of iron appeared to the masses of our population almost as marvellous as the miracle by which the Prophet Elisha caused the iron axe of his disciple to float on the waters of Jordan. Our People became self-glorious at the sight or news of the great iron steamship,—a floating town, which could carry eight full regiments, each a thousand strong, and stow away in its hold merchandise enough for the annual wants of a colony.[1] With equal

---

[1] The career of this great steamship proved a most unfortunate one. The ship at the date of her launch had cost nearly three-quarters of a million sterling, and thereafter required a further outlay to make her fit for sea. She was meant to be a passenger-ship betwixt England and America, but her accommodation was far in excess of the public requirements: fitted up for two thousand passengers, she only obtained two hundred. She was a noble vessel, and of immense structural strength, but her magnitude was much in advance of the wants

marvel did our people see or read of the Thames Tunnel: which, albeit somewhat taxing the highest science of that day, and only constructed after serious mishaps and a repeated drowning-out of the workmen, was extolled as an unprecedented and wellnigh superhuman achievement,—forgetful that three thousand years ago Babylon, the London of primeval civilisation, had similarly tunnelled beneath the mightier stream of the Euphrates; besides enclosing that river between terraced embankments, more fully than London has even yet done, and surrounding the city with vast impregnable defences, which were "a wonder of the world" even in those times of gigantic labour; whereas the wonder of that kind in our day will be when the British metropolis

of the time. She was too big for the Suez Canal, which rendered her useless for the Indian and Australian trade. The only suitable service which was found for her was the laying of ocean-lines of telegraph-cables. The big ship proved as great a commercial failure as she was a triumph of the engineering skill and shipbuilding science of her time. She has been seized by the Sheriff, she has been in Chancery, and she has been constantly in financial shallows. In the very year she was launched, her Directors recommended that she should be put up to auction; but this was resented, as too degrading, and yet this is the issue to which the unfortunate vessel has come at last, with the result that no adequate price has been bid for her. In October last (1881) this leviathan of steam-shipping was put up for sale by auction at Lloyd's Rooms in the Royal Exchange, London, but was withdrawn as the biddings rose no farther than £30,000. Her splendid engines had become antiquated, while her firmly riveted fabric of iron, valuable as it was, would cost almost as much to take to pieces as it had cost to construct. What will be her ultimate fate remains to be seen. Doubtless ships equally large will be built again before long, and with profitable results, as the present taste for voyaging and general diffusion of wealth increase; but doubtless, also, the leviathans of the future will be built upon other plans, both structural and engineering.

goes to the expense of surrounding itself with adequate defences at all!

Such was the many-featured outburst of fresh life and thought which, in its chief phases at least, had immediately preceded the discovery of the great gold-mines; and which, in its mechanical and financial forms, was ready to give employment to, and to further expand under the influence of, the large new supply of gold-money from California and Australia. The engineering inventions of that day were peculiarly fitted to benefit the British Isles, with their rich and economically-contiguous mineral-beds of coal and iron. In truth, the "hot-blast," then recently devised, had largely augmented the capabilities of metal-furnaces, and by its new smelting power had rendered available immense beds of iron-ore (*e.g.* the Scotch "black-band") which had previously been so intractable as to resist economical conversion to the use of mankind. Thereafter, and as invention progressed, Iron became available for a hundred new uses and purposes. Thus the true Iron Age of the world became contemporaneous with the Age of Gold,— together producing many of the triumphant achievements of the Victorian Era of unrivalled material progress and human prosperity. And one of the first consequences of this fresh subjugation of the seas, by the quickening and cheapening of navigation,[1] was vastly to extend the available area of

---

[1] In the Mediterranean, the new navigation owed its chief development to the enterprising Italian, Signor Rubattino, whose excellent

food-supply to our population: which, instead of being limited as hitherto to the adjacent lands of Germany and the Baltic Coast, not merely spread into the steppes of Southern Russia, but overleapt the Atlantic Ocean, and has continuously been spreading westward across the American prairies to the foot of the Rocky Mountains, and even to California and the Pacific slopes. Thenceforth our little Island, so long as markets can be got for our wares, might go on with increasing population, prosecuting her specially favoured or peculiarly fitting trade of Manufacture,—secure in the knowledge that the whole Earth is her granary, so long as we can pay for its produce, and maintain for our shipping the freedom of the seas.

lines of steamers are well known to all travellers on the Mediterranean and in the Levant, and whose death (Nov. 1881) is announced while I write. Raffaele Rubattino, founder and head of the firm of R. Rubattino & Co., was born at Genoa in 1809. The first of his ventures was in 1843, when he began a steamboat service in the Mediterranean with two small vessels, the Castore and the Polluce. The Polluce came into collision with the Mongebella, and foundered. He then built the Cagliari, which he afterwards gave up. The Piemonte and the Lombardo, which transported Garibaldi and "the Thousand" to Marsala, were his vessels. In 1862, at the head of a new company, Rubattino greatly improved the condition of Italian maritime commerce. In 1869 he attempted to open the East to Italy, undertaking navigation to the Indies. He was the first Italian who conceived the idea of a great national steamboat company which should rival that of any foreign land; and he succeeded in his object by uniting his own company with that of Florio of Palermo, to which is now confided such a large part of Italy's commercial future. On board his steamers the name of Raffaele Rubattino was always pronounced with affection. He was a friend to the poor, and provided many an unfortunate creature with work, or took him gratis back to his own country.

Nevertheless, despite this already-sown crop of human enterprise—of widening Trade and cheapened Production—ready to absorb a large addition to the world's currency, the New Gold flowed into Europe, and especially into England, so suddenly and in such abundance that (as before stated)[1] the supply for a time exceeded even the vigorous demand; and the gold-bullion in the Bank of England swelled to twenty millions sterling, despite all the efforts of that establishment to get rid of its plethoric cash in meagrely profitable employment, by a Bank-rate of only two per cent,—that is, at merely one-half of the lowest rate which the Bank had ever before charged for its loans and discounts. It really seemed as if the monetary phenomena of the Silver Age were about to be renewed, and that the reign of Victoria, like that of Elizabeth, was to witness a great fall in the value of Money. Happily, a better fortune was in store for us. Beneficial as "cheap money" is in the main, a revolution, or great and sudden change, in the value of Money also carries with it some serious disadvantages; while even a moderate monetary fall—which implies that the supply is greater than the requirements for it, and consequently that the Miners get less profit on their labour than would otherwise be the case, and that Money itself is not doing fully the work that it is capable of—is less desirable than when, by a happy conjunction of circumstances, there happens a large influx of

---

[1] See chap. iii.

money without any fall in its value,—showing that human enterprise and industry have increased *pari passu* with its indispensable auxiliary, the medium of exchange; and that, large as has been the increase in the stock of money, each particular coin is still doing as much work as before, and (*cæteris paribus*) yielding as much profit to its producer at the Mines. And such, in the main, has been the character of the Golden Age, — albeit some portion of the requirement for the New Gold has been temporarily created by the ambition of rulers or the intemperate passions of nations, manifested in international wars or in civil or domestic strife.

The year 1853 was the most critical stage of the new gold-supplies relative to their monetary effects, especially upon our own country. The new industrial and commercial forces, destined to give employment for the New Gold, were not yet in full action: they were gathering and rising high like waters in a reservoir for whose outflow and utilisation there had not yet been time to construct the requisite channels. But while Trade was preparing its new channels, War, with its imperious demands, curtly relieved the threatening plethora of the precious metal. While the Taeping Rebellion in China—by causing a reduction in the consumption of foreign goods in that empire, and consequently a decrease in the imports of merchandise from Europe—occasioned the employment of a larger amount of specie than usual in that branch of the Eastern Trade; a new demand for the accumulating gold was created in Europe by the outbreak of the Crimean War,—which arose like a new and "ready-money" trade, carried on not only by the primal belligerents, Russia and Turkey, but also by Great Britain and France, followed by the small State of Sardinia. Like the Crusaders of old, the armies of the Western Powers had to be conveyed to the seat of war by sea. So also were the supplies of all kinds for the Allied host,—supplies of food and clothing, of military material, as well as the woful but much-needed adjunct of hospital accommodation. Indeed, severe as were the sufferings of the Allied army during its first winter in the Crimea (the memorably cold winter and spring of 1854-5) encamped on the bare and bleak plateau overlooking Sebastopol, it was then that Civilisation, at length grown humane and tender even in war, suggested, and popular sympathy gave effect to, measures and care for the comforts of soldiers in the field such as had been unknown in any previous warfare.

The Army and the Fleet naturally drew as much of their supplies as possible from the adjacent country; but if the entire supplies of the Allied Expedition did not come from the West, the whole of the expended money did so. The war-chest had to be ceaselessly replenished from the West, from England and France,—which, fortunately, were the two countries into which the New Gold chiefly found its way. Not less important, as producing a drain of specie from Western Europe, were the subsidies which Great Britain and France found it necessary to furnish to their allies, in the shape of the Turkish and Sardinian Loans. In this manner, a considerable portion of the precious metal from California and Australia, coined at the London and Parisian Mints, was despatched to Turkey within a few months after the ore had been raised from the Mines. As the countries which were the seat of war, or which immediately adjoined it, had carried on but little trade with Western Europe, the usual appliances of commercial credit, such as bills, were hardly available for settling the military expenditure. Moreover, those countries were exceedingly poor in coin, or money in any form; and so, when the sluices were opened by the war-expenditure between these regions and wealthy France and England, specie flowed thither through the war-canal as into an empty reservoir.

Although England and France were the two countries of the Old World into which the new Gold-stream was flowing most freely and abundantly, the drain of specie created by the Crimean War very seriously affected the currency of both these countries. But the drain was met, and its effects felt, very differently in the two countries. While, in France, the difficulty was readily overcome without injury to the condition of the community; in Great Britain, with its narrower and more rigid monometallic monetary system, and where no alleviating or counteracting measures were adopted, the drain not only produced its full natural influence upon the currency, but led to a somewhat serious restriction upon the general trade and industry of the kingdom. In fact, although this war-drain of specie was comparatively slight and transient, and although occurring also at a time when the world's supply of gold was at its maximum, its history furnishes another instance of the great influence which the precious metals can, and usually do, exert upon the fortunes of States and nations.

It was not until the second year of the war that the drain of specie began to arrest attention and to create embarrassment in England. In the latter part of 1854, under the apprehensions occasioned by the War and some other causes, the Bank-rate—which in 1853 had stood at the unprecedentedly low point of 2 per cent—was raised to 5 per cent. And at that point it remained until the following April (1854), when the large supplies of the New Gold, from California and Australia, sufficed to put the Bank of England's stock of that metal again upon the increase. Thereupon the Bank-rate began to be lowered again,—falling from 5 per cent at the beginning of April to $3\frac{1}{2}$ per cent in June. All was going merrily. Trade was prosperous,—sound, and moderately active; and—strange as the fact may seem, considering that a Foreign War was in progress—no apprehensions were entertained of coming difficulty: indeed one of the ablest guides of public opinion in Trade and financial matters predicted assured, or even increasing, ease in the Money-market.[1] Midsummer-day, however, saw a reaction commence. The tide then turned, and the bullion began to flow out of the Bank of England even faster than it had been flowing in. The stock of coin and bullion in the Bank, which amounted to £18,200,000 on the 23d of June, was reduced to £10,682,000 on the 26th of October,—a reduction of seven and a half millions sterling in four months, or at the rate of half a million per week throughout that interval. It was not until the beginning of September that the Bank Directors took alarm; but then they began to "put on the screw" resolutely,—so that in the course of six weeks the Bank-rate was raised from 3½ to 6 and 7 per cent, for first-class bills of two or three months' date; while the holders of bills which had longer to run had to submit to still higher terms, and bills which were not of prime quality could not be discounted at all. Not a few traders whose bills the banks would have been eager to receive for discount in June or July, at 3½ per cent, in October could not get banking-accommodation upon any terms. The Bank's reserve of notes had fallen from £11,130,000 at the end of June to only £4,310,000 on the 26th of October. At the same date, Consols, which had stood at 91 on

---

[1] "Looking at the immediate future, there is every probability, if not certainty, that the causes to which we have adverted as influencing the money-market will continue. . . . The whole tendency of the money-market is to reduction, notwithstanding the prospects of the war, which, however, may now be considered to be effectually provided for, during the entire financial year before us,"—*i.e.*, from 1st April 1855 to 31st March 1856.—*Economist*, May 19, 1855.

the 1st of September, had fallen to 87,—a very considerable fall, considering the remarkable steadiness in value of the British Funds. So severe was the contraction of the currency that the note-circulation of the Bank of England became less than three-fourths of what it had been three years previously,—having fallen to £18,142,000, from £24,500,000 in the autumn of 1853, and from £21,000,000 in the spring of 1855.[1]

[1] I was at that time engaged on my first editorship of a newspaper, in my native city; and, observing the signs of the times, and instructed by history, I then predicted a coming change in the Money-market, owing to a war-drain of gold, together with its disastrous effects upon the trade of the country, under the operation of our Currency-laws, or "Bank Acts." On 17th April 1855, when all was sunshine and fair weather both in Trade and in the Money-market, and when even so able a judge of such matters as the *Economist* saw no ground for apprehension, I wrote editorially as follows:—"The recent reductions in the rate of discount have been made by the Directors of the Bank of England in order to get off their reserve-notes; and the process of reduction will be continued until they succeed in this object. Thus tempted, the mercantile class will come forward and take off the notes of the Bank, for the sake of engaging in enterprises which, but for the low rate of money-accommodation, they would not have ventured upon. . . . But suppose that a bad harvest comes, and we have to increase our imports by large purchases of grain, which we have to pay for in so many millions of bullion,—or suppose we have to pay large subsidies to foreign Powers, or have to leave the provisioning, &c., of our army to be obtained by purchases in a foreign country,—then, those disbursements being made in gold, the amount of that metal in the Bank of England will be greatly diminished. The Directors (in order to comply with the Act of 1844, which requires that the paper-circulation shall be diminished as the gold diminishes) must then 'put on the screw,' and draw in their notes by imposing a high rate of discount.

"The effect of this is, of course, to check mercantile enterprise. But it does more than this: it not only prevents new enterprises being undertaken, but it will bring ruin upon many of the speculations which are going on. These speculations may be perfectly sound

This war-drain of specie was also experienced by France, which shared with us the burden of the drain in about equal proportions. France joined equally with Great Britain in the loan to Turkey; and, although France took no part in the loan to Sardinia, this was doubtless more than compensated by the larger specie-requirements for her army in eastern Europe, which was greatly more numerous than ours. Also, the Eastern trade-drain of specie, occasioned by the contemporaneous falling-off in the export of merchandise to China, was especially felt in France, from whose currency the required silver was chiefly taken. But in no country, during the present century, have monetary matters been so successfully managed as in France. Since its estab-

and justifiable; they may be such as, in ordinary circumstances, would return a handsome profit to their projectors; but the sudden and great rise in the rate of discount will at once blast them with disaster. It does so in two ways. Suppose that the speculation be a cargo of foreign goods for this country; and suppose that, before the ship conveying them reaches our shores, the scarcity of money produced by the Bank-regulations has lowered the price of such goods in the market: then it follows that the enterprise may prove wholly abortive, in consequence of the price obtained by the importing merchant falling far short of that which he had calculated upon as sufficient to remunerate him for the speculation. Or, suppose that the merchant is not a millionaire (as comparatively few are), and suppose the Bank puts on the screw and urges him for repayment of its advances, or declines to discount his bills except at exorbitant rates, while his enterprise is still in progress; then he may be forced into the bankrupt-list, although but for those proceedings, compulsory on the Bank, he would have remained perfectly solvent. *A speculation cut short in the midst, however good it may be, becomes necessarily unprofitable;* and the procedure of the Bank in such cases, in accordance with the Act of 1844, is like setting men to sow and not allowing them to reap."—*Edinburgh Advertiser,* April 17, 1855.

lishment or remodelment by Napoleon I., the management of the Bank of France has been a marvel of skill and sagacity; and on several occasions it has carried France unharmed through difficulties which have proved very disastrous to the national industry and wellbeing in England. The dilemma in 1855 was owing simply to a particular commodity, Gold (or, more correctly, Specie), rising in price, because of the War, which created an unusual requirement for it; and obviously, if a country or Bank wanted a supply of specie at that time, it must pay a higher price for it,—just as in the case of any other commodity. There was no absolute dearth of specie,—on the contrary, the supply of the precious metals was then larger than ever before in the whole history of the world, or than it has ever subsequently been. But the commodity was temporarily in greater demand than usual in Europe, so that those who wanted it must give more for it in purchase or exchange. The Bank of France acted accordingly. At that time, owing to our large trade with the new Gold-countries—directly with our Australian colonies, and indirectly with California, as part of the United States,—the chief portion of the New Gold which came to Europe flowed into the Bank of England; and the Bank's stock of gold, when this war-drain commenced, amounted to eighteen millions sterling. At all times there is in the hands of French and other Continental merchants a large amount of bills payable in London; and the Bank of France bought up those bills, or as large a portion of them as it required,—presented them for discount, or else as they fell due, at the Bank of England, and withdrew the amount in gold,—in order to replenish its own reserve of coin and bullion, and thereby enable it safely to carry on its usual operations as a bank of discount and fountain of currency. Gold being then in unusual demand, the Bank of France had to pay a premium (about $3\frac{1}{2}$ per cent) for those bills payable in London, as also upon the purchases which it made from the bullion-dealers or importers of gold. In this manner the Bank of France obtained about four millions of gold from London,— the total amount of premiums paid upon those various purchases being three and a half million francs, or £140,000.[1] The only question which can be reasonably raised in connection with this procedure is, Was this a profitable or beneficial expenditure? It is needless to say that the Bank's procedure was highly beneficial to the commerce and wellbeing of France, inasmuch as the Bank was thereby enabled to sustain the national trade and industry by its advances to the usual extent. Nor was the expenditure in any degree unremunerative to the Bank; because for each ounce of the precious metal thus imported, the Bank could safely issue its notes to three times that value, in the form of loans and discounts at a charge of 4 or 5 per cent, while the

---

[1] This, at least according to an official statement—was the total amount paid by the Bank of France in premiums upon the purchase and import of gold up to the middle of December 1855.

premium which it paid for the gold was only 3½ per cent. In short, the Bank's procedure, while immensely benefiting the nation, was not only remunerative to itself, but to some extent directly profitable.

In England the drain of gold was met in a very different spirit and manner. Acting, it is only fair to state, in perfect accordance with the principles in vogue since the legislation of 1844, the Bank of England took no measures to obtain gold from abroad for the replenishing of its stock. But it contracted its discounts and issue of currency—at the same time doubling its previous charge for discounts,—making money scarce, and thereby raising its value throughout the kingdom. A rise in the value of money means a depreciation of all other kinds of property; and under a fall of prices, combined with a contraction of discounts, or of the ordinary banking-accommodation to traders, heavy losses were imposed upon the general trade and industry of the United Kingdom. The origin and theoretic justification of this procedure was, that the property of the country being depreciated, and the value or purchasing power of money being raised, foreigners would send over gold to make purchases of the depreciated goods and property in this country,—whereby, of course, the Bank's stock of gold would be replenished. The maxim of *laissez faire*, especially in currency or monetary affairs (which are but little studied or understood by our statesmen), is always a favourite one in this country; and the Bank of England—

whose Directors, for a generation past, have entirely repudiated the responsibility for the welfare of the nation which was so sincerely felt and officially acknowledged by the Directors of previous times— may well be content with a system which enables them to meet each successive crisis with folded hands, while deriving increased profits from the so-called "automatic" working of the Bank-machinery; although for every shilling of these crisis-made profits there may be a tenfold or rather hundredfold loss to the labouring, producing, and trading classes —in short, to the general trade and industry of the country. No doubt, Capitalists gain at such times under this Bank-procedure,—as likewise the class of mere consumers, who live by inherited wealth: but the "working bees of the hive," the great mass of the nation, suffer severely,—and usually from circumstances as entirely beyond their control as the occurrence of an earthquake.

It is lamentable to behold a country's trade strangled by its own laws, and bankruptcy and suffering made general by Act of Parliament. It is acknowledged that Trade at that time was perfectly sound, as indeed was proved by the manner in which it withstood the contraction of credit created by the action of the Bank of England. Nor was Trade (as occasionally happens) in want of additional currency or credit: it was strangled purely from an artificially produced dearth of the *ordinary* supply of banking accommodation. I well remember the incidents of that crisis, and the follow-

ing contemporary testimony was extracted by me from the newspapers of the day. On the 13th of October, only a fortnight before the Crisis reached its height, the *Economist* in its Trade-report said:—
" If there be temporary depression in the Manufacturing districts, in consequence chiefly of the alteration in the Money-market, in the real business of the people there seems no falling off." The Bank-restriction had begun to do its work of raising the value of our currency by depreciating the value of goods and property of all kinds; and thereafter the work went on briskly. Of the Manchester market, we read,—" As was to be expected, we have had an exceedingly dull and depressed market this week. However sound commercial matters undoubtedly are, the advance of the Bank-rate above the customary interest charged among merchants and traders in current accounts, could not fail to paralyse all mercantile activity,— more especially as a further advance above $5\frac{1}{2}$ per cent was generally expected. It was not only the speculative portion of the *usual* transactions, therefore, which was wanting in our market, but even the regular trade was visibly affected." A week later, we read of the same market:—" Our market has worn a very unsettled appearance this week. The fact is that commerce, as we have stated repeatedly, is sound throughout; and that some foreign markets are far from being overstocked, and would be willing purchasers of our manufactures, if the monetary pressure did not offer the prospect of a consider-

able saving to them by delay," [that is, owing to a further depreciation of British goods by a further Bank-restriction and rise in the value of the currency]. "But for this derangement of the money-market, business would undoubtedly be brisk. As it is, transactions are reduced to a minimum [foreign buyers holding off until our manufactured goods were further depreciated], and prices of most articles are nominal, with a downward tendency. This last movement of the Bank created a surprise bordering on panic to-day; and people begin to ask, How far is this to go?" Thus pressed, the Manchester manufacturers endeavoured to meet the increased charges upon them by reducing the wages of their workpeople,—the result being a "strike," which caused the stopping of several mills, and threw two thousand hands out of employment. Of the state of employment in Liverpool during the same week, the *Economist* said (Oct. 20):—"The proceedings of the Bank generate apprehensions, which tend to produce the evils of a money-panic. Everybody is hoarding. Money is said to be plentiful, but nobody will lend it; and Commerce, constituting the very sinews of the national strength, is crippled without an adequate cause, by the action of the Bank." Again —"Money is said to be plentiful in some quarters, but nobody will lend. Some banks that usually are extremely liberal, refuse to lend at all!" Thus, we repeat, trade and credit were sound, and no extra accommodation was needed or asked for by the commercial public: it was purely a failure of power on the part of the banks to do their ordinary work which occasioned the severe pressure upon the national industry,— a pressure which the Bank of England did not stir a finger to obviate or lessen. Yet France, under a wiser system, contemporaneously passed through a similar drain of specie without any monetary crisis or sacrifice of the national industry and wellbeing.

It was pleaded then, as always, by the defenders of the Bank Act of 1844, that the cause of the distress produced in this country was not a want of money, but a want of capital. It was maintained that the doubling of the Bank-rate and severe contraction of discounts, within four months' time, was occasioned by a dearth of loanable wealth, in consequence of the expenditure upon the war. To make such an assertion in the year 1856 (a full lifetime after the nation, with far less wealth, had successfully withstood the immensely larger expenditure of the great European war) savours of the grotesque. In the autumn of 1855, the sum expended by this country on the war could not have exceeded forty millions,— raised, too, partly by loan: and the portion raised by loan was, at that time, equivalent to a creation of wealth of similar amount minus the small sum required as current interest thereon. Moreover, the war-expenditure of France was quite as large as that of Great Britain; and how came it that there was no similar distress in France? Nay more: if it was "a loss of capital" which necessitated the undoubted monetary difficulty in this country in

1855, surely this difficulty ought to have gone on increasing as the war-expenditure continued? Whereas in fact, and as is well known, the monetary difficulty was at its height in November 1855, and had greatly lessened—indeed had almost ceased to be felt—at the close of the war. The cost of the war in the autumn of 1855 was trifling compared with the loss of some two hundred millions sterling, in foreign loans, in 1874,—with the difference that a large portion of the war-expenditure gave profitable employment to our people, whereas the greater part of the vast sums recklessly lent in 1872-3 were almost as utterly lost to this country as if they had been sunk in the sea: yet the latter loss of wealth produced no monetary crisis, whereas the comparatively trifling loss in 1855 produced a distinct and tolerably severe monetary crisis. Obviously, there must have been some fundamental difference between the two cases: and the difference was the drain of gold required by the war-expenditure in 1855. As our currency, and indeed our whole monetary system and fabric of credit, is based upon gold, any serious reduction in the stock of gold in the Bank of England tends to produce a grievous monetary embarrassment, or even a temporary collapse of the entire fabric of credit. It is a strange yet well-founded reflection that our country may spend or lose two hundred millions of wealth, yet banking accommodation goes on as before; while a mere shipment of half-a-dozen millions in gold (even though it be a profitable commercial or financial investment) not seldom produces a monetary crisis most disastrous to the whole trade and industry of the kingdom. It was to save us from this that our Banking-system was originated in 1694; yet now, Parliament has placed us again in bondage!

In conclusion, let us follow the stream of the precious metals thus drained away from Great Britain and France, and observe how potently beneficial it proved to the countries to which it flowed. The position of Turkey as a State was then very calamitous. Two of her finest provinces (Moldavia and Wallachia) had been conquered and plundered by the Russian army, and thereafter were held in military occupation by Austria; her fleet was at the bottom of the sea, destroyed by "the massacre of Sinope;" she had been fighting everywhere—on the Danube, in the Crimea, and on her Armenian frontier,—besides putting down rebel Greeks and Montenegrins in Europe, and contumacious Kurds on the banks of the Euphrates. And yet, while Turkey, the State, suffered wofully, the people prospered and the country flourished. The influx of money—the stream of precious metals from Western Europe—operated like a fertilising flood. "All round Constantinople," wrote an eye-witness of this almost magical transmutation, "around the shores of the Dardanelles, the coasts of Asia, the islands of the Archipelago, Candia, and Greece, are verdant with unwonted cultivation. Immense profits are made out of crops that were once hardly worth reaping. Even in Syria, whole districts are being transmuted from rock and waste into the likeness of fertile Belgium or the picturesque Black Forest. As early as last spring, we all heard what was doing at Heraclea. There, the working of the coal-seams had created roads, a railway, a canal, a port, villages,— in fact, a new county of Durham on the shore of the Black Sea. The same process is going on everywhere. Market-stuff is almost as heavy as coal, and there does not exist everywhere in the East a line of road as direct and well-metalled as that which conducts the produce of Turnham Green to Covent Garden. So water-carriage is first sought for, but roads to port soon follow; and even as you coast along the shores of the Levant, you can easily detect everywhere an unusual stir. In fact, the War has proved a California to the dominions of the Sultan, and is opening out regions which have, comparatively, slept since the days of Crœsus, or at least of the Lower Empire." [1]

This was a striking instance and illustration in modern times, of what is recorded by historians (and mentioned in a previous chapter of this book) as to the reinvigorating influence upon Spain of the foreign expenditure and influx or return of the precious metals into the Peninsula during the War of the Succession. Nor was the specie from the West permanently absorbed and retained in these Turkish provinces. It did its work of fertilisation, and then a portion began to return whence it came, through an expansion of the ordinary channels of

[1] Special Correspondent of the *Times*.

trade. And here, also, we have an example of what we have said with respect to not a few of those exports of gold which prove so disastrous to this country under our present laws. A waterspout may pour as much water upon the earth in a few seconds as it will take many days for the sun to draw back again into the sky: but it will all return whence it came, sooner or later. So is it, in most cases, with an export of gold, so long as our country maintains its commercial position in the world. This influx of the precious metals created and diffused prosperity in Turkey; the prosperous population began to desire and to consume a greater quantity of foreign goods: and Great Britain, as the greatest manufacturing country, and possessing also the chief portion of the carrying-trade of the world, became the chief source-of-supply and creditor. In the second year of the war (the third year after the New Gold began to pour into England) the exports of British manufactures to Turkey and the countries adjoining the seat of war, by private merchant trade, became nearly treble their previous amount, quite exclusive of the contemporaneous war-exports of the British Government.[1] A significant circumstance,—illustrating the marvellous power and reproductive operations of wealth in the form of the precious metals; while the rapid back-flow of specie, in payment for these augmented exports, contributes to show how needless and foolish it was to disturb the entire monetary

---

[1] The British exports enumerated in the subjoined table (quoted from the *Economist*) consist exclusively of private merchant-trade, and

system and fabric of credit in this country, and thereby severely oppress the national trade and industry, on account of an almost momentary reduction of the Bank of England's stock of gold, especially when the gold was exported in order to meet an imperious requirement of the State and of the national policy and interests.

At this time, also, our Indian Empire was preparing to make a great drain upon the metallic money of the West. The Marquis of Dalhousie—the most regal of Indian Viceroys, and whose lofty aims and statesmanlike sagacity were displayed at least as much in the arts of peace as in the policy of conquest and the triumphs of war—had projected a magnificent system of Railways throughout India, the construction of which marked a new era of progress for our great empire in the East, while creating a new field of profitable investment for British capital. But unforeseen events arose which, although temporarily obstructing this great project, (while giving fresh proof of its imperial usefulness), of themselves precipitated a flow of the precious metals to the East.

do not include the stores and ammunition of war exported by the Government:—

EXPORTS OF BRITISH MANUFACTURES.

	1853.	1854.	1855.
To Turkey,	£2,029,000	£2,753,000	£5,500,000
„ Syria and Palestine,	306,000	366,000	954,000
„ Egypt,	787,000	1,253,000	1,500,000
„ Malta,	297,000	413,000	515,000
„ Balaklava,	...	26,000	450,000
Total,	£3,419,000	£4,811,000	£8,919,000

It is also to be remembered that the year 1853 was a highly prosperous one in British trade.

Hardly had the Crimean War come to an end than the war with Persia broke out. The latter was a veritable pendant to the former: for the attack of Persia upon Herat had been planned, under Russian influence, for the purpose of distracting the attention and diverting the military forces of England from the Crimean war by creating a danger for our Indian Empire on the side of Affghanistan: just as the Russian Mission to Cabul and the Affghan war of 1879 were a similar pendant and projected diversion to the threatened intervention of England in the Russo-Turkish war of 1878. By what seemed bad luck at the time, while the brief Persian war was in progress, our Government became embroiled with the Chinese Empire. Then, in May 1857, there occurred the opening of the Sepoy War in India, by the mutiny at Meerut, followed by the capture of the imperial city of Delhi by the sepoys, and the atrocious massacre at Cawnpore. Then our embroilment with China proved highly fortunate: for, while Havelock and his regiment arrived promptly at trepidating Calcutta from the Persian War, our Expedition to China was intercepted as it passed through the Bay of Bengal, and brought its troops and Captain Peel's famous Naval Brigade, in the nick of time, to arrest the flood-tide of the great Mutiny, which by that time had raised nearly all northern India against the British rule.

In this way—in connection with these military expeditions, conjointly with the construction of the Indian Railways, strenuously prosecuted after the close of the Sepoy war—there commenced the great drain of specie to the East, which, of all single events, played the most important part in regulating the effects of the Gold-discoveries,—preventing a plethora of the precious metals in Europe and America, while furnishing profitable employment for the thus augmented currency of the world in the richly benefited countries of the East.

Happily, we understand this striking monetary phenomenon, and can follow the course of these events, with a clearness and fulness adequate to the momentous importance which attaches to them. There is no mystery nowadays as to the cause of the flow of gold and silver to the East, nor any uncertainty as to the extent to which such movements take place. For half a century past, the movements of the precious metals have been carefully watched and recorded. At the present day, the coming of every gold-ship to our shores—often bearing, as but a small bulk of its cargo, treasure in specie exceeding that borne by the great Spanish galleons of former times, whose course used to be watched for by hostile fleets, or hovered round by those "water sharks," the Buccaneers—is now recorded in the newspapers: even every £1000 in gold carried into the Bank of England is day by day notified in the journals. In truth, the influx and efflux of the precious metals, and the waxing and waning of the stock of gold in the great national storehouse of specie in Threadneedle Street, is watched by myriads of anxious onlookers. Our whole monetary system and its chief feature, the Bank-rate, together with the conditions and profits of our national trade and industry, are greatly dependent upon the coming or going of the yellow ore. Hence we watch and record the movements of the precious metals to and fro throughout the world. And thus, as regards the Eastern trade, we know from month to month the exact amount of specie absorbed by it; while those who give attention to the subject can tell "the reason why" for the going of almost every ounce of the silver or gold which so persistently makes its way to the East.

Although the underlying influences productive of the drain of the precious metals to the East are well known to men of science, it is their overt sign, rather than the influences themselves, which attracts the practical mind of the public. It is the Balance of Trade, ever in favour of the East, which is the striking object; as undoubtedly, also, it is the proximate and direct cause of the drains of specie. It is a remarkable fact of itself. Between the leading countries of the West, the Balance of Trade—and still more the combined Balance of Trade and Finance—is constantly changing from year to year, and there is a perpetual flux and reflux of the precious metals to settle those balances. But with India, and the East generally, the case is quite different: the current of specie flows always and only in one direction, being absorbed and engulfed in the East as in an abyss which can never be filled up. The Eastern trade is, indeed, a peculiar one. Not merely in present times, but for centuries past, the East has been what is termed an "exporting" region,—its exports of merchandise constantly exceeding its imports. In truth, it holds as exceptional a position in the world as the gold-countries do, but in the contrary manner. California and Australia constantly export the precious metals, as India constantly imports and absorbs them. In the case of the former countries, as likewise of the Silver State of Nevada, the precious metals, being their natural produce or raw productions, may be regarded as part of their merchandise, holding a place in their ordinary Balance of Trade; whereas in the case of almost all other countries, gold and silver are foreign and extraneous commodities, employed to settle the balance of ordinary merchandise.

One circumstance connected with this question is especially worthy of notice in this place. Every influx of the precious metals into a country tends to alter the monetary relation, or it may be equilibrium, between it and other regions,—perchance producing an outflow from a country which previously had been solely an absorbent of specie, and certainly increasing an outflow where it already exists. For example, in proportion as money, owing to its abundance, falls in value in Europe, it becomes profitable to export it to the countries of the East. Indeed, when gold and silver bear a higher value in India than here, the European merchant naturally enlarges his purchases of Indian goods; seeing that, at such times, he obtains not only his ordinary trade-profit but a monetary profit also,—equivalent to the (say) 5 or 10 per cent of higher purchasing power which money (in this case, specie) carries in India. Thus, when the American Mines and treasure were first discovered by Columbus and his followers, there was a twofold cause of the memorable drain of specie which then occurred from Europe to the East. There was not only the reopening of a commercial route to India, but also a peculiar inducement to prosecute it, owing to the superabundance of the stock of specie, and consequently its lesser value, in the West compared with the East. Further, the eastward current of the precious metals, thus established, served to lessen and by-and-by arrest the fall in their value in Europe and America,—thereby rendering profitable the continued working of the Mines. Similar circumstances recurred in the middle of the present century. Besides the improvement of the route through Egypt, by the Cairo railway, and the general quickening and cheapening of navigation, there was an influx of gold into Europe immensely exceeding in amount even the maximum produce of the Silver Age. The phenomenon which had followed the discovery of the New World, was repeated on a scale of such unprecedented magnitude, and also in such novel forms, as almost to make it a new event, — especially if we include the construction of new routes to the East which speedily followed. The sudden and vast expansion of the Eastern Trade during the third quarter of the present century was so great a change as really to parallel the actual Reopening of that trade in the sixteenth century, by means of the new sea-routes and other channels of which we have already spoken. Also, the effects which this Eastern Trade has produced upon the value of the precious metals, are far greater, and in every way more remarkable, than any which happened in previous times. Steam-navigation and the construction of the Suez Canal, together with the great American railway to San Francisco, have revolutionised the communications and commerce with India and China; while the flood of gold and silver from the new mines has of itself been a potent factor in promoting this trade,—and in finding work for these new and better routes, which in turn have provided a happy outlet for the high-gathering flood of the precious metals in the Western world. An action and consequential reaction which has proved of exceeding benefit to mankind.

The great outflow of specie to the East which began soon after the discovery of the new Gold-mines, and the really vast contemporaneous expansion of trade between Great Britain and her Indian Empire, are the more remarkable inasmuch as both of these things were novel to that generation. For two generations, the Eastern Trade had seriously languished. Despite the material progress of Europe and America, the commerce between the East and the West appears to have been smaller during the first half of the present century than it had been throughout the century previous. As the East is commercially an exporting region, this Trade had always been characterised, as it still is, by a balance of trade adverse to Europe, necessitating an export of specie from the Western world to settle the balance,—by payment in the precious metals for that portion of the importations from the East which is not covered or paid for by exports of Western merchandise. Consequently, the fluctuations in this trade with the East are indicated with tolerable exactness by the amount of the Trade-balances, as shown by the export from Europe of the precious metals or other such means of settling the adverse balances. By referring to these exports of the precious metals, we may judge approximately of the extent of the Eastern Trade in earlier times when no commercial statistics of the trade were kept or recorded. And in connection with the recent vast expansion of the foreign trade of India, it is a matter of interest, and also of considerable importance, to observe the striking decline of the Eastern trade, as well as the cause of that decline, during the greater part of the first half of the present century.

As previously described,[1] it was in the latter part of the sixteenth century that the then newly revived trade with the countries of the East assumed an important magnitude. In the first half of that century the new sea-routes to India, and to the remote parts of Southern Asia and the Isles of the

[1] *Vide* chap. ix.

Pacific Ocean, had been discovered: but that was nearly all. In the middle of the century (A.D. 1546) the silver-mountain of Potosi was discovered, and the supply of silver from the New World became permanently large. By the end of the century, the export of the precious metals from Europe to Asia, in connection with the new trade, had amounted in the aggregate (according to Mr Jacob) to fourteen millions sterling,—a very large sum in those days, seeing that, according to Mr Jacob, it exceeded the entire produce of the European mines throughout the same period, viz. A.D. 1492-1600. Thus, at its very outset, the Eastern trade was manifestly dependent upon a new supply of the precious metals to Europe; and but for this supply, the trade could hardly have been prosecuted at all, —a characteristic feature which the trade with the East still preserves.

In the course of the succeeding century (A.D. 1601-1700), the export of the precious metals from Europe to the East more than doubled,—amounting in the aggregate (as estimated by Mr Jacob) to thirty-three millions sterling: a sum which, it is important to remember, equalled the entire estimated stock of the precious metals existing in Europe in 1492, when Columbus sailed for the discovery of the New World. Thereafter the establishment of the Dutch and English East India Companies gave a great impetus to the Eastern trade; and during the eighteenth century the export of specie to the East amounted to fully three hundred and fifty millions sterling, or at the rate of three and a half millions a-year throughout the entire century. The magnitude of this sum will be readily apprehended when it is remembered that, according to Mr Jacob, the total stock of gold and silver coin existing throughout Christendom (that is, the amount of the precious metals after deducting what had been lost, destroyed by wear, or converted into ornaments) was 380 millions sterling in the year 1810: a fact which, allowing for the hundred millions yielded by the Mines between the years 1800 and 1810, shows that the total existing stock of metallic money in Christendom at the beginning of the present century must have been much less than the amount of the precious metals which had been exported to Asia during the single century immediately previous!

"This vast demand for the East," says Jacob, "has been the subject of calculation with several writers. M. Forbonnais supposes that between 1492 and 1724, one-half of the gold and silver which America had supplied to Europe had been absorbed in the trade with the Levant, India, and China. M. Gerboux, in his work on pecuniary legislation, has not merely advocated the same opinion, but has computed the proportion of treasure conveyed to the East at a somewhat higher rate. Baron Humboldt (from whose work on Mexico these views of the two French writers are extracted) has taken pains to estimate the proportion of the exports to Asia of the precious metals which Europe had drawn from America. His estimation—made upon an examination of the exports at the time he composed his work, viz., between the years 1803 and 1806—states the silver and gold annually brought to Europe at that time to be 43,500,000 piastres, of which he supposes there passed to Asia—

By means of the Levant trade . . .	4,000,000 dollars..
By the Cape of Good Hope . . .	17,500,000 ,,
By way of Kiachta and Tobolsk . .	4,000,000 ,,
	25,500,000 dollars.

or, at the rate we have adopted, £5,318,750 sterling. This would lead to the opinion that nearly two-thirds of the gold and silver furnished by the [American] mines were required and supplied to Asia." This large amount, adds Jacob, "seems improbable, considering the general poverty of the numerous inhabitants [of Asia], and the small quantity as compared with Europe of the several commodities which furnished subjects of exchange." Unquestionably so large an annual export of specie as nearly five and a half millions sterling "seems improbable," if judged of by the greatly inferior export of specie to the East in the immediately subsequent period; yet we see little force in Mr Jacob's adverse considerations as opposed to the actual investigations of so eminent and careful an authority as Humboldt. Mr Jacob himself, besides stating that the use of tea in Europe had increased a hundredfold during last century, points out that the circumstances of the time were conducive to a comparatively large export of specie in the Eastern trade. "In 1803 and 1806," he says, while "the amount of gold and silver furnished by America had nearly reached its highest point, the demand for goods from India had not lessened, and the exports to India of British productions were far less than at present," viz., in 1830. Indeed the British manufactures (particularly of cotton goods), with which we chiefly pay for our imports from the East, were at that time in their infancy. Under all these circumstances—considering, too, that the annual export of the precious metals to Asia is estimated to have averaged so much as three and a half millions sterling throughout last century—we see no adequate ground for rejecting Humboldt's calculation that at the time when he wrote (1803-6) the export of gold and silver amounted to fully five and a quarter millions sterling per annum.[1]

[1] In connection with this question, it is not unimportant to remember that, previous to the time at which Humboldt wrote, (1) the entire gold-money and the greater part of the silver-money of Great Britain had been exported in subsidies and war-expenditure, thereby augmenting the stock of metallic money on the Continent; (2) owing to the Bank Suspension Act, the usual demand for the precious metals in this country was greatly diminished; and (3) the large issues of inconvertible paper-currency by Austria and some other States proportionately lessened the requirement for metallic money on the Continent. Further, when the currency of Europe was thus augmented, while the yield of the American mines was at its maximum, the Peace of Amiens brought a temporary cessation of the War, the monetary requirements of which had occasioned this augmentation of the currency; and it was during this period of peace that Humboldt made his investigations. It is difficult to estimate with any confidence the effects of such a state of matters upon the value of the precious metals: but the general effect must have been to lower the value of money in Europe,—thereby tending to promote an export of specie to the East.

Next there occurred the critical period of which we have written in a previous chapter—when the failure of the American supply of the precious metals greatly affected the trade with the East, and indeed the monetary and commercial conditions of the world at large. As already shown, the immediate result of the revolt of the Spanish colonies in the New World was to reduce by one-half the production of the precious metals,—which fell from upwards of ten millions sterling in 1810 to an average of barely five millions during the next twenty years. This disastrous change was strikingly reflected in the export of specie to the East, which, according to Mr Jacob, declined from three and a half millions sterling, which it had averaged from 1700 down to 1810, to only two millions a-year from 1810 to 1830,—not one-half what it had been, according to Humboldt, in the opening years of the century.

For the ensuing period we have no statistics or reliable computation of the export of the precious metals to the East generally; we must, therefore, confine our statement to India, which has always been by far the chief absorbent of gold and silver from the Western world. Between 1834 and 1852, we find from the statistics furnished by Colonel Hyde, late Master of the Calcutta Mint, that in

---

This circumstance, and the others peculiar to that time mentioned above, explain, and seem fully to corroborate, the largeness of the export of specie to the East as stated by Humboldt; but they also tend to show that the export in those years (immediately prior to the stoppage of the American mines, in 1810) was exceptionally large.

India the surplus of the imports of silver over the exports amounted to twenty-nine millions sterling,—which gives an annual average of one and one-third million of silver absorbed by India. During that period there appears a new element in the case—namely, the Home Bills, or Drafts drawn by our Government upon the Indian Government, representing payments due from the Indian Executive to this country. Doubtless such payments had always been in existence to some extent, under the East India Company, although prior to this time we have no official record of them. These home bills, during the period in question (1834-52), averaged one million and three-quarters a-year. Accordingly, the exports of silver to India, together with these home bills equivalent to specie, averaged during this period three and a half millions annually,—just equal to the average export of specie throughout the hundred and ten years ending with 1810. Doubtless there was some export of gold to India during the twenty years ending with 1852, of which we find no official record. But, viewing the whole case, it seems evident that, contemporaneously with the falling-off in the world's supply of the precious metals, there was a stagnation in the trade with the East,—which, we repeat, cannot be carried on without a commensurate supply of specie.

We now come to the concluding and by far the most remarkable and important epoch of the trade with the East, during which that trade has been the most powerful factor in determining the value of the precious metals and of money generally in the Western world. Soon after 1852 this memorable expansion of our Indian Trade set in. The vast supply of new gold from California and Australia created an abundance of metallic money or international currency; and as gold could largely take the place of silver in the currencies of the Western world, a large quantity of the latter metal became available for carrying on an increase of trade with India and the other silver-using countries of the East. The exports of silver to the East from Great Britain and the Mediterranean rose from 1¾ millions sterling in 1851 to upwards of twenty millions in 1857. The silver was obtained almost entirely from the currency of France,—the vacuum being filled by the inflow of the new gold; of which, it is reckoned, France had absorbed £100,000,000 during the eight years ending with 1859.[1] Thus supported, in 1855-6,

---

[1] Previous to 1852 there used to be a surplus of imports of silver into France,—amounting during the six years ending with 1851 to £28,090,102, or at the average rate of £4,680,000 a-year. During the subsequent six years the exports of silver exceeded the imports as follows:—

1852,	£108,669
1853,	4,675,418
1854,	6,547,751
1855,	7,886,385
1856,	11,342,932
1857,	14,500,835
Total,	£45,061,990

This gives an average net export of 7½ millions sterling a-year,—instead of, as formerly, a net import of 4¾ millions. Thus, merely to maintain the old position, the imports of *gold* into France required to compensate this decrease in the supply of silver, needed to show a surplus of fully £12,000,000 a-year.

an immense expenditure of British capital was begun in India for the construction of railways. Mr R. W. Crawford stated in 1876 that the total expenditure for this purpose then amounted to ninety-four millions sterling, of which sum fifty-four millions were expended in India; and the total capital invested in the Indian railways down to the end of last year considerably exceeded a hundred and thirty millions sterling.[1] And just as the first and main portion of this expenditure was coming to a close in 1862, the Cotton Famine commenced, owing to the Civil War in the United States, whereby our cotton-merchants were compelled to have recourse to India for a supply of the raw material of our great textile industry. Under these combined influences a vast amount of money was invested in India, which operated like a fertilising flood,—increasing employment, production, and exports, and enabling the population of India to increase their imports and consumption of foreign commodities. And thus the Foreign Trade of India in merchandise, including both exports and imports, which amounted to thirty-seven millions sterling in the official year 1855-6, rose steadily to ninety-five millions in the year 1865-6,—nearly trebling during those ten years, and exhibiting the most

---

[1] According to official returns, the total capital embarked in railways in India at the close of 1880 was upwards of £129,000,000. The net receipts were £4, 11s. per cent upon the capital, as compared with £4, 7s. in 1879. The guaranteed lines, including the East India Railway, yielded 5·43 and the State lines 2 per cent. The gross receipts derived from the railways of all kinds amounted to £12,099,593, while the gross expenses were £6,192,171.

rapid increase of trade that has been witnessed in any country of the world.

Now, let us see the effect of this remarkable expansion of the India trade, together with the investments of British capital in that country, in creating an increased requirement for the precious metals, which were contemporaneously being poured into the world in unprecedented abundance. There were two separate factors in creating this increased requirement for specie—namely, the Trade balance (the excess of exports of merchandise from India over the imports of merchandise into that country) and the Financial balance. The former was the larger and permanent factor in the case, and we shall deal with it first. Taking the eleven years ending with March 1865, when the Cotton Famine terminated, we find from Mr Waterfield's statistics that the Trade-balance accumulated in favour of India during that period amounted to 207 millions sterling, or at the rate of nineteen millions a-year. The entire production of the precious metals during the same eleven years, according to Sir H. Hay, was 366 millions sterling; of which sum the produce of the new mines (*i.e.*, the supply of gold and silver in excess of what was produced in 1848) amounted to about 190 millions. Accordingly, had it been necessary to pay the whole of the Trade-balance to India in specie, the entire produce of the new mines, both gold and silver, during these eleven years would have proved inadequate, to the extent of seventeen millions sterling. A more remarkable fact in the history of commerce could hardly be imagined. The entire produce of the Californian and Australian mines, when at their best, was exceeded by the contemporaneous commercial debt incurred between merely two countries of the globe—viz., by Great Britain to India!

Happily, as it then proved, there was another means available for settling this debt to India than by sending thither the entire produce of the new Gold-mines, and severely trenching upon the metallic currency of the Western hemisphere. This was the Financial balance: which during the same period embraced two conflicting elements, but which on the whole was largely in favour of Great Britain. Against India, there was the annual amount which the Indian Government had to pay our Government for the "home charges;" in favour of India, there were the annual instalments of British capital, paid through our Government, for the construction of railways in India. In the earlier half of the period in question (1855-60), the railway-payments due from this country appear to have considerably exceeded the amount of the "home charges:" certainly during these five years India received in specie the whole amount of the Trade-balance due to her, and twenty-six millions more,—the Trade-balance during those five years being forty-four and a half millions, while the actual amount of specie received by India was seventy and three-quarter millions. In the subsequent years, however, the "home charges" due from India evidently exceeded the railway-payments from this country; and in striking the Financial balance there has to be added to the "home charges" the private remittances of money made by Englishmen in India to their friends and families in this country, the amount of which cannot be accurately determined. Judging by the result, the aggregate Financial balance during this period (the eleven years ending with 1865) appears to have been against India to the extent of fully thirty millions; and thus, although the aggregate Trade-balances during the same years amounted, as already stated, to 207 millions sterling, the actual amount of specie received by India was 176 millions.

Now, during the same period (1855-65) the total produce of all the mines, both old and new, according to Sir H. Hay, was 366 millions sterling (269 of gold, and 97 of silver): deducting the amount which the old mines would have contemporaneously yielded had their produce remained as it was in 1848, viz., 176 millions, we get, as already said, 190 millions as the produce of the new mines—the addition made to the supply as it stood in 1848. Accordingly, the amount of the precious metals contemporaneously absorbed by the Indian trade (viz., 176 millions) was so great, that of all this stock of *new* gold and silver only fourteen millions, or eight per cent, were left available for the use of the rest of the world! A more remarkable fact can hardly be exhibited; and it sufficiently explains why the confident prediction and general expectation of a vast fall in the value of the precious metals was not realised.

Secondly, let us take the whole period for which we have officially published statistics—viz., from 1855 to 1875. During these twenty-one years, the aggregate exports of merchandise from India amounted to £933,313,000, and the imports of merchandise were £544,907,000 — giving a Trade-balance in favour of India of 388½ millions sterling. How was this enormous commercial debt discharged? During the latter years of this period, owing to the gradual cessation of the railway-payments due from this country, and also from the increase of the home charges due by India, the Financial balance turned heavily against our Eastern Empire; so that the "Council drafts," or bills drawn by the Home Government upon the Indian Government (equivalent to specie, and available for settling the Trade-balance with India) amounted in the aggregate to 113 millions. Deducting this sum from the Trade-balance, there remains 275½ millions still uncovered; but the total amount of specie received by India during these twenty-one years was 250¼ millions,— leaving 25 millions unaccounted for officially, but which doubtless was settled by bills upon India drawn upon remittances from private parties in India to others in this country.

Let us now see what must have been the influence of this greatly expanded trade with India, between 1855-75, upon the value of the precious metals. The total produce of the gold and silver mines during these twenty-one years, according to Sir Hector Hay, was 696 millions sterling: deducting the amount of the "old supply" for a similar number of years (about 336 millions), there remains 360 millions as the additional supply, or produce of the *new* mines,—of which amount, as above stated, 250 millions were contemporaneously exported to India.[1] Thus it appears that during this period the Indian trade absorbed, or caused an actual export of, 70 per cent of the entire *new* supply of the precious metals; leaving only about 30 per cent, little more than a hundred millions (or less than five millions a-year), of this new supply (the produce of the new gold-discoveries) for general use;—that is, to carry on the great expansion of commerce and the other augmented requirements for specie throughout the rest of the world.

The result of these statistics and simple calculations is so extraordinary—as showing what a small portion of the New Supply of gold and silver (*i.e.*, what a comparatively small amount of the precious metals in excess of the annual supply in 1848) remained in Europe and America to promote Trade and affect the value of Money—that I have purposely understated one of the bases of the calculation, viz., the annual amount of gold and silver produced in 1848; thereby somewhat overstating the New

[1] The old reputation of India as "the sink of the precious metals" appears from an official paper recently published in Calcutta to be well maintained. It seems that the net imports of the precious metals during the last twenty-five years—that is, the amount after deducting the quantities exported—has reached the enormous sum of 285½ millions sterling. Last year the registered imports of gold were nearly 80 per cent greater than in the previous year, and the largest of any year since 1870-1.

Supply, and consequently the amount of it which remained in Europe and America. In the two preceding paragraphs, I have reckoned the annual production of gold and silver in 1848 (immediately prior to the new Gold-discoveries) at only sixteen millions sterling; whereas M. Chevalier estimates it at almost nineteen millions. In this estimate M. Chevalier includes three millions of gold and one million of silver as yielded by the Asiatic Archipelago, but of which no mention is made by any other authority on the subject. If this amount be entirely rejected, M. Chevalier's estimate would be reduced to 7·11 millions of gold, and 7·72 millions of silver, —or not quite fifteen millions of the precious metals, as the annual production at the beginning of the year 1848. In the estimate which I employ in the two preceding paragraphs, I accept one million (out of the four): making a total of sixteen millions as the annual production in 1848. But, obviously, the larger the estimate made of the old supply, the less in subsequent years becomes the amount attributable to the New Supply which began in 1849. Accordingly, had I taken the larger amount (19 millions) as the produce of the mines in 1848, it follows that in the eleven years 1855-65, instead of fourteen millions of the New Supply being left in Europe and America, the export of specie to India would have absorbed and withdrawn the *whole* of the New Supply, and fifteen millions more,—part of the produce of the old mines. And on the entire period, 1855-75, the effect of employing M. Chevalier's estimate of nineteen millions (in place of the estimate which I here employ, of 16 millions) as the annual produce of gold and silver in 1848, or "the Old Supply," would be to reduce the portion of the New Supply remaining in Europe and America at the end of 1875 from a hundred millions sterling to only seventy millions. Moreover, according to one authority at least, the produce of the old mines considerably increased during the fifteen years subsequent to 1848: the effect being to reduce that portion of the total supply of gold and silver which is attributable to the new discoveries which began in 1848.[1]

Of the two periods of Indian trade thus passed in review, the former and shorter one (1855-65) is by far the more specially deserving of notice as regards the effect which this Eastern trade exerted upon the value of the precious metals, and of money generally,

[1] PRODUCTION OF GOLD AND SILVER (Annual Averages).

Periods of Years.	Gold.			Silver.
	Old Sources.	New Sources.	Total.	All Sources.
	Million £.	Million £.	Million £.	Million £.
1849-51 (3)	13·5	10·3	23·9	15·5
1852-56 (5)	14·0	24·7	38·7	16·1
1857-59 (3)	14·6	21·9	37·5	17·1
1860-63 (3)	15·3	18·3	33·5	18·2

"*Note.*—The total production shown by these figures in the fifteen years, 1849-63, is of Gold from *old* sources, 215 millions; from *new* sources, 297 millions: Silver from *all* sources, 248 millions. The production of silver is at present 20 per cent larger than in 1849-51; but in the case of gold, the present annual production from all sources is 13 per cent less than in the five years 1852-56."—*Economist's* "Commercial and Financial History of 1864."

throughout the world. It is so for several reasons. In the first place, it was peculiarly the *critical period*—the time during which the new supply of gold would, *per se*, or if unchecked by other circumstances, have produced its maximum effect upon the value of money. In truth, the critical period was passed as soon as the great expansion of the Eastern trade set in. During the four or five previous years gold had been pouring into the markets of the world in unprecedented abundance. Previous to the discovery of the Californian gold-fields—we may say in 1848, for the new mines had hardly begun to be worked in that year—the total production of gold and silver somewhat exceeded sixteen millions sterling, of which rather more than one-half was gold. But in 1849 the gold-supply was increased to about twenty millions by the Californian gold-fields; and in 1851, when the Australian gold-beds began to be worked, the total gold-supply rose to no less than thirty-two millions. In other words, the produce of the *new* gold-mines amounted to twenty-four millions, or three times as much as the yield of the old mines had been; and the total gold-supply became quadrupled since 1848. It is important to bear in mind that the yield of the new mines, both in California and Australia, was largest at the first, or as soon as the tide of immigration allowed of the full working of the gold-fields. At that time it was the "placers" or surface-deposits in the beds of rivers, &c., which were worked, such operations needing only the rudest appliances (the rocker or cradle), which any one could use; and from this cause, together with the wide extent of these purely surface deposits, a much larger population of gold-finders could get employment than was the case afterwards, when those surface-deposits were exhausted, and when skilful appliances and capital had to come into the field.

Owing to these causes—the easier finding of the gold and the larger number of the workers—during these first years the yield of the precious ore was larger than at any subsequent time. Further, it is obvious that, *cæteris paribus*, the first addition to the world's stock of gold must produce a greater effect upon the value of money than any similar addition afterwards: because it will bear a larger ratio to the existing stock of gold. Say that the existing stock is 400 millions, and that the annual supply be suddenly increased to the amount of twenty millions; the first twenty millions being added to the 400 millions will produce a greater effect than the second twenty millions, which will be added to 420 millions; and the third twenty millions, being added to 440 millions, will produce still less effect, and so on. Moreover, as already said, the supply of gold was largest at the first, and thereafter declined. From both of these causes, therefore, it was in the early years of the gold-discoveries that the new supply would naturally produce its maximum effect. Further, it takes some time before employment can be found for a new supply of the precious metals—before new channels of trade can be opened, and before industry generally can avail itself of its new opportunities: which is a farther reason why the new mines were likely to produce their maximum effect upon prices at the outset.

In the years 1852-4, gold was accumulating in the Western world at a prodigious rate; and the confident forebodings of a vast fall in the value of money, expressed so forcibly by M. Chevalier so late as in 1858, appeared only reasonable. Yet the all-important fact was forgotten, that an increased supply of money, by facilitating trade, tends to create an increased requirement, or new fields of employment, for it. And how much and how variously the trade of the world increased during the subsequent period need not be said. But, as we have shown, it was the vast expansion of the Trade with the East which played the chief part in creating the new requirement for specie, and to an extent which throws all the other such causes into the shade. In truth, but for the *previous* accumulation of specie in the Western world (viz., in the years 1850-4), it seems impossible that so vast a drain of specie as that which flowed to the East in the years immediately subsequent to 1854 could have been spared,—the fact being, as already shown, that during the eleven subsequent years the Indian trade required, and India actually received (by the lowest possible estimate), no less than ninety-two per cent of the contemporaneous produce of the *new* mines,—leaving only fourteen millions of their produce for the increased wants of the world at large. No wonder, then, that the expected revolution and vast fall in the value of gold did not occur.

Although the year 1853 was the most critical one, there was a second period when the leading nations of the world were within danger from a plethora of the precious metals. This secondary crisis (so to call it) came in 1864 or thereabouts, during the Civil War in the United States; when the adoption of a system of inconvertible paper-money in that country not only permitted the entire annual yield of the Californian mines to pass to Europe, as the best or only market for it, but also let loose almost the whole specie previously constituting the currency of the warring Republic. Both the North and the South, but especially the Confederate Government, drew a large portion of the war-material from Europe; while the establishment by both Governments of an inconvertible State paper-currency left no inducement for the retention of the gold and silver money, either in the banks or in circulation. The monetary effect was the same as if a surpassingly rich mine had suddenly been opened, and its produce sent to Europe. Also, this transient plethora of money was accompanied by a considerable scarcity of commodities,—notably, of cotton and the raw material of textile manufacture. In this way, Prices were pushed upward by both of the chief operating forces: and, speaking as much from remembered observation as from the tables of Prices, we believe that Prices ranged higher in 1864-5 than at any other time. As frequently happens, too, the War gave a great impulse to certain branches of commerce and manufacture,— notably, the growth of cotton in Egypt, India, and some other countries, to compensate the temporary stoppage of the American supply. Naturally, the rise in the price of cotton occasioned a corresponding rise in the price of the other textile materials. And thus, besides the temporary plethora of gold in Europe, the rise of prices was promoted by a scarcity of some of the leading articles of commerce.

But here again the trade with the East quickly carried off the extra stock of specie thus imported into Europe. After a brief period of redundant cotton-supply, occasioned by the cotton-growing Southern States hurrying every bale to Europe before the war-ships of the North could establish a blockade of their coasts, there ensued a severe period of dearth of this commodity in Europe,—the memorable Cotton Famine, which paralysed the greatest textile industry of the United Kingdom. In this extremity, our cotton-merchants had recourse to new sources of supply, and chiefly to Egypt and India. Every cotton-growing region of the East was energetically applied to for a supply of the much-needed material,—even the most inferior kinds being eagerly purchased for the manufacturers of Europe, and especially of our own country. And so, at the very time when the expenditure of British capital upon the Indian Railways began to decline, the imports of cotton from the East occasioned a continued export of the precious metals, which absorbed the extra supply of specie to Europe arising from the temporary abandonment of a metallic currency in the United States.

Nevertheless, although this export of specie occasioned by the Cotton Famine is well deserving of mention and attention, we repeat that the second of the two periods into which we have divided the course of the Eastern trade—namely, 1865-75—is of much inferior importance to the first, viz., 1855-64. Indeed the greater part of the export of specie in connection with the Cotton Famine belongs to the former of these periods. But, apart from this, and although the Indian trade absorbed a much less percentage of the produce of the Mines in the latter period than in the former, it is to be remembered that this annual produce no longer, of itself, could exert the same influence upon the value of money, as at first. The existing stock of the precious metals had become so very much larger than it was in 1848, that the annual supply, if the conditions and requirements of Trade remained the same, would necessarily, in 1875, produce a much smaller effect upon the value of the precious metals than an equal addition to the existing stock would have done at the beginning of the Gold-discoveries. Moreover, as regards gold, the annual supply had by this time become much diminished: in 1875 it stood at about one-third, or ten millions sterling, below the average maximum yield of the mines—viz., when at their best, in the years 1851-7. On the other hand, the annual supply of silver had largely increased, owing to the discovery of the Nevada mines: so much so that the supply of gold and silver, taken together, in the year 1875 still remained about equal to the highest point ever reached.

The effect of the Eastern Trade upon the value of the precious metals has hitherto attracted little attention from writers on this subject; yet, without a perception and appreciation of the facts which we have now set forth, the events connected with the value of money during the last quarter of a century would be wholly inexplicable.[1] It has been the drain of the precious metals to the East, to meet the requirements of Indian trade and investments, which alone has falsified the confident predictions of all the highest authorities as to a great fall in the value of money, and especially of gold. It is the chief typical event of the Golden Age, and gives the key to the understanding of the unexpected

---

[1] In my *Economy of Capital*, published at the beginning of 1864, I wrote as follows:—" In present circumstances, this drain of bullion is an advantage. The increase of trade with the East, while adding to our wealth, is relieving Europe of a portion of the precious metals of which we have no need, and which it is advantageous to get rid of in this manner. Had all this bullion remained in Europe, the value of gold would have fallen greatly. The prosperity of the world (as affected by the Gold-discoveries) depends upon a continuance of this drain of bullion to the East. As gold flows into Europe, silver flows out; and thus our increased commerce with the East proves to us a double blessing,—at once augmenting employment, and averting any great change in the value of money. It is a waste-pipe by which nothing is wasted. It is a channel by which we not only rid ourselves of a surplus of the precious metals, but turn them to most profitable account."
—See pp. 41-51.

monetary phenomena of this memorable epoch. By its magnitude it stands apart from the numerous contemporaneous expansions of trade: rising above such other events as the Pyramids at Cairo tower above the other grand edifices of the land of the Nile. Accordingly I have dealt with it separately, before considering, in next chapter, the other commercial events and general expansion of trade and production which have characterised the Golden Age, and which have influenced in so happy a manner the value of the vastly augmented precious metals.

CHAPTER XX.

TOTAL AMOUNT OF THE NEW GOLD AND SILVER.
ITS INFLUENCE UPON THE WORLD AT LARGE.

One of the most striking points of difference between the new Golden Age and the prior Silver Age is the rapidity or early vastness of the recent gold-supplies and their quick decline, compared with the slow growth of the stock of the precious metals, both gold and silver, in the sixteenth century, and the gradual and steady increase of the annual supply throughout three hundred years. Another and equally important point, especially relative to the effects of the new supplies of the precious metals upon the value of Money, is the great difference in the existing stock of gold and silver in 1492 and in 1848,—the stock of coin at the latter epoch, according to the accepted estimate, being more than ten times larger than the existing stock at the close of the fifteenth century. Nevertheless, this latter point of difference is very much, indeed incalculably smaller than is represented by the figures (or actual amount of the existing stock at the two periods).

in consequence of the immense expansion in the requirements for money, and for the precious metals in all forms, which had occurred during the three centuries and a half subsequent to the discovery of America. A new world had arisen. Europe, which at the birth of Columbus was but emerging from its Dark Ages, had in 1848 become the heart of the world alike in civilisation and in trade; while America had become largely peopled by the European race, and entirely occupied by European Governments and institutions, from Hudson's Bay to the frontiers of Patagonia. The world at large had become full of commerce and of monetary wants,—a world in which every country longed for more specie, and into which the New Gold found profitable employment and was rapidly absorbed, without redundancy or stagnation: even like as a river descending into the plains, under agricultural engineering, becomes diffused and wellnigh lost to sight in a hundred tiny irrigating channels,—the only sign of its presence being the rich verdure which hides the fertilising waters from whence it springs.

Before following to its uses this bright stream of the precious metals—this Nile or Mississippi of gold and silver,—let us first behold the magnitude of the glittering flood; and then examine what was its influence upon the world, especially in its operations upon Money and Trade. Happily for mankind, the golden stream found ample room and outlet for its waters in the rapidly expanding channels of the world's commerce,—channels which became widened and deepened by its own rushing flow.

The present generation of mankind are not likely to underrate, or form too low a conception of, the magnificent produce of the Californian and Australian Mines,—the discovery of which has been the most notable and widely beneficial event of our lifetime. In the International Exhibitions, which appear to have become an established periodical institution, the public is constantly reminded of the vastness of the new supplies of gold and silver. In our Great Exhibition of 1862, in the Australian department, a gilded obelisk towered aloft, representing in its dimensions the quantity of gold which had been yielded by the Australian mines, at that time amounting to about 120 millions sterling. In the Paris Exhibition of 1878, the colony of Victoria showed in similar fashion the produce of two of its greatest mines: one glittering column representing the gold from the Clunes Mine—352,584 ounces, or about £1,370,000; while another gilded column represents the produce of the Long Tunnel Mining Company's operations — 221,262 ounces, or about £860,000. Yet what are these to the Great Comstoke Lode in Nevada, where gold and silver are found together in nearly equal proportions, and of which £6,000,000, or more, is merely the produce of a single year? As stated by the Director of the United States Mint in 1878, "the yield of bullion from the two mines which embrace the great ore-chimney discovered in 1874 in the Comstoke Lode has amounted, up to 31st October 1877, to 78,852,918 dollars," or about £15,770,000; and, he added, "these mines are now producing at the rate of three million dollars per month," or upwards of seven millions sterling a-year.

Summarising the best authorities, let us now see what has been the course of the supply of the precious metals in the world, or rather in Christendom, during the last four centuries—the statements for the period prior to 1800 being more or less conjectural. As already mentioned, at the time of the discovery of the New World (1492), it is computed, but only as the merest conjecture, that the total stock of the precious metals in Christendom was about forty millions sterling, one-third being gold and two-thirds silver. From 1492 down to 1803 Humboldt computed that 1470 millions sterling were added to the stock of the precious metals,—of which amount 1190 millions were silver, and 280 millions were gold; and in the first years of the present century, down to 1810, he stated the annual supply of the precious metals at £10,367,000,—of which sum £7,732,000 were silver, and £2,634,000 were gold. From 1810 to 1829—a period during which anarchy and revolution were at their height in the great silver-producing countries of South America and Mexico—the supply of the precious metals fell to only one-half of its previous amount; and Mr Jacob computed that the average annual supply during that period was—silver, £3,639,000; gold, £1,598,000;—total, £5,237,000. Thus the supply of silver, which at the beginning of the century, and apparently for several generations previous, had been as 3 to 1 compared to gold, between 1810 and 1830 had fallen to as 2¼ to 1. Thereafter the supply of gold continued to rise rapidly. In 1819 Russia began to produce gold; and during the next ten years (1819-28) the gold obtained from the Ural Mountains amounted to £3,500,000. In 1829 gold began to be found also in Siberia; and during the next eighteen years (1829-46) the total yield of the Russian gold-mines amounted to about £26,000,000 sterling,—a comparatively small, but most welcome, addition to the previously diminished supply of the precious metals.

This brings us to 1847, the year previous to the discovery of the Californian mines. Owing to the gradual increase in the produce of the Russian gold-mines, the supply of the precious metals at the beginning of 1848, according to M. Chevalier, stood at £10,110,000 of gold, and £8,720,000 of silver. Making a deduction from the doubtful portion of the estimate (namely, from the four millions sterling of gold and silver from the Asiatic Archipelago), the annual produce of the mines immediately prior to 1848 may be stated at seventeen millions sterling,—of which rather more than one-half was gold. Thus the supply of the precious metals, which was about 10½ millions sterling at the beginning of the century, and which fell to 5¼ millions between 1810 and 1830, had thereafter gradually increased until it amounted to seventeen millions in 1847, or fully one-half larger than in 1800. At the same time, while the supply of silver had remained stationary, the supply of gold had, according to the lowest estimate, trebled since the beginning of the century. And thus, dethroning silver, Gold at length rose into the supremacy of supply.

In truth, little as the fact was regarded, there was a remarkable heralding of the Golden Age during the previous score of years. Although those years were a period of comparative scarcity, the annual supply of the precious metals actually trebled in amount between 1829 and 1848. But this was an advance upon what had been the lowest point of the supply: and it was not enough, considering the general growth of Trade and of monetary requirements; and under the predominant sentiment of monetary scarcity, even the singularly rapid augmentation of the supply of the precious metals went almost unnoticed, save the momentary large increase of gold in the Bank of England in 1844. So much for the mighty influence of Demand, which then sufficed to obscure from men's minds the rapid, yet quite inadequate, growth of the supply. But then, at length, came the grand gold-burst, striking and welcome as a sunrise,—a sudden and astoundingly abundant outpour of the precious metal from the bosom of Earth, and in countries the most remote from the great centres of the civilised world.

Coming to this new period, inaugurated by the discovery of the Californian gold-mines in 1848, followed in 1851 by the Australian gold-discoveries, and ultimately by the discovery of the marvellously rich silver-mines in Nevada in 1859, the following summary, based upon the statistics of Sir Hector Hay, will show how vast has been the addition thus made to the world's stock of the precious metals, as well as the remarkable change and vicissitudes in the relative supply of gold and silver :—

Average Annual Produce of the Mines.

	Gold.	Silver.	Total annual production.
	£	£	£
1849-51.	14,000,000	8,000,000	22,000,000
1852-60,	28,000,000	8,130,000	36,130,000
1861-71,	22,300,000	10,840,000	33,140,000
1872-75,	19,200,000	14,400,000	33,600,000
Total produce, 1849-75,	£616,000,000	£264,000,000	£880,000,000

Reckoning the produce of the mines during the subsequent five years at 160 millions, we get a total production of gold and silver down to the end of 1880 amounting to considerably upwards of 1000 millions sterling, poured into the world since 1848,—at the rate of 32½ millions a-year, or double the annual supply as it existed immediately prior to the discovery of the Californian gold-fields. Excluding silver, the supply of which has only recently increased, the total production of gold during the thirty-two years ending with 1880 has amounted to about 710 millions, or one-sixth more than the entire production of gold during the three centuries and a half ending with 1848; while, taking gold and silver together, the production of the precious metals since 1848, down to the end of 1880, has amounted to about three-fifths of the entire production of gold and silver from the discovery of America to the middle of the present century. In other words, the annual average production of gold and silver since 1848 has been fully sixfold as great as during the previous three hundred and fifty years.

The combined suddenness and magnitude of the new supply of precious metal rendered the change peculiarly startling and impressive. During the fifteen years beginning with 1852, the New Gold exceeded in amount the entire production of that metal, alike in the New World and the Old, throughout three full centuries after the discovery of America. And still the golden flood continued to pour forth in undiminished abundance from California and Australia,—ceaselessly, and almost as costlessly, as the springs of mineral oil at Petrolea well up from their reservoirs in the subterranean rocks of Pennsylvania. Just as the natural forests of that still wood-named region, in pre-human ages of the Earth, had by vast and slow-operating physical changes, become sunk and embedded, and under mighty pressure distilled off their precious hydro-carbon fluid, forming subterranean lakelets of condensed Light; so, in less remote times, had the auriferous quartz-mountains of California and Australia been disintegrated by physical changes and convulsions, spreading the quartz in alluvial beds or strata over the adjacent plains

—a vast treasure-chamber of Nature, at length discovered by Man, who was now busily gathering the seemingly inexhaustible gold which lay ready to his hand. It seemed like one of those Revolutions of Nature, which, whether good or evil, it is impossible to control or obstruct.

No wonder that many men stood mentally aghast, and, like Chevalier and Cobden, began to calculate the magnitude of the change and its natural or inevitable effects. Two hundred millions of gold and silver added to the world's stock of the precious metals during the century and a half subsequent to the first voyage of Columbus, had reduced Money to below one-third of its former value or purchasing power: and since that date (about 1640 A.D.) the continued influx of gold and silver had kept Money throughout the world at this reduced value.[1] If, then — men reasoned — the addition of less than 1800 millions sterling in gold and silver, spread over 350 years, caused a fall of nearly three-fourths in the value of money, what would be the effect of 400 millions poured into the market within a dozen years? In such questions, of course, Time is everything. Given time (with consequent increase of population, trade, and human wants generally), and the largest conceivable addition to the stock of gold and silver might be regarded without apprehension.

---

[1] M. Chevalier says that the hectolitre of wheat, which in the period prior to 1492 cost at Paris from half-a-crown to 2s. 9d., during the first half of the present century cost about 16s. 8d., or fully six times as much in Money-price.

But an addition of the present kind, both vast and sudden, and therefore acting at once upon the world as it stood, was a very different affair. The question seemingly took the form of a sum in proportion, although the quotient must remain a query. If the addition of so many millions, throughout 350 years, reduced and thereafter kept Money at little more than one-fourth of its former value, what must be the effect of one-fourth of that sum if added within one-thirtieth part of the same time?

And when was the new supply to stop? When was there a probability of the new gold-fields becoming exhausted? M. Chevalier, an accomplished engineer as well as political economist, maintained that the new gold-fields were likely to remain as productive as at first for several generations. A lesser area than that of the county of Middlesex (a mere spot compared with the extent of California) was sufficient, he said, to maintain the gold-production of these countries at its present amount for a century. Farther, as he remarked, "the working of the Mines is an ever-improving industry; and the same law of progress applies to the metallurgic processes for separating the precious metals from the rude ore which is extracted from the bowels of the earth." Thus, in truth, even were the soil of the new gold-countries to become less auriferous, an equal production might continue owing to improvements in the mining processes. Nor did M. Chevalier—who expressed, and partly led, the prevalent opinion of that time, and who also failed to recognise the more or less compensating benefits from the monetary revolution which then seemed impending—find any consolation in the belief that the growth of trade and population, and the wider use of metallic money throughout the world, would go far to mitigate the coming plethora of money. After enumerating, and taking what he regarded as a highly exaggerated estimate of such new outlets for industry and for the absorption of the New Gold, even including the substitution of gold for silver in countries like France, he came to the conclusion that all of these outlets put together would prove quite inadequate to neutralise the effect of the new mines. " In no direction," he said, " can new outlets be seen sufficiently large to absorb the extraordinary production of gold which we are now witnessing, in such a manner as to prevent a fall in its value." Recognising a world-wide fact, yet without observing the real cause of it (namely, as we have pointed out, that gold and silver acquire a new, and their highest possible, value by being minted into Money), M. Chevalier said :—" There is but one way of disposing of these masses of gold—to wit, by coining them, and forcing them into the current of circulation in countries which are already sufficiently provided with a gold-currency. This current will absorb them,—for it is, so to speak, insatiable ; it receives and carries off all that is thrown into it : but the process of absorption and assimilation takes place only on this one condition, that gold diminishes in value ; so that, for example, in those transactions where heretofore ten pieces of gold have sufficed, eleven, twelve, fifteen, or even more, will henceforth be required."

In truth, upon these grounds — namely, if the new gold-fields were to remain as productive as at first for several generations, and since the gold would be added to the circulating medium of the world,—the only limit to the fall in the value of money would be when gold came to possess so little value that gold-mining would cease to be profitable, or otherwise attractive to human enterprise and labour. But what an abyss of possible depreciation here opened to view! Taking California and Australia together, said M. Chevalier, the ordinary earnings of the miner amount to sixteen shillings a-day; and yet, at the present hour, men will labour at gold-finding (witness the gold-washers of the Rhine) even though they only make fifteen or twenty pence a-day! To how low a point, then, must the productiveness of the mines fall before they cease to be worked! But even compare the earnings of the miners at the new gold-fields (viz., 16s. a-day) with the highest rate of wages which generally prevails in temperate climates and among the most prosperous nations of Europe—namely, five francs, or 4s. 2d. How wide a margin is still left! "It follows," said M. Chevalier, "that the value of gold might fall till nineteen francs (16s.) should correspond only to the amount of wellbeing which can at present be procured for five francs (4s. 2d.) By this calculation, the fall in the value of money would in the end amount to three-fourths;—in other words, to procure the same amount of subsistence it would be requisite (other things being equal) to give four times as much gold as at present. According to this, we are very far from the end of the crisis."

The prospect, no doubt, was a very formidable one. The world's money, after having lost nearly three-fourths of its previous value between 1540 and 1640 A.D., seemed now, as in the estimates of M. Chevalier, about to lose three-fourths of its remaining value within a still briefer period. Thus (in round numbers) the £100 of the fifteenth century became equivalent to less than £30 in the seventeenth century,—whereby, by a sudden revulsion, the value of money was perhaps restored to about what it had been in the Roman empire at the beginning of the Christian era.[1] And now, owing to another great discovery of the precious metals, the £100 of the year 1492 A.D. seemed likely to fall to about £7 before the end of the nineteenth century! Coin, even in its best form (gold), would become too heavy for common use; and if mankind were still to adhere to their system of making the measure-of-value out of a valuable material, would they not be forced in the twentieth century to take to pearls or diamonds for currency? Nor, at the time when Chevalier wrote, did there seem to him any way out of the dilemma. As the Money of the World consists both of gold and silver, the value of both of these metals would be reduced in

[1] For a detailed reference to the changes in the purchasing power of Money subsequent to the discovery of America, see Appendix.

the course of the impending monetary revolution. The idea of escaping from the dilemma by demonetising the precious metals was too hopeless to be entertained. It was obviously impossible under the varying circumstances of the world. In truth it was only the wealthiest and chief commercial nations who would be seriously affected by the fall of gold; and to the others, this new abundance of the precious metal would merely bring, for the first time, ordinary plenty. Many countries were greatly lacking in their stock or share of the world's money; while others, not yet brought into the civilised community of Trade, had little or no metallic money at all. Moreover, even if all the trading countries of the world had possessed (what was then deemed) a sufficient currency, would it not have been hopelessly impossible to expect mankind to forsake gold and silver money merely on account of its abundance? As well expect that people will give up eating bread because of a rare abundance of wheat!

But there was another form of the apparently impending dilemma which was less beyond practical control. So long as gold and silver were equally used as money, the plethoric supply of gold would reduce the value of metallic money in general. Nevertheless there was a universal expectation that, as the new mines were of gold, while the supply of silver remained unchanged, the old ratio in value between the two canonised metals would be destroyed; and that silver, as the scarcer metal, would rise in relative value, in proportion as gold fell.

Here, then—to a great extent, at least—there appeared a means of nullifying or preventing the threatened fall in the value of money,—namely, by demonetising gold, and adopting silver as the sole material of money and measure-of-value. Such a change, it is true, was a playing into the hands of capitalists and the moneyed class,—almost as much so as if (to recur to the previous simile), when the wheat-crop by the bounty of Nature became unusually abundant, it were enacted that wheat should cease to be used as food, and the population be compelled by law to use only oats and barley as the material of their bread. Nevertheless there was much to be said, upon the common principles of justice and fair-play, in favour of the substitution of silver for gold as the legal money, and measure of value; inasmuch as silver (the supply of which then continued nearly stationary) would more faithfully represent the value of existing monetary contracts and debts than gold could do, now that, owing to a superabundant supply, that metal seemed on the eve of a great fall in value. Silver would retain its old absolute value—its value as measured in labour and commodities, although not in gold; whereas the value or purchasing power of gold would be changing and falling from year to year as the new supplies poured in. The Dutch—a highly commercial people, and quick-eyed in monetary and financial affairs— were the first to give practical effect to the prevalent opinion. So certain and so serious did the impending monetary revolution appear, that, as early as 1851, the Dutch Government passed a legislative decree demonetising gold, and adopting silver as the sole legal money and measure-of-value in the Dutch dominions. Holland is a small country, and with no great extent of empire, so that a monetary change like this could be effected without much manifest inconvenience, either to the Government or the people; and, remembering the prevalent sentiments of that time, it may safely be said that other Governments would then have taken the same course, but for the greater difficulties which would have beset them, as large States, in carrying out such a change in the monetary standard, or measure of value.

At the present day, it is needless to say how utterly mistaken were those anticipations and gloomy apprehensions as to the effects of the new Gold-discoveries—whether as regards the value of Money in general, or as to the relative value of gold and silver. But it was one of the most striking examples in all History of the incapacity of the human judgment to forecast even the immediate future; and it has contributed, more than any other single instance or incident, to fortify the now current maxim that the only thing certain to happen in the Future is "the unexpected." The disturbing element in all forecasts of the Future is hardly attributable to incapacity of human reasoning, but to the infinite variety of Nature compared with the conceptions of Man. As is to be expected from the harmony which necessarily exists between the constitution of Man and that of external Nature or the system of

Creation of which he is a part (even as a drop is identical in substance with the ocean from which it is taken), the human intellect is well fitted to follow out the natural course of any particular fact, or single condition of affairs: given all the premises, the human mind, at least when of the higher order, is well capable of correctly discerning the issue and conclusion. The difficulty of foresight arises from the infinite variety of Nature, so vastly transcending the conceptions of the human mind,—entirely new events suddenly interposing in the course of affairs, destroying or even reversing their natural tendency and issue. Hence, although it be quite possible for the human intellect, by calculation of the current forces of the day, to foresee deductively the course and result of those existing forces, it is still more likely that the ever-revolving "potter's wheel" of Nature will suddenly cast up some new Event,—begetting a sequence of affairs entirely different from what could have been anticipated, and teaching afresh to the human intellect the ever-needful lesson of humility.

As regards the effects of the new Gold-mines in altering the relative value of gold and silver, the prevalent opinion was for a while supported by current facts of the day,—albeit the support was more in appearance than in reality. And these circumstances are especially worthy of record because they were connected with a great and early absorption of the New Gold, which served the important purpose of averting a serious fall in the value of money at the most critical time,—namely, when the New Gold was pouring into the markets of the world in its maximum quantity, and when commercial and industrial enterprise had not had time to expand proportionately with its new opportunities. But for the *parachute* (as M. Chevalier aptly called it) afforded by the currency of France, it seems beyond doubt that a serious change in the value of money, especially in the gold-currency of our own country, would have occurred in the year or two immediately subsequent to the discovery of the Australian goldfields. France was then, as it continues to be, what is called a Bi-metallic country,—gold and silver being equally legal money in France; and also, fortunately, by far the larger portion of its currency consisted of silver. M. Chevalier, in accord with some other authorities, estimated that at the date of the gold-discoveries, the silver coins circulating in France amounted to about a hundred millions sterling. Thus, as soon as any fall occurred in the value of gold relative to silver, the natural result would be a substitution of gold for silver in the French currency. The "open Mint" of France, in fact, furnished a ready market for the New Gold; and the change which thus occurred in the French currency was a very considerable one. Moreover, the bi-metallic currency of France naturally presented a field wherein any change in the relative value of the two precious metals would become most quickly and readily manifest.

For some years previous to the date of M. Chev

alier's book (which was published in 1858), there had been a considerable change in the relative value of the two precious metals in France, in favour of silver. "In the French market," said M. Chevalier, "silver is now at a premium. To those who bring them a quantity of coined silver, the bullion-merchants give a certain sum beyond its legal equivalent in gold-money. This premium is a notorious fact: it is quoted every day,—every morning the newspapers announce it. During the last two years [1856-7], this premium has ordinarily ranged from 20 to 30 francs per 1000. Sometimes the premium has been lower, but it has also risen to 40 francs"—equal to 4 per cent. As a natural consequence of gold-money thus falling below its legal equivalent in silver-money (or, as it might be, of silver thus rising above its legal equivalent in gold-money), there occurred an extensive substitution of gold for silver in the French currency,—of which operation, in fact, the premium upon silver was an overt sign. The extent of this substitution, and also of the addition by that time made to the metallic money of France in the form of gold, can be measured with tolerable accuracy. As stated by M. Chevalier, during the six years ending with 1857, ninety-six millions sterling in gold had been coined at the French Mint; and, during the same period, the exports of silver from France had exceeded the imports to the amount of forty-five millions sterling. But this positive decrease of the stock of silver in France by no means represents the entire change. On the average of the thirty-five years between 1816 and 1851, the imports of silver into France had exceeded the exports of silver to the amount of three millions sterling a-year.[1] Therefore, in order to maintain the stock of silver in France in its normal condition, eighteen millions sterling of that metal should have been added during the six years subsequent to 1851: whereas, as just stated, during those six years forty-five millions of silver had been withdrawn from France. Accordingly, at the end of the year 1857, the stock of silver in France was less by sixty-three millions sterling than what it would have been had matters continued as they were prior to 1852. Considering the large contemporaneous coinage of gold at the French Mint (equal to £96,000,000), there can be no doubt that the exported silver was taken from the currency,—being a reduction of nearly one-half in the silver portion of the French currency as it existed in 1851; while, as demonstrated by the coinage at the Mint, the French currency had not merely been maintained at its normal amount, but had been increased to the extent of £33,000,00,

---

[1] M. Chevalier states the balance of Imports and Exports of Silver in France, as follows:—

Excess of Imports.		Excess of Exports.	
1846,	£1,870,868	1852,	£108,960
1847,	2,145,163	1853,	4,675,418
1848,	8,557,338	1854,	6,547,751
1849,	9,782,708	1855,	7,886,385
1850,	2,615,378	1856,	11,342,932
1851,	3,117,959	1857,	14,500,835
	£28,089,414		£45,062,281

by the importation and coinage of gold. Under the circumstances of the time, this additional coinage was not calculated to produce any great and palpable rise of prices; but it was of immense value in loosening the fetters upon trade, and alike fostering and supporting new industrial enterprise. The new gold would naturally pass from the Mint into the Bank of France; and so, by enabling that establishment to extend its discounts and loans, without any increased charge or elevation of the Bank-rate, the new gold gave scope to the latent powers of industry and commerce, and served to support the development of the Credit Societies and joint-stock enterprise which the Imperial policy of the day did so much to promote,—and, on the whole, with highly beneficial results to the French people.

Simultaneously with these events, a new force had begun to operate very powerfully, and one which, from first to last, was the chief agent in preventing the great expected Fall in the value of Money, as well as of realising for mankind the full benefits attainable from the Gold-Discoveries. Although the substitution of gold for silver in the bi-metallic currency of France was a natural and readily understood consequence of the great increase of the annual production and supply of gold; it was nevertheless necessary that there should arise or exist some new outlet or external demand for silver. Had France been an isolated country, a little world by itself—or (which for this purpose comes to nearly the same thing), if there had existed a prohibition to export the precious metals from France; then, there would have been no motive for substituting gold for silver in the French currency,—both metals in that country possessing a fixed legal value as money. Gold, as the more abundant and more easily obtained metal, might have been preferably or exclusively employed in the arts and ornamentation,—but that would have been all, or nearly so; while the greater portion of the new gold would have been simply added to the currency, without any displacement of silver, proportionately tending to reduce the value of money.

Happily, as needs hardly be said, the actual circumstances were entirely different from this hypothetical case,—here imagined merely for the purpose of illustration. What was wanted in order to set in motion a drain or outflow of specie from France (making room for the new gold) was an external demand for silver. And this might be found, or created, in other countries where silver was legal money, and where (as was the condition of all countries at that time) the metallic currency was more or less inadequate for the wants or desires of the nation. But the wants of any silver-using country in Europe would very soon have been satisfied: indeed any bi-metallic country (that is, in which both gold and silver are legal money—such as both Germany and the United States then were) would prefer to make additions to its currency in the form of gold-money, as the cheaper or more easily procured of the two metals. Fortunately for mankind, the vast world of the East has steadily adhered to the use of silver-money, as the chief, if not sole, kind of legal currency. And it was from, or in connection with, the East that a new and powerful demand for silver now arose,—not only facilitating, but inciting to, or indeed actually necessitating, the naturally desired substitution of gold for silver in the French currency; and thereby creating a profitable void, which the New Gold must fill before it could operate in changing the value of money.

As shown in our history of the Silver Age, the reopening and expansion of the trade between Europe and the East (after an interruption and virtual closure of wellnigh a thousand years) which followed the discovery of the sea-route to India by the Cape of Good Hope, supplied one of the widest and most profitable channels for the employment of the flood of precious metal which began to pour into Europe from the mines of the New World in the sixteenth century. The revival and remarkable expansion of the same Trade (after a period of comparative collapse), which began immediately subsequent to the recent Gold-discoveries, constitutes a similar and hardly less notable feature in the new Golden Age. The event is highly noteworthy as illustrating what seems to me the peculiar effect, and chief beneficial operation, of the New Gold upon the condition of mankind, or at least upon the leading commercial nations of the world,—namely, not so much any fall in the purchasing power of money, but the great increase in the stock of loanable wealth in its most efficient form for production and trade (viz., as Money), whereby previously unknown facilities and opportunities have been afforded for the development or free exercise of human powers in productive and commercial enterprise, with a consequent increase of profitable employment and wealth-making, — thereby improving the general condition of mankind; first and chiefly, in simple material wellbeing, but also (as Wealth always does) in promoting the cultivation of the Fine Arts, and adding to the higher pleasures and enjoyments of human life.

As previously narrated, during the three centuries subsequent to the discovery of America and the beginning of the present century (viz., between 1492 and 1810 A.D.), three hundred and fifty millions sterling in specie had been exported in course of trade to the East. It is important to observe that during the first of these three centuries, the export of gold and silver to the East amounted to one-twelfth part of the contemporaneous production and supply of the precious metals; in the second period, the export amounted to about one-tenth part of the contemporaneous supply; and during the third period (viz., 1701-1810), the export of specie to the East amounted to exactly one-half of the contemporaneous supply. The annual amount of the production and supply of the precious metals had, throughout all these periods, been steadily on the increase,—rising at length to fully ten millions sterling at the beginning of the present century; nevertheless, as here shown, the export of gold and silver to the East had increased far more rapidly,— the annual export having increased twenty-five fold (from £130,000 to £3,520,000) since the sixteenth century, while the annual production of gold and silver had increased only about five-fold.[1] As the annual export (gradually increasing) throughout last century and down to 1810 amounted in the average to three and a half millions sterling, it is obvious that towards the close of that period the annual amount must have been very considerably larger,—probably, as Humboldt states, between five and six millions sterling. But in 1810, when a serious interruption occurred in the working and produce of the American mines, the disastrous change was at once reflected in the diminished exportation of the precious metals to the East. During the twenty years ending with 1830 the annual export of specie to the East amounted to only two

---

[1] The following table of figures, based upon Mr Jacob's careful yet doubtless only approximately correct estimates, shows the aggregate production of gold and silver, together with the amount of specie exported to the East, in several successive periods :—

PRODUCTION OF GOLD AND SILVER.		EXPORTED TO EAST.		
Aggregate.	Annual Average.	Total.	Annual Average.	Per cent of annual supply.
1492-1600, £177 million	£1.64 million	£14 million	£130,000	8 p. c.
Down to 1700, 514 ,,	3.37 ,,	33 ,,	330,000	10 ,,
,, 1810, 1,396 ,,	7.05 ,,	352 ,,	3,520,000	50 ,,
,, 1830, 1,497 ,,	5.05 ,,	40 ,,	2,000,000	60 ,,
		£439,000,000		

millions sterling, or little more than one-half of the average amount in the preceding century, and little more than one-third of the annual exportation in the opening years of the present century. The annual export, however, *continued to maintain its previous proportion to the annual supply*,—absorbing, during that period of dearth, two-fifths of the entire annual production of the mines: a fact which of itself seems to imply that the change was connected with the contemporaneously diminished supply of the precious metals, and not with a failure in the (ever steadily increasing) demand and purely commercial condition of the Trade with Asia.

This check to the export of specie to the East clearly indicates a corresponding check to the Eastern Trade. This trade has always been attended by a balance in favour of the East, payable in specie by Europe; and it is obvious that, as the precious metals became scarce in Europe, the difficulty of settling these annual balances would become serious, —thereby practically imposing a limit upon the extent of this trade with the East. As the precious metals became scarce, merchants would find greater difficulty in procuring them. Directly or indirectly, merchants would have to pay more for the specie which they required for the settlement of their trade-balance due to the East. They required to settle their accounts by exporting an article which had become unusually dear; and in proportion as this occurred, British merchants (who then held almost a monopoly of the trade with India and the East) would find the trade becoming less profitable, and accordingly would reduce their trading operations within narrower limits,—trading only to such an extent as the available amount of specie permitted them to do, without incurring charges which would destroy their profit from the trade. The difficulty was the same as if the natives of India and other countries of the East required the trade-balances due to them to be paid in coal at a time when coal was becoming scarce and dear: every rise in the price of coal being a reduction on the profits of the Western merchants. Of course, this (hypothetical) demand for coal for the Eastern trade would aggravate the existing scarcity, still further raising the price of coal; whereas, if this Eastern demand were reduced, the price of coal would not rise so high: so that the aim of the merchants would be, so to limit their trade with the East as to allow this restricted portion of it being carried on under more or less profitable conditions. The fact that the export of specie from Europe continued to maintain its old proportion to the supply (viz., one-half) shows the reluctance of the merchants to curtail their trade with the East; and doubtless it also shows the large profits obtained in that Trade, which permitted of very considerable diminution before the merchants felt compelled to suspend their operations. That the Eastern traders, despite the large contraction of their operations between the years 1810 and 1830, had during that period to carry on their actual trade with a considerable sacrifice of the old rate of profits, is suggested by the fact that although the annual export of specie from Europe (required by the Eastern trade) was reduced exactly in proportion to the annual supply of the precious metals, nevertheless this amount of specie could be procurable only upon higher terms than before,—seeing that, instead of being taken as previously from the surplus portion of the annual supply, it must, during that period of scarcity, have been taken from the stock of specie required for general use. In fact, as already stated, between 1810 and 1830 the stock of coin was greatly reduced.

Briefly consider this point. Widely different in many respects as are the qualities of Money and of Bread, they are akin in this, that the former is as necessary to civilised Trade as the latter is to Life. Suppose then—in illustration of the matter here in question—that a country has been in the habit of annually exporting one-half of its cereal produce,—the other half being sufficient for the life-wants of the people. There is no absolute surplus here; nevertheless for one half of the grain-crop there is no competition on the part of the home-consumers, so that this portion of the grain can be bought and exported at a moderate price. But suppose the annual production of grain (like that of gold and silver between 1810 and 1830) falls to only one-half of its previous amount; then, the whole of it will be needed, and competed for, by the people for domestic consumption: so that, even if the exporting merchants curtail their operations in equal proportion to the decrease in the production or supply—that is, to one-half,—nevertheless this portion of the grain being now required for domestic use, will only be procurable (if it were procurable at all) at a very much higher price than before — thereby leaving little or no margin for profit upon its employment in the export-trade. Of course the requirement for Money in trade is far less imperious than the requirement for grain as food, or as necessary to the support of human life: nevertheless this partially parallel case suffices to illustrate the character of the difficulty arising in the Eastern Trade, and of the limitations imposed upon it, owing to the severe dearth of the precious metals which prevailed in the early portion, indeed during the greater part of the first half, of the present century. The difficulty in procuring the means of settling the annual balance in that Trade (always adverse to Europe) was equivalent to a heavy fine or charge imposed by Nature upon that Trade, and limiting the extent of its transactions.

These considerations illustrate in a very striking manner the benefit which the new gold-mines conferred upon mankind in permitting international Trade—indeed every kind of industry, but especially those enterprises for which metallic money is indispensable — to be carried on under more profitable conditions. It is true that, in the Eastern Trade, it was not gold, but silver, that was needed,—silver being the favourite money of Asiatic nations. But, by the above-mentioned substitution of gold for silver in the currency of France (which was then by far the largest metallic currency in Europe), the New Gold at once became available for the wants of the Eastern trade, by setting free an equal amount of silver. A noteworthy feature of the case was, that the premium upon silver (or the rise in the value of that metal beyond its legally fixed ratio to gold) was much larger than was needful to effect this substitution of the one metal for the other in bi-metallic countries like France. As M. Chevalier remarked, experience demonstrates that a difference of one per cent, above or below the legally fixed relative value of gold and silver, suffices to cause gold-money to be substituted for silver-money, and *vice versâ*. But the change which then occurred in the relative value of the two metals amounted to about three per cent,—ranging ordinarily from two to three per cent, and occasionally rising to four per cent. Upon this fact M. Chevalier observed—"That the premium on silver should have reached so high as even four per cent, under the circumstances in which the trade in the precious metals is placed, seems to me to indicate the force with which gold is tending towards depreciation." The correctness of this opinion, however, is questionable. A rise in the demand for silver may have the same effect upon the relative value of the two metals as would be produced by a superabundant supply of gold: and it seems to me that the premium of silver was owing much rather to the former of these causes than to the latter. Considering the vast amount of silver still circulating in France, and with the French Mint open to an unlimited coinage of gold, it is not obvious why or how the process of substitution should be accompanied by a premium on silver threefold as much as is required to produce that substitution. On the other hand, there plainly was an unusual demand for silver, at that time,—chiefly for export to the East, and also in consequence of the adoption of silver, in place of gold, as the currency of Holland. The silver was required to carry on a highly profitable trade with the East, for the sake of which the merchants were willing to pay a premium on the amount of silver which they required,—this competition raising the agio or premium beyond the one per cent which suffices to render profitable the operations requisite for the substitution of gold-money for silver-money, or *vice versâ*. That this external demand for silver, and not the new supplies of gold, produced the whole, or at least the greater part of the premium upon silver in France at that time, seems further proved by the fact that the premium on silver was short-lived and entirely disappeared, despite the continuance of the new gold-supplies from California and Australia, and before any change had occurred in the supply of silver from the discovery of the famous Nevada mines.

Let us pause here for a moment, as at a convenient halting-place, to observe what had been the amount of the New Gold (the produce of the Californian and Australian mines) down to this date—

say the end of the year 1857,—up to which time there had been no increase in the production of silver. The new gold obtained in California in the year 1848 was of so small amount that it need not be taken into account; and the total production of gold in that year may be reckoned at its previous amount, namely, about nine millions sterling. During the nine following years (1849-57) the total production of Gold throughout the world is reckoned as follows:—

1849,	£12,700,000	1854,	£25,490,000
1850,	14,200,000	1855,	27,015,000
1851,	16,600,000	1856,	29,520,000
1852,	36,550,000	1857,	26,655,000
1853,	31,000,000		
		Total,	£219,730,000

Annual average, £24¼ millions (previous average = 9 millions).

Deducting the amount of the old or previous supply (reckoned at nine millions sterling a-year), equal to eighty millions sterling during these nine years, the New Gold produced down to the close of the year 1857 amounted to about one hundred and forty millions sterling. Within the same period (between 1st January 1852 and 31st December 1857), no less than ninety-six millions had been coined at the Paris Mint,—of which amount sixty-three millions sterling went simply to replace an equal amount of silver in the French currency.[1] There has also to be deducted a large sum — not less than twelve millions, and probably a half more — transferred by emigrants and otherwise to

---
[1] See *supra*, p. 411.

our Australian colonies. Further, the whole of the New Gold had not reached Europe,—a very considerable sum being retained for use in America (and also in Australia, after the establishment of the Mint at Sydney). Taking these various circumstances into account, it is manifest that the portion of the New Gold added to the stock of the precious metals in Europe was by no means capable (of itself, or directly) of producing any revolutionary change in the value of money,—although of inestimable value in facilitating trade and production.

In truth the year 1857 witnessed a combined commercial and monetary disaster, overspreading the leading countries of the Western world, which showed how utterly inadequate were even the mines of California and Australia to supply the world's money, and medium of exchange, in such amount as to meet the wants of Trade when left even partially unsupported by the Credit-system. This event was the Crisis of 1857,—the second disaster of this kind in Great Britain, since the passing of the Act of 1844, and the third since the establishment of the British currency on its modern mono-metallic basis by the Acts of 1816 and 1819. The leading features of this Crisis have been described in the third chapter of this book; and, as there remarked, it may be taken as marking the close of the first stage in the Golden Age, which was also the epoch of maximum gold-production.

This Crisis gave a painful contradiction to some of

the most hopeful, and not unreasonable, anticipations with respect to the effects of the new Gold-mines: one of which was, that the New Gold, by greatly enlarging the basis of our currency-system, would insure a low or steadily moderate Bank-rate, and prevent the occurrence of monetary Crises like that of 1847. This anticipation was not incorrect in principle; and although the New Gold has utterly failed to prevent monetary crises arising from a drain of gold from the Bank of England, or from the stock of gold in the Bank being inadequate (under the artificial restrictions of the Act of 1844) to maintain a note-circulation equal to the currency-wants of the community, it is nevertheless certain that but for the New Gold the currency-system established in 1844 *must have utterly broken down*. Coming, as it did, after the fervid views popularly or universally entertained with respect to the new Gold-mines, the Crisis of 1857 gave a startling proof how inadequate is the largest conceivable stock of the precious metals to support the vast fabric of modern trade and industrial enterprise; and also teaching (to those who had eyes to see) that, after all, in the mere system of Credit and Credit-money, properly utilised, mankind may possess a lever of Production and an efficient auxiliary of Trade far surpassing gold and silver, or even making nations wholly independent of those long-canonised metals.

Probably the Crisis of 1857 contributed to produce the somewhat strange impression, then universally prevalent,[1] that the changes to be wrought by the new gold-mines were all in the future. No doubt was entertained as to the inevitable occurrence of these changes. Indeed the apprehension or confident expectation of a great Fall in the value of Gold was then at its height. But no one maintained —certainly Messrs Chevalier and Cobden did not— that any change of that kind, however small, had yet occurred. And yet, by that time, the Mines had reached or even somewhat passed their maximum production, and for nine years had been pouring their marvellous treasure upon the markets of the world. The explanation of this (as it must now seem) very curious state of mind was probably the simple fact that a great Fall in the value of Gold, or of all Money, was a deep-rooted expectancy in the public mind; and the fact that the signs of such a change had not been generally observed only served to increase the confidence that such a cataclysmal Fall was near at hand. As we have repeatedly had occasion to remark, there is no other change more difficult to discern and correctly appraise as a change in the value of Money (as distinct from the transient effects on prices produced by the fluctuations of Trade) at the time when the change is in progress. And doubtless the striking exhibition of a lack of currency in the autumn of 1857—extending, too, over so many countries simul-

---

[1] As previously mentioned, this opinion was not shared by Messrs Tooke and Newmarch, but the views of these able men took no hold upon the public mind.

taneously—must have strengthened the belief that the natural effects of the new Gold-mines had not yet come into operation. Certain it is, that it was after the mines both of California and Australia had overpassed their term of maximum productiveness that the most memorable and emphatic voice of warning and apprehension was raised, as to a great coming Fall in the value of money,—in France by M. Chevalier, and echoed in England by Mr Cobden.

Next, surveying the whole period of the Golden Age—or of that prime time of it embraced by the present work—let us consider what became of the vast masses of gold and silver then extracted from the earth and poured forth upon the markets of the world. The entire production of Gold, from the mines of the world, during the twenty-seven years following the discovery of the Californian gold-beds —namely, from the beginning of 1849 to the end of 1875—is reckoned to have amounted to 616 millions sterling. This was considerably more than the entire stock of gold in all forms (reckoned by Danson at 560 millions) throughout Christendom in 1848; and over fourfold the amount of gold-coin existing at that date. In other words (as there was little time for loss by abrasion and casualties), *the stock of gold in all forms became doubled between the years* 1848 *and* 1875! Further, as the annual production of gold previous to 1848 had been about nine millions (making about 240 millions for these twenty-seven years), the New Gold, or the *additional* supply of that metal, amounted during the same period to nearly 380 millions,—equal to two and a half times the stock of gold-coin in 1848, and all but equalling the entire stock of metallic money (both gold and silver) existing in Christendom in the year 1848, which is estimated at 400 millions sterling.

But the increased production of the precious metals was not confined to gold. During the latter portion of the epoch which we here designate as peculiarly the Golden Age, a great increase took place in the production of Silver—an increase which began about the year 1861, and which became large and very notable after the discovery of the rich silver-mines of Nevada in 1869. The total production of silver during the twenty-seven years ending with 1875 is reckoned at 264 millions sterling : and as the previous production of silver (viz., as in 1848) averaged eight millions a-year, making 216 millions for the subsequent twenty-seven years, the New Silver, or *additional* supply of that metal down to the end of the year 1875, amounted to 48 millions sterling,—all of which (speaking roundly), during the above-mentioned period, circulated at its old value compared with gold.

Accordingly, taking gold and silver together, during the period which we name the Golden Age, the *addition* made to the world's stock of the precious metals—and, potentially at least, to the stock of the World's Money—amounted to no less than 880 millions sterling: equal to two-thirds of the gold and silver in all forms estimated to have been in existence in the countries of Christendom in the year 1848; and more than double the stock of gold and silver coin existing at that date. And of these 880 millions *one-half was an entirely new supply,*—the produce of new mines, additional to the produce of the gold and silver mines which were known and worked in 1848.

Such being the vast additional supply of gold and silver, the first question which naturally arises is, What effect had this new supply upon Prices?—to what extent did it affect the value of Money? In other respects, also, this is the question which claims priority of consideration; because the answer to it really furnishes an indication, if not a key to the ascertainment, of the general and more or less world - wide effects of the new Gold - mines. The effect of new mines of gold and silver upon the value of money is very far from being dependent simply upon the magnitude of the new supply of money, or upon its magnitude relatively to the amount of the previously existing stock of money. An equally important element in the case is the character and acquirements of the population—their industry, skill, and spirit of enterprise. Not less is it dependent upon the opportunities for production and commerce afforded by Nature: and although these, in the truest sense of the term, are as yet (and probably will ever be) illimitable or unexhausted by human power; nevertheless, as actually available by man, these natural opportunities or resources vary greatly in extent from age to age, according to the development of human intellect and the progress achieved in the great work and human mission of the Conquest of Nature. This is but another phrase for material civilisation; or it is at least the fundamental power and spirit, of which "civilisation" is the varied and manifold development. Obviously, therefore, the effect produced upon the value of money by an additional supply of gold and silver is a test or indication of the area and quality of human civilisation,—a sign alike of the extent to which civilisation prevails over the earth, and of the power attained by mankind for utilising the latent or undeveloped resources of Nature, and otherwise expanding the sphere of his industrial energies. In short, the value of money is affected by the amount of the population among whom it is diffused, and also by the extent or degree in which it is profitably employed by them. In this respect, of itself, the question which now presents itself is pregnant with human interest and social importance; while its investigation will serve, among other things, to indicate the extent or urgency of the need of more gold in the middle of the nineteenth century,—which may be pretty accurately measured by the rapidity and extent to which the produce of the new Gold-mines was utilised, and absorbed in the operations of profitable industry.

What, then, has been the effect of these vast supplies of the precious metals upon the twofold value of money?—that is, upon its loanable value and its purchasing power—the Bank-rate and Prices. It may seem a simple matter to ascertain what that change has been. Yet, as regards the exchangeable value or purchasing power, the question is a difficult one. What is requisite is, not only to ascertain changes in the level of prices, but to determine how far, if at all, these changes have been produced by the new Mines. General prices are ceaselessly changing, but the truly difficult point is to determine how far these changes are of a purely monetary character, or, on the other hand, pertain to the commodities which are bought and sold. Is a change of prices due to plenty or scarcity of commodities, or to plenty or scarcity of the medium of exchange with which the commodities are purchased? And beyond that, there is the "state of trade," ever fluctuating and at times inscrutable, yet so powerful in its effects upon Price as wholly to override for a time those produced by an increase or decrease of the stock of money.

Any one who has studied the subject knows that there is no question more perplexingly complicated than that which relates to ascertaining with precision the influence of the supply of the precious metals, or indeed of any individual agency, upon prices. Prices are affected by very many other influences than that of the existing stock of money in the world, or even in any particular country. As regards the extent of Demand, the most potent source of value, increased facilities of conveyance (such as railways and steamships), which augment demand by opening new markets, tend to raise prices in exporting countries; while to importing countries these improved means of conveyance have exactly the opposite effect,—lowering prices by cheapening the means of supply. In this way wheat becomes dearer in Hungary and Russia, and cheaper here. From the same cause, coal tends to become cheaper in the countries which get it from us, and dearer here. In fact, as is well known, improved conveyance (besides its great work of promoting production, by facilitating exchanges or opening new markets) tends to equalise prices, not only among separate countries, but also among various districts of the same country. Manufactured articles, in a question of this kind, may be wholly thrown out of account. Science, in the form of machinery and chemical inventions, is constantly cheapening manufactures of every kind,—altering their price to such an extent as wholly to obscure effects produced by a change in the supply of the precious metals. Raw or unmanufactured commodities are the only ones which can be taken into account in such an inquiry; yet even wheat, which is usually appealed to as the standard in such questions, is more or less subject to all of the above-mentioned influences affecting price. Down almost to the middle of the present century, agricultural operations remained very much the same as they had been for generations before; so that up to that period the price of wheat was a tolerably trustworthy indication of changes in the value of money. But, since then, the conditions of farming have been so greatly altered that the price of wheat now cannot be safely compared with what it was in former times. Bone-dust and artificial manures marked the first stage of agricultural improvement, which has been followed by an extensive use of machinery, such as reaping-machines, the steam-plough, and itinerant steam threshing-machines. Also, in recent times, railways and steam-navigation, while tending to equalise the price of wheat throughout the world, have likewise tended to alter it in particular countries.

Even legislative changes affect prices,—in some cases largely. The abolition of the Corn Laws has lowered the price of wheat in England; and the recent legislation for the protection of miners has added a shilling, or more, to the prime cost of every ton of coal. The price of foreign commodities in the English market, likewise, has been largely affected by legislation,—tea, sugar, coffee, and other imported articles being now much cheaper owing to a reduction of customs-duties. In a country which has little or no customs-duties, the price of foreign commodities is *pro tanto* lessened. Foreign tariffs, too, affect prices by opening or shutting markets, and thereby affecting the Demand which so largely influences prices. Nay more, a bonus on export given by a Government tends to reduce the price of the favoured commodity in other countries,—as we see at present in the case of sugar: the bonus, or exemption from taxation, given by the French Government upon the export of beet-root sugar sufficing to undersell the cane-sugar of our colonies in the English market, and thereby really supplying us with sugar at an artificially low price.

To these manifold agencies which obscure the effect of the new Mines upon the value of money, must be added the vicissitudes of national fortune (whether produced by war, as recently in France and the United States, or by general causes), which of late years have been very great. In truth, the influences at work upon prices are so various and complex as to defy any accurate analysis. Further, there is the State of Trade (using this term as synonymous with the prosperity of a commercial country), which at times most remarkably affects the State of Prices. A depression of Trade is always attended by (although it may be a consequence of) a fall of prices,—in other words, a rise in the purchasing-power of money. For example, referring to the *Economist's* Table of Prices, we find that after the Crisis of 1857 prices fell 17 per cent; after the Crisis of 1866, 25 per cent; and under the long recent depression of trade, prices at the beginning of 1879 stood 30 per cent below their level in 1873. On the other hand, Prices rise when Trade is brisk and the nation prospers,—although the available amount of money may be no larger than before: a fact of no small significance for a correct understanding of the phenomena of Price, or the true causes of change in the purchasing-power of Money.

I shall here offer only one remark more upon the influences which affect Prices. During the last thirty years, Prices have been chiefly influenced by two wholly distinct, and in their operation conflicting, factors. The steam-engine has been employed to annihilate Distance, and cheapen conveyance; and in this way steam-locomotion, both by land and sea, has caused Prices to rise in *remote* places, and to fall in the great towns and in countries which are the hearts of Commerce. On the other hand, the new gold-mines have tended to raise Prices chiefly in the central seats of Commerce. As these and other factors operate more or less together, there is usually a tide-like change in Prices; indeed, even the same cause or factor may produce high-water in some places and low-water in others. On all these accounts, even the State of Prices needs to be scanned with wary discrimination before anything certain can be reached as to the real effects thereon of a scarce or abundant stock of Money.

Moreover, even in the comparatively simple part of the question, relating to the mere ascertainment of the level of prices, the difficulty is by no means trifling. It may seem an easy and simple thing to ascertain what change of prices occurs, at least in any particular country; but, as experience shows, the fact is far otherwise. As previously mentioned, the difficulty of the task compelled Mr Jacob in 1829 to abandon his design of preparing a table of prices which would show the striking change in the value of money in his day. The task is easier nowadays, and there are several Tables of Prices relating to the last thirty years: two of which are usually referred to as authorities,—namely, the table compiled by Mr Jevons, and also the table annually published in the *Economist*, and of which the author and originator was Mr Newmarch. Both of these tables are carefully compiled by able men, practised in this kind of work, yet the one table in some years shows a change of prices twice as great as in the other! Thus, in what appears, and indeed is, the surest and most computable of the factors which indicate the value of money—namely, the statistical department, or the actual state of prices,—there exists a striking variance and discrepancy, which makes it impossible to attain anything like accuracy of detail. We can say that prices have risen or fallen (in other words, that the value of money has changed) so much according to this or that Table, but it seems hopeless at present to reach anything like perfect accuracy. On the whole, we must repeat, it seems as hopeless to accurately appreciate changes in the value of money when these changes are in progress as it is to map the features of a woodland through which we are passing. When we reach a height beyond, or above, then the task becomes comparatively easy: we see things in truer shape, in perspective and mutual relation. In much the same way does the lapse of Time—which alone gives perspective to History—enable us to discern with substantial accuracy those changes in the value of Money, which are alike so subtle and so vitally important in their influence upon human affairs.

As soon as the great extent and richness of the new gold-fields became known, the apprehension arose (very naturally) of a coming fall in the value of money; nevertheless for several years even men who gave their attention to public and monetary matters remained in a state of doubt as to whether any depreciation of gold was actually in progress. Mr Newmarch in 1857 and Mr M'Culloch in 1858 both doubted the existence of any depreciation.[1] Almost simultaneously, however, M. Chevalier published his well-known book (presented to English readers by Mr Cobden in 1859), in which he confidently predicted a fall in the value of gold and money of such serious magnitude as to threaten a social revolution. But neither M. Chevalier nor Mr Cobden ventured to affirm that a fall in the value of money had already occurred; and yet, as seems certain to me, by that time the maximum effect of the New Gold upon the value of money had already been produced!

In 1863 Mr Jevons took up the subject, after the new gold-mines had been pouring their wealth into the world for fifteen years. He held that prices had then risen to the extent of 10, 15, or 20 per cent;[2] and he expected that this rise of

[1] See the concluding volume of Tooke's *History of Prices*, and the article on the "Precious Metals" in the *Encyclopædia Britannica*.

[2] "While I must assert the fact of a depreciation of gold with the utmost confidence, I assign a numerical amount to it with equal diffidence. The lowest estimate of the fall that I arrive at [in 1863] is 9 per cent; and I shall be satisfied if my readers accept this. At the same time, in my own opinion, the fall is nearer to 15 per cent. It

prices, or fall in the value of money, would soon increase to 30 per cent,—at which point he thought that a combination of circumstances would stop the further fall in the value of money, by arresting or diminishing the labour expended upon gold-mining. Mr Jevons stated that his attention had first been attracted to this rise of prices, when he was engaged in the preparation of a list of prices, by a rise which he observed in the year 1853; and although he fully admits that this elevation of prices had been interrupted, he considered that the facts at the time when he wrote (1863) justified him in holding that a permanent rise of prices had been established to the extent of at least 15 per cent. In opposition to Mr Jevons, Mr Newmarch (in a paper which he read before the Statistical Society in May 1878) continued to maintain that there had been no fall in the value of money which could be attributed to the New Gold; but he acknowledged that a list of prices which he had compiled showed a rise of 10 per cent for the years 1870-77 compared with the period immediately prior to the Gold-discoveries. As regards the actual rise of prices, we think Mr Jevons was right. Also, as already stated, we hold that in 1853-4, when the produce of the new gold-mines was accumulating in the Western world, before it

may even be more than this. Many years, however, must pass before numerical estimates can be properly stated to possess more than a slight degree of probability."—*A Serious Fall in the Value of Gold Ascertained*, p. 2.

obtained an outlet—just before the Crimean War occasioned a considerable expenditure of specie in Turkey, which was immediately followed by the great and permanent drain of specie to the East, produced by the expansion of the trade with India—the rise of prices may be attributed directly to the new supplies of gold.

Prices were at their very lowest point (for nearly three centuries past) in the four years immediately prior to the arrival of the New Gold in the markets of the world,—prices in 1849-52, according to one of Mr Jevons's Tables, averaging 8 per cent below even their low level in 1845-50. In 1853-4 the rise of prices amounted to about 20 per cent above the level of 1845-50, and still more as compared with 1849-52,—a sudden rise, in fact, of nearly 30 per cent within two years. Then came a relapse, occasioned by the Crimean War. In 1857, aided by a brisk and partially speculative outburst of Trade, prices rose to their first acme; but *thereafter*, as it seems to me, *the rising force of the New Gold was wholly stayed*,—merely supporting the level of prices already attained. In 1864-6 there was a second wave of high prices,—owing not to any further effect of the New Gold, but to the letting loose of the metallic money of the United States (together, of course, with a stoppage of the annual absorption of gold and silver in that country), combined with the purely commercial cause of a scarcity of certain commodities, combined with much speculative enterprise, chiefly of a financial kind. After a second relapse, prices for a third time rose to an acme in the years 1772-3, when Trade "proceeded by leaps and bounds," but upon somewhat inflated bases. Thereafter prices fell continuously, until in 1879 they all but returned to their old low level in 1845-50.

From a comparison of the several Tables of Prices for this period (viz. Mr Jevons's, the *Economist's*, and the latter as modified by Mr Bourne), it may be said that throughout the nineteen years beginning with 1857 and ending with 1875, prices averaged nearly 25 per cent above their old level: in other words, the exchangeable value or purchasing-power of money became less by about one-fourth in 1857-75 compared with the eight years prior to 1853,—the rise ranging from 18 per cent as a minimum, in the year or two immediately following each of the Crises of 1857 and 1866, up to a maximum of fully 33 per cent in 1857. With respect to the second acme of prices, in 1866, the Tables vary greatly,—prices then standing, according to Mr Jevons, at 28 per cent above the level of 1845-50, but at more than double that height (62 per cent) according to the *Economist*. For the four years 1863-6, Mr Jevons gives the level of prices at 23½ per cent above that of 1845-50; the *Economist* gives it at no less than 63; and Mr Bourne, in his modified form of the *Economist's* Table, at 43½ per cent. In their third acme or culminating point, in 1873, prices were fully one-third above their level in 1845-50. From that year prices continuously fell—in other words, money grew dearer,—until in 1879 the purchasing-power of money had risen to within one per cent of what it had been prior to the gold-discoveries.

The year 1879, it is true, witnessed the lowest depth of the great agricultural and commercial depression which began in 1875 (or earlier), and from which our country has not yet fully recovered; and bad Trade, as already said, is always accompanied by low prices. Nevertheless, it can hardly be affirmed that the state of Trade in 1879 was worse than it was during the years 1845-50, with which period this comparison is made. And thus we have the remarkable fact that although nearly a thousand millions sterling of gold and silver have been poured into the world within the last thirty years (of which more than one-half was an extra supply, from entirely new mines), the world's requirement for this new supply of specie has been sufficient to bring back money almost to its old value.

These facts in the history or course of the new gold-supplies, if properly considered, suffice of themselves to exhibit a conclusive proof (if such were needed) that since the central year of the century the world must have passed through a period of exceptional prosperity,—that there has and must have been a great augmentation of those transactions which, while employing money, normally yield profits and promote an accumulation of wealth. Despite the enormous amount of new gold poured into the world, that metal has wellnigh returned to its old value. Whether this state of the matter be desirable or not, it at least shows that, in the interval (since 1850), there must have occurred a vast increase in the world's requirements for gold,— which, primarily and chiefly, means an increase of trade and profitable industry. There must have been a greatly increased employment of money, in the grand work of production, down to ordinary buying and selling and the mere retail work of "shopping,"—which latter operations only increase when, together with more produce, there is more money to buy with. The rapid expansion of commerce and industrial enterprise, especially in an international form, which followed the discovery of the new goldfields, created a new requirement for their produce; and the very means of conveyance for that Trade (railways and steam-ships) have given employment to a vast amount of Money, alike in their construction and in their working and maintenance. Indeed a most striking peculiarity of the commercial prosperity of the last thirty years is, that its main adjuvants have been similar, or indeed identical in character, and have increased Trade and Production solely or chiefly through the means of Exchange. The new Money, in short, has played a *rôle* identical with that of the new Iron-roads, oceanic steam-navigation, and telegraphs,—which Inventions and their development rival the Gold-discoveries themselves as memorable features of the Golden Age.

The internal or domestic trade of every country, even of our own, vastly exceeds the foreign trade;

but of this domestic trade there are no certain criteria, at least not in the form of statistics. But when we come to foreign trade, wherein a supply of the precious metals is indispensable, the statistics are readily obtainable as regards the leading commercial countries of the world, such as Great Britain, France, India, and the United States. Putting into a compendious form the commercial statistics of those countries, we subjoin a synopsis of the course of international trade since the discovery of the gold-mines. To show the full power of the recent commercial expansion, and also to allow of a fair comparison being made between the progress of these different countries, we shall first take the periods when the trade of each country proceeded undisturbed by extraneous disasters. Therefore we stop our statistics for the United States at 1860, the year before the Civil War began, and for France before the calamitous war of 1870. In like manner, although with less cause, we stop the statistics for our own country at 1865, in consequence of the severe monetary crisis of 1866, with the subsequent year or two of commercial prostration,—and of India at the same point, when the great increase of the Council drafts, representing the national indebtedness of that country, took place.

The figures in the subjoined table represent the "special" trade of each country (*i.e.*, exclusive of the Transit-trade), in millions sterling, for the period immediately subsequent to the Gold-discoveries:—

Great Britain.				France.			
Year.	Exports.	Imports.	Total.	Year.	Exports.	Imports.	Total.
1850	71½	115	186½	1850	42½	31½	74
1855	95½	122½	218	1855	62½	63¾	126
1860	136	182	318	1860	91	75	166
1865	166	218	384	1865	128	101⅓	239⅓
Increase (15 yrs.) = 106 per cent.				Increase (15 yrs.) = 224 per cent.			

India.				United States.			
Official Year.	Exports.	Imports.	Total.	Year.	Exports.	Imports.	Total.
1855–6	23	14	37	1850	27½	32⅔	60
1860–1	33	23½	56½	1855	49¼	46½	96
1865–6	65½	29½	95	1860	74½	67	141½
Increase (10 yrs.) = 156 per cent.				Increase (10 yrs.) = 136 per cent.			

It here appears that, taking the total trade during the first year of each series as 1, the foreign trade of England in the next ten years rose to fully 1⅔; that of France to rather more than 2; of the United States to 2⅓; and of India to 2½. And in the fifteen years subsequent to 1850, the foreign trade of England doubled, and that of France more than trebled.

In the more recent years, trade has been subjected to great extraneous disturbances. In the United States, owing to the Civil War, trade continued in a state of depression for eight years, not beginning to expand anew until 1869. French trade recovered from the effects of the German War after only two years of depression. The culminating point of the remarkable prosperity which followed 1850 was reached in the golden year 1873,—by which time we may state (without further encumbering our pages with statistical tables) the foreign trade of France, India, and the United States had quadrupled and that of Great Britain fully trebled.[1] The tide then turned, and all over the world Trade underwent a remarkable revulsion, actually retrograding in some countries, and becoming temporarily stagnant in all.

In any general history of the last thirty years, great prominence must be given to the remarkable inventions which have signalised that period,—notably railways, the electric telegraph, and steam-navigation with its iron-built ships, besides the numerous improvements in Production effected by mechanical and chemical science. It is those manifold inventions which have operated most manifestly in producing the great expansion of commerce. The discovery of the gold-mines was contemporaneous with a vast development of industrial power. The Railway Age had just commenced, and steam-navigation had begun to manifest its great capabilities. And thus, when the new supplies of gold came, the development of these new powers was instantaneous, and became progressive; while the electric telegraph soon came to lend its powerful aid to the movement. It is these above-mentioned agencies which, as

[1] Unfortunately the growth of our Trade is not so remarkable as these statistics show. Owing to a grievous official blunder, our Board of Trade returns, while supposed to show the progress of our Foreign Trade, now exhibit chiefly the mere current changes in Price, or in the purchasing power of the British currency!—See Appendix C.

originally latent forces, provided the new powers for human enterprise to develop,—opening new channels for Trade, resulting in a great expansion of the world's commerce; and but for their operation, the new supplies of gold and silver would have been comparatively little needed, and, in so far as not needed, would soon have been checked. Moreover, these new agencies of traffic and locomotion have directly affected the New Gold itself, by giving a rapid and wide diffusion to the produce of the mines,—preventing a plethora or redundant accumulation of gold in the countries adjoining the mines, or even in the central seats of commerce. The flood of the precious metals which came across the Atlantic in the sixteenth century, producing the great fall in the value of money, was poured only into Europe, or rather merely into some countries of Europe; whereas now the golden flood has poured freely into every part both of Europe and America, while the surplus flows off rapidly to the other regions of the globe.

As regards our own country, especially, the expansion of foreign trade during the last thirty years has been promoted by the Free Trade policy, which had been adopted a few years previous to the discovery of the new gold-mines. Free Trade (which means the abolition of import-duties) has promoted the foreign commerce of our country by abolishing some and reducing others of the duties upon imported commodities. Such duties constitute an obstacle to imports; they are an addition to the cost of foreign commodities as brought into our markets, and consequently they restrict the sale and use of them. Accordingly, since we abolished or reduced these customs-duties, foreign countries have had a greater inducement to send their produce, both raw and manufactured, to our markets; and thus our system of Free Trade has tended to increase the foreign trade of other countries as well as our own. But the influence of Free Trade has played only a very small part in the commercial progress of the world at large. No country but our own has yet adopted this commercial system. In fact, since 1850, when the recent expansion of international commerce began, protective tariffs in other countries have been at least as much in vogue as before, and, unfortunately, much more so in our own colonies, which have signalised their recently obtained powers of self-government by adopting fiscal systems directly antagonistic to Free Trade. Moreover, Free Trade had been in operation for several years, while the condition of our country remained as bad as, or indeed even worse than before; and undoubtedly it was the arrival of the vast supplies of New Gold in 1852-3 which first set Trade again in motion,—bringing a bright Revival of national prosperity; even neutralising for years the depression of British agriculture which is the unavoidable drawback upon the many advantages which Free Trade confers upon this country. Also, as a matter of fact, shown in the preceding table, the foreign trade of Great Britain since 1850 has progressed very much less than that of the other leading commercial Powers who adhere to Protection.

It was the New Gold which gave wings to the manifold inventions of the age—to the new agencies both of traffic and production. But for the new mines, those inventions would have been stunted from lack of the means of development, and commerce and production could not possibly have attained the remarkable expansion which has actually taken place. More money was the medium through which human power could operate upon, or set in motion, the new forces and opportunities then lying at its disposal. The new supplies of gold have afforded new facilities to Trade; and Trade is illimitable with its opportunities. Every man desires to trade more, if he can do so at his previous rate of profit. And the two most important auxiliaries to trade are Roads and Money,—which things, in this respect, as Adam Smith long ago said, are substantially similar both in their character and functions. Roads are at first a subtraction from productive power: they occupy a portion of the land more or less capable of production, and also they absorb a certain amount of labour in their construction. In like manner, the production of gold and silver absorbs an amount of labour in working the mines. But in both cases it is an expenditure which more than repays itself, by facilitating, and therefore cheapening, trade and production.

Money, in truth, creates Trade, just as Roads

create Traffic. The prime motive to Production in civilised countries, where subdivision of labour is the universal system, (and the motive to *all* production except that for consumption by the producers themselves) is Exchange: *i.e.*, to give the produce in exchange for something which the producer wants more. To carry out this exchange, there must be roads and money; and in proportion as either of these are lacking, the exchange becomes more difficult or costly, proportionately reducing the profits of the producer and the motive to Production. An absolutely secluded district has no motive to produce more commodities of any kind than are sufficient for its own wants: hence a portion of its soil or of its labour may remain unemployed; and in no country is production carried (except temporarily and by miscalculation) beyond the demand, or limits of consumption. The Demand for goods or labour is extended and enlarged by Roads; and so the value both of the labour and of the goods increases. In consequence of the new markets thus opened, there is more employment for labour and more production of goods: every man's labour becomes more valuable, while the stock of commodities in the country or community is simultaneously augmented. Money acts in an analogous manner; not only by facilitating exchanges of goods, but by supplying the only means or medium by which labour is paid, industry employed, and productive or commercial enterprises carried on—at least in civilised countries, under the effective system of " the division of labour." In short, in proportion as the means of conveyance and of exchange are supplied, not only does the Trade of the district tend to expand — exporting some commodities which are more valuable abroad than at home, and importing other commodities in return—but Production also increases, in consequence of the new markets or demand which renders further production profitable. The natural result of more trade and industry is more wealth,—more goods or property to every man than before. There is more employment for the people, and more profits from production and commerce to pay for and further extend that employment.

This increase of trade, or of exchanges, requires more money,—indeed, presupposes it. As Adam Smith says, "A greater quantity of coin becomes necessary in order to circulate a greater number [or value] of commodities"—in other words, more trade. If this additional quantity of money is not obtainable, the greater circulation of commodities, or increased trade, is impossible, and cannot be undertaken,—no more than there can be journeyings before there are roads or routes. The means of exchange are as requisite as the means of conveyance: indeed, in the case of merchandise, the sole object and purpose of conveyance is Exchange. Moreover, the means of conveyance of themselves cause an absorption of Money, alike in their construction and maintenance. Since Adam Smith's time, a vast economy of coin has been effected.

Nowadays, the universal employment of bank-cheques in payments between individuals, and of the "clearing system" in payments between the banks themselves, has immensely diminished the requirement for coin: indeed the fluctuating expansions and shrinkage of the vast fabric of Credit, reared and resting like an inverted pyramid upon the coin, tend to obscure and at times override the variations in money itself. But, despite those changes, Adam Smith's statement is as correct now as ever. Relatively to the banking and financial processes of each age, a greater circulation of commodities, more numerous or more valuable exchanges of property — in short, more trade — requires a greater quantity of money: that is, of property in a loanable and perfectly exchangeable form, adapted alike for the employment of capital, for the payment of Labour, and for the exchange of commodities.

In practice the operation is this:—Trade is set in motion and carried on by means either of capital or credit, or both,—frequently by advances of money, and almost always by the discount (*i.e.*, conversion into money or banking-accommodation) of bills payable at fixed dates. Of course these loans and banking-accommodation are limited by the amount of money on loan. Suppose that payments in coin were alone in use: then, as trade and discounts increased, coin would become scarce in the banks, which thereupon would charge more for the use or loan of their coin; and the merchant would find that the increased payment which he has to make to the banks leaves him no profit on this extended trade,—or he may even find it impossible to get advances from the banks upon any terms. Thereupon, since money cannot be had in one way, it must be had in another. Loans being scarce or unprocurable, sales have to be "forced," and made in unusual quantity: whereupon, money being in unusual demand, Prices fall,—credit becomes shaken and contracted, rendering still more sales necessary, and further reducing prices and the value of property: until the case ends with heavy losses, numerous bankruptcies, and a long collapse or depression of Trade. A disastrous issue of this kind is not seldom occasioned or precipitated by some untoward accident, beyond foresight or calculation. Nevertheless, in the main, the trading classes, after suffering, learn to keep their operations within the limits which they find profitable,—and which, as said at the outset, are dependent at bottom upon the available stock of money. Despite the employment of cheques, the process is exactly the same at the present day. The tether may be longer, but its limit is as definite and its check as stringent as ever. As gold is withdrawn from the banks to carry on an extension of trade (notably, foreign trade), the banks raise the rate of discount; and merchants must regulate their operations accordingly, keeping their trade within limits which may allow a profit to themselves, yet which fail to supply the usual employment and maintain the ordinary prosperity of the community. And, of course, if the lack of currency be not merely a sudden and single event, but progressive, the period of disaster to the general community becomes proportionately lengthened, proceeding by successive stages of disaster,—as actually happened for generations prior to the discovery of America, and again during the first half of the present century.

It is often said that a lack of money can be remedied without any addition to its quantity, by means of a rise in its value. Double the value of money, and its purchasing power will be simultaneously doubled; and thereafter things will go on as before. This seems a very simple operation; and it seems a most natural thing that money, when it becomes scarce, should rise in value just as other commodities do. But we all know, as regards a scarcity of any commodity, that a rise of price tends to check itself, by checking the consumption or employment of the scarce commodity; and this is true to an unusual extent as regards money. The use of money is not like that of food,—which at all times is indispensable at whatever price, while the extent of its use is determined imperatively by the number of mouths to be filled. The demand for money in Trade (which furnishes the chief requirement for money) is checked in proportion as the advantages of employing it are lessened, and is stopped at the point where those advantages disappear. The hardships produced by a rise in the value of money are so great that the classes upon whose requirements the value of money chiefly depends — viz., the trading and producing classes

—prefer to check those requirements so far as is possible, rather than suffer the diminution of their profits inseparable in the first instance from a rise in the value of money.

These considerations explain, or reveal the cause of, the strange and hitherto unnoticed fact that there may be a scarcity of money, and a very considerable one, without public attention being drawn to the fact by a commensurate sign. Prices are low, it is true: but (as it is usual to say) does not that mean cheapness?—forgetful that it is equally a sign of Poverty! Again, the Bank-rate is low—money on loan is plentiful; because traders have no motive to employ it. They can hardly employ their own capital profitably; still less could they make a profit on borrowed money, for the use of which they must pay. Were they to extend their business-transactions under such circumstances, the requirement for money would be increased,—the stock of money would become more inadequate than before; and while the Bank-rate went up, prices would fall lower than ever. But, under such a state of matters, an expansion of Trade would be a hopeless venture, and is never engaged in. And thus it is only the truth to say that, during a protracted dearth of money and of falling prices, the full extent of the dearth is never cognisable; seeing that the ordinary amount of Trade is not engaged in, and therefore the full monetary inadequacy is never made apparent. Rather than submit to the loss or ruin inflicted by a high Bank-rate, together with a fall of prices and in the value of all existing property, the classes whose operations create the chief requirement for money accept the lesser calamity of stationary or restricted Trade and production. Thus the effects of a scarcity of money may be, and usually are, much more severe than can possibly be perceived. During the brief monetary Crises (occasioned by mere transient fluctuations of Trade) with which the present generation are only too familiar, the signs of dear money are everywhere manifest: there is both an exorbitant Bank-rate and a great fall of prices. On the other hand, under a protracted dearth of money, traders have to accommodate their operations to the existing monetary restrictions. The scarcity, beyond a certain point, ceases to manifest itself by a further fall of prices, but operates severely through a restriction of the transactions upon which the value of money depends. There may be great losses and suffering, owing to an inadequate supply of money, without the cause becoming manifest in the expected way. The supply of the precious metals was vastly inadequate during the greater part of the first half of the present century; yet the fact itself was little noticed. But the universal distress was intense, remarkable, and at the time mysterious or inexplicable. Other causes, no doubt, co-operated in producing the distress, as some circumstances tended to alleviate it; but one chief and unmistakable cause was the restriction of trade necessitated by the lack of money, and enhanced by the constant tendency towards a fall of prices and in the value of labour and of realised property of all kinds. Obviously the scarcity of specie must have been very great when the produce of the mines (as previously described) was barely sufficient even to replace the wear and tear of the stock of coin in circulation!

In this respect, the difference between money and all other commodities of universal use has not hitherto been sufficiently observed. Had grain fallen one-half in quantity, as gold and silver did in 1810-30, the price would have risen beyond all calculation. A very small decrease in the ordinary supply of food sends up the price in a geometrical ratio, or indeed, as in a besieged town, beyond all ratio. When money *must* be used to the ordinary previous extent — when a scarcity of it occurs abruptly, interrupting the ordinary course of business, and current engagements have to be met,—*then* its value rises almost as exorbitantly as that of food during a dearth. For example, when the credit-system breaks down, as occurs during our great commercial and monetary crises, a peremptory requirement for more money arises, together with a drain upon the banks; and although this increased demand may not exceed three or four millions sterling (in notes and coin), the value of the part of the currency thus drawn upon—viz., the reserve or loanable portion — doubles and even trebles instantaneously: the Bank-rate rising from 3 to 6, 9, and even 10 or 12 per cent in the course of a few weeks. Upon such occasions *the trading classes have no time to contract their operations;*

and hence a dearth of money operates with full force, producing a corresponding rise in its value. But, we repeat, under ordinary circumstances, the transactions which produce a demand for money are to a large extent voluntary: it is a question of balanced advantages and disadvantages: " Whether shall I gain or lose more by carrying on operations which (of necessity) enhance the value of money, or by abstaining from them, and thereby keeping money and my existing goods and property at their ordinary value?" Doubtless the community do not usually reflect in this manner; indeed there is nothing which so eludes general observation as a change in the value of money *per se;* but such is the real character of the operation. The trader, whether merchant or producer, farmer or manufacturer, finds that he must keep his industrial enterprise, with its necessary loans and discounts, within certain limits; or else he must pay more for these advances than his profits will bear,—and also encounter a fall of prices which will reduce the value of his whole property, not merely his stock of goods or produce on hand, but his plant, factories, warehouses, &c. — in short, property in every shape except money itself,—and with these, of course, a corresponding loss of credit. And although the moneyed class benefit from such a change, they lose, like the general community, upon that portion of their wealth which does not exist in a moneyed form.

The first and special benefit derived from the new

gold-mines was that they removed this incubus—this imperious restriction upon the world's Trade, using this word in its widest sense. The new gold, after adding California and Australia to the populated and trading countries of the globe, flowed into the banks, the reservoirs of money, thereby enabling the industrial classes to get increased discounts for carrying on an increased trade, and at no higher rate than before. This is an immense advantage to trade and production in all its forms,—every increase of trade being profitable when conducted at no higher cost than before; and this advantage has unquestionably occurred. Trade has increased enormously without any rise of the Bank-rate above its ordinary level, either in our own country or elsewhere. In this way, we repeat, the industrial energies of mankind have been freed from the restriction imposed by the dearth of the precious metals, which prevailed during the forty years previous to the discovery of the new gold-mines. Observe the course of events. In 1852 the new supply of gold visibly affected the value of money; and, naturally, it acted first upon the Bank-rate. We agree with Mr Jevons in thinking that the preceding period of commercial depression reached its lowest point before the end of the year 1850, when (December 26) the Bank-rate, which had stood at $2\frac{1}{2}$ per cent for more than a year, began to move upwards, being raised to 3 per cent,—at which point it remained throughout 1851. But in January 1852, when the new gold was arriving in large quantity, the rate was lowered again to 2½, and in April to 2 per cent (for the first time), *although a revival of trade was in progress.* Consols also throughout that year (1852) stood above par, and touched 102—the highest price ever reached. A lowered Bank-rate during a time of progressive trade certainly indicates an addition to the stock of money, of which the Bank of England is our great reservoir and source of supply. And such an addition actually occurred. The stock of Money— the amount of capital in a loanable form, available for the promotion of trade and industry — was largely augmented; the average stock of bullion held by the Bank became more than doubled; and thus the merchants, manufacturers, and agricultural classes of the Western world, suddenly found that they had more scope for their operations, and better markets owing to the general prosperity. It was as if the working-hive of the world had become enlarged; and the busy occupants forthwith engaged in new or extended operations, such as previously had been beyond their reach.

How far the change in the value of money has gone beyond this, and further benefited industry by producing a rise of prices, cannot be accurately determined. The vicissitudes of trade and of commercial credit (which may arise from many different causes) of themselves potently affect prices;— frequently wholly overriding for a time, and temporarily obscuring, the effect of any change which may contemporaneously occur in the value of money *per se*,—that is, owing to changes in the stock or supply of the precious metals. The action of the New Gold was most rapid and distinct, and hence most visible, at the outset. As already remarked, prices were then at their lowest, also the stock of money to be acted upon was at its smallest, while the production of gold in 1851-3 was at its maximum. Thus the rise of prices was then most manifest, and most clearly attributable to the new supplies of gold. Thereafter, it is exceedingly difficult to determine with even approximate accuracy the further effect of the New Gold upon the value of money. On the whole, the varying evidence of the Tables of Prices may be held to show a rise of prices, or fall in the purchasing-power of money, to the extent of about twenty-five per cent above their previous level, or as they stood throughout the years 1845-52. An important change, no doubt; but not great compared with the previous long-continued fall between 1810 and 1852, and trifling compared with the revolution in the value of gold which had been so fully expected and alarmingly predicted. Further, the rise, or period of high prices, was all over in a quarter of a century! And at present, despite a slight revival since 1879, the purchasing-power of money shows hardly an appreciable difference from what it used to be a generation ago.

Wholly unexpected, and *à priori* improbable or impossible, as such a result was, a careful analysis of the facts, and especially of those relating to the diffusion of the precious metals, altogether changes the complexion of the case; so much that, upon the ordinary hypothesis—namely, that the rise of prices was produced simply and directly by the numerical addition made to the world's stock of coins, or money—the wonder rather is, how the New Gold could have produced any appreciable rise of prices, at least in Europe and the central portions of the civilised world of commerce—or, to use the common phrase in such questions, within the area of Christendom. In the previous chapter, we called attention to the speedy loss or neutralisation to the Western world of a very large portion of the produce of the new Mines by the remarkable export of the precious metals (chiefly silver) to the East. For the entire period, 1849-75, the total production of the precious metals throughout the world may be taken, roundly, at 900 millions sterling; of which amount (reckoning the annual production at the beginning of 1848 at seventeen millions) just over one half, or say 450 millions, was a new or additional supply; while the gold and silver absorbed in India alone, during the same period, amounted to 270 millions: leaving for the rest of the world only 180 millions, spread over a full quarter of a century of the most rapid commercial expansion which the world has ever beheld. Thus, for the general and domestic use of the great Western world, the New Supply added only $6\frac{2}{3}$ millions a-year, or barely one-third, to the amount of the previous notoriously inadequate supply, as it existed at the beginning of 1848.

Moreover, during what may be called the very height of the Golden Age—namely, the eleven years 1855-65—India absorbed fully 90 per cent of the contemporaneous new portion of the supply,—leaving barely fifteen millions sterling of it, or less than one and a half million a-year, for the use of the rest of the world throughout these years: an insignificant addition, considering the contemporaneous energy of industrial enterprise, and rapid increase of trade, population, and monetary requirements. The money was gone from Europe: this vast proportion of the new gold or silver hardly circulated at all in the Western world — merely passing through it, as through a sieve. Yet although this new money was gone, exported to the East, no small profit or new wealth was left behind, created by the new Trade which this gold and silver had sufficed to promote and sustain.

These facts are fitted to suggest, or indeed to challenge, a reconsideration of the received theory or explanation as to the effect of additional money upon Prices—its exchangeable value or purchasing power; and, in particular, as to the mode in which the New Gold operated in producing a Rise of Prices. For, how could a mere addition of £15,000,000 of new money suffice to raise prices full twenty per cent throughout Europe and America during the eleven years 1855-65, when the Golden Age was about its best and prices were at their highest? The common doctrine is, that an addition to the currency increases prices by or through a simple depreciation of money, in the same way as the doubling of the counters in a game at cards. An utterly barren operation,—a mere waste of the precious metal, and, with that, the labour of the Miners! But such a doctrine (which is correct in principle with respect to a State-issue of paper-money, not needed by the community, and forced out solely as a means of paying the State's debts) is quite inapplicable and erroneous in a case like that of the New Gold; where the money is solely obtained by voluntary labour from the earth, and thereafter from banks in exchange for "money's worth"—suitable property of various kinds; and which, being only obtainable by being paid for, never goes into circulation unless it be needed, that is, can be profitably employed,— as for an extension of trade or the undertaking of new industrial enterprises. It is only money in circulation (*i.e.*, in use) which affects Prices, or the purchasing-power of money. And more money in use, —what does this imply? Having to be paid for, the additional money is taken (say from the banks) not to be hoarded, but to be profitably employed. And more money in profitable employment means more employment for labour, a greater demand for goods, more production, and more trade in this increased production: all which operations being presumably profitable, the result is more Wealth or Property. Thus there are more goods, and more exchanges both of labour and goods,—while the greater demand raises the value both of goods and labour; and the increase of the circulating medium suffices to pay these higher wages and prices without creating a monetary scarcity, —the occurrence of which would put a check upon the whole round of those beneficial operations. Also, it must be remembered, a million in gold supports, or renders available, a much larger sum in credit-money of various kinds; while the increased prosperity strengthens Credit, which of itself is equivalent to more money. Moreover, the quickened circulation of Money during prosperous times (enabling each coin to do more work) further adds to its potency, and augments its influence upon prices.

One more point to be remembered is, that ultimately these operations check themselves; and that the original force which at first induced and pushed on the industrial progress, becomes simply adequate to maintain the expansion which has been reached. It is a progress which tends to bring itself to a halt, somewhat as a locomotive on a snow-blocked line only advances by heaping up obstacles in front, which ere long bring it to a stand. Or rather, it is like a man's pushing back of an iron spring, which reaches a point beyond which he can do no more, while if his own strength diminish, the spring will proportionately recoil into its old position. Dropping the simile for the facts,—the industrial and commercial transactions which cheap or ample Money set agoing in due course make Money scarce, and reimpose upon Trade the old monetary checks. There are more commodities to be exchanged and a larger number of those exchanges;

and thus, at every step, the beneficial operation of the New Gold created new requirements for itself, until the cheap money was actually nullified by the result of its own operations. And thus, as we see, Prices have at length all but returned to their old level. Yet what does this imply but that the world has reached a higher level of existence? There has been an enormous increase of human prosperity in the interval,—so much so, that the doubled currency of the world is no more adequate than before for the amount of profit-making transactions daily carried on! Moreover, this very greatness of prosperity is proportionately exposed to danger; and it becomes statesmen to consider how a permanent return to an inadequate monetary supply is to be avoided, together with a painful, troubled, and humiliating descent from the higher and happier level which under Providence we have reached, and as yet still enjoy.

As I have repeatedly remarked, an addition to the currency (provided, of course, it be not forced out by the State, but voluntarily taken into circulation in the ordinary manner) does not raise prices save while creating and increasing Wealth. New and profitable enterprises of trade and production are undertaken,—increasing the demand for labour and the consumption of goods, whereby the value both of labour and of goods is enhanced; while a portion of the simultaneously accruing production or wealth pays for the additional coin. On the other hand, if trade is bad—if there be no profitable openings for industrial enterprise, or if, owing to some of the numerous vicissitudes to which Trade is liable (and which may arise from an inadequate currency), enterprises prove unprofitable in character, or are cut short ere they can bear fruit, wealth is lost, bankruptcies ensue. Credit is shaken and contracts: wages and prices fall; money circulates slowly, doing less work than before, or lies wholly stagnant and barren in the banks: no one being willing to borrow money, because no one can profitably employ it,—hardly, at such times, even his own capital. "High Prices and Plenty; Low Prices and Want!"—such is the old saying, and it is a true one; albeit it was not the deduction of a philosopher, but has sprung from the simple instincts or crude experience of the masses.

The condition of our own country, and indeed the general history of the world, suffices to show that the third quarter of the present century has been a most notable and hitherto unparalleled epoch of prosperity. It was like the Augustan Age of Rome (which was the acme of the old Mediterranean World) enlarged to the limits of wellnigh the globe itself. The sphere of civilisation, the area of internationalism, extended into previously barbarous or jealously excluded regions; and the bonds of Trade and Finance were cast far abroad from the heart of the civilised world,—like grappling-irons of peace and humanity, tending to bind together in mutual prosperity distant regions and alien peoples. In consequence of the vast amount of capital conveyed in the form of the precious metals to the East, our Indian Empire, covered by a system of railways, sprang into active industrial existence; and the multiplied trade between the East and the West added greatly to employment and production, to the comforts of life and national prosperity, in both of these regions,—each of which found a complement of itself in the other. Australasia and the Pacific coast of North America, by becoming occupied by a civilised population, served to extend the girdle of Commerce all round the earth. And all the wealth which arose in those remote regions, or which was transferred thither from the old centres of Western civilisation, was reflected back upon Europe, quickening industrial life and augmenting social wellbeing: constituting new markets and channels for trade, and opening new fields alike for population, labour, and capital. In truth, the face of the whole world has been changed, and the general condition of mankind happily improved during the past thirty years: each man and each nation is now the centre of a far larger world,—conferring a universality of industrial freedom and of opportunities for action such as cannot be too highly estimated. Although there has been no discovery of a New World, nor even a practical re-discovery of old regions, such as marked the Silver Age, there has been a general utilisation of the world for the benefit of mankind, and in commerce and finance an almost world-wide development of Internationalism, which in its completeness must be the crowning stage of the human career.

The beginning of this epoch of world-wide changes and prosperity was undoubtedly synchronous with the gold-discoveries at the middle of the century; and although opinions may differ as to the degree or extent to which those changes are directly attributable to those discoveries, the connection between them is too manifest to be questioned. As regards the peculiar action of the New Gold—of the remarkable addition made during that period to the precious metals, the World's stock of Money,—let us put the case in a shape somewhat curious, yet substantially correct, and which may render readily intelligible in broad outline facts which, we admit, are too vast and vague to be satisfactorily dealt with in detail. Keeping in mind the exposition which we have given, in a previous chapter, of the true nature and operations of Money—a thing of man's invention which stands alone, without its like in any other commodity,—consider what is necessarily implied in the fact of the enormous addition recently made to the world's stock of the precious metals. Between the years 1848 and 1875, wellnigh 900 millions sterling of gold and silver were produced; the greater part of which has been employed as Money—chiefly in coin, and partly in those stamped ingots which are much employed as international currency. Make any allowance for depreciation, or fall in the value of money, since 1848: still, after every reasonable deduction, the amount of Money put in circulation during the Golden Age has been enormous. Well, then, what has this new money been doing? and what must have been the general result or effects of its operation?

All of this new money has been ceaselessly employed as the medium of exchange,—in effecting exchanges of various kinds: in buying goods, paying for labour, and in other suchlike transactions. All these exchanges are normally profitable: they are meant to be profitable—profit is their sole object,—and ordinarily the object is attained. Each exchange gives a profit to both the parties engaged in the transaction,—alike to buyer and seller. And, as already said, and as is obvious, all the New Money since 1848—not only the hundreds of millions of metallic money, but also the credit-money or paper-currency of various kinds which has been issued upon or supported by the new gold and silver—has been engaged in carrying on these exchanges: commercial or industrial transactions which could not otherwise have been carried on, and the increase of which has alone prevented the predicted monetary revolution. *Consequently, the New Gold has been ceaselessly engaged in making profits.* The effect has been the same as if, upon each exchange thus effected, a portion of the gold adhered to or remained in the palm of each hand through which it passed,—while the gold-money itself passes on undiminished in value, to effect an ever-new series of exchanges! If a producer sells a thousand pounds worth of goods, he makes (say) ten per cent of profit: so that he is richer by £100. In like manner the merchant-purchaser re-sells the goods, in retail or otherwise, with a profit of ten per cent on the transaction. Thus in these two exchanges the money has given rise to a profit, gain, or new wealth, amounting to £200; while the thousand sovereigns remain in undiminished value, and continue circulating and effecting exchanges,—every one of which presumably yields a profit, correspondingly increasing wealth. This, then, and not the mere profit on production, as marked by the "first exchange" of the gold, constitutes the benefit accruing from the Gold-mines,—a benefit (as previously explained) arising from the fact that Gold as Money, besides being wellnigh imperishable of itself, is the commodity possessing the strange quality that it is *used without being consumed*,—its value is developed without exhaustion: and consequently, in its use (being employed in effecting profitable exchanges), it gives rise to a long series of profits, or of new wealth, which have to be added to that original profit, which belongs to it in common with other useful commodities—namely, the profit upon its production. It is true that the New Gold did not of itself create these exchanges—no more than the mere existence of Roads creates traffic: but this new Trade and these additional exchanges could not have been effected without the new or additional gold. Moreover, the mere existence of a power impels to its use. If, as has been remarked, the existence of a great army tempts a monarch or nation to a line of policy tending to utilise that military power; so, still more, does the existence of an ample or adequate stock of the circulating medium suggest, and create a reasonable motive for, engaging in those exchanges which constitute trade, and for which this medium of exchange was specially designed. Money, in truth, besides being the mere medium of exchange, is Wealth in its most mobile, exchangeable, and potent form: it is wealth in the very form most powerful and suitable for carrying on industrial and commercial enterprise—both the production of commodities, and the exchange of them. Hence, we repeat, Money creates Trade and thereby begets Profits, just as Roads are now well known to create Traffic and promote both production and trade.

Startling, or at least striking, as is the case as we here put it, it is no exaggeration of the truth. And who can calculate or estimate, even in imagination, the sum-total of the new profits, the additional wealth thus flowing from the employment of the New Gold—or of both the gold and silver?—for both of those metals retained their old value as money down to 1875. We repeat—novel as this doctrine may be [1]—the vast amount of metallic money, and of paper-currency supported by it,

---

[1] In reviewing my *Economy of Capital*, published in 1864, in which this view was briefly expressed, a critic remarked (as if to destroy my opinion by a *reductio ad absurdum*)—"If this view were right, the value of the new gold would not be terminated by the first exchange, but would be renewed every time the piece of metal changed hands." In substance, this is just what I affirm.

added to the circulating medium between 1848 and 1875, was engaged in a ceaseless round of profit-making: the sum-total of which represents the real gain reaped by mankind from the new Mines, together with the consequent addition to the well-being and improvement of the condition of the civilised world from the Golden Age.

CHAPTER XXI.

CLOSE OF THE GOLDEN AGE—(1876–80).

THE two grandest epochs of the modern world, as well as two of the finest and happiest periods of English history, have been synchronous with and comprised in the reigns of two British Queens. The Elizabethan Age has only been equalled or excelled by that of Victoria; while the intermediate reign of Queen Anne ranks second to them, and was famous alike in arms and in literature. The reign of Elizabeth was the prime of the Silver Age, when a New World had been added to the Old, and when European trade and enterprise sprang into energy; when the ventures of commerce were eminently profit-yielding; and when the bare and bleak conditions of human existence, which had prevailed throughout the Dark Ages, began to soften under the influences of new and rapidly growing wealth. The masses of the population rose in the scale of existence, under the vast increase in the demand for their labour, which came with the multifarious opportunities for its profitable employment. Wise

Ministers, of a patriotic Queen, guided the bark of the State; and both in Art and in Arms there was a galaxy of famous men, such as a nation gives birth to only in some brief and rare flowering-time of the national spirit, and which in the Elizabethan epoch extended almost equally over the leading nations of Europe, begot and inspired by the momentous, exciting, and imagination-firing discoveries and events of the time. The people of seafaring England, especially, were stirred to daring and to fervid enthusiasm by the circumstance that it was *upon the seas* that the grand new life of the times was to be played,—that new oceans were then revealed and opened to human enterprise, containing in their still shadowy expanse men hardly knew what not of marvels, magnificence, and wealth. Besides a New World, with strange peoples and vegetation, new empires of strange civilisation, like those of the Incas and of Montezuma, had been discovered only to vanish with magic-like suddenness; while tales of the far-distant realms of Cathay and the Indies replaced, with the superior interest of reality, the vanishing fabulous Empire of Prester John. Under these various influences, a "sea-change" came over the spirit and thoughts of our people, as over the other Western nations of Europe; while, combined with the general spirit of adventure thus engendered, there was the urgent necessity, as well as high desire, to defend the freedom and uphold the fortunes of England; and the same bold "sea-dogs" who, pushing to sea from every bay and creek in their little vessels, grappled and worsted the "Invincible Armada" in the British Channel, also sailed as rovers and discoverers around the shores of the New World,—fighting the silver-laden galleons as they voyaged, and haunting the Spanish Main as a "Land Debatable," whereon the triumphs of victory went to Old England, while the spoils sufficed to defray the costs of these volunteer expeditions of naval war. Such was the Volunteer System in the days of Elizabeth—anticipating, in the more warlike and aggressive fashion of that age, the defensive Volunteer force evoked by national peril under George the Third, and the more disciplined and powerful Volunteer force which has sprung up to guard the British Isles under our beloved Victoria. The silver from the mountain-mines of the New World enabled Queen Elizabeth to restore the English coinage from the debasements almost necessarily imposed upon it by her royal predecessors; and, by-and-by, the growing plenty of the precious metals served to displace the dismal incubus of Barter and payments in kind—which, despite knowledge and intellectual civilisation, had previously kept European commerce under the conditions of barbarism. Yet what was even this fundamentally great change, and enfranchisement of trade and labour, but a bagatelle compared with the whole mass of benefits to civilisation and to the wellbeing of mankind conferred by the Silver Age under the reign of Elizabeth,—which contributed to make the Elizabethan Age one of the brightest epochs of England, and contemporary with the Renaissance of the European peoples and the momentous birth of the Modern World?

After the lapse of three centuries, the Victorian Age has come as the truly Augustan age of England, and as an historical epoch on the whole as grand, albeit in different fashion, and certainly more happy than even the reign of "good Queen Bess." When the youthful VICTORIA ascended the British throne, her country still lay in that "winter of our discontent" which had so strangely set-in after the Napoleonic wars, in lieu of the splendid prosperity which, according to all human anticipation, was to engirdle the British empire on the return of Peace. During the first dozen years of the young Queen's reign, the distress continued to predominate, interrupted only by the sunny burst which attended the new gold from Russia and the splendid madness of the Railway Mania,—which in a mere year or two equipped our Isles with the iron road and the rapid steam-car, preparing us in advance of the rest of the world with a mighty enginery of trade, in most fortunate anticipation of the Golden Age which, although close at hand, still lay undreamt of in the womb of Time. And with the predominating Distress there existed much popular discontent, of which the first Reform Bill had brought no cessation, and which not only appeared in the half-social half-political shape of Chartism, but gave birth to a virulent Trades-unionism, of which the Glasgow cotton-spinners' conspiracy was a murderous outcome. Then came the famous

Gold-discoveries; and in the year 1853 the country finally left its long drear winter-time behind, and rose into a new spring, under the sunshine of the Golden Age. Even our Agriculture, menaced as it seemed with coming destruction from the free competition of more favoured grain-regions, rose quickly into a prosperity which for a while gave the lie to its wellnigh despairing apprehensions; while commercial and manufacturing industry, aided by our railways and by cheapened food for its labourers, more than realised the high expectations for the sake of which the new Free-trade legislation had mainly been ventured upon. Ten or twelve years thereafter, that golden epoch reached its summer-time; and in other ten years we reached its autumn and fullest golden fruitage in 1873,—when Trade progressed " by leaps and bounds ;" but when, as we now know, the fruitage had begun to rot.[1]

The Golden Age in England has been especially fortunate in the Sovereign of the time, and whose auspicious name of " VICTORY " foreshadowed the triumphs of her reign, and fitly marks the zenith-time of the British Empire. Happily, compared with Elizabeth's, the reign of Victoria has been free from any dire external peril,—mainly, a period of peace abroad and a halcyon-time of calm contentment at home. The special triumph of Victoria, and

[1] It is now well known that a considerable portion of our Exports in 1872-3 were purchased *with our own wealth*—with the proceeds of the large and reckless Loans to foreign countries, the greater part of which sums were wholly lost to their owners, and to this country, by the bankruptcy or repudiation of the borrowing States.

the brightest glory of her reign, has been in winning the hearts, by ceaselessly caring for the wellbeing of her people,—especially of the humbler and less fortunate classes, to whom the sympathy of the beloved Queen has come directly in many an hour of sorrow and bereavement. Future generations, looking back upon this prosperous time, will admiringly remember that the Golden Age was also the reign of Victoria, who is as truly the *chère Reine* of England's people, as was Queen Eleanor to the first and greatest of the royal Plantagenets,—Victoria, the most well-beloved of monarchs in all history, and whose whole reign has been prosperous even as this briefer golden Epoch which, sunny as "the Queen's weather" itself, surrounded her path, and contributed to add domestic happiness to external prosperity.

Agriculture is the trade wherein changes of its condition are most readily visible to common observation. And in the course of my own routine of life I have had yearly opportunities of observing its changes, especially in one of the not least notable agricultural districts of the kingdom. Year after year from boyhood, as autumn came round, I have visited in brief but happy sojourn the Scottish Border counties: first, the Lammermoor hills and the banks of the bright-flowing Whitadder; and thereafter the vales of the Teviot and Tweed, with their tributary glens, sparkling with trout-streams—from Kelso westward through the gap in the Dumfries-shire hills into green Ewesdale and sunny Langholm. Since I first, as a released school-

boy—mounted on the four-horsed mail-coach of the
time, the "Blucher" or the "Chevy Chase"—crossed
the flat bleak summit of Middleton Moor, and rolled
down the narrow strath of the Heriot and Gala
Water; or, by the other route from Edinburgh over
Soutra Hill (where the mail-coach used frequently
to be blocked by winter snow-storms, and more than
one guard lost his life when gallantly struggling
on with the mail-bag through the deep drifts),
entered the vale of the Leader at Carfrae Mill; since
then, cultivation like a green tide has risen higher
and higher up the bare stone-covered hill-slopes
on either hand—so steep, and where the soil is so
thin, that it is prone to roll down the hillsides with
the yearly furrowing passage of the plough: until
now the conical hill of Cowdenknowes hardly preserves a green circlet of Nature's growth on its
summit (Cybele cramped on her throne by the
industrial inroads of Man!) So also with Penilheugh
and Ruber's Law, and the whole sweep of the hillsides which enclose the valley of the Teviot,—where
the old moorland and grouse-shooting have all but
vanished under the progress of tile-draining and
tillage, favoured by long leases and fair co-operation
on the part of the Buccleuch and other great landowners of the Scottish Borders.

I have seen changes, also—I may say natural
and corresponding changes—in the life and fortunes
of the Farmers. The closing years of the first half
of the century were hard times for the Farmers.
There had been two or three unwontedly good years

just before—some fine harvests, together with good prices under the large and general spending during the Railway Mania; and possibly the Border farmers had caught some part of the contagion, living with less careful economy than before. Anyhow the years 1847-8-9 played serious havoc; and agricultural discontent, bred by distress, still widely prevailed in 1851, when the recent abolition of the Corn-law (although at that time it had hardly had time to bear its fruits) was as loudly complained of as ever. Yet lo! and with almost magical suddenness, these complaints ceased, in 1852,—not to be heard of again until recently, under the return and renewal of hard times. With the year 1853, British Agriculture became highly prosperous—for the first and only time since the Peace of Waterloo. The new generation of farmers enjoyed a very different life from what their fathers had known. Among the Farmers of the Scottish Border counties[1]— most notably in Teviotdale, I think—the present generation so greatly advanced in fortune after 1853 that their habits and mode of life became like those of the "country gentleman,"—with fine houses (en-

---

[1] Owing to the superior education long ago established in Scotland, I have frequently had occasion to observe that the Farmer on the English side of the Border—even though he be a "statesman" or yeoman, owning the ground which he cultivates—is hardly distinguishable in mind and manners from the "hind" or regular farm-labourer of the Scottish Border counties. Also the Farmers of these latter counties, as commonly throughout Scotland—owing to the largeness of their farms, which necessitates the possession of capital to hold and work them— belong in most respects to a superior class compared with those of other countries.

larged and improved chiefly at their own expense), conservatories, hothouses, &c.; keeping not merely the customary gig or dog-cart, but handsome carriages; engaging in coursing and fox-hunting,—not merely riding with the hounds as outsiders, but as members of the Hunt, wearing "the Duke's" buttons, or other insignia of membership. Besides hunting, and the ordinary sport on river or moor, steeplechasing, even racing, became included in the amusements of the wealthier few; choice greyhounds are to be seen at many a farm-house; and even bloodhorses are bred, here and there—certainly as a luxury or pleasant speculation, rather than as a profitable department of the farm. And Farming itself, as we have said, has been well cared for,—conducted with the aids of science, and with no small personal skill and enterprise. Nor must it be thought that all the profits of the new and prosperous time went to the Farmer. Rents have been raised and raised again,—especially on the pastoral farms, where the usual lease runs for only half the length of the nineteen years' lease accorded for grain-farms.

The happy change which has come over our country since the middle of the present century—and the effects of which have not been exhausted even by the long and severe Depression which (like the seven lean years of Pharaoh's Dream) has lain so heavily upon the national fortunes—has pervaded all trades and all classes of the nation, and has been brightly reflected in the improved conditions and usages of daily life. Any one who, like myself, has attained to threescore years, or even who has reached the full middle of the allotted span of human life, must have been struck by the softer and happier life which surrounds our children, compared with the Spartan-like bareness of our own youthful upbringing. How often must such an observer have rejoiced, in quiet thankfulness of heart, to see the softer ways and numberless little luxuries and pleasures which are now regarded as a reasonable right of our children, and a justifiable indulgence on the part of parents,—remembering, not grudgingly nor regretfully, how entirely such pleasures and pleasantness were absent from the homes of our own childhood and youth. True, it may be said that a change of ideas, the growth of gentler sentiments and of a quicker sympathy, has had much to do with this kindlier and more indulgent treatment of the young. And in part this is true: and I should be sorry to think otherwise. Nevertheless, generosity and self-sacrifice for the happiness of others are but limited, very limited, sentiments in human nature in the general. And any observer to whom I here appeal, possessed of a tolerably long experience of mankind —and, if he can look within, of himself also—will be ready to acknowledge that a mere change of ideas or sentiments, howsoever powerful, would fail to produce so widespread a change of habits, and one which makes so considerable a drain upon the purse and pocket. Not a few natures, thank God! feel the truth of the Divine teaching that "it is more blessed to give than to receive,"—that it is a luxury of happiness to give, not merely out of abundance, but at what may seem some sacrifice to one's self,—and that to impart pleasure is the sweetest enjoyment either of Nature's gifts or of worldly fortune. But depend upon it, the greater costliness (to sum it up in one dry ugly word) which is nowadays accorded to the upbringing of the young, would never have become a general usage had there not simultaneously been a marked increment of wealth in the community. In truth, this increased expenditure upon children has not stood alone—a monument of parental self-denying,—a marvellous, if not impossible expenditure out of a half-full purse. It originated in greater wealth, and has been accompanied—has it not?—by softer living and increased expenditure upon our own selves.

Look, too, at the hours of work; and remember that these hours cannot be shortened except the work be more profitable, (unless, of course, the condition both of employer and employed is deteriorated — which admittedly was not the case during the period in question). In my early life, in Edinburgh, even professional men—solicitors, accountants, &c.—and the more or less wealthy heads of firms, managers of companies, proprietors of works and factories, remained at business as a rule till eight or nine o'clock at night; besides a similar, though lesser, difference in the morning hours of attendance at business. Of the changed hours of the working-classes I need not speak: it is so obvious and well known. Indeed in their case, had the "golden period" lasted until now, they would probably by this time have realised the new charter of British labour:—"Eight hours' sleep; eight hours' play; eight hours' work; and eight shillings a-day!" In some kinds of work, did not labourers wellnigh, or actually, realise this ideal (albeit in a desultory if not dissolute way) in the heyday of 1873? And according to much evidence, has not the British workman, even in those subsequent years of depression, been perilously asserting his claim to this ideal condition, at least in that part of it attainable by himself — namely, the shortening of working-hours by regular or irregular absence, or abstention from work?

True, to this part also of my inferential argument, as to the preceding one, an obvious objection may be taken; and one which, as in the previous case, I am glad to recognise so far as it is founded on fact. It may be said, although the hours of work have been shortened, the matter is explainable by the improved quality of the work. I admit that this may be a partial explanation,—even in face of complaints that ordinary labour now lacks the thoroughness and conscientious care and diligence which previously was common. For, whether that complaint be correct or not, it is true that, in not a few departments of industry, human labour has become more potent or productive, through steam-driven machinery and other suchlike material appliances by or through which it operates. Indeed (as has been fully recognised in these pages), the numerous inventions and industrial appliances which have come into operation within the last forty years—railways, oceanic steam-navigation, telegraphs, the steam-hammer, the reaping-machine, and even the still embryo steam-plough, &c.—have played the foremost part in our recent prosperity,—albeit propelled (so to speak) by the New Gold, while also furnishing new channels for its profit-making action and circulation.

And now the world has come to the close of a very memorable epoch. The present generation has seen come and go the most remarkable outburst of material prosperity which has ever visited the nations of mankind. The epoch has been short-lived as a northern summer,—brief and brilliant as the sunshine which suddenly clothes with almost tropical luxuriance the plains of the Red River Settlement, where rich crops ripen and fruits and flowers of the South blossom and mature, all in the course of a few weeks, betwixt long periods of frost and snow. The world has fallen into winter again; but a large portion of the fruits of the golden summer enduringly remain, —a rich heritage for subsequent generations. New regions have been peopled, and the trading world widened and enriched. Countless new and large factories of human industry, even whole townships of labour, have been established widely throughout our own and other countries. Enlarged harbours and new docks and quays line the shores of our bays and estuaries, and a mightily increased forest of shipping has sprung up for the maritime conveyance of the augmented produce of the world; Earth's isthmuses are being canalised, and its great mountain-chains tunnelled; while thousands of miles of the iron road have been constructed to give play to the increased locomotion both of men and merchandise: these railways showing like a network on the map of each country, and internationally girdling the continents from sea to sea,—spanning America at its widest, and thickly traversing all Europe, from the British Channel eastward to the Caspian and the Euxine, and southward to almost every point on the shores of the Mediterranean Sea.

The change has been so great that even the aspect of the earth's surface visibly bears witness to it. Compared with the third and fourth decades of the century, how manifest is the changed aspect of our own islands! The country is now all in motion, swarming like a hive of ants. Motion and locomotion are everywhere. Instead of the quiet highways along which the mail-coach with its dozen passengers passed but once a-day, and only the occasional blare of the guard's horn broke the rural silence, an aeronaut would now hear beneath him a perpetual roar of sound, and see hundreds of smoking railway-trains moving in swift succession along the far-stretching lines of the iron road, receiving and disgorging crowds of passengers at each terminus and halting-station. By sea, the change has been hardly less striking. Along the great highways of the ocean, instead of a thin and straggling line of ships, baffled by wind and tide, there is a steady procession of swift-going leviathans of the deep,—marking the great sea-routes by an almost continuous trail of smoke, signalising the steam-engine at work in its latest and most far-journeying form.

This epoch of rich commercial progress, pervading all the leading countries of the world, culminated, and also came to a close, with the eminently prosperous years of 1872 and 1873,—ending suddenly when at its height, rocket-like, with an outburst of fresh splendour. Since 1873 the course of events has resembled the "dissolving views" of the diorama, wherein a glowing summer landscape is seen to pass swiftly, yet by distinctly marked gradations, into the bleakness and snowy garb of winter. As by the wave of a magician's wand—certainly from causes which in their entirety cannot be readily explained,—the golden "tide in the affairs of men" rapidly ebbed away, until there came low-water again all over the world, leaving stately industrial enterprises like stranded ships strewing every shore. The numerous factories erected during the golden epoch stood idle, or with doors half-closed; crowds of splendid shipping lay idle in the harbours of the world from Liverpool to Calcutta, from San Francisco to New York; and the railways, although still making their hourly journeys, would have been glad to carry behind each rapid locomotive a heavier burden of goods or passengers. But they all remain —factories, shipping, railways,—a heritage from the golden past, and ready for work again as soon as the present "winter of our discontent" is over.

Besides these very visible and tangible signs of the past prosperity, and of existing potential power and usefulness, the third quarter of the century has left an enormous legacy of moneyed wealth. Statists have sought to become eloquent over the vast accumulations of wealth in the United Kingdom. Even if their computations were less correct than they appear to be—even were it requisite to make no small abatement from some of their conclusions, the broad and unquestionable facts of the case show an increase of wealth altogether unprecedented. No writer has resumed the work of Mr Porter—the pioneer in this branch of digested statistics, whose *Progress of the Nation* required for its compilation an amount of labour unneeded nowadays, when Government returns and other sources of information readily supply a continuous record of the national fortunes. But the part of Mr Porter's subject which in one respect sums up all the others—namely, the Wealth of the Nation—has of late years been ably and carefully dealt with by the late Mr Dudley Baxter, Mr Newmarch, and Mr Giffen, each continuing the work of his predecessors. What is the tale thus told, in dry figures, of our national progress during the epoch of which we write? It is not until 1855 that, by the extension of the Income-tax to Ireland, the official records comprise the incomes of the whole kingdom. In that year the *assessed* incomes of the nation (exclusive of the larger amount of unassessed income, belonging chiefly to the wage-receiving classes) amounted to 308 millions sterling; in 1865 this yearly income had risen to 396 millions; and in 1875 to 571 millions. Thus, this portion of the national income increased so rapidly that in 1875 it was no less than 263 millions larger than it was in 1855. And if the increase had affected all persons equally, the income of each individual belonging to the class who pay assessed taxes would have increased 80 per cent during these twenty years. In like manner the property, or realised wealth, of the nation has increased from barely 4800 millions sterling in 1854 to 6100 millions in 1866, and in 1875 to 8600 millions. During the last decade of the period—namely, from 1865 to 1875— the amount of property per head of the population increased from £200 in 1865 to £260 in 1875.

What has become of the enormous mass of wealth thus rapidly accumulated,—equivalent to one-half of the National Debt, and *exceeding the entire amount of the previously accumulated wealth of the British nation?* Only in one year of the recent long Depression did the returns of the national income retrograde, and merely to a trifling extent. What, then, has become of this vast additional wealth— of these 380 millions sterling accumulated, and added to the previous stock of wealth, by our nation during the brief quarter-century of the Golden Age?

A considerable portion of this New Wealth exists in a form invisible to the public sight, and is difficult to reckon even by the most capable authorities. Such are the investments of British wealth in other countries—the foreign and colonial investments; in the shape of State-loans, investments in railways, and other public works, chiefly made through the agency of joint-stock companies. But by far the larger portion of this new wealth remains in our own country, in forms visible to the instructed eye, and more or less to all men, whether they think of it or not. A large portion of it has been invested in Agriculture, in improving cultivation and the produce of the soil; in reclaiming marshes and moorland; in constructing thousands of miles of field-drains and fences, erecting new and better farm-buildings, purchasing agricultural tools and machinery; raising hamlets into villages, and brightening the rural districts with elegant mansions. Another portion of the new wealth has been devoted to the extension and improvement of our railway-system, canals, harbours, docks; to the multiplication of industrial factories, coal-mines, iron-furnaces, workshops and machinery, and other suchlike agencies of production and manufacture; and to building the splendid shipping which now does the larger part of the maritime carrying-trade of the world. Look also at our cities,—how they grow, and how they brighten. What has been the growth of London alone, in mere structured bricks and mortar, within the last thirty years? How much, from the spare surplus wealth of individuals, has been spent upon town-halls, public parks, schools, colleges, churches, hospitals? Costly works of "sanitation," undertaken by municipalities, are gradually rendering our towns as healthy as the country. How great, too, has been the improvement and increase of theatres, concert-halls, picture-galleries, and other places for public pleasure or amusement. Within our homes, how much more is there both of comfort and of beauty,—houses more spacious and airy, beautiful furniture and improved domestic appliances. And for the person, more carriages and horses, better cookery, more pleasing or attractive dress. In short, more "sweetness and light" in the material fashion of our dwellings; and a general and not unsuccessful striving to rise into a higher level of daily life.

Here we end our task. The book has reached its allotted limits; and the close of the quarter-century following the gold-discoveries affords a tempting and natural boundary for a work of this kind. We had designed to bring the subject down to the present day. We had purposed to describe the partial renewal of the Silver Age: the new and singularly rich silver-mines in the Washaw Hills of Nevada, and the extensive demonetisation of that metal in Europe,—the consequences of which appear destined to be of extreme gravity. It would have been deeply interesting, also, to have traced out the leading features of the remarkable Depression of Trade which set-in in 1875, or earlier—which indeed was heralded, if not inaugurated, by the semi-crisis of November 1873, which like a thunderclap in a clear sky startled the American and British public while rejoicing in the extraordinary trade-prosperity of that culminating year. And, lastly, there are the new gold-mines of India, in which this country is deeply concerned, and upon the issue of which discoveries the fortunes of the commercial world at large will be considerably dependent.

The aspect of affairs at the present time still remains somewhat discouraging. We do not confine this remark to our own country,—albeit our condition is now seriously fraught with those perils which are inseparable from a nation which is so largely dependent upon other countries both for food and employment,—a nation whose numbers are so much in excess of the natural powers of its territory that no less than a hundred millions sterling are annually consumed, utterly extinguished or destroyed every year, in the importation of foreign necessaries and luxuries of life; while an almost equal amount of foreign produce has to be imported to supply materials for our manufacturing industry and profitable employment for our people: while, further, our whole manufacturing industry, and our means of paying alike for foreign food and foreign raw material, are dependent upon the willingness of other countries to purchase our manufactured goods, instead of themselves producing them. Our present condition, in truth, is only possible and maintainable in consequence of our little Isles being the head and centre of a great Empire,—the loss of which would at once reduce Great Britain to a third-rate rank among States. Nor can any thoughtful observer shut his eyes to the fact that, under the recent shiftings of political and governing power—necessary, and in many respects beneficial as these are—the maintenance of our Empire has now passed into unstable hands and insecure keeping.

Democracy never created an empire, and is ill-fitted to preserve one. Admirable as a democratic government may be as regards domestic affairs and legislation, inasmuch as the majority of a people may be trusted to know its own everyday wants—quickly feeling "where the shoe pinches;" such a government is ill-fitted for the management of imperial policy,—for dealing with foreign countries and rival nations, of which the mass of our population know little or nothing, and for framing and maintaining a system of policy requiring foresight and prompt resolution, qualities lacking in the multitude,—occasionally, too, demanding quick strokes and apparently aggressive (although really protective) enterprises, the wisdom or necessity of which is not manifest to the masses, and in opposition to which the multitude may easily be roused by the Party out of office, whether under the plea of sentiment or of economy. Moreover, the masses are not only ignorant (in such affairs) but passionate, whereby the government may be forced into a war at a time when the odds are entirely against their country. In the United States of America, Democracy is in a favoured home. There, no empire is needed—the country is self-supporting; or rather, it contains an empire within itself, to be won simply by settlement and cultivation,—the State steadily growing in magnitude by homogeneous population and integral additions of territory. *There*, the State and its prosperity are alike secure, immortal, except it perish by suicide, destroyed by its own people,—a peril from which, owing to happy circumstances, they are more exempt than any other civilised community. But *here*, the case is far different; and any one who may attempt to forecast the future of Great Britain must not only remember that our prosperity—nay, even the existence of one-half our population—is dependent upon foreign countries, and chiefly upon our colonies and dependencies— in fact, upon our Empire; but also that the ruling power has passed from those classes who created the empire, and who for successive generations have extended and upheld it, into the hands of a numerical majority, who, howsoever patriotic in heart, are deficient alike in the moral and in the intellectual qualities which are requisite for the ruling and maintaining of empires. Is it not a significant fact (whatever else may be thought of it) that the movement or desire—apparently a popular one—for the establishment of a Customs' Union between Great Britain and her colonies and dependencies — an imperial Zollverein — should be merely a desire for the system established by Pitt, and which this present generation threw away?

One can hardly take note of the peculiar prosperity of Great Britain (which, in truth, is one of the greatest marvels and proudest achievements of the modern world—a Carthage of the two hemispheres, as compared with its Mediterranean prototype) without feeling some disquietude as to the precarious basis of all this power, wealth, and splendour—nay, even for the continued existence of that dense population which fills our country with great cities, rivalling or surpassing in inhabitants mighty Babylon, imperial Rome, or the "hundred-gated Thebes" of the Pharaohs.

But it is not of these things, nor specially of our own country, that we here write: but of changes alike world-wide and inevitable which came in sequel to the now closed or closing epoch of the Gold-mines. The world has progressed remarkably since 1848,—so much so that despite the vast quantity of the precious metals produced during the last thirty-three years, money has become wellnigh as dear as it was before the gold-discoveries in California. Such a change bodes ill for the world; and if statesmen be not alive to the change, the course of affairs may become very seriously, or even perilously, troubled.

As already said, there still exists a grand legacy of benefits from the Golden Age. Everything is better than it was in 1848. The condition of all classes, certainly of the masses of the population, is improved in material wellbeing; and Education makes each individual more powerful, whether for good or evil. Nevertheless in currency affairs, the nations are sliding back into the old position from which they were happily lifted by the Gold-discoveries. And in some respects the position of Society and Civilisation is weaker than it was then: props and stays have been removed in the interval, whose absence must be severely felt under any renewal of the old trials. Not to speak of the growing sentiment of

Equality in its levelling form, nor of the at least apparent increase of money-greed and personal indulgence, how vast has been the progress of Irreligion, Atheism, and Materialism? And when Man makes this brief earthly life his all—without the comforts as well as moral restraints of Religion,—when he owns no God, and sees no future life in which goodness will have an immeasurable reward of happiness in better worlds of immortal joy: then, in truth, must come a fiery trial for all Governments and Societies. Civilisation will be tested and pried into in all its parts, to see if it be in accord with the wants and desires of the new time—of human life without a God or a Future—of a developed Ape, passionately craving for material enjoyment, and believing that he must get it *here*, or *nowhere!*—here, too, within the limited span of half a century! In 1848, Europe was in throes of Revolution, in which the *nouvelles couches sociales* held the foremost place. It was a sequel, a further stage of the merely embryo Socialism of the first French Revolution (which was too occupied with Destruction, with the easy work of slaughter and abolition, to have time or thought for the difficult task of Reconstruction),—a conversion or transference of the revolutionary spirit from politics and Government to Society and Civilisation. The Gold-discoveries came, like the waving of a fairy's wand, to check that evil spirit,—throwing oil on the troubled waters of popular discontent; and men became satisfied under the golden prosperity, the brightest and most nearly universal that the world has ever seen. Yet the evil spirit lives. What means the cry, "*Ni Dieu, ni Maître*"? Have we not seen the lurid fires of social revolution flare up briefly but terribly in the Parisian Commune of 1871? And one has only to note the French Communism, German Socialism, Russian Nihilism—not to speak of the Irish Jacquerie, the Intransigeants of Spain, and a similar class in Italy—to feel how Europe has glided forward in popular demoralisation since 1848, and how the fires of anarchy and destruction visibly smoulder, like the furnace of a brick-kiln, under the whole base of Government and Society,—even menacing with destruction the existing order of things, the long-established system of Civilisation in Modern or post-pagan Europe.

General prosperity has had its wonted effect of begetting general contentment. It has for a generation lulled to sleep the awakening spirit and powers of evil. Prosperity is the great peace-preserver: and in proportion as "hard times" return, must we not likewise expect a return to those Revolutionary forms of Discontent which frown upon Europe from the Past,—giant-like shapes of Despair and Hate, at present but dimly seen across the broad expanse of the Golden Age, through the golden haze of an epoch of unparalleled prosperity? Abundance of gold, as the world's Money, has assuredly been one potent cause of that general wellbeing; and if the world be now entering upon an opposite, as certainly a different, monetary epoch, it becomes nations and their guides or rulers to note well the change, and consider how far Legislation, availing itself of the growth of international civilisation, may be employed to mitigate the not novel phenomenon of the exhaustion and closure of the great treasure-beds of Nature. The difficulty is hardly a new one; and the book of the Past is open for our instruction; while the mature civilisation and riper social compact of the present day offer previously unknown means and opportunities by which, surely, we may accomplish with ease what was not unsuccessfully achieved by our forefathers under far less favourable circumstances.

There are some parts of this book which probably will prove interesting to the general reader, owing to the somewhat picturesque or romantic character of the events therein narrated. Yet not for this did I engage in the work; but because I saw that my generation has been passing through a strikingly exceptional epoch,—fraught with important lessons, which legislators hitherto have been slow to appreciate, as the masses have been slow to understand. I beheld a grand illustration illuminating the whole period, and visible to all eyes,—a maxim or lesson written in gold across the broad face of the epoch— as to the potent and dominating part which Money plays, and must play, in the affairs and fortunes of civilised mankind. Not merely as Wealth or Property: in that respect, mankind have been agreed as to the value of Money, even in an exaggerated form, from the earliest times of history, and not least since the commencement of the current era, when Jesus of Nazareth was betrayed for forty pieces of silver! The value of Money which I here speak of is that which pertains to it as a promoter and indispensable auxiliary of civilised trade, industry, employment — the potent agent or instrument in augmenting Production of all things useful to man; while making that production profitable to the producers, and its produce more useful to the world, by the circulation and exchange of the commodities produced. Money is not only the most potent form of Property, but the *only* form of it which is suitable and thoroughly effective for the undertaking and prosecution of those manifold industrial and commercial enterprises which add to the power and wellbeing of mankind at large, while profitably sustaining the people engaged in those transactions. But, even viewing Money simply in the former of these aspects—simply as Property,—how momentous is its influence upon Society, upon its individual members and separate classes: seeing, for example, how each step towards scarcity augments its value, and the value or weight of those moneyed contracts and engagements with which civilised life is full. Debt, in truth, the prevalence of contracts to pay, is one of the concomitants of civilisation—being only possible where good faith is reckoned a public duty and an indispensable requisite of a community. And where—as is usual in civilised communities— these contracts or obligations are payable in money, any change in the quantity or supply of money is immediately and severely felt (though it may not be intelligently perceived) through all classes of the community.

Such changes, too, are most frequently towards scarcity,—chiefly owing to the fact that the spread or normal growth of civilisation ever tends to make money scarce and dear, by multiplying the requirements for it. And what is such a dearth of money, and rise in the measure-of-value, but an injustice to the many to the gain of the few,—an unfair exalting of the power of the Past over the Present—an unfair and undesirable aggravation of the poverty of the poor and of the wealth of the rich—a stereotyping of classes according to wealth, until they tend to become permanent and distinct like castes. We have seen how powerful and beneficial was the influx of the precious metals from the New World four centuries ago, in breaking the social bondage which had settled upon Europe during the long night of the Dark Ages; enabling that generation to escape from the heritage of the Past, and bound forward upon the new career then opening to mankind. Such times come from the hand of Providence, and with an exceeding rarity even in the long career of civilised mankind. But at least let us avoid the opposite, and never allow successive generations to be unfairly — nay, most unjustly, though it may not so be meant—handicapped, each in its own race, owing to a growing dearth and dearness of money; whereby the Past throws its chains over the Present to an extent exceeding that natural and rightful heritage — that sequence which pervades all Nature; and any rupture of which would rob Virtue and Wisdom of their best inducements, loving self-denial of its sweet reward, and children or family-successors of their honourable and rightful inheritance.

In justice, it cannot be too frankly and fully acknowledged that there is no matter in which legislators may so readily err as in appreciating the monetary wants of an epoch when changes are in progress in the supply of the precious metals. And such a difficulty exists at present. In more than one part of the *Wealth of Nations*, Adam Smith refers to the prevalent opinion in his time, that the value of the precious metals was still falling; whereas he explicitly states as his own opinion, or rather as a fact demonstrated by the state of prices, that for nearly a century previous—viz., from the closing years of the seventeenth century down to the time when he wrote—there had been a slight but distinctly perceptible rise in the value of money. The popular opinion thus referred to was perfectly natural. Money had fallen immensely in value during the century and a half subsequent to the discovery of America with its mines of the precious metals; and as the produce of the mines in the eighteenth century was very much larger than it had ever been before, it was only natural to believe that the fall in the value of the precious metals was still in progress. Ordinary observers overlooked the fact, pointed out by Adam Smith, that the requirements for money had contemporaneously increased vastly; indeed to such an extent that the increased produce of the mines was inadequate to fully meet the increased requirements for it.

An analogous or parallel state of public opinion has prevailed in connection with the peerlessly rich new mines of America and Australia. In 1873 prices were very high, and people were still believing-in or expecting a continuous fall in the value of money. Although the gold-mines had declined from their maximum production, little attention was given to that circumstance; moreover, the annual yield of gold was still more than double what it was in 1848; and also, the comparative falling-off in the produce of gold was compensated in amount by the increased supply of silver from the new Nevada mines. This was the state of matters in 1873.

Soon afterwards, a great fall began in the value of silver compared with gold. The baneful work of demonetising silver had commenced; yet the necessary result of that work in lowering the value of the discarded metal failed to be recognised. As no one then thought that gold was becoming scarce and rising in value, the change in the value of silver appeared to be simply a depreciation of that metal owing to superabundance—a fall not merely relatively to gold, but also to labour and commodities in general. The House of Commons, when appointing the Select Committee of 1876, adopted the prevalent opinion; and the Committee in their Report proceeded upon the same view of the matter, although some of the evidence then adduced pointed to a different conclusion. On the other hand, the Commission simultaneously appointed by the Congress of the United States, reported in the clearest and most confident terms that there had been no fall in the value of silver, except as compared with gold, and that the value of gold had risen: in their own words, "Since 1873, the purchasing power of gold has risen in all countries, and the purchasing power of silver has fallen in none." The report of the American Commission failed to attract attention in this country: indeed, as the United States are interested in upholding the value of silver, for the sake of the splendid Nevada mines, the opinion of the American Commission was open to the suspicion that "the wish was father to the thought." Recently, however, it has become acknowledged in this country that the view taken by the American Commission is not a baseless one,—that the "depreciation" of silver in Europe and America is really aggravated or increased owing to a rise in the value of gold; and that, in consequence of the large decrease in the produce of the Californian and Australian mines, the civilised world is entering upon a new period of monetary scarcity,—and a serious one, at least relatively to the previous thirty years of monetary plenty.

But however discernible the change may be to the few who study such subjects, the change has obviously not yet been appreciated by legislators and the public at large. The question of Mono-metallism we have not space to discuss, except to remark that what may be styled the theoretic part of the question—or simply as to whether, in the abstract (that is, irrespective of existing circumstances), it would be preferable to have a double or a single measure of property—albeit easily answered in the study, is of but small importance in the Cabinet and Legislature. If there be enough of both gold and silver to furnish an adequate currency of either metal, then, but then only, ought the abstract merits of Mono-metallism and Bi-metallism to become an affair of practical politics. But if there be only enough, or hardly enough, of both the canonised metals taken together to meet the present and ever-growing requirements for this world's money, then surely the demonetisation of one or other of these metals is an act of legislative insanity, suicidal to the wellbeing of the whole civilised world.

The common and strongest arguments in favour of a single gold standard are, firstly, that gold is best suited for wealthy countries where large payments are common. But even in England, as we all know, no large payments are made in coin at all; and as regards international payments, it costs no more to send silver than to send gold, because the cost of conveyance is not reckoned by the weight of the bullion, but by its value. The other and more important argument in favour of a single standard (but one which, be it noted, is as much in favour of silver as of gold), is, that a standard which rests upon the two metals is doubly unstable, because liable to a double set of fluctuations. I venture to

say, there could not be a greater mistake than
this. If the two bases were things wholly different
and independent, the argument would be correct;
but it is wholly incorrect when the two things are
mutually interchangeable,—when they can be used
for the same purpose. No one will say that a man
can stand better upon one leg than on two! I have
never heard any sane man complain of having two
legs because thereby he has to support himself upon
"a double set of fluctuations." Or put the case in
another way :—Would any one think of maintaining
that the cost of food fluctuates more when men can
live both upon animal and vegetable food than if,
with both kinds of sustenance within reach, they
chose to live upon bread or butcher's-meat separately? If either of these two kinds of food be in
such abundance that people can wholly do without
the other, then undoubtedly the people may indulge
their preference, and live upon that one kind of food
alone. But if, as is actually the case, there is no
such superabundance of food, people would be foolish
indeed if they created an *artificial famine*, and
starvation for themselves, by refusing to treat as
food what *is* food. In like manner, for Governments or Legislatures to forbid and prevent the use
of silver as Money at a time like the present, when
metallic money is growing scarce, is as extraordinary an aberration as legislative wisdom can possibly
exhibit. Yet it is merely a repetition of what was
done by our own Parliament in 1816,—when silver
was demonetised, at a time when the annual supply

both of gold and silver had fallen to only one-half of the previous ordinary amount.

How stands the case at present? The total production of the precious metals when the new gold-mines were at their best, viz., in 1852-60, was 36 millions sterling annually. At present it appears to be almost the same. But there has been a great change in the character of the supply. In 1852-60, the annual produce of gold averaged nearly 28 millions, and of silver a trifle over 8 millions. Of late years the supply of gold has averaged about 19½ millions, and of silver about 15 millions. Thus, if the Double Standard of gold and silver conjointly generally prevailed, no effect at all upon Prices could be produced by the present state of the annual supply of the precious metals. But in countries under a single gold standard, Money ought to be rising in value; and in countries under a single silver standard, Money ought to be falling in value. Nevertheless, silver still maintains its old purchasing-power in India, or indeed has risen in value there, while in England the purchasing-power of silver has likewise risen; and gold in both countries has risen still more. For instance, in 1879 the purchasing-power of gold (its value relative to general commodities) had risen 24 per cent since 1872, while, relatively to gold, the value of silver had fallen barely 14 per cent,—that is, silver had risen 10 per cent, and gold 24 per cent, above their previous value in 1872.[1]

[1] See a Paper which I read before the Statistical Society in December 1879, entitled, "Is the Value of Money Rising, in England and throughout the World?"

No one can read this brief statement, especially relative to the large decrease in the produce of the gold-mines, without strongly suspecting, if not feeling convinced, (wholly irrespective of the available evidence of Prices) that Money must already be growing scarce in countries which have a single gold-currency, and that the scarcity will inevitably become greater and severe. It is a noteworthy fact that if the Double Standard of gold and silver conjointly, generally prevailed, there would be no scarcity, nor seeming approach to a scarcity, under the recent and present state of the annual supply of the precious metals. As above remarked, the increased production of silver (from the new Nevada mines) almost exactly compensates the great decline in the produce of the gold-mines: so that, under the old Double Standard, the value of Money would continue perfectly stable and unchanged. But men will not "rest and be thankful," nor be content with the blessings which they possess. And in seeking for something which seems to them better, they are apt to sacrifice their present advantages.

The extensive demonetisation of silver has suddenly and seriously disturbed the position of affairs. Inevitably, the demonetisation of one of the precious metals carries with it a rise in the value of the other. The amount of silver demonetised must be replaced by, and cause to be absorbed in new transactions, an equal amount of gold. If there were a great plethora of gold, such a change might be advantageous, and could not be embarrassing. But there is no such plethora of gold; and the amount of this metal required to take the place of the demonetised silver must inevitably produce a scarcity of gold,—*dear Money*, in this and every other country which has adopted a single gold standard. The amount of gold required for this *new* use must be very large, and each year in the future will make the amount larger. If the world had remained as it was in 1870, the seven millions a-year of *new* silver from the Nevada Mines would have been readily absorbed; indeed such a sum would hardly have done more than annually replace the mass of lost and worn-out silver throughout the world. But since 1872, besides the collapse of Trade, several of the leading Governments of the West have followed the example of England in adopting a single gold standard; while France and the other States of the Latin Union have, in self-defence, stopped the coinage of silver. Thus a vast amount of silver-money has been actually demonetised, while, almost throughout the whole Western world, the entire replacement of the worn metallic currency or coinage, and also all the additions to it, must henceforth be made in gold. And it will hardly be questioned that these requisite additions will be of no small amount.

A scarcity of gold, under such circumstances, seems inevitable. Three years ago, the leading merchants and bankers of the City of London addressed a memorial to the Prime Minister, complaining that metallic money is growing scarce. Too commonly, the event is spoken of as if it were a visitation of Providence,—a thing as much beyond man's power of prevention as the bad seasons with which we have recently been afflicted; and yet this scarcity of metallic money is entirely of man's making. The demonetising of silver is *a destruction of a large part of the world's currency*, wilfully produced,—a measure voluntarily adopted by Parliaments or enacted by Governments. Legislation creates this difficulty, and legislation could remedy it. I see much ground for believing that, but for the wide demonetisation of silver in the Western world, there would have been no fall in the value of that metal relatively to gold,—at most the fall would have been slight and transient. How stood the facts? The use of silver-money, especially in the East, is so extensive as to require a large amount of that metal for the mere maintenance of those silver currencies, as well as for the additions which are naturally required, owing to the growth of trade. Before 1873, the expenditure of British capital for the railways in India had come to an end; and, owing to the world-wide Depression of Trade, the foreign trade of India became, not retrogressive, but stationary. And under these circumstances silver, which had previously *risen* in value compared with gold, returned to its old and traditional price in gold. But thereupon the work of demonetising silver commenced in Europe, and the gold-price of silver has fallen greatly. But for this arbitrary change (viz., the demonetisation), I think any change in the value of silver relatively to gold would have been slight and transient. Since the world proved able to absorb some twenty millions of new gold annually, is it not probable (to say the least) that now, when the gold-supply has diminished to the extent of eight millions sterling, the world would have been able to absorb the seven millions of new silver from Nevada? In fact, but for the demonetisation of silver, would not the recent deficit of gold have been just compensated by the increase of silver,—thereby preventing that "scarcity of metallic money" which the leading merchants and bankers of the City of London deplore in their recent memorial to the Prime Minister.

When one of the metals which constitute Money is becoming scarce, it is a strange procedure to demonetise the other.

Money is an invention of Civilisation, created by it to meet its own wants: it is the offspring of Agreement, ratified and enforced by Law; and it is either from Agreement or by Law that money carries its peculiar value, and is able to perform its allotted work, fulfilling the purpose for which it is created. The chief and paramount requirement both for gold and silver nowadays is *as money;* consequently the chief and paramount source or element of their value arises from the fact that *they are money.* The common saying that gold owes its value as Money simply to its natural preciousness as a commodity, I hold to be exceedingly incorrect. As money, gold acquires a legal value, *besides* its ordinary value as merchandise. Demonetise both gold and silver (as it is quite conceivable may be the fate of those metals ultimately in the remote future), and the value of those metals would at once be immensely reduced—it may be to a half, or even to a quarter of the value which they at present possess as the costly counters which nations have agreed to trade with and accept as a measure of value or property. Already, in the most advanced countries, gold and silver might be, and to a large extent are, dispensed with in domestic circulation. Even now, specie is indispensable only in international payments—or rather, for a small part of them, viz., the "balance;" and if the nations come to suffer severely from changes in the relative value of the two metals—the depreciation of one and the appreciation of the other,—they will be tempted to see whether such fitful measures of value cannot be still further supplanted by other means of exchange, even in international transactions.[1]

Meanwhile—and this alone is urgent—should gold become scarce again, let my countrymen remember that there is an adequate remedy for the evil within their reach. Let them remember that, nigh two centuries ago, there was established both in England and Scotland a monetary system, a means of supplying currency in accordance with the requirements of the national trade and industry—amply sufficient to

---

[1] Upon this question, see my *Science of Finance*, chap. xxiii., on "an International Monetary System," wherein I describe the pernicious "War of the Banks," now in vogue, and suggest a new and better system, and one in accord with the international character of the age.

meet any probable, or almost possible, scarcity of the precious metals for years to come. A system, too, which in substance has been revived as the best, and adopted in the United States, after the world's experience of such matters throughout little short of two centuries.[1] In England that system was speedily dwarfed, and its further adoption forbidden, by the monopoly conferred upon the Bank of England in 1708; next, in the middle of last century, silver was deprived of its functions as legal money for sums above forty pounds sterling; then, in 1816, the complete demonetisation of silver curtailed by more than one-half the basis of our currency and the power of issuing it; and finally (not to speak of the abolition of £1 notes[2]), in 1844-5 our monetary system was curtailed again; so that now, vastly useful though it be, it is but a fragment of what it was in its origin, nearly two centuries ago. Surely, what England was fit for in 1694, and what Scot-

[1] State-security, without State-issue, is the best requisite of a national currency: a principle or system devised and originated by Paterson when founding the Bank of England,—the notes of which establishment were based upon Government security, the Bank (a joint-stock company) maintaining their convertibility, and issuing them at 4 per cent in discounts and advances to the public.

[2] As a currency measure, the abolition of £1 notes in England was a miserable mistake,—the blunder of politicians who did not see that the only way to get a sound currency is to get strong banks—instead of the private banks of issue which alone could be established under the monopoly of joint-stock issue-banking conferred in 1708 upon the Bank of England. On the other hand, as a matter of State-policy, it seems to me highly important to possess a metallic currency. Our gold-circulation is a War-chest, immediately available to meet national emergencies,—and it is the only thing of the kind which popular distrust or a misplaced economy will permit to be kept in this country.

land practised with freer spirit and on a fuller scale for a century and a half (down to 1845), our nation is, *à fortiori*, capable of rightly using at the present day. Nay more, even though there come no notable scarcity of gold, do we not suffer periodically from transient ebbs or "drains" of the precious metal, which, under our now cramped and curtailed monetary system, recurrently strangle our trade and industry, and therewith the prosperity of the industrial classes, every ten years or less. If my countrymen allow themselves to be so overweighted in the race of trade-competition—or if industry is thus to be robbed of its profits, and the power of capital to be at such times unfairly augmented, the blame must lie with themselves. The remedy is within their reach. Do not blame statesmen and politicians, who as yet comprehend so little of these things, for the continuance of a regime of recurrent Trade-suicide, from which the industrial classes suffer most; yet which is hardly of permanent advantage even to that portion of the moneyed classes who can turn these crises to their profit.

Any dethronement of Gold and Silver as the money of civilised countries is a change which, manifestly, lies afar off; nor, in several respects, is it desirable that it should come soon. "There is a time for everything under the sun," said Solomon of old: and how much—so far as man's eye can discern—would have been lost to the world had gold and silver been dispossessed of their monetary value some thirty or more years ago! And does not this peculiar value, which civilisation has so long imputed to those metals, appear one means for carrying out what seems to human eye to be that scheme of Providence which guides and overrules the course of human affairs, by attracting, as no other force can, the flow of civilised nations into the secluded regions of the earth: thereby not only extending civilisation and developing it in new forms, but even prolonging its existence in its old seats, and so permitting human thought and society to attain to a greater maturity, and consequently more novel developments, than were possible but for the hiving-off of swarms of the less fortunate classes—whose slowly accumulating forces would otherwise prove destructive to the Society and organised communities which engender them, or at least within which they grow up,—parasites of suffering and discontent from which no human civilisation has yet known how to keep free. I am not so confident as most men are that European Civilisation is secure against a new inroad of the younger and rude peoples, styled Barbarians; but few thoughtful minds can doubt that our Civilisation (like others before it), while liable to the effeteness of age, contains barbaric forces which may of themselves work out a cataclysmal overthrow.

The present is not a time for dogmatism, much less for prophecy. The actual signs of the times, the state of our own country and of Europe at large —readily intelligible as the letters of the alphabet although they will be to a later generation which has beheld their sequence and outcome—plain and patent as they are to our objective sight, are nevertheless like hieroglyphics whose true and full meaning has not yet dawned upon us. What but failure, error glaring and entire, has attended the numerous and confident predictions, current almost as Gospel a quarter of a century ago, as to the Gold-mines and their effects? Taught by that experience, I shall not venture upon ground where so many have failed, nor seek to measure with mortal eye the infinite and varied possibilities of Nature and Providence. Not even as to the duration of the present gold-beds shall we offer an opinion. Apparently there are still great depths and stretches of gold-bearing detritus in those ancient river-beds, relics of an elder world, in California; and much gold may still lie hidden in those equally strange beds of alluvial clay in Australia, now sunk many fathoms deep, yet which originally spread over the surface of the country, seemingly vomited from the cavernous depths of vast volcanoes. And who can speak with confidence as to the treasure which may be won from new and still undiscovered mines of gold or silver? Humboldt saw reason to believe, even in his comparatively recent day, that the whole chain of the Andes was so silver-bearing—that its rocks were so widely permeated by argentiferous veins, that from this source alone Europe might be flooded with silver until that metal became a drug. And are not the Nevada mines—a second and richer Potosi—an indication that this remarkable prediction may not be exaggerated? Yet, more than three centuries elapsed between the parallel discoveries of Potosi and the Comstoke Lode, even though the search for silver has never ceased; and may not another long interval elapse, and generations suffer again from a dearth of the precious ores, ere another suchlike discovery be made of the hidden treasure-beds of the American Cordillera?

India, too, now promises gold; yet who at present can tell how far the promise will be kept? Who as yet can say how much of the precious metal remains in the Wynaad rocks after the rude labour and exploration of the ancient workers? It is marvellous —as the old Spanish and Hungarian mines testify— how well the ancients cleared out the veins of precious metal, despite their rude appliances; and my hope of good profit for the Indian Mining companies rests not so much upon the rudeness of the old labour, as upon the conjecture which I entertain (from the reading of Indian history) that these gold-mines of Southern India were abandoned rather owing to the troubles in the country, chiefly owing to successive hostile invasions from the north, than in consequence of the mining operations ceasing to be profitable to the old Princes and Rajahs of the region. Finally, who shall say how soon the finding of rich new gold-mines in Central Africa, or in the Altai Mountain-chain of Upper Asia, may attract a new flood of migration from the central seats of civilisation into the two greatest remaining solitudes of the earth? Nay, even just beyond our own Indian frontier, among the inner ranges of the mighty Himalayas, are there not mines of great mineral wealth awaiting mankind, and the very existence of which (although doubtless imperfectly known) inspires the Chinese authorities in their peculiarly stern exclusion of all foreigners from that *terra incognita* of British travellers and explorers?

But, whatever may lie in the womb of Time, the Golden Age of which I write is past. Possibly the world may never see its like again,—so largely has it been composed of several entirely distinct elements. The Silver Age had its New World, and a course of marvellous discovery, unveiling the face of the Earth, which stimulated alike the reason and the imagination of infant Europe; while the new treasures of the Transatlantic Mines furnished to our then half-barbarous continent the means of employing its awakening powers in commerce and industry. In its turn, the Golden Age combined, with the discovery of the richest treasure-beds which the eye of man has beheld, a remarkable development of mechanical and chemical invention,— especially a suddenly acquired mastery of the powers of locomotion alike by sea and land, and consequently a rapid growth of Internationalism, vastly enlarging each man's sphere, while widening the spirit and sympathies of nations. The glories of the Silver Age pertained directly to monarchs and princes, and not less to that wider upper class of humanity, whom nature had endowed with the gifts of intellect and the gallant spirit of daring adventure. The benefits of the Golden Age came primarily and chiefly to the poor multitude,—to the masses of humanity alike neglected by worldly Fortune and unendowed with the gifts of Nature. The former Age came to awaken Europe, both intellectually and socially, from the troubled slumber of the Dark Ages, and to give birth and growing maturity to a new Civilisation,—one more (albeit far the widest) in the long series of organisations of human government and society which, with a natural yet startling mortality, the world has seen flourish and expire. The latter Age—that of our own time—came to give a fresh start to that Civilisation when it was beginning to grow old,—relieving it, in its old and native seats, from perilous masses of social and political discontent,—thereby transferred by migration into new or virgin regions where they are chiefly the makers of their own circumstances or surroundings, and can mould to their liking the old civilisation into newer forms.

When, or how soon, a renewed trumpet-call of "Gold! Gold!" from Upper Asia or Central Africa, may again draw forth an exodus from the plethoric centres of civilisation, and migratory myriads rush forth afresh into the solitudes—making the lone waste places to bloom, and covering the face of the Earth with civilised mankind, "even as the waters cover the channels of the sea"—no man can tell. But if, as may be, a long interval occur, it seems to me probable that ere then the magic of the gold-spell will be broken, and civilised communities will find that Man can make for himself, by mere agreement and legislation, that indispensable thing Money, the medium of exchange and measure of property, — for a supply of which hitherto he has been, often painfully, dependent upon accidental discoveries of the treasure-beds of the Earth.

APPENDIX.

A.

TOTAL PRODUCTION OF GOLD AND SILVER.
Period, 1492-1848.

M. CHEVALIER in his 'Remarks on the Production of the Precious Metals,' published in 1853, said:—

"M. de Humboldt was the first writer who produced calculations, founded for the most part on trustworthy data: but he did not carry his inquiry beyond the beginning of the present century. I have continued his calculations, and brought them down to 1848—the year in which the discovery of the mines of California took place, and which forms a new era in the history of the precious metals." M. Chevalier's estimate of the production of gold and silver in the New World and in the Old, between A.D. 1492 and 1848, is as follows:—

PRODUCED IN THE NEW WORLD.

Countries.	Value in Millions of Francs.		
	Silver.	Gold.	Total.
United States,	...	76	76
New Mexico,	61,985,522	1,341	15,115
Grenada,	259,774	1,952	2,010
Peru, }	58,765,244	1,172	14,231
Bolivia, }			
Brazil,	...	4,623	4,623
Chili,	1,040,184	862	1,093
Totals,	122,050,724	10,026	37,148

PRODUCED IN THE OLD WORLD.

Countries.	Value in Millions of Francs.		
	Silver.	Gold.	Total.
Europe, exclusive of Russia,	2,000	500	2,500
Russian Empire,	330	1,100	1,430
Africa and Islands of the Malay Archipelago,	...	2,500	2,500
Totals,	2,330	4,100	6,430

Making a total weight of 132,535,724 kilogrammes of silver, and 4,131,207 kilogrammes of gold,—equal in value to 43½ milliards of francs, or 1740 millions sterling,—produced during the three centuries and a half ending with 1848.

PRODUCTION OF GOLD AND SILVER SUBSEQUENT TO 1848.

The following estimates of the total produce of the gold and silver mines of the world (exclusive of China and some other parts of Asia) are here quoted from the *American Almanac* and from a paper by Sir Hector Hay, put in evidence before the Parliamentary Committee on the Silver Question in 1876. Allowing for the fact that the *American Almanac* includes four years more than Sir H. Hay's estimate does (representing 100 millions of gold and silver), it will be found that, as regards the total production, the two estimates are in complete accord.

The figures represent millions sterling and decimals of a million. Thus, £12·7 means £12,700,000 :—

| | American Almanac. | | Sir H. Hay. | | | American Almanac. | | Sir H. Hay. | |
	Gold.	Gold & Silver.	Gold.	Gold & Silver.		Gold.	Gold & Silver.	Gold.	Gold & Silver.
1849,	£12·7	£20·4			1863,	21·4	31·2	21·39	31·23
1850,	14·2	22·			1864,	22·6	30·2	22·6	32·94
1851,	16·6	24·4			1865,	24·	32·6	24·04	34·43
1852,	32·0	40·	36·55	44·67	1866,	24·2	34·2	24·22	34·365
1853,	31·	39·	31·09	39·21	1867,	23·2	34·2	22·805	33·65
1854,	25·4	33·4	25·49	33·61	1868,	24·	33·2	21·945	31·99
1855,	27·	35·	27·01	35·135	1869,	24·2	34·0	21·245	30·745
1856,	29·5	37·6	29·52	37·65	1870,	23·2	33·6	21·37	31·685
1857,	26·6	34·6	26·65	34·785	1871,	21·6	33·4	21·4	33·61
1858,	25·	33·	24·93	33·06	1872,	20·8	32·2	19·91	32·96
1859,	25·	34·6	24·97	33·12	1873,	21·4	34·0	19·24	33·29
1860,	23·8	35·0	23·85	32·01	1874,	19·6	32·8	18·15	32·45
1861,	22·8	35·0	22·76	31·3	1875,	19·8	33·6	19·5	35·6
1862,	21·4	32·0	21·55	30·59	1876,	20·2	35·6	...	...
			Total,			£642 0	£916·46	£ 572 195	£814·085

Thus the *American Almanac* states the annual average production of gold and silver during the 28 years 1849-76, at £32,730,000—of gold alone, at £23,000,000; and of silver at £9,800,000. The Nevada silver-mines were discovered in 1869: and of these, a single ore-vein, the famous "Bonanza" of the Comstoke Lode, on 31st October 1877, had yielded no less than £15,770,583. The total yield of silver from the famous Potosi mine since its discovery in 1544 down to 1850 is estimated at 27 million kilogrammes, equivalent to £240,000,000.

B.

CHANGES IN THE VALUE OF MONEY SUBSEQUENT TO A.D. 1492.

According to Mr Jacob, money was so dear at the time of the discovery of America that the average money-price of the Winchester bushel of wheat was two ounces of silver in the latter part of the 15th century—say 1450-1492; and it fell to a still lower price in the opening years of the 16th century—say 1500-1520. But after the middle of that century, the price rose rapidly, until, about A.D. 1630, it stood at 7½ ounces of silver: a fall in the value of money in the proportion of from $7\frac{1}{2}$ to 2. Mr Jacob's figures are as follows :—

Price of Wheat (Winchester bushel).

Prior to A.D. 1350,		4 ounces of silver.
1351 ,, 1570,		2 ,,
1571 ,, 1620,		6 ,,
1621 ,, 1636,		7·5 ,,
1637 ,, 1700,		7·2 ,,
1701 ,, 1755,		7 ,,

M. Chevalier, in his 'Remarks on the Production of the Precious Metals,' published in 1853, says :—

"At Paris, the hectolitre of wheat, which prior to the discovery of America was exchanged for 15 grammes of silver, could not be bought for less than threefold that amount in 1620, or after the depreciation of that metal first became perceptible."

This was the extent of the change in the value of silver. "The effect on gold," adds M. Chevalier, "was not so great, but it was nevertheless widely felt."

After A.D. 1640, the purchasing-power of money remained steady until near to the end of that century, when a slightly upward movement set in. As Adam Smith remarked, the value of money was somewhat on the rise throughout the 18th century, down to the time at which he wrote. Nevertheless, although the value of Money as a whole was moving upward during that period, M. Chevalier states that a perceptible fall occurred in the value of silver about A.D. 1750, in consequence of the discovery of some famous rich silver-mines in Mexico,—those of Zacatecas and Guanaxuata.

Judging by the price of wheat, says M. Chevalier, "we find that the value of silver declined more than fifty per cent between the middle and end of the last century. In short, the hectolitre of wheat, which was worth 15 grammes of silver at the close of the 15th century,—which rose to 45 grammes of the same metal after the first quarter of the 17th century,—and which was exchanged for 40 grammes about 1750, commanded

90 grammes by the beginning of the 19th century. The value of gold has undergone less fluctuation." Finally, speaking of the entire change in the value of money between 1492 and 1850, M. Chevalier says :—" We may assume that at the time of the discovery of America, a given weight of gold used to be exchanged for fourfold the quantity of wheat it can now command; whereas the purchasing-power of silver has diminished sixfold."

CHANGES SUBSEQUENT TO 1848.

Prices were at their lowest point for the present century in the years immediately prior to the arrival in the markets of the world of the New Gold from California and Australia. Mr Jevons exhibits the ratio of prices during the years 1845-62 as follows:—the level or average of prices for the six years ending with 1850 being represented by 100:—

1845, 104·4	1851, 92·4	1857, 128·8
1846, 105·4	1852, 93·8	1858, 114·2
1847, 110·8	1853, 111·3	1859, 116·0
1848, 94·1	1854, 120·7	1860, 117·9
1849, 89·6	1855, 117·6	1861, 115·1
1850, 92·1	1856, 122·5	1862, 119·4

For subsequent years, we have the *Economist's* Table, and the same Table as modified by Mr Stephen Bourne. In the *Economist's* Table, textile fabrics are assigned a very weighty influence,—correctly enough, on the whole, but which somewhat impairs accuracy in years like 1863-4, when these commodities were unusually high-priced. On the other hand, coal and iron are excluded from the Table, on account of the excessive fluctuations of value to which these commodities are liable. Mr Bourne's modification of the *Economist's* Table consists in adding to its elements, or including in it, coal and iron,—commodities which undoubtedly figure prominently in our national trade and industry.

In the Table, as here given, the number 100 is taken as representing the level or average of prices for the years 1845-50 :—

APPENDIX. 525

	Economist. 1845-50 = 100.	Bourne.		Economist. 1845-50 = 100.	Bourne.
1857,	136	140	1871,	118	118
1858,	119	123	1872,	129	133
1859,	115	118	1873,	134	142
1860,	122	123	1874,	131	136
1861,	124	124	1875,	126	130
1862,	131	125	1876,	123	123
1863,	158	144	1877,	123	126
1864,	172	151	1878,	116	118
1865,	162	138	1879,	101	106
1866,	162	141	1880,	115	—
1867,	137	128	1881, Jan. 1,	108	—
1868,	122	122	1881, July 1,	104	—
1869,	121	118	1882, Jan. 1,	110	—
1870,	122	119			

CHANGES IN THE WHOLE PERIOD A.D. 1782-1865.

Also, in a Paper read before the Statistical Society in June 1865, Professor Jevons gave the following Table showing the general variation in price of forty leading commercial commodities, during the three-quarters of a century ending with 1865:—

Proportional Variation of Prices, 1782-1865.

Year.	Ratio.	Year.	Ratio.	Year.	Ratio.
1782,	100	1810,	142	1838,	84
1783,	100	1811,	136	1839,	92
1784,	93	1812,	121	1840,	87
1785,	90	1813,	115	1841,	85
1786,	85	1814,	114	1842,	75
1787,	87	1815,	109	1843,	71
1788,	87	1816,	91	1844,	69
1789,	85	1817,	117	1845,	74
1790,	87	1818,	132	1846,	74
1791,	89	1819,	112	1847,	78
1792,	93	1820,	103	1848,	68
1793,	99	1821,	94	1849,	64
1794,	98	1822,	88	1850,	64
1795,	117	1823,	89	1851,	66
1796,	125	1824,	88	1852,	65
1797,	110	1825,	103	1853,	74
1798,	118	1826,	90	1854,	83
1799,	130	1827,	90	1855,	80
1800,	141	1828,	81	1856,	82
1801,	140	1829,	79	1857,	85
1802,	110	1830,	81	1858,	76
1803,	125	1831,	82	1859,	77
1804,	119	1832,	78	1860,	79
1805,	132	1833,	75	1861,	78
1806,	130	1834,	78	1862,	79
1807,	129	1835,	80	1863,	78
1808,	145	1836,	86	1864,	78
1809,	157	1837,	84	1865,	78

C.

ILLUSIVE CHARACTER OF THE BOARD OF TRADE RETURNS SINCE 1853.

In the text (vol. ii. p. 444) I have, in the usual fashion, quoted the Board of Trade returns as exhibiting the growth of our Foreign Trade since the date of the Gold-discoveries. A very gratifying picture they present. Unfortunately, the Board of Trade returns under the present system (owing to a lamentable change adopted in 1854, and continuously prevalent ever since) have become thoroughly illusory and worthless for their main purpose,—which we take to be to show the condition of our Foreign Trade through the successive rises and falls in quantity of goods or merchandise; whereas by the present system there are great rises and falls which are merely apparent, produced simply by changes of Price: in other words, by every change whether in the quantity of Money or in the state of Trade.

Until 1854 the Board of Trade returns included an "Official" value as well as the Real or current value as declared by the owners, the exporters or importers of the goods. This "official value" was reckoned from a scale of prices compiled so long ago as 1698; and, the prices being thus fixed, every increase or decrease in the amount of the Exports or Imports represented an exactly equal increase or decrease in the amount of the merchandise which the nation exported or received. Naturally, however, Prices in course of time came to diverge considerably from this standard price-list. As regards raw materials, the prices had not changed much; but as regards manufactured articles, owing to machinery and inventions, the alteration of prices had become very considerable. In fact, the difference which since 1698 had grown up between the "official" value and the "real" or current value seems in 1853-4 to have amounted upon the whole Exports and Imports to about one-third, or 33 per cent.

Such a difference, of course, could not fail to be observed. But the peculiar and important use of the "Official Value" was entirely overlooked. It seemed merely an old-fashioned arrangement which it was incumbent upon enlightened officials to sweep away. So the column showing the official value was struck out; and since then the values assigned to our Exports and Imports are simply the current values as declared by the owners of the goods, and which fluctuate from year to year with the state of the Money-market and the vicissitudes of Prices!

Such a change was not merely a great blunder, robbing the Board of Trade returns of their special usefulness, by abrogating (as a useless and antiquated thing!) the sole element and standard by which the increase or decrease of our Foreign Trade was ascertainable and exhibited to the public; but also it was committed at the very time when such a blunder was most disastrous to the public interest,—namely, at the very time when the great Gold-discoveries were about to make an important change in the value of money, and consequently in the "real value" by which is now reckoned the progress or decline of our Foreign Trade.

Indeed, if any one considers the matter, he will see that (although doubtless unthought of at the time) it was the very operation of the New Gold which first served to attract to the old price-list the unfortunate because shortsighted and undiscerning attention of the Board of Trade. It was the further divergence between current values and the standard price-list, occasioned by the monetary effects of the New Gold, which determined the officials to drop the standard price-list altogether; although the very fact of the changing prices, and fall in the value of money, ought to have demonstrated the exceeding usefulness of the old standard.

So the change was made in 1854,—at the very time when, owing to the gold-discoveries and other causes, Trade had entered upon a new epoch,—which called for anxious and careful consideration alike from politicians, economists, and philosophic historians; yet, by this unfortunate change, these investigations have been obstructed, and the deductions therefrom vitiated,—the Board of Trade returns, the official calendar of our Foreign Trade, giving throughout the whole period hardly any clue to, and throwing a wholly illusive light over, this important branch of our national industry and enterprise. Since the change was made, the public have lost the means of knowing the real condition of our Foreign Trade. If prices rise, our foreign trade appears to be increasing, although it may be perfectly stationary. If prices fall, then our foreign trade appears to be declining, although it may be as large as before. In truth, the effect of the change made in 1854 is even worse than this. It is twofold. As is well known, a fall of prices always accompanies a bad state of trade,—in which times, of course, the growth or progress of our foreign trade diminishes. Thus, when there is an actual decrease in the actual amount, volume, or extent of our foreign trade, there is also a fall of prices, whereby the decrease appears much greater than it really is. In like manner, when prices have risen, and our foreign trade is likewise increasing, the increase becomes twofold, and is made to appear much above the reality. In short, the money-value and *apparent amount* of our Foreign Trade, exhibited in the Board of Trade returns, during the third quarter of the century has been magnified by a double set of influences, —namely, the New Gold, and an abundant or redundant currency, together with a prosperous state of Trade, which of itself produces high prices. Such is the illusory nature of the Board of Trade returns as "improved" in 1854.

And so the state of matters remains. Not for the first time do I here call attention to this defect in our national Trade-records,—which renders the Board of Trade statistics so illusory or ambiguous that they can even be made a mere shuttlecock of Party politics! For example, for a quarter of a century after 1852, did not politicians ceaselessly point with enthusiasm to the "growth" of our

Foreign Trade as annually reported by the Board of Trade, in proof of the great success of our modern commercial legislation; yet when in 1874 the tables turned, and the Board of Trade figures sank lower and lower, all at once the same politicians discovered that this steady and alarming decline was merely apparent—the consequence of "a mere change in the value of money"? Yet was not this equally true during the prior period of apparent increase, when these official statistics were so boastingly appealed to? In times like the present, it is impossible to guard against the glosses and misrepresentations of Party politicians; but at least let us place the official records of our Foreign Trade on a basis of mercantile truth, exhibiting to the nation (as used to be the case) the real state, progress, or decline of this great source of the national prosperity.

Tables of Prices now lie to hand, in ready substitution for the old Official list, so mistakenly discarded in 1854. But do not the annual returns deposited with the Board of Trade suffice for the revision and rectification of our commercial statistics since 1854,—whereby the public may come to see and know what has been the real growth and fluctuations of our Foreign Trade during the most remarkable commercial epoch that the world has ever beheld?

D.

THE GROWTH OF WEALTH.—1853-80.

(See vol. ii. p. 489.)

An Inland Revenue Report, just issued, contains an account of the Property and Income Tax since it was reimposed in 1842: including a table which shows *inter alia* the total assessments in each year, and also the net produce of each penny of the Income-tax, after making all deductions and allowances. The statistics, as subjoined, help to show clearly when the new epoch of prosperity began—namely, as soon as the New Gold arrived in the markets of the world :—

Year.	Gross Amount of Property and Profits assessed.	Net Produce per 1d. of Tax.
1842-43,	£251,013,000	£772,000
1852-53,	262,375,000	809,000
1862-63,	359,142,000	1,192,000
1863-64,	371,102,000	1,218,000
1864-65,	395,828,000	1,312,000
1865-66,	413,105,000	1,376,000
1866-67,	422,883,000	1,412,000
1867-68,	430,368,000	1,427,000
1868-69,	434,803,000	1,434,000
1869-70,	444,914,000	1,473,000
1870-71,	465,478,000	1,587,000
1871-72,	482,338,000	1,650,000
1872-73,	513,807,000	1,724,000
1873-74,	549,422,000	1,842,000
1874-75,	571,056,000	1,916,000
1875-76,	579,405,000	1,935,000
1876-77,	570,331,000	1,881,000
1877-78,	578,341,000	1,894,000
1878-79,	578,046,000	1,867,000
1879-80,	576,896,000	1,840,000
1880-81,	585,224,000	...

Referring to this table, *The Statist* remarks :—" From this table it will be seen that the progress of the tax, though it is enormous for the whole period, and increases practically at the rate of 50 per cent in every ten years, has not been at all uniform. *In the first ten years of the period*—namely, from 1842-43 to 1852-53—*there is hardly any progress of any kind.* The yield of a penny in 1842-43 was £772,000 ; in the following two years it fell to £749,000 ; in 1846-47 it had increased to £798,000 ; but after that the yield fell again to £782,000 in 1849-50, only recovering to £799,000 in 1851-52, and advancing in the following year to £809,000. *In all these ten years, therefore—the first of the Free-trading period—there was comparatively little progress*: the yield of the Income-tax may be said to have been all but stationary.

"After that period, however, the improvement came very rapidly. In 1862-63 the yield of the penny was £1,193,000, or just about 50 per cent more than it was ten years previously. In 1872-73, again, the yield of a penny was £1,724,000, or almost exactly 50 per cent more than it was ten years previously.

"*Now* there is comparatively little increase since 1872-73,—the total being £1,867,000; and, the maximum reached since that date having been £1,935,000 in 1875-76, the conclusion can only be that we are going through *a period not unlike that which existed in the first years of the Free Trade period.*"—*Oct.* 14, 1882.

E.

QUEEN VICTORIA.

(See vol. ii. p. 477.)

In reference to the auspicious name of our beloved Sovereign, it is a curious coincidence (as recently stated by an eminent Welsh scholar) that the name of the great queen of the early Britons, Boadicea, is manifestly the Latinised form of *Budig*, or "Victory." Truly, under Boadicea's illustrious successor and name-bearer, England has attained to an empire vaster and grander than that of Rome, including regions "which Cæsar's legions never knew," and which Cæsar himself never dreamt of.

Also, when Queen Victoria visited Glasgow (after a similar visit to Dublin) in 1849, immediately after the revolutionary agitation in that city, as well as in Ireland, a stone had been dug up a few days previously, on the site of the ancient Wall of Antoninus, the work of the Legions, on which is inscribed the singularly apposite legend, "*Victoria reduce, Pax rediviva.*"

INDEX.

AFRICA, as a producer of gold, i. 428, 430.
Agriculturists, condition of, between 1810 and 1830, ii. 200 *et seq.*, 206 —changes in their state during the reign of Queen Victoria, 478 *et seq.*
Alaric, King of the Visigoths, i. 295.
Albert, Prince, and the Great Exhibition, i. 40 — his Memorial in Hyde Park, 41, and also *note.*
Alexander the Great, a factor in the dispersal of gold, i. 279.
Alison, Sir Archibald, on the Californian gold-mines, i. 12 *et seq.*—on gold-rock mining, 16—on the supposed auriferous rocks of California, 17—on the new gold-supplies as promoting commerce, 19 *et seq.*—on the alteration of prices, 21—on the wide-spread distress between 1819 and 1829, ii. 180.
America, discovery of, and Silver Age in, i. 320 *et seq.*—effects of the latter on money, 322—the supply of silver from, 324—first tales from the New World, 326—little effect upon Europe, 328 *et seq.*—monopolised by Spain, 333—results of Spanish rule, 337—discovery of gold and silver in, 338 *et seq.*—Balboa in, 339—Cortez in, 340 *et seq.*—"Kingdom of Granada," 343 —golden products of S. America, 344 *et seq.*—further discoveries of gold, 349 *et seq.*—the fertility of, 350 *et seq.*—the short-sightedness of Spanish rulers in, 352 *et seq.*—trade under these with, 355 *et seq.*—introduction of British factories into, 359—revival of Spanish trade with, 360 *et seq.*—the Church of Rome in, 365 *et seq.*—production of precious metals from American mines during Silver Age, 422 *et seq.*—decline in their richness, 424 *et seq.*—aggregate amount of gold and silver from, between 1492 and 1600, 428—and in after-years, *ib.*—Spanish colonies in, freed from the mother country, ii. 8 *et seq.*—their decline, 10 *et seq.*—decline of American mines, 74 *et seq.*—British enterprise in S. America, 93 *et seq.*
Assignats, note-issue of the First Republic of France, ii. 15 *et seq.*
Attwood, Mr, M.P., on the Fall of Prices after the Monetary Act of 1819, ii. 80 *et seq.*, 204.
Australasian colonies, statistics of the, in 1860, i. 229.
Australia, discovery of gold in, i. 3, 21 *et seq.*—emigration to, prior to the gold-discoveries, 56—after the discoveries, 57—the Golden Age in, 165 *et seq.*—Cockneys as observers of, 167 — the athleticism of, 168—sporting and intellectual pursuits, 169—recent origin of its history, 170 — first colonisation, 171—Victoria, 173—principal immigration from Great Britain, 173 —various settlements founded on Wakefield principle, 175 *et seq.*—advantages of this system to, 177 *et seq.*—the squatter system, 179 *et seq.* — advantage of gold-discoveries to squatters, 181 — the gold-fever in, 182 *et seq.* — the transformation of, 184 *et seq.*—

INDEX. 533

discovery of gold by Mr Hargreaves in, 185—result and immigration, 187 et seq.—gold-finding population of Victoria, 188—earnings of diggers, 189 et seq.—gold-production of Victoria and New South Wales, 191 note—high prices in, 192—wages in, during the gold-fever, 194—supply and demand as regards imported goods, ib. et seq.—effects of excessive supply, 197 et seq. — revival of trade in 1856, 201 et seq.—the banks in, 202—scarcity of money in 1855, 203 et seq.—its cause, 204—banks in South Australia, 207 et seq.—establishment of the Sydney Mint, 209—resultant advantages, 210 et seq.—self-government granted, 214—the aspect and climate of, 216 et seq.—its cities, 218 et seq.—its progress during the last thirty years, 221 et seq. — its influence upon the more civilised countries of the world, 225 et seq.—statistics of, for 1878, 229—gold-mining life in, 239 et seq.—discovery of a rich gold-bed beside the Buckland River, 242—famous nuggets found in, 244—quartz-mining in, 264—layers of auriferous deposits in, 265 et seq.—perpendicular mining in Australia, 269.

BABYLON, the destruction of, ii. 11 et seq.
Bacon, Lord, on the scarcity of money, ii. 178.
Balboa, discovery of Pacific Ocean by, i. 339.
Bancroft, Secretary, and California, i. 102.
"Bank Acts" of 1844-5, ii. 140 et seq., 152, 356.
Banking, the trade of, ii. 266 et seq.
Banks and their note-circulation, i. 31 et seq.—banks in Australia, 202 et seq.
Banks, private, in England, i. 465 et seq.—joint-stock, ii. 131.
Barter, the system of, i. 297—necessitated by dearth of money, 313.
Beaconsfield, Lord, on the Californian and Australian gold-mines, i. 9 note.
Bebulo, a silver-mine in Spain, i. 283, 429.
Bills, commercial, ii. 267.

Bourke, Governor, i. 218.
Bourne, Mr, his modification of the Economist's Table quoted, i. 524 et seq.
Brougham, Lord, on increased pauperism, i. 181 et seq.
Buckland River, a rich "placer" discovered beside, i. 242.

CABOT, Sebastian, i. 380.
Cabral, of Portugal, i. 381.
California, discovery of gold in, i. 3—Sir Archibald Alison and the auriferous deposits of, 12 et seq., 17—as a home for emigrants prior to the gold-discoveries, 53 et seq.—the discoveries, 54 et seq.—flooded at this period by British, 80 et seq.—the Golden Age in, 98 et seq.—Drake and its gold deposits, ib. et seq.—the Spaniards in, 101 et seq.—added to the United States, 102—gold discovered by "General Shutter" in, 104—immigration into, ib. et seq.—as it appeared in 1848, 107—its population in 1852, 109—landing of Johan Sutter in, 114—results of gold-discoveries in, 117 et seq.—quartz-mining in, 119 et seq.—disappearance of quartz-rocks in California, 120 et seq.—capital now working its gold-mines, 124 et seq.—San Francisco, 127—population and capital engaged in gold-finding in 1852, 128—in the general business of the country, ib.—the development of high prices, 129 et seq.—coins at this period in, 132—life amongst the diggers, ib. et seq.—a firm government necessary, 133—disparity of the sexes in, 136 et seq.—revulsion of prices in 1852, 138—strikes in, 139—influence of Panama Railway on, 142 et seq.—becomes a new country, 143—quartz-mining in, 145 et seq.—the supposed existence of quartz-mountains in, 147 et seq.—geological speculation, 148 et seq.—the third and present period of life in, 151 et seq.—the Central Pacific Railway, 152—California as it now is, 153 et seq.—its Constitution, 154 et seq.—travelling from New York to, 156—the climate of, 160 et seq.—the cereal crops, 161 et seq.—fruit and

INDEX.

flowers, 162—present population, *ib.*—the Chinese Question in, 163—gold-mining life in, 239 *et seq.*—earnings of gold-diggers in, 248—hydraulic mining in, 259 *et seq.*—the Spaniards in, 347 *et seq.*

Canal-mania in Great Britain, i. 74, 472 *et seq.*

Chevalier, M. Michel, on the gold-discoveries of 1850, i. 14 *et seq.*, 22 *et seq.*—on the daily earnings of gold-miners, 247—on production of the precious metals in 1847, 117 *et seq.*—on the reduction of the value of money by the discovery of new mines, ii. 263—on the production of precious metals in 1848, 382—on the productiveness of the new gold-mines, 401—on the relative value of silver and gold in France, 409 *et seq.*—on the total production of gold and silver, 1492-1848, 520 *et seq.*—on the value of money after 1492, 523.

Chinese, emigration of, to goldfields, i. 58 *et seq.*—in San Francisco, 158 *et seq.*—the Chinese Question in California, 163 *et seq.*

Christianity, influence of, on Europe, i. 301 *et seq.*

Cineguilla, the gold of, i. 349 *et seq.*

Civilisation, the enemies of modern, i. 48 *et seq.*

Coal, as compared with gold, ii. 291 *et seq.*

Cobden, Mr, on the gold-discoveries, i. 22—on the value of Chevalier's 'Probable Fall in the Value of Gold,' 26.

Cockneys as observers of Australia, i. 167 *et seq.*

Colonies, the, as a pillar of Britain's supremacy, i. 71.

Columbus, on the fertility of America, 350 *et seq.*—discovers America, 380.

Commerce, gold-discoveries giving a vast extension to, i. 62 *et seq.*—commerce as tending to increase of production, 63—good effects of foreign commerce, *ib.*—the principle of, 64—beneficent operation of, on the progress of the world, 66 *et seq.*—the religion of, 68.

Consols, influenced by gold-discoveries, i. 87 *et seq.*

Corn-law, the old, and the new Bank Act, ii. 138 *et seq.*

Cortez in America, 340 *et seq.*—in California, 346 *et seq.*

Cotton-famine, the, ii. 388.

Crimean War and the gold-discoveries, i. 91.

Crown-lands in France, ii. 16.

Cruikshank, George, and the Crystal Palace, i. 44.

Crusades, the, as creating the history of European trade, 304—lessons of the First Crusade, 306 *et seq.*

Crystal Palace, i. 42 *et seq.*—failure of the original design of, 48.

"Currency Principle," influence of, i. 31 *et seq.*

Danson, an authority on the precious metals, i. 433 *note.*

Darien Canal, the future, i. 141.

Democracy and Empire, ii. 493 *et seq.*

Deposits in banks, the cause of the 1797 dilemma, ii. 49 *et seq.*

Diodorus on gold-mining in Egypt, i. 233 *et seq.*

Drake, discovery of gold in California by, i. 98 *et seq.*, 371.

Dutch, the, and silver as a standard money, i. 30 ; ii. 407.

East, trade with the, i. 408 *et seq.*—its various routes, 409 *et seq.*—Pliny on the Eastern Trade, 411—close of the traffic, 413—its revival, 417 *et seq.*—great trade with the, ii. 333 *et seq.*—drain of specie to, 363 *et seq.*—dependence of, on Europe, for supply of precious metals, 368 *et seq.*—Mr Jacob on the Eastern Trade, 370 *et seq.*—exports of gold and silver to, at various times, 415 *et seq.*—difficulty of maintaining trade-balance with the East, 417 *et seq.*—silver requisite in such a trade, 421.

Economist Table of Prices, value of, ii. 436, 440—quotation from, concerning changes in value of money after 1848, 524 *et seq.*

Egypt, Ancient, gold-mines in, i. 233 *et seq.*—precious metals in, 276.

Elizabeth, Queen, the Silver Age of, ii. 474 *et seq.*

Emigration, the great, inspired by gold-discoveries, i. 52 *et seq.*—transference of population to gold-fields from every quarter of the globe, 57 *et seq.*—the Chinese emigration,

58 et seq.—effects of this golden exodus, 59 et seq.—emigration from Great Britain, 77 et seq.—the emigration of 1848, ii. 216 et seq.

England, Bank of, entering the Bankers' Clearing-House, i. 76 note—influx of gold after the new gold-discoveries into, 86 et seq.— its establishment, 457—Paterson's connection with, 464—favoured by Government, 465—supporting great wars, 470—during the crisis of 1797, ii. 28 et seq.—resumption of specie payments, 33—commercial paper under discount at the Bank of England, 1792-1831, 65 note—the Bank and the Act of 1819, 82—the monetary crisis of 1825, 96—loan to banks of the United States, 123 et seq.—the Bank-rate, 125—monopoly of joint-stock banking by, 131 et seq.—the monopoly of 1708, 147 et seq.—first break-down of the Bank, 154 et seq.—her action during the Crimean war, 352 et seq.

England, recoinage of the currency of, i. 437—value of money in, about 1575, 438 et seq.—scarcity of precious metals created by war in, 452 et seq.—dearth of money in, on the accession of William of Orange, 455 et seq.—abolition of small notes in, ii. 132, 512 note.—Vide Great Britain.

Epping Forest, i. 7, and note; ii. 193.

Eucalyptus globulus (the Blue Gum), i. 251 note.

Europe, chief sources of gold and silver in, i. 281 et seq.—its trade born with the Crusades, 304 et seq.—stock of precious metals in, about 1492, 314 et seq.—influence on, by the discovery of the New World, 319—effects of Silver Age on, 374 et seq.—invaded by the Turks, 375—Europe of the Middle Ages and the East, 408 et seq.—productiveness of mines in, 422 et seq.—emigration from, on the discovery of gold in California, ii. 222.

Exchange, the "first," defined, ii. 296 et seq.—exchange the prime motive to production, 449 et seq.

Exhibition, the Great, i. 33 et seq., 37 et seq.—reappearance of, as the Crystal Palace, 42 et seq.

FARM-LABOUR, influence of gold-discoveries on, i. 84.

Fawcett, Mr, on foreign trade between 1815 and 1845, i. 5 et seq.

Fawkner, John Pascoe, i. 170.

France, issue of notes by First Republic of, ii. 15 et seq.—money in, under the reign of Napoleon, 18 et seq.—imminent bankruptcy of the Bank of, in 1805, 20 et seq.—the action of the Bank of France during the Crimean war, 350 et seq.—France as a bi-metallic country, 409—synopsis of French foreign trade, 1850-65, 444.

Free Trade, growth of, ii. 159 et seq.—completion of, 189—influence of, 446 et seq.

Freiberg, the mines of, i. 287.

Fremont, Colonel, i. 103.

GAMA, Vasco de, i. 380.

Gaul, in ancient times a store-house of precious metals, i. 284.

Geelong, i. 220.

Geologists and the Golden Age, i. 10 et seq.—on gold-rock mining, 16—their theories and the Australian gold-discoveries, 263.

Gladstone, Mr, conversion of portion of Three-per-cents into Consols by, i. 87 et seq.

Gmelin on mining in Siberia, i. 277, and note.

Gold, discovery of, in Australia and California, i. 1 et seq.—wearing of gold coinage, 6, and also note—influence of the discoveries of 1850, 7 et seq.—these despondently regarded by the Learned Class, 9 et seq.—scientific opinion adverse to the continued productiveness of the new mines, 10 et seq.—Sir Archibald Alison on this view, 12 et seq.—M. Michel Chevalier on the discoveries, 14 et seq.—gold in the Urals, ib.—in the Valley of the Rhine, ib—in Siberia, ib.—gold-rock mining, 16—influence of gold discoveries on value of money, 19 et seq.—M. Michel Chevalier and his 'Probable Fall in the Value of Gold,' 22 et seq.—gold as a barren increment of the volume of metallic money, 27 et seq.—as a reducer of the Rate of Interest, 28—Mr Lalor on this view, *ib. et seq.*—gold and silver, relative values of, 29 *et seq.*—optimist view of the new discoveries verified by experience, 30 *et seq.*—the Golden Age, an epoch of enthusiasm, 33 *et seq.*—as the most brilliant period of Modern Civilisation, 50—gold-discoveries incentives to emigration, 52 *et seq.*—as giving vast extension to commerce, 62 *et seq.*—the New Gold and the New Commerce, 66—influence of gold discoveries on Great Britain, 76 *et seq.*—on the shipping trade, 82—on wages, 83—on Prices, 85—as causing Strikes, *ib.*—influx of gold, 86—influencing Consols, 87—restoring Balance of Trade, 90—the yield of gold and the Commercial Crisis of 1857, 92 *et seq.*—the Golden Age in California, 98 *et seq.*—the Golden Age in Australia, 165 *et seq.*—the coinage of gold, 209—life at the gold-mines, 231 *et seq.*—gold-mines in India, *ib. et seq.*—in Ancient Egypt, 233, 276—in Samos, 235—in Russia, 238—mining life in California and Australia, 239 *et seq.*—profits of gold-mining, 246 *et seq.*—hydraulic mining in California, 259 *et seq.*—perpendicular mining in Australia, 269 *et seq.*—gold in Ancient Asia, 274 *et seq.*—usage of gold by ancient monarchs, 279—Rome inaugurating a new golden age, 280 *et seq.*—gold in America, 338—in American Granada, 343 *et seq.*—further discoveries in America by Spaniards, 349—Africa as a producer of gold, 428—total supply of precious metals between 1492 and 1830, 431 *note*, 434 *et seq.*—supply of gold in 1800, ii. 4—price of, at the beginning of the century, 30 *et seq.*—in 1797, 32 *note*—production of, in the Old World, 115 *et seq.*—mines of Russia and Siberia, 116 *et seq.*—primal acquisition by Labour of Wealth after the new gold-discoveries, 289 *et seq.*—gold as being then immediately negotiable, 290 *et seq.*—exceptional position of gold among the earth's products, 295 *et seq.*—its prime and chief use, 299 *et seq.*—exchangeable value of gold the "Mystery of Money," 307 *et seq.*

—area of employment extended by gold-discoveries, 311—quic diffusion of the new gold, 314 *et seq.*—attractions of gold-countries for Capital, 318 *et seq.*—gold-fields pay on the spot for their own working, 320 *et seq.*—the miners' earnings regulating the value of labour, 326—local influences of new Gold, *ib.*—exportation of new Gold, 328 *et seq.*—actual processes of its diffusion, 331—local consumption, *ib. et seq.*—European demand, 333 *et seq.*—consumption of new Gold by War, 343 *et seq.*—influence of new Gold on Turkey, 358 *et seq.*—gold accumulation in the Western world in 1852-4, 386—plethora of 1864, 387—productiveness of the new gold-mines, 401 *et seq.*—their influence upon the value of money, 401 *et seq.*—demonetising of gold by the Dutch, 407—relative value of silver and gold, 408 *et seq.*—production of gold from 1849 to 1857, 423—doubling of stock of gold between 1848 and 1875, 427—new Gold affected by modern inventions, 446—causing increased discounts at the usual rate, 458—ceaselessly making profits, 469 *et seq.*—close of the Golden Age, 473 *et seq.*—a single gold standard, 504 *et seq.*—the present growing scarcity of gold, 508 *et seq.*—future gold, 514 *et seq.*—*Vide* Money.

Grain, as a standard of value, ii. 302.

Granada, American, i. 343.

Great Britain, scarcity of money in, about 1800, i. 26 *et seq.*—peculiar conditions of note-issue about this time, 39 *et seq.*—British trade expanded by Napoleonic wars, 52 *et seq.*—its agriculture during the same time, 54 *et seq.*—its loans during the Wars a help to the people, 57 *et seq.*—monetary condition of, in 1813, 59 *et seq.*—the iron trade of the time, 61—influence of the closing of the Napoleonic Wars upon, *ib. et seq.*—upon Agriculture, 63 *et seq.*—resultant general distress, 64 *et seq.*—growth of internationalism in, 70 *et seq.*—dearth of Money in, after Peace of 1815, 74 *et seq.*, 108 *et seq.*—fall of Prices in, after 1819, 80 *et seq.*—

INDEX. 537

British export trade after the Wars, 87 *et seq.*—prosperity of 1822, 89 *et seq.*—resultant commercial enterprise, 93 *et seq.*—the monetary crisis of 1826, 95 *et seq.*—agricultural distress and political discontent, 109 *et seq.*—crisis of 1837, 120 *et seq.*—crisis of 1847, 136 *et seq.*—the old Corn Law and the new Bank Act, 137 *et seq.*—the commercial adversity during the quarter of a century after the great war, 142 *et seq.*—the monetary system of, 144 *et seq.*—depends for her prosperity upon Foreign Trade, 160—increase of pauperism about 1832, 181—condition of the country in 1843, 183—condition of, between 1842 and 1852, 184 *et seq.*—cessation in the growth of population and increase in crime, 187—increase of pauperism, 188—general distress and discontent, 190 *et seq.*—causes of this decline after 1815, 194 *et seq.*—synopsis of Foreign Trade, 1850-65, 444—the Silver Age of Britain, 473 *et seq.*—the Augustan Age of, 476 *et seq.*—present conditions of life in, 481 *et seq.*—recent accumulation of wealth in, 488 *et seq.*—present position of, 492 *et seq.*—invention of steam-engine in, 473 *et seq.*—her development, 475 *et seq.*—chiefly by Foreign trade and Foreign venture, 478—freeing the Spanish colonies, ii. 8 *et seq.*—position of, at the birth of the Golden Age, 69 *et seq.*—as the heart of commerce, 72 *et seq.*—marvellous development of her powers, 74—her mineral resources, 75—her Monetary Economy, 76—influence of gold-discoveries on, *ib. et seq.*—emigration at that period from, 77.—*Vide* England.

"Great Eastern" Steamship, ii. 338, and *note.*

Guiana, gold-beds of, i. 343—Raleigh's expedition to, 345 *et seq.*

Gum, the Blue, i. 251 *note.*

HANSEATIC League, the, i. 311.
Hargreaves, Mr, discoverer of gold in Australia, i. 185.
Hay, Sir Hector, on the average annual produce of mines of precious metals since 1849, ii. 398—on the production of gold and silver after 1852, 521 *et seq.*
Hayter, Mr, on the remuneration of gold-miners, i. 228 *note.*
Hispaniola, the gold-mines of, i. 338.
Holland, and silver as its standard money, i. 30.
Huancavelica, quicksilver mine of, i. 425.
Humboldt, on the auriferous character of the Andes, i. 16 *et seq.*—as an authority on the production of the American mines, 433 *note*—on the Eastern Trade, ii. 270 *et seq.*
Hungary, a producer of precious metals, i. 286 *et seq.*, 429 *et seq.*
Hydraulic mining or "hydraulicking" in California, i. 259 *et seq.*
Hyde, Colonel, late master of the Calcutta Mint, ii. 373.

INDIA, gold-mines in, i. 231 *et seq.*—the precious metals in, 277 *et seq.*—probable results of a monetary dearth on the taxation of, ii. 240 *et seq.*—influence of new Golden Age upon, 361 *et seq.*—specie in India between 1834 and 1852, 373 *et seq.*—Home Bills, 374—Indian railways, 376—influence of Indian trade on the requirement of precious metals, 377 *et seq.*—its influence on the value of the precious metals, 380 *et seq.*—India and temporary plethoras of gold in Europe, 386 *et seq.*—synopsis of Foreign Trade, 1855-65, 444—the future of the Wynaad Mines, 516.
Interest, Rate of, gold as a reducer of, i. 28, 87 *et seq.*, 92—influence of the Commercial Crisis of 1857 on, 95—the increase of, in 1839, ii. 125—result of a high Bank-rate, 254—as an influence on national industry, 272—high rate of, in 1854, 346—of 1855, 347.
Internationalism, the growth of, ii. 70.
Ireland, a principal factor in peopling America and the gold-fields, i. 78 *et seq.*
Italy, dearth of money in Ancient, i. 289 *et seq.*—the Renaissance in, 298 *et seq.*—as a shipping nation in the Dark Ages, 308.

JACKSON, General, and the Bank of the United States, ii. 122 *et seq.*
Jacob, Mr, on the stock of precious

metals in Europe, about 1492, i. 314 *et seq.*—as an authority on the supply of precious metals, 433 *note* —on the change in mercantile relations during the fifteenth and sixteenth centuries, 445 *et seq.*—on the production, distribution, and consumption of money from 1492 to 1829, ii. 25 *note*—on the dearth of money after 1815, 196 *et seq.*—on increase of population in Europe and America from 1810 to 1830, 198 *et seq.*—on agriculture during that period, 200 *et seq.*—on the supply of specie to the East, 370 *et seq.*

Jevons, Professor, Table of Prices of, i. 143—on the daily earnings of gold-miners, 247—on the nomadic habits of Australian gold-diggers, 253 *et seq.*—his Table of Prices quoted, ii. 32 *note*—on prices prior to 1852, 202—value of his Table, 436—on the fall in the value of gold, 436 *note*—on the ratio of prices, 1845-62, 524—on proportional variation of prices, 1782-1865, 525.

Jews, the, as dealers in money, i. 314—in Spain, 394—annulment of debts among the, ii. 279 *et seq.*

KÖNIGSBERG, the mines of, i. 287.

LALOR, Mr, and his 'Morals and Money,' i. 28 *et seq.*

Lava in Australia and elsewhere, i. 268.

Laveleye, M. de, on the distress between 1820 and 1830, ii. 203—on the contemporaneous condition of Europe and America, 204 *et seq.*

Law of Lauriston, and the Mississippi Scheme, i. 485 *et seq.*

Lloyd, Mr Jones (now Lord Overstone), on note-circulation, i. 32 *note.*

Loans, the making of, by Great Britain, ii. 73 *et seq.*

Locke on scarcity of money, ii. 178.

Lombards, the, i. 209.

Louis XIV. and his wars, i. 450 *et seq.*

MACAULAY on the blessings of the year 1851, i. 45.

Macleod, Mr Dunning, on credit and banking, ii. 145 *note.*

Magellan, i. 381.

Malthus, on the monetary legislation of 1816 and 1819, ii. 179.

Marshall, James, i. 117.

Martineau, Miss, on the condition of Great Britain in 1843, ii. 183 *et seq.*

M'Culloch, Mr, author of 'Commercial Dictionary,' on the precious metals, i. 21.

Melbourne, the development of, i. 188—land-prices in, after the discovery of gold, 193 *note*—description of, 218 *et seq.*—its social life, 220 *et seq.*

Mint, establishment at Sydney of a, i. 209.

Mitchell, Major, on Australia, i. 172.

Money, influence of new gold-discoveries on value of, i. 19 *et seq.*—M. Michel Chevalier and the probable fall, 22 *et seq.*—gold as a barren increment of metallic money, 27 *et seq.*—Great Britain's monetary economy, 76—monetary crisis succeeding commercial crisis of 1857, 95 *et seq.*—scarcity of money adverse to production, 203 *et seq.*—the Australian monetary crisis, 204 *et seq.*—scarcity of money in the Roman world, 289 *et seq.*—value of, in the Middle Ages, 311 *et seq.*—necessity of, in the promotion of national life, 317 *et seq.* —necessity of keeping money in a country, 389 *et seq.*—the phenomenon of money-draining from Europe to the East, 418 *et seq.*—effects of Silver Age on value of money, 436 *et seq.*—subsequent fall in the value, 440 *et seq.*—cessation of this fall, 443 *et seq.*—loss on money by casualties and abrasion, 447 *et seq.*—war an absorbent of, 451—note-circulation, 456 *et seq.*—a dearth of money the probable result had no banks of issue been established, 483 *et seq.* —quantity of money in Europe in 1800, ii. 3—the supply at the same time, 4—scarcity of, at the end of the eighteenth century, *ib. et seq.*—influence of Napoleonic wars on, 12 *et seq.*—production, distribution, and consumption of, from 1492 to 1829, 25 *note*—prices of gold and silver bullion in Bank of England notes during the suspension of specie payments in

INDEX. 539

1797, 32 *note*—paper-money of this time in Britain, 42 *et seq.*—bank-deposits a cause of the 1797 dilemma, 49 *et seq.*—return to specie payments in 1815, 67 *et seq.*—consequent dearth, 75 *et seq.*—the Resumption Act of 1819, 82 *et seq.*—monetary crisis of 1825, 95 *et seq.*—suspension of Act of 1819, 97—causes of the crisis, 98 *et seq.*—advantages of spending money at home, 101 *et seq.*—export of gold cause of the 1826 crisis, 103—the new monetary system, 104 *et seq.*—production of precious metals from 1829 to 1847, 117 *et seq.*—crisis of 1837, 120 *et seq.*—change in British Monetary Laws, 129 *et seq.*—crisis of 1847, 136 *et seq.*—the old Corn Law and the new Bank Act, 137—the depression during the quarter of a century after great wars, —142 *et seq.*—the monetary system of this country and its changes, 144 *et seq.*—the Acts of 1816 and 1819 and the decrease of metallic money, 150—evils of transition from inconvertible to convertible currency in 1819, 151—the Act of 1844, 152—its consequences, 154 *et seq.*—baneful influence of currency restrictions, 157—increase of money with population, 165—considerations with reference to produce of precious metals, *ib. et seq.*—position of world at various times with respect to total amount and annual supply, 169 *et seq.*—the great Napoleonic wars and money, 176—results in Britain of the resumption of specie payments,177—change in the value of money and agriculture, 206—capitalists profit during a scarcity of money, 209 *et seq.*—influence of gold-discoveries on value of money, 229 *et seq.*—effects of a reduced currency, 234 *et seq.*—relations to taxation of the value of money, 236 *et seq.*—its relations to classes and individuals in ordinary transactions, 243 *et seq.*—and to monetary contracts, 244 *et seq.*—difficulty of ascertaining changes in the value of money, 247 *et seq.*—general results of the falling of prices, 248 *et seq.*—shifting of wealth from one country to another, in bullion or coin, 251—two separate kinds of value of money, 252—an exorbitant Bank-rate, 254—a drain of gold and consequent refusing to discount, *ib. et seq.*—a dearth of money a process of decay, 259 *et seq.*—value of money reduced by discovery of new mines, 262 *et seq.*—the coin more valuable than metal, 265—the trade of banking, 266 *et seq.*—effects in the fall of the value of money *per se*, 275 *et seq.*—the 'Mystery of Money,' 299 *et seq.*—state of money during the Crimean war, 346 *et seq.*—the monetary crisis of 1855, 356 *et seq.*—production of gold and silver, 1849-1863, 383 *note*—gold accumulations of 1852-4 and 1864, 386 *et seq.*—total amount of the new gold and silver, 392 *et seq.*—course of the supply of precious metals during the last four centuries, 395 *et seq.*—supply in 1848, 396—average annual produce of mines since 1849, 398—influence of new gold on the value of money, 401 *et seq.*—the plethoric supply and metallic money in general, 405 *et seq.*—relative value of silver and gold, 408—silver in France, 409 *et seq.*—the crisis of 1857, 424 *et seq.*—the world's money in 1875, 428 *et seq.*—effect of this on the value of money, 429 *et seq.*—vast increase in the requirements for, 442—money the creator of trade, 448 *et seq.*—money and trade, 451 *et seq.*—effects in the rise of the value of money, 453 *et seq.*—dearth of, rarely recognisable, 455—effects of a peremptory money requirement, 456—effect of additional money on prices, 462—new gold ceaselessly making profits, 469 *et seq.*—money at the close of the Golden Age, 495 *et seq.*—money as property, 499—value of gold and silver in 1873 and afterwards, 502 *et seq.*—demonetisation and scarcity of money, 508 *et seq.*—total production of gold and silver, 1492-1848, 520 *et seq.*—subsequent to 1848, 521 *et seq.*—changes in value of money after 1492, 522 *et seq.*—changes subsequent to 1848, 524 *et seq.*—proportional variation

INDEX.

of prices, 1782-1865, 525—growth of wealth, 1853-1880, 529 *et seq.*
Mono-metallism, ii. 503 *et seq.*
Moors, expulsion of, from Spain, i. 394 *et seq.*
Murchison, Sir R., on a "Currency Restriction Act of Nature," i. 11 *et seq.*

NAPOLEON, and the finances of France, ii. 19 *et seq.*—his principle of war supporting war, 21 *et seq.*—influence of the wars of, upon the European Powers, 24 *et seq.*—upon Great Britain, 26 *et seq.*—his "Continental System," 46 *et seq.*
Negroes in America, ii. 225 *note*.
Nevada, silver-mines of, i. 143—the Great Comstoke Lode of, ii. 394.
Newmarch, Mr, on the dearth of precious metals before 1849, i. 20 *note*; ii. 202—on the value of new gold-mines, 274.
New South Wales, gold-production of, i. 191—present prosperity, 225.
New Zealand, i. 215 *et seq.*
Note-circulation, i. 31 *et seq.*, and also *note*—in South Australia, 208—originated by William Paterson, 456 *et seq.*—prohibition of small-note issue in England, 468—issue of notes by the First Republic of France, ii. 15 *et seq.*—paper currency throughout Europe the result of the Napoleonic wars, 24—in Great Britain, 29—peculiar conditions of note-issue under Napoleonic wars, 37 *et seq.*—paper-money *versus* paper-currency, 41—abolition of small notes in England, 132—bank-notes of our monetary system, 145 *et seq.*

PANAMA Railway, i. 140.
Papacy, rise of the, i. 300 *et seq.*—its influence on modern Europe, 303.
Paper-currency, ii. 41.
Paper-money, definition of, ii. 41.
Paterson, William, the Bank of England established through, i. 456 *et seq.*, 464 and *note*—power and usefulness of his banking system, 469 *et seq.*; ii. 154 *et seq.*
Paton, Sir Noel, "Pursuit of Pleasure" by, i. 231.
Pauperism, in Great Britain, ii. 181 *et seq.*—the new Poor Law Act, 182—increase in, 188.

Peel, Sir Robert, and note-circulation, i. 32 *note*—Bank Act of 1844, ii. 152.
Peru, the silver-mines of, i. 236 *et seq.*—gold and silver in, 341—steeped by Spaniards in bloodshed, 363—discovered by Pizarro, 381.
Peto, Sir Morton, on farm-labour in 1852, i. 84.
Pinkerton, on the auriferous deposits of California, i. 100.
Pitt, William, the commercial war-policy of, i. 70 *et seq.*—the developer of England's greatness, 475 *et seq.*—as a Minister, ii. 40 *note*.
"Placers," the gold-beds of Guiana, i. 344.
Pliny on the Eastern Trade, i. 411.
Poland, the defender of Western civilisation, i. 376 *et seq.*
Population, increase of money with, ii. 165.
Porter, Mr, 'Progress of the Nation,' by, ii. 488.
Porto Bello, i. 355.
Potosi, discovery of the mines of, i. 424—their productiveness, *ib. et seq.*—deterioration of quality, 425—increase in yield, 426—their decline, ii. 74 *et seq.*
Portugal, as a factor in civilisation, i. 379.
Preston, strike of 1853-4 at, i. 85.
Prices, influence of gold-discoveries on, i. 85—in California, 129 *et seq.*, 138—Table of, by Professor Jevons, 143—*Economist's* Table, 144—fall of, in Great Britain, after Monetary Act of 1819, ii. 80 *et seq.*—Sir A. Alison on the fall of, between 1819 and 1829, 180—after 1815, 198 *et seq.*—prices prior to 1848, 202—seriousness of a fall in, 256—effect of the world's money in 1875 on, 430 *et seq.*—state of trade and state of prices, 434—other influences on prices, *ib. et seq.*—prices between 1857 and 1875, 440—effect of additional money on prices, 462—Jevons on the ratio of, 1845-62, 524—on proportional variation of, 525.—*Vide* Money.
Production, first effect of the new gold-mines on, i. 81; ii. 449.
Property, exchange of, for money, ii. 266, 499.

INDEX. 541

Protection, cry for, during 1820-30, ii. 207.

QUARTZ-MOUNTAINS, disappearance of, in California and Australia, i. 18—quartz-mining in California, 119 et seq.—disappearance of auriferous rocks in California commented on, 120 et seq.—hydraulic quartz-mining in California, 146—mountains of auriferous quartz, 147 and note—quartz-mining, 257 et seq.—in California, 259 et seq.—in Australia, 264.

RALEIGH, Sir Walter, expedition of, to Guiana, i. 345 et seq.
Rhine, gold in the valley of the, i. 14.
Roads, an auxiliary to trade, ii. 448.
Rome, inaugurating a new Golden Age, i. 280—fortunes of private individuals in Ancient, 288—restoration of Roman wealth to the East, 289 et seq.—irruptions of barbarians destructive to the monetary treasure of, 293—resurrection of the empire in the Papacy, 300 et seq.—wealth of the empire, 311 note—suspension of cash-payments in Ancient, ii. 35—taxation during the later years of the empire, 238 et seq.
Rooke, Sir George, introducer of snuff into England, ii. 7 note.
Rubattino, Signor, ii. 340 note.
Russia, gold-mining in, i. 238; ii. 116 et seq.—introduction of Russian Gold to western markets, 128 et seq.

SAMOS, gold-mines of, i. 235.
San Francisco, i. 127—five times burned, 135—as it now is, 157 et seq.—present population, 163.
Scotland, Bank of, i. 457—advantages of note-issue to, 460 et seq.
Scotland, the banking system of, i. 463.
Shipping-trade, influence of gold-discoveries on, i. 82.
Siberia, gold in, i. 14—early mining in, 274—old silver-mines in Eastern, 277.
Silver, the value of, i. 29 et seq.—Holland and silver as its standard money, 30—mines in Mexico and Peru, 236 et seq.—in Spain, 282 et seq.—in Hungary, 286 et seq.—the Silver Age in America, 320 et seq.—great effects of the discoveries on money, 322—American supply of silver, 324—silver in Peru, 341 et seq.—effects of Silver Age on Europe, 374 et seq.—yields of, from American mines, 424—amalgam process with quicksilver, 425—total supply of precious metals between 1492 and 1810, 431 note, 434 et seq.—effects of the silver age on the value of money, 436 et seq.—rise in value of, at the close of the seventeenth century, 480—supply of silver in 1800, ii. 4—demonetisation of, 77—close of the Silver Age, 114—the partial demonetisation of, in Britain, 148 et seq.—relative value of silver and gold, 408—silver in France, 409—in the Eastern trade, 421—silver and mono-metallism, 504 et seq.—extensive demonetisation, 507 et seq.—the 1861 increase in the production of silver, 428.
Sismondi on European distress after the peace of 1815, ii. 211 et seq.
Smith, Adam, on the change of conveyance in his time through Great Britain, i. 472 et seq.—on the rise of the value of silver, 480 et seq.
Snuff-taking, introduction of, into England, ii. 7 note.
Socialism, advance in, during the Golden Age, ii. 496 et seq.
Soetbeer, on the annual production of gold and silver between 1781 and 1840, ii. 199 note.
Sovereigns, tear and wear of, i. 6 note, et seq.
Spain, silver-mines in, i. 282 et seq.—monopolising America, 333 et seq.—short-sightedness of Spain in America, 352 et seq.—decay and revival of their American trade, 358 et seq.—expulsion of Moors from, 378—the latter result effected by her wealth, 387—her consequent power, ib. et seq.—evil effects of the discovery of America upon her domestic career, 392 et seq.—expulsion of Jews and Moors from, 394 et seq.—Spain and her American colonies, 397 et seq.—scarcity of precious metals in, 403 et seq.—its causes, 404 et seq.—its remedy, 405 et seq.—effects of Silver Age upon the value of money

in, 438—money in, during the War of Succession, 455—revolt of her colonies, ii. 6 *et seq.*—attacks by British on the galleons of, 7—Britain and the Spanish colonies, 8 *et seq.*—their decline, 10 *et seq.*

Squatter system of Australia, i. 179 *et seq.*

Steam-engine, invention of the, i. 473 *et seq.*—application of, to navigation, ii. 337 *et seq.*

Strikes, originated by the gold-discoveries, i. 85—in California, 139.

Sugar, in Spain and in America, i. 399 *et seq.*—price of, ii. 433 *et seq.*

Supply and demand, the laws of, i. 212 *et seq.*; ii. 164.

Sutter, Johan, the discoverer of gold in California, i. 110 *et seq.*—reduced to beggary by gold-discoveries, 117 *note.*

Sydney, establishment of Mint at, i. 209.

TAXATION, various kinds of, ii. 236 *et seq.*—relations of, to value of money, 238.

Taylor, Mr Bayard, in California, i. 106 *et seq.*

Tooke, Mr, on the effects of the new supplies of gold, i. 28—on the rise of wages, 83—on the Rate of Interest, 88—on the Mexican silver mines, 427—as an authority on the precious metals, 434 *note.*

Trade, Board of, Returns since 1853, delusive character of, ii. 526 *et seq.*

Trade, state of, before the gold-discoveries of 1850, i. 4 *et seq.*—influence of these on, 7 *et seq.*—the precious metals and the state of, 20—good results of foreign trade, 63—influence of international, on the progress of the world, 66 *et seq.*—first effects of the new gold-mines on, 81—history of European trade begins with the Crusades, 304—origin of American trade, 355 *et seq.*—the Eastern Trade, 408 *et seq.*—state of trade during the Crimean War, ii. 353 *et seq.*—Balance of Trade with the East, 364—Trade-balance with India, 377 *et seq.*—synopsis of Foreign Trade, 443—influence of Free Trade, 446 *et seq.*—influence of New Gold on, 448—of Roads and Money on, *ib. et seq.*—the life of, 451.

Turkey, influence of new gold-discoveries on, ii. 358 *et seq.*—exports of Britain to, 360, and *note.*

Turks, invasion of Europe by, i. 355 *et seq.*

UNITED States, Bank of the, ii. 122 *et seq.*, 126—struggling with Britain for gold, 122 *et seq.*—the Civil War and the gold plethora of 1864, 387—synopsis of foreign trade, 1850-60, 444.

Ural Mountains, gold in the, i. 14—early mining in the, 274.

Usury Laws, the, ii. 278.

VALUE of money — *vide* Money: world-value, ii. 301—individual value, *ib.*—grain as a standard of value, 302.

Victoria, Queen, and Epping Forest, i. 7—on the Great Exhibition, 39 *et seq.*—the Victorian era the Augustan Age of Britain, 476 *et seq.*—the name of our Queen, 531.

Victoria, State of, development of, i. 173—gold-finding population of, 189—gold-production of, 191—value of Crown lands of, 193—its prosperity, 222 *et seq.*—famous nuggets found in, 244—perpendicular mining in, 269.

WAGES, influence of gold-discoveries on, i. 83.

Wakefield system of colonisation, i. 175 *et seq.*

War, an absorbent of money, i. 451—as a trade, ii. 56 *et seq.*

Wellington, and the Napoleonic wars, ii. 30 *et seq.*

Western Bank of Scotland, fall of, i. 93 *et seq.*

Wheat, prices of, from 1450 to 1775, i. 441 *note*—price of, as an indication of change in the value of money, ii. 432 *et seq.*

Wynaad Mines, ii. 516.

YORKTOWN, the siege of, ii. 5, and *note.*

www.ingramcontent.com/pod-product-compliance
Lightning Source LLC
Chambersburg PA
CBHW031944290426
44108CB00011B/675